SPACE PLANNING FOR COMMERCIAL OFFICE INTERIORS

SPACE PLANNING FOR COMMERCIAL OFFICE INTERIORS

SECOND EDITION

Mary Lou Bakker, AIA, IIDA, LEED AP

Fairchild Books
An imprint of Bloomsbury Publishing Inc

B L O O M S B U R Y
NEW YORK · LONDON · OXFORD · NEW DELHI · SYDNEY

Fairchild Books

An imprint of Bloomsbury Publishing Inc

1385 Broadway	50 Bedford Square
New York	London
NY 10018	WC1B 3DP
USA	UK

www.bloomsbury.com

**FAIRCHILD BOOKS, BLOOMSBURY and the Diana logo
are trademarks of Bloomsbury Publishing Plc**

This edition published 2016

First edition published 2012

© Bloomsbury Publishing Inc, 2016

Library of Congress Cataloging-in-Publication Data

Names: Bakker, Mary Lou, author.
Title: Space planning for commercial office interiors / Mary Lou Bakker,
AIA, IIDA, LEED AP.
Description: Second edition. | New York : Fairchild Books, 2016.
Identifiers: LCCN 2015039449 | ISBN 978-1-5013-1050-8 (paperback)
Subjects: LCSH: Office layout. | BISAC: ARCHITECTURE / Interior Design / General.
Classification: LCC NA2856 .B35 2016 | DDC 729—dc23
LC record available at
http://lccn.loc.gov/2015039449

ISBN: PB: 978-1-5013-1050-8
ePDF: 978-1-5013-1052-2

Typeset by Lachina
Printed and bound in the United States of America

CONTENTS

EXTENDED CONTENTS

PREFACE

This second edition of *Space Planning for Commercial Office Interiors* is an exciting update, incorporating the latest workplace practices and code sections throughout the book. As more and more firms and workers adopt telecommuting and mobility of work and work locations, office requirements and layouts have also adopted new footprints and functions. Rather than occupying large permanent workstations, many workers now reserve smaller work areas for a day or week, and store personnel items in a nearby locker. They use small collaborative rooms or open areas and videoconferencing equipment to work jointly together, in person, or remotely. *Work is not where you are, but what you do and how you do it.*

All code references are replaced with the most recent code years—2015 IBC Building code, 2012 IgCC Green code, 2010 ADA code, and 2013 LEED IC+C. The Green code section appears for the first time in this book. Finally, a new client profile, which incorporates these new practices and code updates, has been added in Appendix A.

Interior design is a very graphic profession; illustrations, figures, and plans are liberally used in the book. Even though the computer is now used extensively to draw floor plans, it is still important for designers to draw small sketches of office and workstation layouts, suggestive elevations, and isometrics by hand. Hand sketching is quick, fluid, and conceptual vs. the locked-in hard lines with CAD drawings. Hand sketching is impressive, especially when done in front of a client. Therefore, exclusive of the CAD floor plans shown in the later chapters, all graphics are hand-drawn to scale, although because of enlargements or reductions for page layouts, they should not be scaled for dimensional information.

I love the interior design profession. It involves a full range of life. In addition to integrating colors and creativity, interior design is a people profession. It is also a technical and logical profession, a numbers and math profession; it is a research profession, and it is a profession requiring discipline, organization, and communication skills. It is a rewarding profession because interior design provides a great deal of latitude, allowing designers to develop their own personal styles.

When I started college at Iowa State University, the interior design profession, as we know it today, was a nascent profession. Over the years, the profession has evolved from a little-recognized career to a profession now requiring certification or licensing in most states, along with continuing education or CEUs. Much of the information imparted in this book is an accumulation of knowledge I gained over time, through my experiences working at some excellent interior design firms and through my collaboration with coworkers and other designers in the industry. With this book, today's students can now benefit, at the beginning of their careers, from all the tools and insight the design industry has acquired.

Of all the design services and tasks, it is my experience that designers find space planning to be one of the most exciting, challenging, fun, and frustrating tasks. Good space planning is the basis of great design; yet it can often be difficult to define the exact meaning of space planning.

Successful space planning and space plans are achieved through understanding the space planning process; through asking many questions and truly listening to the client; through trial and error; through teamwork and peer critics; through years of experience, acquired industry knowledge, and understanding aspects of the building and other influences of the design world. Although the specific types of interiors and client requirements will vary from project to project, the general design process, tasks, guidelines, and organization for space planning and laying out interior spaces remains consistent: it is for the designer to apply the process and procedures as outlined in this book to all types of interior spaces. Once these concepts are understood, the designer can often deviate in the process, with technical variances or in allotment of space, to create that fabulous space plan and design. First, however, it is essential for the principles and process to be understood.

Many interior floor plans, *space plans*, are rotated on a 45-degree angle within the building footprint, conveying excitement to an otherwise ordinary layout. Plans at other angles, such as 20/70 or 30/60 degrees, often set up a wonderful dynamic tension within the space. Curved corridors or foyers can soften a harsh grid of numerous offices and other rooms. Some layouts are able to project linear planes, lines, and shapes well beyond the confines of the building envelope, giving an endless feel to the interior space. Yet other plans, many plans, provide an orderly sense of space within their rectilinear lines and forms.

These multitudes of plans are conceived and developed by space planners who bring countless planning elements and components together, in both creative and functional ways that meet their clients' many needs and expectations. This task of incorporating, laying out, or planning each client's list of needs and wants—or program requirements as it is known—into a two-dimensional floor plan is one of the first opportunities in the design process for creative expression. When effectively applied in space planning, creativity can help generate the many great and exciting plans described above. Creativity alone though, is not enough. According to the NCIDQ Definition of Interior Design glossary of terms, "**Space planning** means the analysis and design of spatial and occupancy requirements, including, but not limited to, space layouts and final planning".[1]

Space Planning for Commercial Office Interiors, second edition, uses commercial office interiors, also known as contract design, as the primary focus for space planning pedagogy. The design process, and thus space planning, begins only when a signed contract is received from a client who has a need to remodel or relocate their existing space. Once a project begins, but prior to the start of space planning, parameters such as budgets and schedules are established through verbal dialog with the client; room quantities and ambience requirements are determined via programming and building selection; building codes and new products to be used within the space may need to be researched. All information is communicated to the client for approval and documented in writing.

As a college or university textbook, this book is targeted primarily toward second-year or sophomore students who already have had prerequisite classes in design principles, drafting, and drawing on CAD. The book can continue to serve as a good reference source for students as they complete their interior design degree and start to work in the professional world. Facility managers and administrators may also use the book as a guide when embarking on remodeling or relocation projects. Additionally, the book can be enjoyed by the general public to better understand the interior design profession; the spaces we inhabit; how those spaces came into being; and how they can be changed, rearranged, or influenced by any myriad confluences in the world.

While the book is not specifically broken into parts, there are essentially five areas or tasks presented as part of the design process for space planning.

- Client make-up and information gathering, Chapters 2, 3, and 12
- Code review and circulation requirements, Chapters 5 and 13
- Typical drawings, parts of Chapter 4 and Chapters 6, 7, and 8
- Other rooms and areas found within a space and on a floor plan, parts of Chapter 4 and Chapters 9, 10, and 11
- Bringing all components together in a space plan for presentation to the client, Chapters 14 and 15

To acclimate readers to the task of space planning, Chapter 1 provides an overview of space plans, planning components, and the space planner.

Chapter 2 discusses general background information about all clients, including their legal framework, building code classifications, work area mixes, the importance of job titles, and clients' expectations for their newly designed spaces.

Programming, or ascertaining the specific space requirements, needs, and wants for a particular client, is covered in Chapter 3, along with some basic project parameters such as meeting procedures, establishing daily contacts, and defining typical layouts.

Office furniture, or contract furniture as it is known, is described in Chapter 4. This chapter can be read in its entirety or divided and read in sections as applicable. For instance, the section on casegoods can be read in conjunction with Chapter 6, "Room Envelopes and Typical Private Office Layouts," while the section on tables can be read with Chapter 8, "Conference Rooms."

Chapter 5, "Circulation and Clearances," serves as a companion to Chapter 4 by indicating appropriate amounts of circulation required in front of and around the furniture along with primary and secondary corridor code requirements.

Chapters 6, 7, and 8 present typical layouts, rooms, or areas that are duplicated throughout a client's space, for private offices, workstations, and conference rooms. Typical layouts, drawn and distributed at the beginning of each project and regularly included as part of the programming questionnaire, help initiate design discussions and serve as the basis for programming assignments and space planning. Chapter 6 also explains the make-up of a room envelope.

The remaining rooms and areas commonly found in most space plans, including receptions areas, food or coffee rooms, and other support rooms are addressed in Chapters 9, 10, and 11, respectively. Most of these rooms or areas are single rooms within a plan, often serving as either highly visible public areas or as backroom functions.

Using the planning components from previous chapters, Chapter 12 demonstrates the necessary steps to turn program information acquired in Chapter 3 into a Program Report for review and approval by the client. Adjacency diagrams are presented as part of this chapter.

Chapter 13 covers building footprints, location and jurisdictions, tenant occupancy, and code-related information such as public corridors and means of egress. This chapter also discusses *tests fits* or preliminary space plans that are often generated for a client when they are considering several different buildings for their new location.

In Chapter 14, plans and accompanying text show how to start space planning, by either hand drafting or on the computer, beginning with either rooms and offices or workstations, starting at exterior window walls and moving inward or from an interior position and moving outward; using straight lines and walls or curved, angled, or other lines and walls. Once an initial plan is drawn, it is analyzed and adjusted to make it more functional and exciting. Chapter 15 discusses ways to present plans for client review.

Each chapter leads into the next chapter and builds from the previous chapter. Yet each chapter can be read and studied on its own. Since many people are familiar with reception areas or rooms, it can be fascinating to understand the design thought process of how or why reception rooms evolve into a final shape without the designer actually knowing the specific sizes and style of furniture used. Finally, while the chapter on discovery and programming, Chapter 3, is located near the beginning of the book, it might be helpful to reread this chapter before reading the Program Report chapter (12) because the later chapter is calculating results based on information gathered in the earlier chapter.

While the manner in which program requirements are arranged within a space plan affects the final outcome of the design, various arrangements also affect the ability of people to interact within and around that space, and how they emotionally feel. Personal space differs from one culture to another. Personal space differs whether we are among friends, at work, or with total strangers. In addition to program requirements, space planners must also consider culture— culture of both the people to occupy the space and the nature of the business for which the space is being designed. Each space must be analyzed and planned according to its occupants and their unique needs.

To achieve a successful space plan, and then a finished designed environment, it is important to first listen to clients, understand what they are saying and asking for, and then to incorporate their ideas into a space plan based on the designer's knowledge, ability, and creativity.

Mary Lou Bakker

ACKNOWLEDGMENTS

I am very appreciative of the various designers with whom I had the pleasure of working over numerous years and for all the technical information, drafting, sketching, and lettering techniques they offered along the way. Some of my most valued space planning experiences were gained while working for a furniture dealer, CI, who often had clients with large quantities of workstations. Later, when working at design firms GHK and RGA, I was able to apply the planning skills I acquired previously to full-scale design projects with great success.

Then I had the wonderful opportunity to bring those space planning skills to even greater fruition when I was asked to teach space planning at the Illinois Institute of Art–Schaumburg (formerly Ray College of Design). Each year, I looked for a textbook on two-dimensional space planning for office interiors, but to no avail. So, each year I distributed many handouts to the students and drew other visuals on the whiteboard. I am indebted to Susan Kehrer, then an assistant librarian, now an academic adviser, who encouraged me to write my own space planning book. This book is a result of that encouragement; it incorporates the extensive outlines, handouts, and drawings from my lecture notes.

I also want to acknowledge and thank Tom Dryjanski, a furniture specifier with whom I worked, who first planted the concept of teaching in my mind by his example of teaching at a local college. What a marvelous idea: teaching—what a great way to give back to my profession! I began to collect articles and other data relating to interior design, which became the basis for the many class handouts and illustrations in this book.

Two other people instrumental in my teaching success were Carolyn Buchach, chairperson at the Illinois Institute of Art–Schaumburg, and Emmelou Wilson, my first point of contact there. I am grateful for their efforts in securing the teaching position for me.

All sales reps are to be commended for their tireless efforts in continually educating designers on product details and nuances as products change or are newly introduced. Their wealth of knowledge is a great asset for assisting designers as design development unfolds. In particular, I want to thank sales reps from Allsteel, Haworth, Herman Miller, Hon, Kimball, Knoll, Steelcase, and Teknion, who provided tours of their respective showrooms when I was researching the most recent versions of work area systems.

When I wrote the section on videoconferencing for the first printing, back when videoconferencing was up-and-coming, I had the opportunity to visit two international design firms, to see and experience their two very different videoconferencing set-ups. I greatly appreciated those occasions. As videoconferencing technology advanced and became a regular presence in many conference rooms, I am thankful to have worked as a tenant representative on several government projects, General Services Administration (GSA) and Department of Justice, Office of Justice Programs (DOJ, OJP), whereby I gained first-hand knowledge not only of design and construction requirements for the equipment, but also how to operate the various gizmos to run orderly and smooth conferences for both videoconferencing and in-house AV presentations.

I want to give special thanks to Dom Ruggerio, Ruggerio & Associates, and James Landa, past chairperson at International Academy of Design & Technology–Chicago, for reading many chapters of the of the book early on. Their comments and insight were very helpful.

Several case and feasibility studies that I conducted for some clients earlier in my career, and the resulting written reports, were beneficial preparation for learning to clearly articulate and communicate information in this book. In particular, for a booklet we worked on together, I would like to thank Stewart Skubel, Heery International, and his list of adverbs—*generally, usually, typically, normally, customarily*—and on the list went. He is correct: in the design industry, there are almost never any absolutes: for every condition, for every solution or design option offered, another designer may suggest an equally compelling alternative.

David Keck, a past client and now a friend, has given me much verbal encouragement over the years. In addition to reviewing this book, he pushed me to get my architectural license and LEED accreditation. A very big thanks.

Another past client and friend, Al Keller, provided unique projects where I first gained insight into alternative work styles, the importance of costs per SF per employee, and the metric system. Thank you.

It was prudent to validate numerous points throughout the book. I truly value the various people and designers who responded via the telephone and emails to my diverse number of questions.

I am very happy to have had the opportunity to work with Cheryle Rome-Beatty over the years. She is a wonderful designer and artist, which is reflected in the numerous figures that she drew for the book. Other designers and past coworkers who contributed chapter-opening photographs of their work are Jeffrey J. Cohen, Todd Ezrin, Mike Given, Matthew Nichols, Ernst Pierre-Toussaint, Cheryle Rome-Beatty, Jeff Wirt, and Kevin Wyllie. I cherish their friendship and mentoring.

I am also grateful for the review and constructive criticism of reviewers Elizabeth F. Pober, University of Oklahoma; Amy Rogovich, New England School of Art and Design; Jacie Johnson, Weber State University; Lubomir Savov Popov, Bowling Green State University; Kathleen Anne Ryan, Washington State University.

I want to thank Fairchild Books and their associated staff for publishing this book. I also want to thank all of my friends and family who listened to me talk about this book for many years, wondering when it would become a reality.

Finally, I am thankful for the diversity of clients with whom I have had the privilege to provide space planning and design services for the renovations, refreshes, and relocations of their office spaces. Through these clients and their projects, I had opportunities, challenges, and experiences to gain a well-rounded scope of knowledge in the wonderful profession of interior design.

It has been a real pleasure to write this book. It took many years: I moved from one city to another city, changed jobs, and watched the industry go from drafting boards to computers. Work habits have changed for many people from a "must come into the office every day" to having alternative work location options. I also changed from working at design firms where I did the space planning to working on the client side where I now review plans provided by other designers and space planners. While working on this book I had the pleasure of sitting outside, writing chapters and text long-hand; going from desktop to laptop, sipping a cappuccino at a coffee shop, or sitting inside at the computer; all the time reflecting on the best way to present space planning principles and procedures. Life never stops changing; yet the process of space planning remains the same—acquire a client; listen to the client; obtain program requirements; create a space plan; develop the design, finishes and furniture specs; document all decisions through notes and drawings; participate during construction; and watch clients move into their fabulous, new office spaces. I believe this book will be a valued tool for every designer, whether he or she is just embarking on a space planning and design career, mentoring other designers, or working with a client on that *fantastic space design*.

Mary Lou Bakker

ABBREVIATIONS AND ACRONYMS

CODES

ADA	Americans with Disability Act	IgCC	International Green Construction Code
BOCA	Building Officials and Code Administrators	IRC	International Residential Code
IBC	International Building Code	NBC	National Building Code of Canada
ICC	International Code Council	SBC	Standard Building Code
IEBC	International Existing Building Code	UBC	Uniform Building Code

CONSTRUCTION DOCUMENTS

A/C	Air Conditioning	D or d	Deep or Depth
AFF	Above Finished Floor	DIDs	Design Intent Drawings
@	At	EXTG	Existing
CA	Contract Administration	EQ	Equal
CAD	Computer-aided Design	FLR HGT	Floor Height
CADD	Computer-aided Design and Drafting	GFCI	Ground-fault Circuit-interrupter
CF	Cubic Feet	GFI	Ground-fault Interrupter
CH	Ceiling Height	GSF	Gross Square Feet
℄	Center Line	GYP BD	Gypsum Board [Sheetrock] *Drywall*
CDs	Contract Documents [unofficially, CDs will occasionally also mean construction drawings]	H or h	Height
		HVAC	Heating, Ventilation, and Air Conditioning
		L or l	Length
CMU	Concrete Masonry Unit	MAX	Maximum

CONSTRUCTION DOCUMENTS (continued)

MEP	Mechanical, Electrical, and Plumbing Engineers	RFI	Request for Information
MIN	Minimum	RSF	Rentable Square Feet
NSF	Net Square Feet	SF	Square Feet, Square Foot
OA	Over All	SIM	Similar
OC	On Center	TYP	Typical
OPP	Opposite	UNO	Unless Noted Otherwise
PL or PLAM	Plastic Laminate	UON	Unless Otherwise Noted
psf	Pounds per Square Foot	USF	Usable Square Feet
P&D	Power and Data	VAV	Variable Air Volume
QTY	Quantity	VCT	Vinyl Composite Tile
RCP	Reflected Ceiling Plan	VOCs	Volatile Organic Compounds
		W or w	Wide or Width

INTERIOR DESIGN PROFESSION

A&D	Architects and Designers	RFP	Request for Proposal
CD	Chair Depth	R/U	Efficiency Ratio—RSF/USF
COL	Customer's Own Leather	SOW	Scope of Work
COM	Customer's Own Material	TFO	Tenant Fit Out
CW	Chair Width	TI	Tenant Improvements
DD	Design Development	TL	Table Length
Dr or dr	Drawer [for file cabinets]	TW	Table Width
KD	Knocked Down	3-D	3-dimensional
LCA	Life-cycle Assessment	WS	Workstation [occasionally worksurface]
PED or peds	Pedestal		

ORGANIZATIONS

AIA	American Institute of Architects	LEED	Leadership in Energy and Environmental Design
ASID	American Society of Interior Designers	LEED CI	Leadership in Energy and Environmental Design Commercial Interiors
BOMA	Building Owners and Managers Association	LEED AP	Leadership in Energy and Environmental Design Accredited Professional
CREW	Commercial Real Estate Women, Inc.		
IDEC	Interior Design Educators Council, Inc.	NCIDQ	National Council for Interior Design Qualification
IFMA	International Facilities Management Association	UL	Underwriters Laboratory
IIDA	International Interior Design Association		

OTHER

EX	Example
JIT	Just-in-time
PR	Public Relations

TECHNOLOGY

ATM	Automated Teller Machine	LAN	Local Area Network
A/V	Audio/Visual	PC	Personal Computer
CRT	Cathode Ray Tube [computer terminal]	VTC	Video Teleconferencing
		VDT	Video Display Terminal [computer terminal]
EDP	Electronic Data Processing		
IT	Information Technology	WAN	Wide Area Network

TITLES

CEO	Chief Executive Officer	HR	Human Resources
CFO	Chief Financial Officer	VP	Vice President

"No matter what he does, every person on earth plays a central role in the history of the world. And normally he doesn't know it."

—Coelho, Paulo. *The Alchemist*,
(HarperSanFrancisco, 1988), p. 164.

1

INTRODUCTION TO SPACE PLANNING

Space Planning!

What does that term mean—*space planning*?

As a young girl I used to pore over and study house plans that appeared in the newspaper each Sunday. I compared how the plans were repetitious or how they differed from one week to the next, how the plans might be similar to houses with which I was familiar or were the plans unique. Did the plans present new ideas and concepts for the inhabitants or did the plans seem conventional? Did the plans look logical [to my young eyes]? Did the plans have enough rooms or the right rooms? Were the rooms large enough? Was there a good adjacency and flow to the rooms? Did the plans contain a desired wish list of rooms, or only the basic necessity of rooms? *What did the perfect Dream House look like?*

Sometimes the plans received high praise! Sometimes I replanned the layouts. *If the architect had just switched this room and that room around—it would be a much better plan. Perhaps another room should have opened directly to the exterior or been located on a different floor level. Oh—there were so many thoughts about, what if . . . !* It was the spatial layout of the interior rooms and spaces that interested me the most. Ah—space planning!

Although most houses and residential buildings are designed, laid out, and drafted by architects as a complete package for both the exterior facade and interior walls and rooms, many commercial office buildings are designed by architects as *core and shell* buildings with unfinished and unconditioned space on each floor level (see cover). This approach provides opportunity for interior designers to space plan and finish out the interior floors and spaces.

According to *Encyclopædia Britannica*:

Because of the technological complexity of contemporary planning and building, it is no longer possible for a single architect or designer to be an expert in all the many aspects that make up a modern building . . . While the architect usually concerns himself with the overall design of buildings, the interior designer is concerned with the more intimately scaled aspects of design . . . and Although the desire to create a pleasant environment is as old as civilization itself, the field of interior design is relatively new . . . The field of interior design already has a number of specialized areas. One of the newer areas is space planning, *i.e., the analysis of space needs, allocation of space, and the interrelation of functions within business firms.*[1]

SPACE PLANNING—this specialized area of interior design is the essence of this book.

In the interior design profession, the term *space planning* refers specifically to the process whereby a *space planner* methodically and creatively lays out or plans an initial two-dimensional floor plan, known as a *space plan*, based on a client's program requirements and other planning components. It is a task performed during the conceptual design phase, the second of five basic design phases. (Box 1.1)

THE PROCESS OF SPACE PLANNING

Space planning, however, is more than just arranging rooms on or within a building floor plate. Space planning is a many-faceted task that incorporates not only clients' program requirements (needs, wants, and wishes) but also their current and future conditions, workflow, culture, and vision. It involves using both leading-edge and tried-and-true techniques, listening and explaining, and other seemingly opposing methods.

Space planning takes into consideration other aspects of the design phases as well as outside influences, such as budgets and schedules, building and ADA (Americans with Disabilities Act) code requirements, the use of new or reuse of existing furniture, "green" products and concepts, and other components as identified during the programming process. Space planning requires an understanding of the client, the building envelope, and the location of the space being planned; general knowledge; industry and design knowledge; logic, experience, and a sense of history; a willingness to listen; keeping an open mind and the ability to conceptualize how people will use and interact within the finished, built space—all reflected on a two-dimensional plan (Fig. 1.1).

There is no single criterion for the approach taken to space planning. Designers, or space planners, as they are known during this phase, will develop their own unique abilities that will allow them to achieve exciting, innovative, and efficient space plans. Experienced space planners are able to bring all concepts, both

FIGURE 1.1 Planning spaces

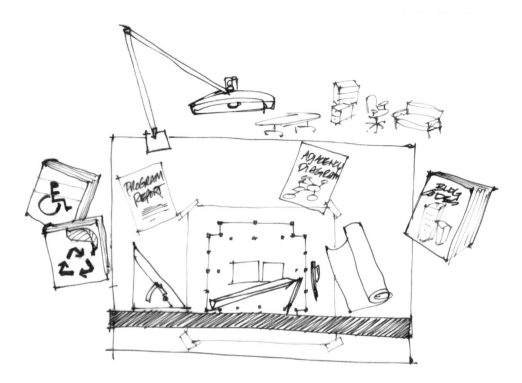

tangible and intangible, together in functional and creative layouts to optimize the space and floor plan within the building constraints.

Space Analysis

Prior to starting a new project or space plan, it is important for the designer to understand both the space to be planned and the culture of the client for whom the planning is being done. Space is three-dimensional, yet the planning task is based on a two-dimensional plane, often seen from above and at a reduced size or scale; most plans are printed at scales of $1/8$ in. or $1/4$ in., sometimes even at $1/16$ in. Even on the computer, drawings are generally viewed at reduced sizes, often displaying only partial sections of a plan at any given time.

"The seventeenth-century engraving (Fig. 1.2) . . . poses a question that persists today: Is the designer thinking of his work from the lofty bird's-eye viewpoint of a disembodied intellect, or is he able to project himself into the person of the participator, and so conceive his design in terms of the effect it will actually have on the senses of the people who use his buildings?"[2]

Design philosophy as well as the amount of workspace required per person can vary from locale to locale and from business type to business type. Some buildings are designed and constructed to house a particular client with tailor-made rooms and spaces to accommodate specific needs or desires. Other buildings are designed as speculative buildings to house a variety of clients and businesses. Older buildings are often renovated and converted from the original intended use for completely different types of occupants and usage.

Not only must designers understand the proportions of the intended space, they must also be able to address how the space will be used based on a client's building, location, business, philosophy, and needs and desires. John Wood, the Younger, provided his approach to designing cottages in Bath, England: "In order to make myself master of the subject, it was necessary for me to feel as the cottager himself . . . no architect can form a convenient plan unless he ideally places himself in the situation of the person for whom he designs."[3]

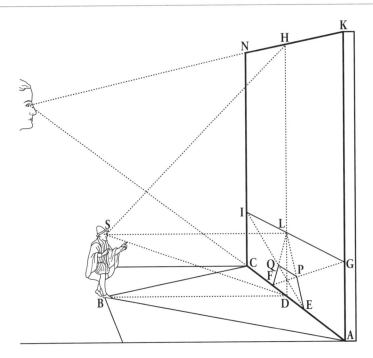

Romance of Space Planning

Many people are inclined to think of interior design, and thus space planning, as fun, creative, imaginative, artistic, and sort of romantic. The average person believes that they do not have these artistic capabilities, so they look to designers to provide inspiring designs and built spaces.

Occasionally, designers plan their own spaces, but most of the time designers are planning spaces for other people: spaces in which people work, live, vacation, shop, and worship; spaces in which people have time to stop and analyze as many details as they wish; spaces barely seen as people rush by from one place to the next; spaces that are public or private, official or makeshift, seen once or every day; spaces that last for an eon; and spaces that are demolished almost before the paint is dry.

Ultimately, designers have no control over how their designed spaces are used or for how long those spaces will remain intact. However, designers can and should take responsible steps to satisfy the immediate direction as provided by their clients. In the process, they can be creative, have fun, record or photograph the finished space, and know that nothing lasts forever—no matter how beautiful the space might be.

Space Planning Process

At times, the space planner will need to take a macro approach in order to grasp the holistic requirements. At other times, the space planner will need to focus on specific facets of the plan—to place files or recycle containers in precise locations, for example. Space planning requires the designer's focus to zoom into a tiny section of the plan then out to the overall plan and back again in order to incorporate all of the many aspects and requirements needed to achieve a well laid-out and energetic space plan.

Before space planning actually begins, other design services and tasks are normally performed as part of the pre-design phase. Some tasks are completed at the designer's firm: drafting typical layouts, researching code issues, reviewing the client's lease or building standards. Other tasks are completed at the client's present location: programming the client's current and future needs, inventory of existing furniture to be reused, discussing budgets and schedules, and finally, ascertaining the desired ambience for the new space. Certain tasks can be performed simultaneously, whereas other tasks are conducted sequentially.

Sometimes the space planner will work alone, sometimes as a team member, and sometimes as a team leader. The space planner may gather and compile the client's program requirements or simply be handed a list of requirements supplied by either the client or another design team. Many of these factors depend on the size and scope of the project, location of the project, nature of the client or the client's business, or the design firm makeup and structure.

Space Planning and Design Development

While in the process of space planning, designers should initiate and contemplate design development—a raised ceiling here, an exposed brick wall there, a change of flooring materials. However, in a sequential order, it is better to first present the space plan to the client, discuss technical aspects of the plan, receive approval of the plan from the client, and then further develop the design concepts to show the client in a future meeting.

During early planning phases, clients are habitually more focused on making sure that their program requirements are met rather than envisioning the finished design. In other words, have all rooms been placed on the floor plan? Are rooms the right size? Are rooms that need to be adjacent actually next to or sufficiently near each other?

Upon first reviewing the initial space plan, clients tend to physically point at rooms on the plan while they count out the required number of offices, workstations, conference rooms, and so on. Clients want to make sure that there are appropriate numbers of work areas for their employees' needs. This is more important, at this moment, than looking at the curvilinear corridors, angled furniture, or the imagined raised ceiling.

This is also the time to discuss how the building code or any specific issues as required by code might impact the plan or finished space and how the latest technology advancements will be incorporated into the finished space as a planned enhancement, not as an afterthought. It is best to meet and discuss all of the practical aspects as applicable prior to generating excitement over plans that look and sound great, but do not satisfy functional requirements. Once these and other technical aspects are met, then the designer can freely move on to the creative aspects of design development.

SPACE PLANS

There is no one correct or perfect space plan for any given space, building, or client. There are good plans. There are exciting plans. There are plans that work today and that will work for the client at the time of move in. There are plans that work today, but that will need to be changed after the time of client move in. Two or three or five designers can start with the same program requirements and the same building footprint; they will create different space plans. The plans may be similar or vastly different. Most likely, any one of the plans will adequately fulfill the needs of the client. There is no exact science for creating good space plans. It is for each designer to ascertain the needs and wants of the client for each new project, and then combine all of the aspects of space planning into a final plan that is pleasing and acceptable.

SPACE PLAN COMPONENTS

All interior spaces and space plans, regardless of the nature or size of the business, are made up of the same basic components. These include an entry or reception area, typical rooms, semi-typical rooms, food rooms, support rooms, employee or staff work areas, furniture and equipment, circulation or corridors, building core, public-accessible rooms or areas, building and ADA code requirements, and building structure and infrastructure. A quick review of the Table of Contents lists these components as individual chapters, first to be studied and understood, then incorporated within the discovery process and Program Report outlining each client's needs, wants, and desires, and finally, integrated into an overall space plan.

Individual room names or terminology may be consistent from one client to the next or from one type of business to another type of business, or different names may be used for the same type of room. Terms such as *restrooms* and *washrooms* usually mean the same thing as bathrooms, but not always. Company offices in a manufacturing plant may need a lounging area in its restrooms, and a company with an exercise room may wish to include changing areas or showers in its washrooms. A library in an interior design firm will mean something very different from a library requested by a law firm. Designers should always verify and understand the component list, terminology, and makeup for each new project prior to space planning the components on a floor plan.

There is no official designation, but in general, components can be divided into five categories.

1. **The space**: building, location, history
2. **The client**: type of business, program requirements, desired ambience and vision, budgets and schedules, "baggage"
3. **Elements of the space**: furniture, room size, circulation, construction
4. **Technical requirements**: building codes, ADA codes, infrastructure
5. **Occupants and the environment**: health, safety, and welfare, universal design, going green

The Space

What is known about the space? Does it have many windows or just a few? Are there views to be considered, either picturesque or unattractive? If the inside of the space can be seen from a distance when standing outside the building, will this affect how the space is planned? Are there bay windows or balconies, which often solicit remarkable first impressions but are not very conducive for functional space?

The designer should understand why the client selected the particular building or space to be planned, designed, and inhabited. Was it the only space available? Did the building offer the best rent negotiations? Or, does the client have an affinity for the space and building? Will that affinity or lack thereof affect the planning process?

The Building

Buildings can be of any type—historical, contemporary, modern, neoclassical, or nondescript. They

FIGURE 1.3 Initial space plan: Offices along front windows of a building

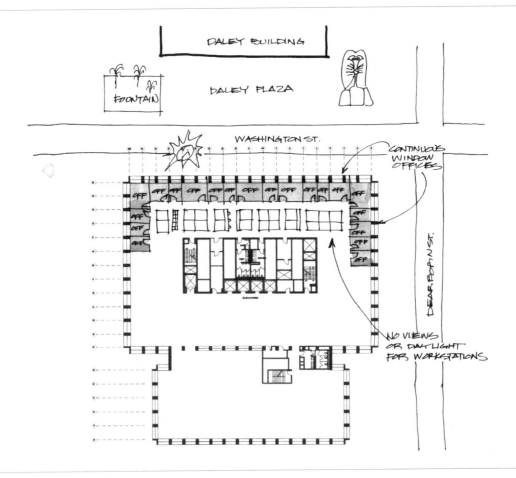

may be low rise, high rise, or single story. They may be constructed of wood frame, solid core material such as brick or concrete masonry units (CMUs), brick veneer, steel and glazing, steel and unit panel assemblies, and green or other materials. The building type may or may not affect the size or configuration of the interior rooms and open areas. A floor level may or may not influence the placement of the entry door. Building construction type, however, can and does bring into play different design options for exposing construction materials or raising the ceilings (see Chapter 13).

Many landlords set regulations and standards to be considered when planning the space, such as public area colors and finishes or suite entry door styles. How will these stipulations affect the space plan?

Building Location

Building location can affect both the planning and design of a space. For a gas and oil pipeline project to be located in Prudhoe Bay, Alaska, where year-round the local area consists of frigid temperatures, snow, and caribou, furniture and layouts needed to reflect soft edges and curves. Designers were instructed not to specify any chrome or other "cold" materials. Finishes were to have "warm" and even "fuzzy" feelings. Many psychological aspects were considered to help alleviate the feelings of depression and isolation that can develop in such remote conditions.

On a more local scale, the selected building for another project sat across the street from one of the few open plazas in downtown Chicago. By positioning offices along the side windows, as opposed to the front windows, the plan not only provided natural daylight for more people within the space but also extended the boundaries of the space beyond the confines of the building. In this way, everyone enjoyed the feeling of being part of the outside world (Figs. 1.3 and 1.4).

FIGURE 1.4 Final space plan: Offices along the side windows of a building with an overlay illustrating daylight access and exterior views[5]

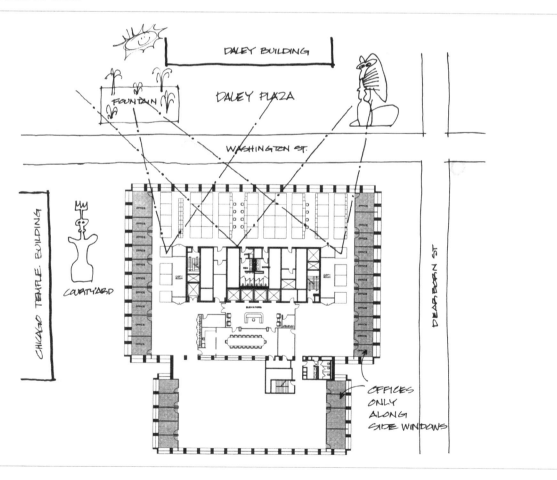

Building History

Some buildings and spaces have more history than do others. Sometimes it is possible to preserve that history. Other times there is no reason to preserve it.

Buildings may be assigned historic protection by local and national historic preservation committees that need to approve any changes made to the space, especially on the outside of the building. Designers should be aware of any such historical status, as stated guidelines may control or influence parts of the space plan.

For those buildings not under historic protection, the designer may still want to consider its history when planning new spaces within. The designer may want the plan to reflect the symmetry or the angles or modernism of the building. Many older cities, for instance, have angled streets, which in turn often dictate angled buildings. To see those angles reflected in a space plan can provide added value and harmony to the overall space.

In addition, it is frequently beneficial for designers to examine the surrounding building site and community at large. This holistic approach can often generate abstract ideas or assist with applicable LEED credits for public transportation (see Appendix B).

The Client

There is no typical client; they come with many backgrounds and points of view. Clients may be remodeling or relocating for the tenth time or the first time. This may be their only space, or it may be a new branch location. The space may require an expansion to house a growing employee population, or the client may be reducing space due to selling off a part of the business. The client may be an old and staid company or a nascent, up-and-coming company.

The Client's Business

Not only will the designer want to understand the makeup of each client's company, but the designer also needs to understand the client's type of business. Some design solutions will work for many clients, even clients of varying business types. Other design aspects will work for only one client or business type. Even when the same design feature works in more than one

space plan, it is still important for the designer to make that feature unique for each client. No company wants to look like another company, unless they are branding their own locations.

Programming Requirements

Many people tend to think of the program requirements as just a list of the number of employees and rooms or other areas needed in the space. Program requirements do provide the number of rooms and areas, but they also offer much more. They present an ideal model, both written and graphic, of the client's needs, desires, wishes, and makeup. Through programming efforts, the client can articulate the management style and structure of the company—progressive, autocratic, laid-back, traditional, customer-driven, employee-owned, and on and on.

What do these adjectives tell us? Well, if the company is employee-owned, it might want nice space but have a conservative budget in order to keep money available for other investments, or it could mean an expensive space to show off its business success. An autocratic structure may indicate that the largest offices should be corner offices with more than one window, with all other offices placed as space allows. A laid-back structure may suggest that the majority of employees and workstations are placed along the window walls with offices occupying interior spaces.

Desired Ambience

Many clients cannot conceive of or imagine the final design. They often cannot articulate the desired ambience for their new spaces. To aid clients, designers frequently use metaphors to initiate space planning concepts and even to follow through on the design development.

For new offices of a major magazine publisher, the project manager elaborated: "[The] floor was treated as an open loft broken up with elements endemic to city planning . . . the connective traffic route became a grand promenade. Thematic derivatives extend to other circulation lanes (boulevards, streets), informal meeting enclaves (parks), private offices (high-rent districts), angled workstation blocks (workers' housing), etc."[6]

In another office space overlooking Times Square, "often referred to as the 'crossroads of the world.'" . . . The designer, using a similar metaphor, "remarks that the boulevard design concept was used on each floor, which presents thoroughfares extending through the space."[7]

By using metaphors, the designer can draw analogies to help the client conceptualize various designs.

Budgets and Schedules

Every client has a budget, even those clients who wish to spend a lot of money due to their desired décor or the size of the space to be designed. Although some clients may be reluctant to divulge their intended budget, it is imperative that designers be aware of the amount of money the client wants to spend. With this knowledge, designers can often recommend solutions that may curb expenditures in one area for a much-needed trade-off with another area of the design.

The same can be said about schedules. How much time has been allowed not only for design development and documentation but also for construction of the space? Is there enough time to design a custom reception desk or glass entry doors, items that regularly have long lead times? Or should the designer propose standard products that are typically stocked in local warehouses for immediate delivery and that are generally just as well designed as custom pieces but are normally less expensive?

By discussing budgets and schedules with clients up front for each new project, designers demonstrate their capabilities and acumen in other areas of business and life in addition to their creative competencies.

Client "Baggage"

All clients have some sort of "baggage" in the form of furniture to be reused; a required high-volume, smelly copy room; ideas of how much money, or lack thereof, they are willing to spend on the food room; or strong ideas regarding the style of entry door they wish to use. Much of this baggage is made known to the designer at the beginning of the project.

There is no point in fighting clients about this baggage. It is better for the designer to ask questions and know all the facts at the start of space planning. Then each issue can be dealt with in such a way as to minimize its impact on the overall design. It may be possible to repaint existing file cabinets or reupholster a sofa that will be reused. Maybe the copy room can be located on the other side of the supply room. Although people may need to walk a bit farther to get copies, the ammonia smell will be far enough away from the work areas to justify the walk.

Elements of the Space

Just as the overall space plan is based on the quantity and size of rooms and circulation corridors, individual rooms are based on the quantity and size of furniture or other items within the room, along with a determined amount of circulation space needed to navigate around these items. But how do these elements affect and interact with each other?

Furniture, Equipment, and Other Elements

The selection of specific furniture, equipment, and other elements can affect the final room size and shape. For example, many training rooms are sized to seat approximately 20 participants. When occupants sit in rows of fixed, auditorium chairs with tablet arms, such seating, per building code, allows 7 square feet (SF) per person (see Table 13.1) or 140 SF total for the seating area of those 20 participants. Aisles and the lectern area are in addition to the 140 SF.

When participants sit in movable tablet-arm chairs or in chairs at individual or group-occupied tables, building codes require 15 SF per person (see Table 13.1) or 300 SF total for occupant seating plus additional square footage for the aisles and speaker areas. Obviously, the furniture and layout can greatly influence the room size.

Room Size and Ambience

Customarily, rooms are sized to be no larger than needed to adequately house the furniture to be placed within the room along with an appropriate amount of circulation space. Sometimes, however, it is desirable for selected rooms, such as a reception area, to be grander than the amount of required furniture might dictate (see Figure 9.7b).

In terms of pure space planning or space requirements, the furniture in this reception area could fit into a smaller space or more furniture could be placed in the space. Space planning, however, is more than just providing the appropriate or minimum amounts of square footage for individual elements within a space. Room sizes and layouts can also be thought of in terms of the desired relevance or ambience for the built space.

Circulation

It stands to reason that a certain amount of space, otherwise known as circulation, is needed around each piece of furniture and equipment in order to access those items. Circulation within rooms and around individual items of furniture or equipment is usually based on common sense, logic, and minimum clearances required for servicing the equipment.

When circulation connects rooms, it is commonly referred to as *hallways*, *aisles*, or *corridors*. Specific code requirements for this circulation are governed by the classification of the business and the number of people being served, as well as whether the building has a sprinkler system (see Chapter 5).

Construction

Typically, people think of interior walls as being constructed with drywall. We are accustomed to seeing rooms separated from each other in this way: a wall, a room, a wall, a room, a wall. The rooms are accessible by either a door or a cased opening.

Actually, many alternate materials can be used for "construction" of walls or as dividers, which can be included in the space plan from the very start. Glass walls—framed or frameless, translucent, clear, or laminated—or acrylic panels can divide spaces for privacy, yet allow some light to transmit to the next space. Corrugated metals can be used around conferencing centers or teaming areas. Back-lit glass block can form the basis of a reception desk or gaming area. Within their standard product-lines of furniture, many manufacturers offer full-height panels that can be installed to the ceiling to appear as a permanent wall, yet can be demounted and reinstalled as the client's needs grow and change (see Fig. 7.7b). Even hanging solid or perforated fabrics

and textiles give the illusion of privacy and walls.

Technical Requirements

Technical requirements are many and varied: they may be official requirements or comfort requirements. They may be requirements for pieces of equipment in terms of the amount of space clearance or electrical power or temperature control needed, or they may be requirements for the overall space. Oftentimes, an engineer will calculate many of the technical requirements, but the space planner will provide for the rooms and layouts to incorporate those requirements.

Building and ADA Codes

Building codes cover building construction, both exterior and interior, and the health, safety, and welfare of the people who will occupy those buildings. ADA codes not only prohibit discrimination against any persons but also require all public areas to be accessible to everyone (see Chapter 5). Codes must be met and clearly shown on all space plans and accompanying construction documents in order to receive a construction permit.

Infrastructure

Heating, ventilation, and cooling (HVAC), while not strictly a part of the designer's responsibility, must fit into the space plan as an integrated part of the overall design. Ductwork needs to go through or under the ceilings or floors, up through the walls, or down through the space. Sometimes the ductwork can be hidden by constructing a soffit around it. It can be exposed; it can hug the ceiling or be dropped down a foot or more (see Fig. 13.1). However it is handled, there will be ductwork. It can be planned into the space or dangle as an eyesore.

Trading floors and computer intensive companies have high volumes of computer and electrical usage that require huge amounts of electrical wiring and data cabling. Like the ductwork, these wires and cables can be hidden in walls, under raised floors, or above ceilings, or they can be exposed and carried via horizontal ladder trays for a high-tech designed interior space.

With experience comes knowledge. Planners can increase closet sizes or strategically place bump-outs to house the vertical duct risers or wiring. Void spaces formed in angular or curved plans can also be used for risers, cabling, and other electrical wires. By analyzing these elements up front, the space planner can assimilate these varied necessities into the space plan from the beginning.

Occupants and the Environment

Designers were, and are, leading proponents of accessibility and usability of spaces by all people. Designers lead the charge to curb global warming by selecting more efficient light fixtures and lamps. Designers also specify many recycled and renewable products for all aspects of the designed space. With so many building dictates behind them, many designers are now taking a proactive focus to execute the National Council for Interior Design Qualification (NCIDQ) mantra regarding the health and welfare of the occupants in these newly sustainable and environmentally friendly buildings.

Health, Safety, and Welfare

With the aging of the population and the problem of obesity becoming more prevalent, everyone, including designers, will need to learn how to best address these issues. Designers can build health and other wellness aspects into the space plan from the start. For example, when designers strategically place a staircase in the center of activity, employees are equally likely to use the stairs as to walk a greater distance to use the elevator. Clearly, walking is good exercise, but climbing stairs is even better. While working on a General Services Administration (GSA) project, I was able to observe firsthand the efforts of this government agency to promote stairclimbing; they displayed posters stating that climbing stairs burns five times as many calories as taking the elevator—*How many calories have you burned today?*

Mental wellness can play a large part in our daily activities as well. By addressing employees' comfort, efficiency of their work areas, and ease of communication with coworkers, designers have been credited with reducing absenteeism. According to one article, "Studies show that people who are stressed tend to have more colds and body aches." It goes on to say, "[the] environment is just as important as what goes on in . . . rooms . . . considering the intricacies of the unseen elements, such as plumbing, air conditioning, and lighting, so that the temperature is just right, the air doesn't diffuse over the client, and the light doesn't shine in anyone's eyes." According to the article, "that which a person is not conscious of can still be incredibly affecting."[8]

Universal Design

Design and space planning should consider all who will use it; it should be inclusive. As designers, we should always design and plan for universal use, for everyone and by anyone. When we consider disabled people, we habitually tend to group people according to physical disabilities, such as impaired sight or hearing, reduced mobility to the point of using a wheelchair or cane, or shortened stature owing to a medical or genetic condition. However, a disabled person could be anyone; consider someone who is temporarily using crutches, or someone using both hands to carry a load of boxes, or even someone recovering from eye surgery. Thus, through the ADA Act (see Chapter 5), we have many codes that address the need for tactile surfaces, audio in addition to visual danger warnings, minimum and maximum installation heights, levered hardware, and other appropriate requirements.

In the past, where not specifically regulated by code requirements, furniture and other manufacturers have generally designed and scaled their products to be comfortably used by 85 percent of the "average" population. But what about others who are not physically disabled yet fall outside of what we consider to be average stature?

One of the most famous incidents occurred when Queen Elizabeth II visited the United States in 1991. While giving a speech in the US Congress, "[she] became a 'Talking Hat,' . . . by virtually disappearing behind a lectern scaled for President Bush [Sr.], she generated both amusement and a perfect example of the need for Universal Design."[9]

So amazing was this feat, that it was recalled more than 16 years later when she again returned to the United States for a visit. According to an article in the *Washington Post*, "Zantzinger's job is to make sure everything goes exactly as planned.... What could go wrong? During the queen's last visit, in 1991, it was the too-tall lectern—all you could see was a royal hat."[10]

When the Queen spoke in 1991, a small box was found and placed behind the lectern on which she could stand. When she returned in 2007, the lectern had been replaced with a new one designed to be lowered and raised as needed for each individual speaker.

Going Green

Recyclable, renewable, reusable, energy efficiency, sustainable, postconsumer products, and *waste reduction* are all various terms used to describe the concept of *green*. As Websites are constantly updated, words and wording may be slightly altered from these quoted internet definitions on green buildings, but the concepts remain the same:

> *Green building is a design and construction practice that promotes the economic health and well-being of your family, the community, and the environment.*[11]

> *Green building is the practice of increasing the efficiency with which buildings use resources—energy, water, and materials—while reducing the building impacts on human health and the environment, through better siting, design, construction, operation, maintenance, and removal—the complete building life cycle.*[12]

From this passion and awareness to create friendlier solutions to the environmental challenges facing the plant and to reduce the negative environmental impacts, the US Green Building Council developed the Leadership in Energy and Environmental Design (LEED), introducing the first version in 1998. It has been updated several times as new markets, advances in practices, and technology have evolved. "LEED is a framework for identifying, implementing, and measuring green building and neighborhood design, construction, operations, and maintenance. LEED is a *voluntary*, market-driven, consensus-based tool that serves as a guideline and assessment mechanism ... [for] commercial, institutional, and residential buildings ..."[13]

As more and more clients chose to achieve LEED certification (there is a fairly hefty cost associated with the process) or simply to implement some of the LEED framework without specifically registering their projects (thus eliminating certification costs), the building code organization, International Code Council (ICC), recognized the many benefits of green construction. In 2012 they introduced The International Green Construction Code (IgCC) as part of the overall family of code books (see Box 5.1).

Interior designers can participate equally with architects in designing more green spaces. By maintaining as many existing interior walls as possible when space planning a new project in recently vacated spaces, designers can help keep landfills from being overwhelmed with old construction debris. By reusing existing furniture wherever possible, exhaust fumes from trucks delivering new furniture are reduced. Providing access to daylight for all building inhabitants not only reduces electrical use when daylight harvesting is used (see Box 14.3), but also helps to reduce overall stress, which in turn can reduce employee turnover and medical costs. Planning for recycling containers is just as important as planning for reception areas. There are many ways that interior designers can plan for better health, welfare, and safety of people by taking responsibility for helping to protect our planet.

SPACE PLANNERS

Interior designers and space planners express many viewpoints, styles, and personalities. To illustrate this outlook, the design director at one firm drew circles and arrows showing how three designers at the firm went about producing a space plan (Fig. 1.5).

Designer A took a list of requirements, set each requirement down on the floor plan in an orderly, precise manner, with little time given to trying other options. After all, everything fit neatly into the plan, so it must be okay.

Designer B played with the requirements. If they made sense, they were added fairly quickly to the plan. If the requirements did not make sense, they were not included in the initial layout. In addition, some of the requirements were embellished, altered, or adjusted to help the overall plan look visually pleasing. Items were arranged, rearranged, and moved a dozen times before they came together in the final plan.

Designer C took a course somewhere between the two extremes. All required items were included in a final plan. Some time and thought was given to planning various layouts, but every idea under the sun was not exhausted before reaching a final plan.

All three designers are successful. Each of their respective clients liked their designer very much and continued to use that designer from one project to the next. Although their methods of planning varied, each of these designers had some of the same traits, traits that are essential for all designers and space planners.

All designers should have good follow-up and follow-through when planning for all of the client's program requirements. They need to pay attention to detail. They need to be in constant communication with their clients. And most of all, designers need to listen to what their clients have to say. It is the method of producing the final product that varied, not the product itself.

Planning Strategies

Differences in methodologies or planning strategies most likely extend from left or right hemispheric dominance of the brain, where "the left side of the brain processes in a logical and sequential order, while the right side is more visual and processes intuitively, holistically, and randomly."[15]

Neither left- nor right-brain dominance is totally right or totally wrong. Each side of the brain just processes information in a different way. With a holistic approach, the planner can start with the overall building and then work from large spaces down toward the smallest items, such as placement of files and coat closets. Under a sequential approach, the planner may start with individual items of furniture to build typical rooms, add corridors

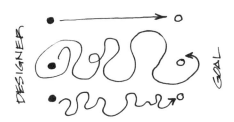

FIGURE 1.5 Path of travel taken by various designers for space planning[14]

as needed, and adjust all components into the building. One project may require one approach, and the next project may require the opposite approach. Sometimes a combination of planning strategies is the best approach. As designers, we can feel comfortable with our style, be it linear, holistic, or somewhere between. Then again, by striving to develop both sides of the brain, our designs can be greatly enhanced when all of our senses are used to produce a final package.

Implementing the Space Plan Components

Quantitative components such as furniture sizes, room functions, circulation factors, and the program lists can be documented, calculated, memorized, looked-up, or researched. They can be counted and verified on the plan.

Qualitative concepts concerning ambience, philosophy, and vision are harder to capture; these concepts cannot be learned or memorized, calculated, or explicitly taught. Examples demonstrate a particular solution for a curved conference room or angled workstation runs. Each one of these examples, however, is unique to a particular client, business, or building. The conference room could just as easily have been rectangular or hexagonal. The workstation runs could have been at 90 degrees to the building perimeter or on an angle of 70/20 degrees. Incorporating qualitative solutions are acquired through experience, trial and error, intuition, research, and observation.

Hand Sketching

Some designers start by hand sketching random concepts and layouts on tissue paper, also known as *sketch* or *trace paper* or *bum wad*. Sometimes the tissue is taped to a hard copy of the building base plan; at other times, it is simply laid over or on top of the base plan. Designers might doodle first or draw in typical rooms using single lines. They might chart out bubble diagrams or arbitrarily place suggestions of furniture on the tissue paper: something, anything, to make a start at laying out the various program requirements.

Drawing and Planning

Once a space planner is ready to start planning, he or she should gather everything together:

Program requirements

Building information
Client outlook
Coffee
Computer
Sketch paper
Soda
Client wishes
Codes
Markers
Pens

The space planner should then do the following:

Clear the mind!
Start.
Draw something—anything!
Move it around.
Play with it.
Walk away.
Throw it away.

Start over.
Take a break.
Look at it again.
Relax and have another coffee, a soda, some crackers, or fruit.

Show the plan to a codesigner.
Write down thoughts.
Reconsider the plan.
Try another idea!

Look at the requirements again.
Push the plan.
Look at other plans.
Reconsider the first idea.
Refine the ideas and plans.
Decide?

Yes, it's a good plan.
Step back and reconsider it one last time.
Finalize the plan for presentation to the client.

Expect to make some minor changes based on feedback from the client, and that's okay. It is not possible to get a final plan on the first try.

Once the designer is reasonably satisfied with the planning efforts, a new piece of paper can be taped to the base plan, and the resulting space plan is drawn as an initial "final" plan.

Computer-Aided Design and Drafting (CADD)

Other designers go straight to the computer to lay out and plan the rooms of each space. Ideas or layers can easily be copied over and over to add new thoughts or layouts; revise lines, corridors, or rooms; delete areas that do not work well; and rearrange program requirements as needed to provide a pleasing outcome. Layers can be turned off to save desired areas of the plan, and then turned on for printing a "final" plan once all parts and pieces of the layout come together.

Designers will develop personal methods for achieving the best space plan for a project. One designer may wish to start by sketching a few ideas on tissue paper and then go to the computer. Another designer may start on the computer and then sketch some ideas on tissue before finalizing the computer drawing. Some designers may be able to develop complete plans using only the computer. Each designer will develop a personal style of working, planning, and laying out space plans.

Peer Review

Whether sketching on tissue or the computer, it is important for space planners to collaborate with codesigners and peers throughout the design project, including the space planning task. The best designs generally do not happen in a vacuum. Suggestions and thoughts offered by associates may be the needed punch to finalize the layout. Even when the designer has laid out the "perfect" plan, it never hurts to have someone validate the plan prior to showing it to the client.

Space planning is intuitive. Space planning is logical. Space planning is creative. Space planning is fun. Space planning is methodical. Space planning is responsible.

In summary, and as an introduction to space planning, following are quotations from three exciting authors. These authors are site planners, planners in nature, and planners of movement within the city, yet their words speak to the essence of planning interior spaces.

According to site planner Kevin Lynch:

Design is a process of envisioning and weighing possibilities, mindful of past experience. . . . Each initial solution will fail to achieve the outcome sought. Failure points to another way of thinking about the problem.

Some [designers] prefer to make decisions along the way, moving deliberately from one step to the next, while others engage in a free-flowing inquiry in which nothing is frozen until all aspects seem right.

Designers . . . choose the mode in which to begin their design. . . . It is a schizoid business. At times, the designer is relaxed and uncritical, allowing her subconscious mind to suggest forms and connections, most of them fantastic and unworkable. At other times, she turns sharply on those suggestions, probing and testing them. So she swings from doodling to stern and critical review, and part of her skill lies in managing those two states of mind.[16]

Design ecologist Ian L. McHarg believes:

The ideal is seldom a choice of either/or, but rather the combination of both or all. One dreams of the museum and cabaret, concert hall and ball park within stone's throw, but it would be as splendid if the mountains, the ocean and the primeval forest were at the doorstep. . . .[17]

In his book, *Design of Cities*, Edmund Bacon says:

The idea itself must grow organically over time. It cannot and should not be produced in all its manifestations at a single moment.

As soon as we are able to think simultaneously about a range of systems and our thoughts relate one to the other, we are able to create a feeling of continuity and harmony in architectural designs.[18]

Space planning is a state of mind!

PROJECTS

Images with narrative

Project #1: Write a 2–3 page essay

Analyze existing interior office projects to better understand how design develops from nothing to a finished, built space.

1. Research design industry magazines to locate articles on two commercial office projects that include both floor plans and photographs.
2. How are the projects similar; how are they different? *materials*
3. Did the designers use metaphors to describe the elements?
4. How does the space plan relate to the building architecture?

5. How did the designer incorporate green design or code requirements into the final plan?
6. How were the budget or schedules addressed in the articles?
7. Was this a good approach for the plan and design, or should a different approach have been taken?
8. How can these lessons be applied to future space plans?

Project #2: Round table discussion

During class, students should discuss and compare their findings on the featured office articles.

American Architectural Rewards

Interior design rewards

BD.com

Due Monday

Looking at space compare/contrast impressions visual

2

CLIENTS AND THEIR ORGANIZATIONS

"The customer is always right!" "Even when wrong—the CUSTOMER is still right!"

The store manager used to explain this customer philosophy during staff meetings at an upscale, residential furniture store where I first worked for a short time after graduating from college. He went on to say that without the customer there would be no sales, no commissions, and no opportunity for design; customer interest always came first.

The same should be true for designers and their business clients who want new or remodeled space designs. To provide the best design and help each client make the best decisions, it is crucial for the designer to listen to and understand their clients and learn as much about their needs and desires as possible. The designer must come to understand: how are clients and their respective business setups similar? How are they different? How is each client or business unique?

Once the project is completed, the designer may never revisit the site. Ultimately, the designer does not even have to like the outcome of a project. Granted, the experience is much more rewarding when the designer is pleased, but it is most important for the client to be happy and satisfied. The client must live with the end results long after the designer finishes. In addition, satisfied clients are more likely to reuse the same designer or firm on future projects and to recommend the designer to other potential clients. Therefore, it is in the designer's best interest to incorporate their clients' needs and desires whenever possible, to design to the clients' highest expectations, and to let them be right.

When starting each new project, a designer should first take a macro approach to grasp the overall makeup of the client. Once the broad implications are identified, the designer can then focus on the nuances of each aspect of the design and space plan. Macro topics to consider for each client include:

- Client needs, desires, and expectations
- Legal classifications
- Use and occupancy classifications
- Work area mix
- Job title descriptions

Budget Always ask

Range

CLIENT NEEDS, DESIRES, AND EXPECTATIONS

Design projects are initiated based on clients' needs or desires to renovate or relocate their existing office spaces. Whatever the situation, the clients should know what to expect during all phases of the design process and after moving into the new space. Can they afford the project? Have they allowed enough time for the space to be adequately designed and constructed? Do they have a realistic idea of what the space will look like upon completion?

Often times, it behooves the designer to take an active role in educating the client, to explain the steps and phases that will occur during the design process. According to the Washington, D.C., chapter of the American Institute of Architects (AIA), "In today's economy, an architect's (and designer's) vision and skills are needed beyond the drawing board, in the board room."[1]

Single-Location Clients

Clients with a single location tend to relocate, remodel, or refurbish only once or twice every 5 to 20 years or so. They generally do not know much about what to expect or what to do during the design process. They may not know what things cost or how long it takes for the project to be completed. Some clients may conduct research or ask a lot of questions, but many clients may be too embarrassed or intimidated to ask questions. These clients will probably need much guidance from the designer.

Clients with Multiple or Branch Locations

Clients with multiple or branch locations are typically more familiar with the design process. They customarily have a facility or real estate group that is responsible for coordinating, overseeing, and managing the design process as new projects occur for their various branch locations. Though this client may be accustomed to the design process, it is still wise for the designer to review and discuss the essential design phases of the project.

Building and Site Analysis

Sometimes a client says, *"This is the building. This is the space. Now design the project. Help*

us spend money!" At other times the clients may wish to consider several locations. They may look to the designer or other consultants for recommendations or reasons to select one building over the next building (see Chapter 13).

Lease Review

In general, it is wise for the designer to review the lease or specific building requirements before starting to space plan. On one project, the client's lease clearly stated that there could be no vending machines within client spaces as the building had inadequate dock clearance for weekly vending truck deliveries. Though this was a small deterrent, by reviewing the lease, I was able to inform the clients not to anticipate any vending machines in their space plan. This step prevented the client from encountering surprises on the move-in day.

Preliminary Budget

Although many projects start without discussing budgets, it is important to discuss this topic as early in the process as possible: "[W]ithout knowledge of your client's intended budget, it is virtually impossible to determine the viability of the proposed project, arrive at an appropriate fee arrangement and, most importantly, determine whether your client's design expectations can be achieved through the financial resources that the client is prepared to commit."[2]

High-end budgets often allow for wider corridors, more open space, larger conference rooms, curvilinear rooms, special ceiling treatments, and other amenities that can be suggested in a space plan. Lower or moderate budgets may not allow for the same grandiose concepts, but these plans can be made just as exciting by incorporating an abundance of daylight or outside views into the overall space plan. If the designer does not know the intended budget, he or she may miss the opportunity to provide the client with the best space plan possible right from the start.

Listening to the Client

Although it is important to listen to your clients and incorporate their needs and desires, this does not mean the designer should do everything exactly as requested by the client. After all, if the client knew everything, there would be no reason to retain a designer. Sometimes it is necessary to offer several solutions to a request: a solution to meet the client's minimum requirements and then a better or more expanded solution that may increase the client's gratification and ultimately be greater than what they might have known to be possible.

At other times, the client's ideal or requested solution may be beyond their budget or time frame. In this situation, the designer should present alternate solutions that are equally capable of meeting the requirements and yet staying within the budget and schedule.

In all situations, it is for the client to decide if they will select the first solution, an upgraded solution, a solution that takes the project over its budget, or an alternate solution that keeps the project on schedule. It is the client's decision to wait or move ahead, insist on what they requested, or try a new option. Designers can only recommend solutions. It is the client who must feel comfortable with those solutions and make final decisions.

Understanding the Client

On occasion, clients are not always as explicit as they might wish to be. Sometimes the designer has to read between the lines to understand what the client is really trying to say.

Over time and with each experience, designers gain general understanding and comprehension of the needs and desires of their clients as well as design applications that can be used in succeeding projects. More understanding can be gained through research, especially when the designer encounters new or unfamiliar business entities. Some understanding comes from natural creative ability and intuition. Further understanding is gained during each programming phase and subsequent design phases, when the designer sees first-hand how a client operates on a daily basis. Understanding can also come while collaborating with peers and codesigners.

Basic Client Makeup

Most companies, regardless of their business function, have similar program and space planning components (see Chapter 1).

Differences between clients and space plans are a result of the specific type of business, classification of the business or occupancy group per code requirements, building configurations, and nuances or philosophies of each firm. The number of offices and workstations will vary based on the type of business. Building codes vary based on the type of occupancy. Job titles can vary greatly from one business to the next. Day-to-day differences may include hours of operation or leniency for taking breaks to use the lunchroom. Dress attire differences may range from business-casual dress codes accepted by many companies to the required uniforms worn by service staff or the suits and ties preferred by well-established corporate businesses. These attitudes and practices often translate into accompanying design philosophy, which can be incorporated into the new space plan and, eventually, the built space.

By recognizing the many similarities and differences between clients, the designer is often able to offer suggestions or solutions that have worked in other situations. However, the designer should not categorize clients into stringent groups that all receive the same design solutions. Despite similarities, each client remains unique. For instance, while many law firms generally prefer a more traditional appearance, in Los Angeles a number of law firms that cater to Hollywood clientele have requested contemporary, even trendy, offices.

LEGAL CLASSIFICATIONS

When filing for a business permit, companies can register under several legal entities. Legal classification establishes the firm name, lists primary activities of the firm, and serves as a basis for tax purposes. Various classifications include:

- Government sector
- Private or public sector
- For profit or nonprofit
- Corporation, partnership, or sole proprietor
- Headquarters or branch office
- Main location or off-site location
- US or foreign company

A firm may have more than one classification, but it cannot fall under all of the categories.

Two distinctive law firms might include an attorney partnership providing legal services for profit in Canada or a group within a government body providing nonprofit legal services as public defenders. A publicly held manufacturing company will probably have both a corporate headquarters and branch locations, while a non-profit women's shelter may have only one main location.

At the same time, all of the categories can contain more than one type of business. Accounting firms, law firms, brokers, psychologists, doctors, restaurant owners, and construction or dot.com companies can form partnerships or corporations, for profit or nonprofit, US-based or outside the United States with one or more locations. Each firm can choose how they legally set up their organization and business functions.

With few exceptions, such as physical site separations required by the Securities and Exchange Commission (SEC) for some groups within financial institutions, legal classifications of a business have little bearing on space planning or design development. Legal classification can, though, play a role in the assignment, quantity, and hierarchy of the work area mix.

Program Requirements

In general, program requirements and room types—along with job descriptions—are consistent for similar types of businesses, regardless of their legal classifications. In the law organizations mentioned previously, both types of firms typically request larger offices for senior attorneys, smaller offices for the balance of the attorneys and paralegals, workstations for administrative assistants, a library and Lexus for research, and a reception area that "speaks" of the ambience the firm wishes to convey. Interior design firms and designers require access to a samples library, flat files, and larger than average worksurfaces and layout tables, whether the designer is a sole practitioner or one of many in a large firm.

Differences in requirements and design ambience between similar types of businesses are usually a consequence of size of the organization, clientele served, and philosophy.

Size of the Organization

Obviously, the size of an organization dictates the quantity of rooms. Though many rooms are the same, larger businesses can afford to request individual rooms for particular functions that a smaller company will want to be shared. For example, a local graphic agency may use its conference room for training employees on new computer programs, whereas a major advertising agency will probably have two separate rooms, a conference room and a training room.

Clientele Served

Clientele can greatly influence a space plan and design. For a law firm or public defenders' offices, the general philosophy and interior finishes may be similar, provided the law firm caters to average citizens. Primary differences will probably be the size and configuration of the reception room. Law firms typically provide seating for six to eight people, while a defender's office normally requires a much larger room to seat as many as 20 to 30 persons. The defender's office may also want a secured door that opens with a buzzer between the reception area and offices beyond.

On the other hand, if the law firm is large or handles exclusive clients, the interior finishes are customarily of much higher quality. The reception area may be very large, even though there is seating for only a half a dozen people or so. This graciousness and atmosphere translate into higher attorney fees without the attorneys having to state such blunt facts. Even so, this firm would still have senior attorneys or partners, lesser attorneys or associates, paralegals and clerks, all needing a library and Lexus to do research.

Philosophy

In the past, many firms, both large and small, tended to locate private offices (see Chapter 6), along perimeter window walls and workstations in interior rooms. With the advent of *greening* and *sustainability*, some firms are now reversing those layouts. Glass-fronted offices occupy interior positions, and workstations enjoy the benefits of daylight along the window walls. Some companies are also requesting more open workstation areas rather than enclosed offices to help promote collaboration and an open-door policy.

Similarities and differences or nuances between firms abound. Designers can and should use all aspects of client background, research, and experience to lay out and plan each new project.

USE AND OCCUPANCY CLASSIFICATIONS

For purposes of construction and obtaining building permits, all buildings, structures, and interior spaces are classified with respect to use or occupancy in one or more groups as defined by the local jurisdiction and governing building codes (Box 2.1). Although code terminology may vary slightly, in general most codes list use and occupancy groups similar to those defined by the International Building Code (IBC).

Use or occupancy and legal classifications are not related to each other. Use Group B, Business, includes buildings or structures for office and professional services (architects, attorneys, engineers, dentists, physicians, etc.), along with other service-type transactions found in banks, barber and beauty shops, dry cleaning and laundries, laboratories, post offices, and radio and television stations, to name a few. Companies and organizations can be for profit or nonprofit, private or government sector, large or small, yet they all have the same code requirements because these types of companies are in the business of making, buying, or selling goods or providing services in exchange for money. Companies or organizations in another occupancy group, such as healthcare or assembly, will have other code requirements.

Designers must state the occupancy group on the cover sheet of each set of construction documents when submitting them for a permit (see Chapter 13). Based on the occupancy group, code requirements provide for the appropriate type of construction, means of egress, fire protection systems, and other architectural configurations to best serve the occupants within each space. To state an extreme example, it stands to reason that while exiting a burning one- or two-story house, a family of four will most likely act more coherently than a hundred office workers

---

BOX 2.1 IBC Use and Occupancy Classification[3]

SECTION 302 CLASSIFICATION

1.	Assembly:	Groups A-1, A-2, A-3, A-4, and A-5
2.	Business:	Group B
3.	Educational:	Group E
4.	Factory and Industrial:	Groups F-1 and F-2
5.	High Hazard:	Groups H-1, H-2, H-3, H-4, and H-5
6.	Institutional:	Groups I-1, I-2, I-3, and I-4 (hospitals and jails)*
7.	Mercantile:	Group M
8.	Residential:	Groups R-1, R-2, R-3, and R-4 (hotels and dorms)*
9.	Storage:	Groups S-1 and S-2
10.	Utility and Miscellaneous:	Group U

* Description breakdowns inserted by author for further clarification.

---

exiting a burning high-rise building. A house is classified under Group R where hallways can be as narrow as 36 inches (in.) wide, while an office building is classified under Group B where corridors must be at least 44 in. wide. With so many more people in the office building, it makes sense that the means of egress needs to be wider than in a house.

Single or Multiple Classifications

Typically, a building or business is classified as an entity under the most appropriate use or occupancy group. But occasionally, certain rooms within a space may fall under a different use group, such as a large conference or training room within an office space. When these rooms meet or exceed 50 occupants (750 square feet, SF), the rooms are reclassified from Group B, office space, to Group A, assembly or a gathering of people (Box 2.2). All codes applicable to each use group must be met for their respective areas.

Code Variances

Occasionally, it may be difficult to meet certain code requirements due to building configuration, location of the space within the building, or client desires and wishes. Depending on each explicit application, a code reviewer may allow a variance, as it is known, from a specific code requirement if the designer can demonstrate that it would be difficult to comply with that particular code and that the variance would not compromise the overall health, safety, and welfare of the occupants. For instance, if the Americans with Disabilities Act (ADA) code requiring 18 in. of clear space on the strike pull-side of one office door (see Box 6.2a) cannot be met due to the column pattern in the building, a reviewer may allow a variance of less clear space for that one door as long as the balance of doors meet the 18 in. requirement.

At other times, it will be necessary to adjust a space plan to meet code requirements even though the new plan may not fully meet the client's program requirements. When a movie theater headquarters relocated its offices in Chicago, the firm wanted a 50-person viewing studio incorporated on the same floor as its new office space. Applicable codes for occupancies of Group A, assembly, required two means of egress for spaces serving 50 or more persons.

Due to that building's floor-plate configuration, it was impossible to provide a second means of egress from the studio. Upon reviewing the proposed layout with the city permit office, the designer and client agreed to a compromise. Per code, only one means of egress was required for spaces containing fewer than 50 occupants. By eliminating one seat and documenting that all seats were fixed or permanently attached to the floor, thus ensuring that additional chairs would not be brought into the studio space, the permit office allowed the studio to be reclassified

as part of Group B, business space, rather than its intended usage as an assembly area, Group A.

It is important for the designer to review how code requirements may affect the overall design. The designer can then discuss varying requirements with the client, as necessary, to arrive at an acceptable solution.

WORK AREA MIX

The mix of offices and workstations in corporate settings has come full circle from a few offices with many open area desks, to many offices and fewer workstations, and now back to fewer offices and more workstations. Having a private office has always projected a higher status than sitting out in the general office area. In the past, companies offered offices as rewards to valued employees. However, as real estate costs and lease rates escalated over time, many companies began to reevaluate the number of actual offices needed vs. the number of offices desired.

Each private office requires from two to three times as much space as a workstation. It is conceivable to put two 100-SF workstations in the same area as one 225-SF office or two 64-SF workstations in the same area as one 150-SF office and thus either reduce the total amount of required overall office square footage or increase the number of personnel to be housed within the existing square footage.

Offices vs. Workstations

In addition to reducing the overall square footage required for a specific number of employees, replacing private offices with workstations can lower yearly rent costs, decrease construction and operating costs, and improve tax write-offs and life-cycle costs. While designers should present these advantages to their client, they should also encourage a company to take the time to present this potential change to their employees.

Displaced Personnel

Few people voluntarily make the change from enclosed offices to an open environment of workstations. After all, having a private office is a coveted perk. To offset this reassignment of work area type, designers can recommend that the client consider upgrading those workstations for displaced personnel. An upgraded workstation can imply special attention for higher-level staff, so they can continue to feel like an important asset to the company (see Chapter 7).

Yearly Lease or Rent Costs

Workstations require less square footage than private offices. If a client decides that all employees will occupy workstations rather than offices, the amount of required office square footage is reduced. Thus, the rent is also reduced because the client will be leasing less space.

Construction Costs

Typically, each private office receives at least one door, one light switch, one sprinkler head, one air supply, two to four light fixtures, and drywall on three to four sides. Granted, drywall can be shared by offices on either side, but it is still required.

Workstations share most of these construction items. There may be one light switch for 10 to 50 stations, one sprinkler head for every four to six stations, one light fixture for every four stations, and no doors or drywall. The cost savings can be significant.

Operating Costs

Instinct tells us that with fewer light fixtures and air supply, less electricity is required, thus reducing the monthly electric bill. Fewer light fixtures also mean fewer lamps to replace, thus reducing both yearly office expenses and labor for changing the lamps.

Life-Cycle Cost Analysis (LCCA)

Not all trade-offs reduce up-front construction costs. In fact, sometimes the selected materials and installation of those materials actually increase construction costs. When workstations replace offices, the data and electrical outlet installation is more expensive since outlets typically come up through the floor rather than through an office wall. However, by considering total cost of the items, including both the initial purchase costs and operating costs over the period of their existence (called *life-cycle* cost

analysis), the client usually saves money in the long run.

Tax Write-Off

Whether clients choose offices, workstations, or a combination of the two, they can write off certain items on their income tax returns to help reduce the amount of taxes to be paid on gross yearly income. Expenses such as office supplies are generally written off every year. Furniture and other movable items are amortized and written off over a seven-year period, while write-offs on fixed items such as drywall and other construction extend over the life of the lease, often from 15 to 20 years. Generally, companies like an earlier write-off, particularly if they anticipate a larger gross income during ensuing years.

In simple terms, if both workstations and offices cost the same amount of money, say $100,000, the furniture is written off (reduces the gross income) at $14,286 per year for seven years, while construction costs are written off at only $6,670 to $5,000 per year.

Typically, the designer does not need to explain specific write-offs or how they work. It is usually enough just to mention that furniture can be written off in a shorter time period. The client, as a rule, is astute enough to grasp the implications of such a choice, which he or she can later discuss in greater detail with his or her accountant.

By bringing these incentives and options to each client's attention, the designer is demonstrating a dimension beyond strict creativity. This shows the clients that they are the designer's true concern and not just seen as the opportunity for a great design.

Mobility and Telecommuting Personnel

Advanced technology has allowed the following paraphrase to take hold in many organizations: *It's not where you work, but the work you do—any place, anywhere.*

To further reduce overall office square footage and yearly lease payments, both government and commercial firms are encouraging a percentage of their employees to telecommute, or be more mobile, meaning that when there is no explicit reason to come into the office, those employees can work from home, a nearby coffee shop, library, or any other convenient locale as long as the employee is able to complete their daily work. Even when these employees need to participate in conference or other meetings, they do not necessarily need to come to the office. They are able to connect, using their laptops, with other participants within VTC rooms (see Chapter 8).

With this philosophy, mobile people normally do not have an assigned work area. After all, why should a work area sit vacant for three or four days each week? However, when employees do come into the office, they do need a place sit, hang-out or store their daily items. To satisfy these needs, firms are implanting reservation systems, similar to selecting an airline seat when booking a plane ticket. On days when employees come into the office space, they can select a mobile or touch-down work area for the day, week, or other time frame based on the firm's scheduling guidelines (see Chapter 7). Generally speaking, most employees will probably not be able to sit in the same work area from week to week, as other employees are also reserving work areas when they need to come into the office for the day.

Although this approach can save considerable square footage and lease costs, it is a very different way of working from the way that corporate America and other countries have been working for a very long time. When contemplating this new way of operating, organizations may want to retain outside change management firms to explain to and train employees about new practices, and then implement new procedures for the organization as a whole.

Philosophy

The eventual work area mix of offices and workstations is often predicated on the type, size, and similarity of each company for which the space is being planned. For example, design firms of all sizes are apt to have two to six offices for principals and management and open office space for the other employees (designers, CAD operators, etc.). Some firms may provide high panels around workstations, but many firms have low or no panels to allow for easy collaboration on team projects.

Most insurance companies, corporate headquarters, and other large firms also seat most of their personnel in workstations. The high–low panel mix tends to vary with the type of work performed. Underwriters who need to concentrate or claims adjusters who talk on the telephone a lot might have high panels for some privacy, while data entry people who experience fewer distractions might have low panels.

On the other hand, firms with many partners, such as law and accounting firms, for the most part have all personnel except administrative assistants behind closed office doors. Not only does this type of work regularly call for privacy when seeing clientele, but partners all have equal status: if one receives an office, then all receive an office.

While partner firms tend to have mostly large, equal-sized offices, sole proprietorships and large corporations are likely to have proportionally fewer large offices, a select number of middle-sized offices, and many smaller offices, plus workstations. These trends, though not absolute, seem to fall naturally according to business classifications.

Privacy: Closed Door vs. Open Area

Office doors can be closed when the occupant conducts confidential meetings or does not wish to be disturbed. Workstations, upgraded or not, do not accord that same amount of privacy. No matter the cost savings, before committing to replace offices with workstations, many companies still consider other factors such as the need for privacy.

First, how much privacy is required for telephone conversations? When personnel discuss sensitive information via the telephone, coworkers hear only one side of the exchange, which is not the same as listening to both parties in person. For topics that involve projects or products, not people, it is often felt there is slightly less need for total privacy, so workstations can adequately house most employees.

Second, recognizing there are times when a need for total privacy exists, for both telephone conversations and in-person meetings, many companies incorporate telephone booths and a few small meeting rooms into their space plans to handle these situations (see Chapter 11).

Managers of People or Managers of Products and Projects

When requesting that offices be replaced with workstations, companies must select which employee level or grade within their organization will remain in offices and which will now occupy workstations. The workstation level is often established as everyone below the director or senior management level. Still, this choice can create a quandary. Should all managers be treated equally? When grade and pay scale are the same, then most managers say yes; if one manager occupies an office, then all managers should occupy an office. However, when there are many managers, the concept of putting more people in workstations is defeated if all managers receive an office.

Often a distinction must be made between the manager titles. Managers of people tend to see employees for disciplinary reasons, to discuss personal matters, or for other sensitive issues held in confidence.

Managers of products or projects oversee a concept and thus typically do not have the same confidentiality requirements as managers of people. True, these managers have staff with whom they work on products or projects, but the same sensitive types of issues are not involved as with managers of people. Therefore, when the company decides to reduce the number of offices at a new location, it is often felt that product and project managers can function in a more open work area setting, while managers of people require an office.

Average SF per Person

Companies use an average square foot (SF) per person as a benchmark to compare their real estate needs and employee provisions with other, primarily similar—but also dissimilar—businesses. Average SF per person includes not only the actual work area for each employee but also a portion of all other rooms and circulation within the office space. By multiplying the average SF of work area allotted to each person times the total number of personnel in the office, management is able to calculate an approximate amount of usable square feet (USF) required for new office space, construction and furniture costs, and design fees. Three basic methods are used to establish the average SF per person: existing average SF per person, industry-accepted standard for average SF per person, and average SF per person based on a programming effort.

Existing Average SF per Person

Based on their lease (rental) contract, clients know the amount of total square footage currently occupied. They also know the number of personnel occupying their existing space. By dividing the total square footage by the total number of employees, clients are able to calculate their existing average SF per person. If they are satisfied with the spatial *feel* of their existing space conditions, clients can initiate a new design project using those existing average square footages. When the existing spaces feel either cramped or too spacious, clients can adjust the average SF per person up or down based on intuition, industry-accepted standards, or a programming effort.

Industry-Accepted Standard for Average SF per Person

Similar types of businesses tend to provide similar amounts of SF per person, but there is no one standard average that fits all companies. Law firms, which are generally designed exclusively with private offices, tend to provide the highest amount of square footage, often as much as 300 to 325 SF per person. At the opposite end of the business spectrum are call centers that may average only 50 SF per person. Accounting firms that make regular use of touchdown stations and hoteling (see Chapter 7) may average around 135 SF per person, while other accounting firms offering more traditional office and workstation settings may average around 185 SF per person. Today, many firms now look for an overall average between 190 and 225 SF per person for typical office space or between 150 and 185 SF when more benching workstations and collaborative areas are designed into the space.

Average SF per Person Based on a Programming Effort

During the programming effort (see Chapters 3 and 12), the designer, together with the client, compiles a list of all space planning components requested by the client for their new office space. Square footages for each room and area are tabulated, totaled, and then divided by the client's total number of employees to achieve an actual average square foot per person for that client.

Once the average SF per person is calculated, the designer, based on direction from the client, can increase, decrease, or manipulate the square footage to some extent. Options include:

- Eliminate or add support areas
- Eliminate or add special use areas
- Reduce or increase office sizes
- Reduce or increase workstation sizes
- Replace offices with workstations
- Replace workstations with offices

Obviously, adding or increasing areas will increase the total amount of required square footage, thus increasing the average square foot per person. Conversely, eliminating or reducing areas will reduce the total amount of required square footage, thus reducing the average square foot per person, which in turn reduces the rent.

JOB TITLE DESCRIPTIONS

People spend nearly one-third of their life at work. This is more time than they spend doing anything else in their lives. So a job title is personal. It identifies who we are, what we do, the amount of experience we have accumulated, and the status we enjoy at our place of work.

Some titles tell more than other titles, and sometimes the same title means vastly different things. For example, interior designer and interior architect are basically the same title or job position. However, the general public usually associates the first term with residential decorators and the second term with building architecture. When I described myself as a space planner while living in Long Beach, California, many people automatically thought of the space shuttles under design and construction at nearby aircraft plants rather than interior design.

Specific Job Titles

To avoid possible confusion, it is wise to obtain accurate titles from each client and to use those titles on each respective project. There are hundreds of job titles, so it is not possible to list all titles here. To illustrate the use of various titles,

a small cross section of titles from a selected group of business entities is provided (Box 2.3).

Titles can be so similar and yet mean such different things. Partner, or senior partner, is the highest title held by attorneys within a law firm. Yet, in an accounting firm, principal is the highest title, not partner.

Just as titles vary from one type of business to the next business for similar job positions, there may be different job titles for the same position depending on whether a firm is located within the United States or another country. In the United Kingdom, the term *chambermaid* would be used in place of *housekeeper* in the hotel industry and *barrister* or *solicitor* in place of *attorney* in the legal profession. It would be a *faux pas* to reverse or misuse titles on a client's space plan.

The Meaning of *Manager*

Of all the job titles, manager is probably the most subjective. It carries several meanings and levels of status:

- Branch manager
- General manager
- Office manager
- Manager of people
- Manager of products or projects
- Facility manager

A branch or general manager is in charge of or responsible for a particular office location. This manager reports to a vice president (VP), director, or other executive-level person who is customarily located at the corporate headquarters. Because there is typically only one branch manager, this person most likely occupies the largest private office at this location.

An office manager, also a single position, is responsible for the day-to-day functions required to run an office smoothly. This manager usually occupies a smaller office and reports directly to the branch manager or other high-level person within the immediate office.

Managers of people, products, and projects are generally mid-level positions in a large corporation. As previously discussed, these managers carry different responsibilities and occupy either offices or workstations.

Facility managers are responsible for the maintenance and care of commercial and institutional buildings. The title may refer to the head of the department or a position within the department.

Contact with the Client

Depending on each project, designers interact with many levels of people, from the highest position to the lowest—CEOs, CFOs, administrators, partners, facility managers, high school librarians, factory supervisors, government people, doctors, entrepreneurs, and mailroom clerks. It is essential for designers to develop a well-rounded education and the communication skills to interact effectively with each client member.

There are many ways to communicate with the client and other members of the design team. Often times it is verbal, but sometimes a good drawing, rendering, or spreadsheet will communicate the information more readily. Writing is undoubtedly one of the most important forms of communication. Though the first written document a client may see is the design firm's marketing material, a well-written design contract is probably the most important task on any given project. A project should never, ever start without a signed contract. A contract should clearly state the scope of work (SOW), a scheduled time frame, fees, and any other pertinent information relating to the project. Both the client and designer should fully understand from the contract what to expect from each other and the anticipated outcome. Without a well-written contract, anything is up for grabs.

Other important written documents in the design process include meeting minutes, specifications, thank you letters, email correspondence, and marketing presentations. It is crucial to know how to write well. Well-written information leads to fewer surprises, misunderstandings, or confusion.

Two other "forms" of communication include math and reading. Yes—math! Math is perhaps the most used skill in the design and space planning process. As mentioned above for the contract, the designer must calculate fees and a schedule for the project. Each month

the designer will review billable hours worked on the project and then invoice the client accordingly. In between, there are site measurements to be taken, floor plans to be scaled, furniture and other dimensions to be considered for planning within a given room size or to determine a new room size, elevations to be detailed and dimensioned for construction documents, quantities of furniture to be specified and associated budgets, and on the math requirements go.

Reading is a constant and continuous task, even between design projects. There are always tons of magazines and articles to show us what other designers are doing and give inspiration for our projects or information about the latest manufacturing advancements for improving materials and finishes or incorporating sustainable products into projects. There are Requests for Proposals (RFPs) for the next projects. There is research for current projects. There is endless information about new products; new ways of doing existing tasks; and new, updated code requirements every few years. Use of all skills leads to good communication and relationships with our clients and successful projects.

BOX 2.3 Job Title Descriptions

Courts	Law Firms	Accounting Firms
Deputy Director	Partners	Principals
General Counsel	Associates	Partners
Research Attorney	Paralegals	Managers
Senior Attorney	Clerks	Auditors
Librarian	Administrator	Supervisors

Manufacturing	Bank	Brokerage Firms
President	President	President
Vice Presidents	Vice Presidents	Vice Presidents
Directors	Loan Officers	Branch Managers
Managers	New Accounts Officers	Account Executives
Supervisors	Bank Tellers	Facilities Managers

Hotel	Hospital	Clinic
General Manager	Director	Medical Director
Director of Rooms	Administrator	Administrative Director
Desk Clerk	Admitting Coordinator	Clinical Case Manager
Controller	Doctor	Trial Specialist
Housekeeper	Head Nurse	Counselor
Executive Chef	Chief Dietitian	Nurse

For a successful project, it is important for everyone to have a clear understanding of the client's expectations. *The client may always be right,* but the client does not always have all of the answers. That is why the client retains design professionals—to assist in providing the best design project possible, within the budget and on time. It is essential for all parties involved to communicate openly and well.

PROJECTS

Project #1: Write a 3–4 paragraph essay

To build a portfolio for a final project, select a client from one of the profiles shown in Appendix A to use for all exercises and assignments throughout the book. There are four client profiles representing distinct scenarios for typical client program requirements:

- A majority of offices with a few workstations—law firm
- A majority of workstations with a few offices—accounting firm
- Approximately 50-50 offices and workstations—advertising firm
- Mobility and collaborative work areas—nonprofit organization

1. State why the particular client was selected.
2. Provide some thoughts on the requirements as provided for the selected client.
3. Do these seem like real clients—why or why not?

Project #2: Write a 3–4 paragraph essay

To gain knowledge about your selected client, their needs, and daily work habits, research similar types of firms.

1. Research information on similar types of firms featured on the internet, in trade magazines, in a local community business directory, or at the library.
2. Interview people employed in similar types of businesses.
3. Before calling or meeting in person for an interview, prepare a list of questions. Be sure to include the list of questions with the essay.

3

DISCOVERY PROCESS

When a design firm learns that it has been awarded a new design project, there is cause for celebration. In fact, some firms have even been known to break out a bottle of champagne when awarded a coveted project.

However, for all of those wonderful feelings, for all of the creativity and ability to design a beautiful space, for all of the talented staff that will collaborate on the project, there are other aspects equally important to achieving success with each project. First and foremost, the designer must ask, *"Who is this client? What are this client's needs?"*

DISCOVERY PROCESS

The first response to "Who is the client?" might simply be the client's name. However, what does the name of the client tell the designer about the company itself? Oftentimes, not much.

Through a discovery process, the designer *gets to know* the clients to the fullest extent possible. Designers learn about clients' existing and future needs—their requirements, goals, visions, desired changes, and wish lists—at the start of each respective project. Designers use this information for organizing and managing a project, space planning, and later during design development. In fact, it is often said that by the time a project is completed, the designer knows more about the clients than the clients know about their own company. To a certain extent, this is true. Designers look at both macro and micro information. They take direction from upper management and plan for the general employee population. Designers must meet ergonomic and Americans with Disabilities Act (ADA) requirements in the workspace, yet satisfy the budget. To create a successful design, the designer must meet and fulfill the individual needs and the broad perspectives of the client.

With most projects, the designer takes the lead in running a project and culling information from the client. A primary way of gleaning data is through a process called programming. However, before the start of programming, several other key means of data gathering should occur, beginning with a kickoff meeting.

Kickoff Meeting

Most new projects start with an initial meeting known as the kickoff meeting. Attendees customarily include all known participants and disciplines who might be involved at some point during the project, even if their involvement is minor or not required for several months. Everyone wants to be included from the beginning; this meeting sets the tone for a successful and collaborative project. Future meetings are generally attended only by participants appropriate to the subject of the meeting, but for the kickoff meeting it is beneficial to meet all other team members face-to-face.

This is the time to start a project directory: establish procedures for future meetings and meeting minutes; identify primary day-to-day contacts for the client, design firm, and other involved consultants; confirm chains of command; and set up other regulations as necessary. It is also the time to review typical layouts (see Figs. 6.5, 7.2, and 8.8) and program questionnaires (see Appendix C), discuss their relevancy, make changes as needed, and outline procedures for distributing and collecting the questionnaires.

Meeting Minutes

Throughout the project, there will be many meetings, some spontaneous, others scheduled well in advance. Some meetings may have a specific agenda; other meetings may be general or *"we haven't gotten together in a while"* types of meetings. Meetings may involve only two or three people or the entire design team, including all consultants. Whatever the type of meeting, it is of utmost importance to document every meeting with well-written minutes.

Over the course of a project, many decisions are made, unmade, remade, revised, changed, added, deleted, forgotten, or remembered inaccurately. In general, there are enough decisions to tax anyone's brain in trying to correctly remember all things discussed and agreed upon. Minutes should always cover current decisions, open issues, action items, and persons responsible for completing identified tasks.

A copy of the minutes from the last meeting should be distributed to each member listed in the project directory, either before or at each successive meeting. It is wise to review the latest minutes at each meeting while the information and decisions are still relatively fresh in everyone's mind. Corrections can be agreed upon and made so that the minutes serve as documented fact in the future.

Project Directory

Most people exchange business cards at the kickoff meeting. However, the best means for a designer to keep track of all persons involved in the design process is through an electronic project directory. This directory can easily be added to and updated as new members join the design team or as people leave.

Day-to-Day Contacts

Although email and other internet programs have made mass communication easier, when so many people from such a variety of disciplines are involved in each design project, it can still be time consuming to contact each person with new information or requests or to answer questions. Therefore, it is important to identify the primary day-to-day contact for each team discipline: client, design firm, engineer, consultants, and so on.

Primary contacts can converse with each other on relevant issues and then disseminate the information within their respective disciplines. For design firms, the contact is normally the lead designer or project manager; for the client, it may be a facility manager, senior partner, administrator, or company owner. Other disciplines select their daily contacts accordingly. In this manner, a clear chain of command for communication is established.

Chain of Command

A clear chain of command ensures greater control of the decision-making process. That said, it is not always possible as this approach can be very time consuming for the primary contacts.

A better procedure might be to establish major and minor levels of command that specify which team members are responsible for what kinds of information. For instance, a junior designer could contact the mailroom clerk directly to schedule a time to measure existing mailroom equipment that will be reused in the new space plan. The primary contacts would be notified that such a meeting has been scheduled and then receive a written report or communiqué documenting the meeting and information gathered. This approach saves time, yet ensures that everyone is kept abreast and decision-making boundaries are not overstepped.

Not only is it important to lay the ground rules for contacting other team members, but it is also necessary to understand or establish who has the ability to make decisions on the project and at what level each person can make such decisions. For instance, the client daily contact may be able to make schedule changes or monetary decisions up to a certain time delay or dollar amount. Beyond that point, the CFO or company president may need to be involved for these changes. Establishing the chain of command at the beginning of the project helps ensure an organized process throughout the project.

PROGRAMMING

Programming consists of two parts. First, the designer gathers and discerns information from the client by means of questionnaires (see Appendix C), typical work area layouts (see Chapters 6–11), interviews, and a walk-through of the existing space. Then, using written summaries, spreadsheets, diagrams, and charts, the information is tabulated and compiled into a Program Report that presents an ideal concept for the client's new space (see Chapter 12).

Who Is the Client?

Answers to this question are complex. There is the client that exists today and the client as they desire to be in the new space. Some clients can articulate the difference between the two spaces; other clients find it difficult to comprehend change and even more difficult to express their desires. A few clients are happy with their existing spaces and want to duplicate what they have, while many clients want something radically different.

Although each client and project is unique, the process and types of information gathered and validated for each project are typical from one project to the next. Starting from a macro approach, the designer poses broad questions to client management regarding their overall quantitative, qualitative, and philosophical outlook for the new or remodeled space.

- How many employees are there?
- What percentage of work areas will be offices?
- What percentage of work areas will be workstations?
- Will offices be replaced with workstations?
- Will the furniture be new or reused?
- Does the client want branding?
- Do they want a unique space?
- Do they have an idea of what the new space should look like?
- What goals should be achieved in the new space?
- What is their philosophy towards their customers?
- What is their philosophy towards their employees?
- What is the client's mission statement?
- What is their vision for the future?
- Why is the client moving anyway?

QUESTIONNAIRES

To gather more detailed information, a standard questionnaire (see Appendix C) can provide a consistent means for gathering data from each client and from each group or department within the client firm. Use of questionnaires allows time for client personnel to contemplate answers as opposed to answering off the cuff during a meeting. Answers give the designer a basis for comprehending each group's individual makeup regarding daily workflow, existing conditions, anticipated organizational changes, future requirements, current business trends that should be incorporated, and criteria for moving to new space.

Classic questions asked of each group normally cover such topics as:

- Department function
- Department organization chart
- Existing and projected personnel
- Assignment of typical work areas
- Special requirements
- Adjacency requirements

- Support area requirements
- Security requirements
- Miscellaneous requirements

Although typical by nature, standard questionnaires can be edited and tailored for each client. Keywords such as *department*, *division*, *group*, and *section* should be changed to match the client's organizational terminology. Additional questions can be included to address a law firm's library, a brokerage firm's trading floor, expanded security for government projects, or any other special business needs.

Questionnaires should be user-friendly. The average person is not familiar with the design process and is generally not as comfortable with dimension sizes and square footages as designers are. Questions should be phrased to ask about the client's needs rather than specifics about room sizes, layouts, and configurations. For example, the client will probably not know how large the conference or file rooms should be, but they will know how many people they want to seat around the conference table or the quantity of files that need to be housed in a file room. Therefore, questions should be phrased to obtain information that clients can easily provide, such as, "How many people attend a typical conference meeting?" rather than, "What size would you like to make the conference room?" The designer can calculate the room sizes later, based on the number of people or items to be accommodated within the room (see Chapters 8 and 11).

Before questionnaires are distributed, clients should be given the opportunity to add questions or instructions. They may want feedback from their employees on using off-site storage, or they may ask departments to limit future personnel growth. Involving the client in creating the questionnaire will help the client control square footage requirements, excessive needs and wants, as well as communicate direction to everyone.

Questionnaire Format

Questionnaires can be formatted in either portrait or landscape. Design firms may standardize in one format or the other, or they may give latitude for each new project. Questions can be rearranged for a specific client, but in general, it is better to start with quantitative questions—how many personnel are within the department, and then move towards less quantitative, more qualitative questions—how do they envision the reception area?

Questionnaires can be set up in Word, Excel, or some other user-friendly program that allows direct input by client personnel, and later, editing by the designer, as appropriate.

Distribution

Most projects will benefit from a questionnaire, although there are exceptions. For smaller projects, up to approximately 10,000 square feet (SF), an official questionnaire and report may not be required. The client team leader generally knows most of the company's wants and needs and can simply provide the information to the designer as a predetermined *list of requirements* along with appropriate square footages.

When projects are very large (anywhere over 600,000 SF), complex, or spread throughout several buildings, the information gathering and resulting report may also be more complex than an average project. These reports may be called Strategic Reports or Visioning Outlooks.

For medium-sized projects or projects with a few specialized areas, the client team leader distributes a questionnaire to the heads of each group or department within the company. Upper management can either fill out the questionnaire on hard copy or electronically, or they can ask subordinate personnel who are more familiar with the daily workflow to provide specific information for some or all of the questions.

Each high-level department or group within the organization should receive its own questionnaire. This allows each group to list their specific requirements without compromising another group. It also allows the designer to arrange the information according to the client's organizational chart (see Figs. 12.1 and 12.2). In some cases, a group may wish to have separate questionnaires for lower-level specialized areas such as a mailroom, computer lab, or library. These questionnaires are then arranged based on their respective upper-level groups.

Answering the Questionnaires

In general, two weeks is an appropriate amount of time to allow company personnel to complete the questionnaires. Many of the questions are of a quantitative nature. They ask how many, dimension sizes, and who should be located next to whom. Some of these questions are easy to answer quickly, while others require physical effort to assess existing equipment and storage units. The qualitative questions frequently are left unanswered because department heads may wish to defer to upper management. Nevertheless, designers will want to address these issues during the interview to obtain a broad company perspective.

Additionally, some questions are of a sensitive nature or can seem intrusive. For instance, one group may be planning a reorganization that will downsize a portion of the personnel. Another group may want to purchase a major piece of equipment that has not yet received financial approval but needs to be planned into the new space. Sometimes department heads are reluctant to reveal this information, especially to

an outside source (the designer). It is crucial for the client leader to emphasize the importance of thoroughly answering the questionnaires and to assure respondents that the questionnaires will be kept in strict confidence.

Completed questionnaires should be returned to the client leader, who will in turn provide copies of each questionnaire to the designer.

TYPICAL WORK AREA LAYOUTS

As a rule, commercial businesses have a series of offices, rooms, or areas that are nearly identical in layouts, functions, furniture, ambience, and aesthetics (Fig. 3.1). In conjunction with the programming phase, designers typically draft, or draw up to scale, one to three versions of each duplicate room and area. These drawings, known as typical layouts, form a basis for initial discussions with the client at the start of the project. Based on the client's preferences, selected typical layouts are attached to questionnaires for visual clarity; they also

FIGURE 3.1 Floor plan showing typical work area layouts[1]

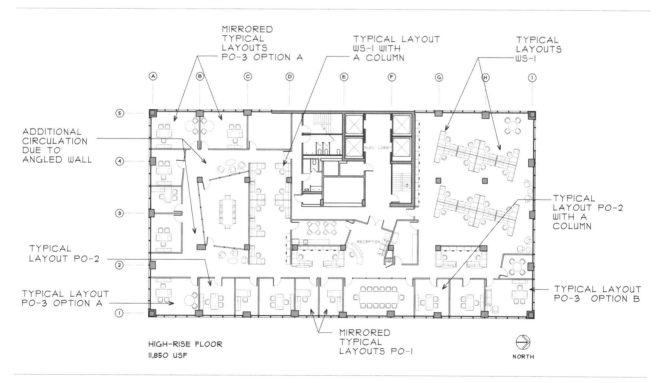

are included in the Program Report (see Chapter 12) as support documentation. Moreover, selected or final typical layouts serve as part of the building blocks for space planning and design development.

Defining Typical Layouts

A typical layout is made up of the items within an area or room and, when applicable, the room itself—walls, windows where relevant, doors, floor, and ceiling—known as the room envelope (see Chapter 6). There are three determining factors for each typical layout: size, function, and furniture.

1. When two or more rooms are the same size with the same function and furniture layout, such as two 10' × 15' private offices, they are considered to be the same typical layout. This typical layout can be abbreviated as **PO-1** (see Fig. 6.11a).
2. When two or more rooms have the same function but are different sizes, such as a 10' × 15' private office and a 15' × 15' private office, they are considered different typical layouts. Abbreviated, these drawings can be labeled **PO-1** and **PO-2** (see Figs. 6.11a and 6.11c).
3. When two or more rooms are the same size but have different functions, such as a 15' × 15' private office and a 15' × 15' conference room, these rooms are different typical layouts. Abbreviated, they can be labeled **PO-2** and **C-1** (see Figs. 6.5 and 8.8).

Number of Typical Layouts

As many typical layouts as necessary can be drawn for each project. If the client requests ten typical private offices, then the designer should draw up ten different office layouts. However, at a certain point, too many "typicals" become neither typical nor practical, but rather a unique room for each employee. Generally, designers provide two to three typical room sizes per function and then offer optional furniture layouts for each room size.

Optional Layouts

Because people come and go, are promoted, or move around internally, it is far easier for firms to offer alternate furniture layouts within the same-sized rooms than to have many different room sizes. Rooms that are the same size and serve the same function but have optional furniture layouts are still considered a typical room. Abbreviated, optional layouts can be labeled **PO-1 option A** and **PO-1 option B** (see Figs. 6.11a and 6.11b).

Minor Architectural Discrepancies

Any number of small discrepancies may occur in the final floor plan. The designer may find that one or two rooms end up with a column on one wall that is not found in other similar rooms due to building architecture. A room may have an extra window or one less window, or it may be two inches shorter or five inches wider. However, if the room is basically the same size as all of the other rooms, serves the same function, and has the same furniture layout, it is considered the same typical layout as the other rooms (see Fig. 3.1).

Mirrored Rooms

Often, rooms along a corridor are mirrored, meaning the doors are next to each other and the furniture layout is flipped inside the room (see Fig. 3.1). If the rooms are the same size and serve the same purpose but differ only by having mirrored layouts, the rooms are considered to be the same typical rooms.

Typical Layouts

On office floor plans, private offices and workstations constitute the two primary typical layouts. When applicable, particularly for larger firms with many groups, typical layouts are also drawn for conference rooms and some support rooms.

Typical layouts are drawn for two reasons. First, they are a visual tool to help the client allocate an amount of square footage to each employee during the programming task. Second, they document the final layout for each private office, workstation, and any other typical rooms as agreed upon by the client personnel and designer.

Visual Presentations

Typical layouts are customarily drawn at quarter-inch scale as a single room or workstation and then printed on an 8½" × 11" sheet of paper, either portrait or landscape, along with pertinent information such as the type of room displayed, square footage, scale, date, client name, and design firm name (see Figs. 6.5, 7.2, and 8.8). When the designer wishes to show optional furniture layouts for the same room, both plans may be printed on the same sheet or each plan may be displayed on a separate sheet.

Approved Typical Layouts

Before including typical layouts as part of the programming questionnaire or drafting furniture on the final floor plan, the designer should present several options for a typical room layout to the client for review and approval. The client may select one or two of the plans, make some minor changes, or request that other options be presented before making a final selection for typical layouts. When the typical layout has been approved, then the designer can draw all of the furniture in all of the rooms, knowing that the client will approve the final plan and request very few changes.

Draw, Draft, Space Plan Typical Layouts

Although the designer is technically planning spaces, room sizes, and furniture layouts for typical offices and other rooms, it is a more accepted practice to use the terms *draw* or *draft* typical layouts rather than *space plan* typical layouts. Typical layouts, even though they may vary a bit from one client to the next or from one building to the next, are still fairly standard layouts. Little creative planning is involved at this point. Typical layouts are tools to communicate common information to the client. True space planning and creativity come later in the design process when the designer brings all the typical layouts and other program requirements together in a cohesive, fascinating overall floor plan within a given building space.

PROGRAMMING INTERVIEWS

Once the designer has received the questionnaires from the client, he or she should schedule interviews with the client to elaborate on any issues that may or may not have been addressed. As mentioned in Chapter 2,

designers and clients do not always speak the same language. Questions that seem straightforward and simple to the designer can turn into complex, twisted, and totally unknown requests in the client's mind. Some client personnel are too busy, or not interested, in fully reading and filling out the questionnaire. They may not understand the necessity to provide the requested information.

By scheduling an interview with each group or personnel, the designer can review and discuss the completed (or partially completed) questionnaire with all parties. In addition to the group representative for the questionnaire, the designer, and any subordinates who were involved with the questionnaire, the client team leader should be present at each interview. This gives the group representative an internal comfort level when discussing sensitive information with the designer, a person outside of the company. The client team leader can also answer general or specific questions relating to the company's design project. It is important to remember that the designer is there strictly to gather information as required for space planning, not to disseminate information about the actual move itself or the client's new policies and direction.

It is beneficial for the designer to receive a copy, preferably a live electronic copy, of the completed questionnaires for review before each interview. Then during each interview, questions that have not been completed should be addressed. Answers that are unclear should also be discussed. Even questions and answers that seem clear should be reviewed. New or clarified information can be added directly into the questionnaire, with updated copies sent to all parties. The interview is one of the few occasions for the designer and individual groups to meet face-to-face and discuss the group's daily needs and wants.

Interview Time Allotment

The designer should block out two hours for each interview. Review of the questionnaire and answers often takes a full hour. A walk-through of each group's space will take 15 to 30 minutes. Follow-up time may be required to discuss new items added to the list of requirements during the walk-through. Between interviews, it is a good idea for the designer to take some time to make notes or comments about each interview while the information is fresh in his or her mind. If the interview was intense, the designer may need five or ten minutes to regroup before the next interview. Finally, there should be adequate time to proceed to the next interview without rushing.

As a word of caution, it is best to schedule an interview for each group rather than interviewing several groups at once. Each group has its own agenda, needs, and desires. Individual group interviews give the designer time to focus on each group's individual needs.

Interview Summaries

Notes, questionnaire information, and other points of discussion raised during each interview should be documented in much the same manner as meeting minutes. Some design firms like to include these summaries as part of the Program Report while other firms keep the summaries as backup information. Copies of interview summaries should be sent to all respective interviewees and the client team leader for review of accuracy and agreement. Changes should be forwarded to the designer for immediate correction with updated copies sent to all parties.

WALK-THROUGH

A physical walk-through of each group's existing workspace may help the designer better understand some of the client's answers or requests on the questionnaire. Inevitably, clients forget about or overlook a part of their space, such as a light table or a large file, when answering questions. Clients are used to "fitting" these items into their floor space and assume they will do the same thing at their new location. During the walk-through, designers can spot these overlooked items, ask questions, or take photographs for later reference, and document the items on the questionnaires as necessary. Later, the designer can return to inventory all items within that client's space that will be reused on the project (see Chapter 4).

A walk-through normally takes place directly following an interview, but it can occur before the interview or can be scheduled for another time. No matter when it occurs, a walk-through must take place.

COMPILATION OF INFORMATION

Information from the questionnaires and interviews is organized by group according to the client's organization chart and then compiled into a Program Report (see Chapter 12), which is made available to the clients, their broker, landlord, and other vested parties. The questionnaires themselves, interview notes, and other gathered materials are generally filed in a three-ring binder, file cabinet, or similar system within the design firm for internal use and occasional backup reference during the design development and construction document phases.

PROJECT

Complete a questionnaire (see Appendix C)

Gather data and information about your selected client using a standard programming questionnaire. This information will be used to calculate square footages for a Program Report in Chapter 12. There are two options for selecting a client to provide information for the questionnaire.

1. The selected client profile from Appendix A can be used. Fill in the information provided in the client profile.
2. Find a client within the local community and ask them to fill out the questionnaire.

The client should have approximately 20 to 25 employees, or approximately 5,000 USF of existing office space.

Although some data can be input into the questionnaire at this point, in reality, specific data for many of the questions, and the ability to calculate the square footage for the report in Chapter 12, are detailed in Chapters 5 through 11. Therefore, the questionnaire will remain a working document until submitted with the Program Report in Chapter 12.

4

CONTRACT FURNITURE

To a great extent, furniture, equipment, and freestanding accessories determine the size and layout of individual rooms and in turn, the general space plan for commercial interiors. For example, a conference room needs to be large enough to accommodate the table, accompanying chairs, and any other items desired within the room. It makes sense that a 20-ft-long conference table cannot fit into a 15-ft-long room. Therefore, before space planning can begin, it is beneficial for the designer to understand the sizes of and general information about items found within rooms as well as human requirements for using those items.

CONTRACT FURNITURE

Because of the amount of use it sustains, furniture for commercial interiors, normally referred to as contract furniture, is generally more durable than furniture found in residential settings. Contract furniture is typically constructed with heavier-gauge metal, sturdier framework, and tougher fabrics than materials commonly used for similar residential furniture items. As a result, contract furniture normally costs

more than comparable residential items. In addition, contract furniture items are generally manufactured according to industry-accepted standard sizes, regardless of furniture style or manufacturer.

Standard Furniture Sizes

Standard sizes of furniture refer to the interior design industry's accepted average sizes, which normally include only two stated dimensions—the width (or length) and depth as seen on plan views of the items. Although heights are provided for many of the items shown in this book, heights are more often used as background information and during design development, and not as much during the phase of space planning.

Furniture dimensions are ordinarily referenced by inches. For example, a desk is listed as 36" × 72", not 3' × 6'. A bookcase is listed as 12" × 36", not 1' × 3'. Since the standard is to use inches, it is common practice to list dimensions without the inch symbol, such as 36 × 72, for furniture. For single dimensions, such as 29" high, the inch symbol should be included as part of the dimension.

There are two exceptions when feet and inches are used rather than inches only: huge conference tables and workstations. When tables are longer than 144 inches (in.), the dimensions are generally referred to by feet and inches since dimensions like 156 in. or 216 in. do not readily compute for most people. Then it is acceptable to refer to a 13'-0" or 18'-0" table. Workstation sizes are also listed in feet and inches: 8 × 10 or 6 × 7-6. Here too, it is customary to drop the foot (') and inch (") marks.

Many manufacturers conform to standard sizes, but some manufacturers will vary the sizes slightly. A standard desk size is 36 × 72, however, the specific desk selected may actually be 35 × 74 or 36 × 70. Generally, these slight variances will not affect the overall space plan. If the specific desk and size is known, the designer should use the exact sizes on all drawings, especially in the final floor plans. If the desk or other items have not been selected, then industry-accepted average sizes can be used in planning most work areas and other rooms within office spaces, especially during the initial stages.

Standard Product

Occasionally reference is made to a manufacturer's standard product, which should not be confused with standard sizes. Standard products are the items that each manufacturer makes and offers for sale on a regular basis. These items may or may not conform to the industry standard sizes. Standard product from one manufacturer will not be the same as standard product offered by the next manufacturer.

Regardless of style, size, or manufacturer, contract furniture has unique features that need to be considered when space planning. Office furniture items customarily fall into one of 11 categories.

1. **Casegoods**: desks, credenzas, bookcases, storage units
2. **Filing and Storage**: lateral files, vertical files, pedestals, storage cabinets, lockers
3. **Panel Systems**: panels, worksurfaces, overheads, storage
4. **Tables**: conference, training, lunchroom, informal, occasional
5. **Seating**: desk chairs, conference chairs, guest chairs, sofas, lounge chairs, stools, stack chairs, benches
6. **Shelving**: open, closed, movable
7. **Custom Furniture**: desks, tables, counters, workstations, seating
8. **Accessories**: planters, letter trays, desk lamps
9. **Equipment**: copiers, printers, fax machines, scanners, etc.
10. **Other**: pigeon/mail slots, carts, recycle bins, etc.
11. **Existing or Reused**: any or all of the above items

CASEGOODS

In today's market, the bulk of office furniture consists of private office casegoods, general staff workstations, and file cabinets. Casegoods often set the tone or style of the overall office design by using traditional, transitional, or contemporary styles. Although found mainly in private offices, casegoods can also be used in reception areas and other rooms on the floor plan.

Finishes

The two materials used most often in casegood construction are wood and painted metal. Many, many woods are available for making furniture, but manufacturers tend to use five or six basic woods and veneers: oak, walnut, mahogany, cherry, sycamore, and maple. Manufacturers usually offer several stains for each wood, including a natural finish. If another finish is desired for a particular project, most manufacturers are willing to do a custom stain for a small upcharge.

Metal casegoods are painted, generally by an electrostatic process in cleanrooms at the factory. Most manufacturers offer a wide selection of standard colors, often in neutral tones, or custom colors for a slight upcharge. Standard colors are typically updated every three to five years. Metal desks and credenzas generally receive a plastic laminate top.

Other casegood materials include all-plastic laminate; glass tops; exposed metals such as stainless steel, chrome, brass, or bronze; and any other finish or material that will provide structural support. When available, these materials typically come in several colors and finishes to coordinate with other products.

Style

Casegoods come in many styles and variations. Manufacturers may offer one, two, or more versions, or lines, as versions are called, of each item as a traditional, transitional, or contemporary piece in wood, metal, or other material. Each manufacturer determines its particular product lines and styles, which may or may not be similar to those of the next manufacturer. Product lines customarily include companion pieces to allow for a fully coordinated design.

Executive Desks

Executive desks serve as the primary work-surface for an office occupant. Desk features may include pedestals, modesty panels, a center drawer, top inlay, grommets (Illustrated Table 4.1), drawer pull, and edge detail options. Most of these options do not affect the space plan, but they do need to be finalized at some point in the design process.

Size

Most executive desks are 36 × 72. Occasionally, when a private office is very large, the desk may be 42 × 84. Very small offices routinely require a 36 × 66 desk. Desk sizes are based on the size of the desk top, which may be flush with the sides of the desk, overhang along the front edge or side edges, or be bowed. There is no rule as to which dimension is listed first—width or depth. Some manufacturers and designers prefer to list the depth first (36 × 72) while others prefer to list the width first (72 × 36.) Either practice is acceptable. Desks are 29–30 in. high (Illustrated Table 4.1).

Pedestals

Most desks come standard with a set of pre-installed pedestals on both the left and right sides. Pedestals (peds) are either three-quarter height or full-to-the-floor. Three-quarter peds typically consist of two sets of drawers containing one box and one file drawer (written

as "box/file" or "bx/file ped") (Illustrated Table 4.1g). Occasionally some manufacturers provide a set of three box drawers (written as "bx/bx/bx ped") in place of one of the box/file pedestals.

With full-to-the-floor peds, the left side is often a double file ped, and the right side is a bx/bx/file ped (Illustrated Table 4.1h). However, the designer should verify specifics with each manufacturer because some manufacturers provide other standards. The designer must also verify if locks are standard or an extra.

Front Modesty Panel and Top

Modesty panel refers to the front of the desk. Panels may be three-quarter panels or full-to-the-floor. Some desks, with floating desktops, may not have panels at all. Desktops may be flush with the front and side panels, overhang along the front panel only, or overhang along both the front and sides of the desk. There are no standards, although a full overhang is more common on traditional styles while recessed modesty panels are more common on contemporary styles (Illustrated Table 4.1a–f).

When full-to-the-floor peds are specified, the front modesty and side panels must also be full-to-the-floor. If three-quarter peds are specified, either a three-quarter panel or full modesty panel may be used (Illustrated Table 4.1g and Illustrated Table 4.2d).

Credenzas

Credenzas provide additional storage and work-surface apart from the desk. They are typically positioned 40–45 in. directly behind the desk, allowing the user to swivel around in his or her chair between the two positions (Fig. 6.10). Although a credenza is not as deep as the desk, it costs as much or more than the desk because it usually provides more storage.

Size

The width (or length) of the credenza is normally the same width as the desk with which it will be used. If the desk is 72 in. wide, then the credenza will also be 72 in. wide. If the desk is 66 in. wide, then the credenza will be 66 in. wide. This is not a hard-and-fast rule, but a general guideline. Individual circumstances must always be considered (Illustrated Table 4.2a and b).

ILLUSTRATED TABLE 4.1 Case Goods: Executive Desks

AXONOMETRIC DRAWINGS FRONT SIDE OF EXECUTIVE DESKS	PLAN VIEWS DASHED MODESTY PANEL LINES ARE SHOWN FOR UNDERSTANDING; THEY ARE NOT TYPICALLY DRAWN ON A FURNITURE PLAN	ELEVATIONS AS SEEN FROM USER SIDE
a. Three-quarter recessed modesty panel	d. 36 × 66 Desk with recessed panel	g. Three-quarter pedestals and modesty panel
b. Traditional-style desk with top overhang	e. 36 × 72 Desk with top and side overhangs	h. Full-to-the-floor pedestals and center drawer
c. Recessed front with bowed top	f. 42 × 84 Desk with bowed top and recessed front	i. Double file ped left, 4 box drawers right

Depths, which vary from 20–25 in., will depend on the function of the credenza. If the credenza is used strictly for storage or aesthetics, a lesser depth is sufficient. When a computer monitor is placed on the credenza, the greater 25 in. depth is required. If a company provides mostly laptops or flat-screen monitors to its employees, a lesser depth will suffice. Credenza heights correspond to the matching desk height of 29–30 in. (Illustrated Table 4.2d and e).

Storage

A credenza is made up of various storage components such as file pedestals, box drawers, lateral files, sliding door cabinets, hinge door cabinets, or an open kneehole space (Illustrated Table 4.2e and f). Some manufacturers provide standard credenzas with a pre-selected arrangement of components. In more expensive lines, the designer often has the option of selecting and arranging the components at no upcharge. As with desks, the components come in three-quarter or full-to-the-floor styles.

Upper Storage

When even more storage is required or for aesthetic purposes, upper cabinets or bookshelves can be installed on top of the credenza.

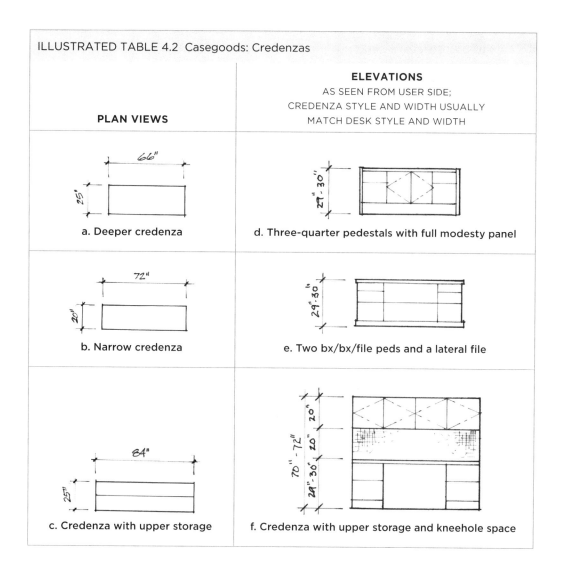

ILLUSTRATED TABLE 4.2 Casegoods: Credenzas

PLAN VIEWS	ELEVATIONS AS SEEN FROM USER SIDE; CREDENZA STYLE AND WIDTH USUALLY MATCH DESK STYLE AND WIDTH
a. Deeper credenza	d. Three-quarter pedestals with full modesty panel
b. Narrow credenza	e. Two bx/bx/file peds and a lateral file
c. Credenza with upper storage	f. Credenza with upper storage and kneehole space

These units may have tackboards on the lower half, task lights, or other features. Each manufacturer should be consulted for specifications (Illustrated Table 4.2f).

Returns

Another option for additional worksurface, and adjacent convenience, is a return. The return is attached directly to the desk on either the right or left side in lieu of a pedestal, which is then eliminated (Illustrated Table 4.3). The return is referred to as a left or right return based on its position from the perspective of a person sitting at the desk or user side. In the same manner, the desk is now referred to as a left- or right-hand, single-pedestal desk, depending on the position

of the remaining pedestal. A right-hand return attaches to a left-hand, single-pedestal desk and vice versa.

When used in a private office, the return is usually located on the side of the desk against the wall. In the event the desk is not against a wall, the return may be located on either side based on the room layout or the user's preference.

Size

The width of a return is measured perpendicular to the desk. It is typically available in 36, 42, 48, and 54 in. widths with 42 and 48 in. as the most common sizes. The selected width often depends on the available space in the room layout or the chair size.

ILLUSTRATED TABLE 4.3 Casegoods: Returns

PLAN VIEWS	SIDE ELEVATIONS
DESK AND RETURNS	DESK AND RETURNS AS SEEN FROM USER SIDE

a. Right-hand single-ped desk with left-hand return

c. Three-quarter panel desk and return

b. Left-hand single-ped desk with right-hand return

d. Executive desk with return and front overhang top from user side

Return depths vary from 19–25 in. When specifying the return depth, the designer must keep several things in mind, including the computer to be used, desk size, and room size. The desk width must accommodate a pedestal, generally 16 or 20 in. wide, approximately 30 in. of knee space and the return depth. Provided the desk is 72 in. wide, there should be adequate remaining space for a 24-in.-deep return (72 – 20 – 28 = 24). However, if the desk and return are going into a narrow office, it may be necessary to use a smaller 66-in.-wide desk, which in turn will require a smaller return depth to allow for adequate knee space (Illustrated Table 4.3).

U-Shaped Desks

In a private office setting, it is difficult to use both a credenza and a return. Part of the credenza may be blocked by the return and thus unusable, or the desk and return must be moved far enough forward to allow access to that part of the credenza, or the credenza must be offset from directly behind the desk (Fig. 4.1). To alleviate these potential issues, the return can be attached to the credenza in the same manner as it is attached to the desk to create a U-shaped unit (Fig. 4.2). As with the desk, the pedestal at the return and credenza junction is eliminated. The return is now referred to as a bridge.

Bookcases

The most common size for a bookcase is 36 × 12 × 2 shelves (approximately 30 in. high, depending on the top and base thicknesses) (Fig. 4.3). Some manufacturers make a narrower 30-in.-wide unit; wider 42-in. units are very uncommon as these wider shelves tend to sag under too much weight. Many traditional lines have a 54-in.-high unit with three adjustable shelves. A few manufacturers offer other, taller units.

FIGURE 4.1 Plan views: Optional layouts for desk and return with credenza

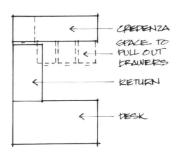

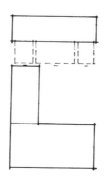

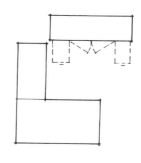

a. Desk sitting immediately in front of credenza blocks one pedestal

b. Desk and return pulled forward to allow access into credenza pedestal

c. Credenza off-set to the side to allow access into all pedestals

Storage Units

Casegood storage units are normally constructed of wood. These units are expensive and are used primarily in special locations. They are usually one of two sizes: 36"w × 24"d × 30"h or 36"w × 24"d × 65"h.

The shorter units are sometimes referred to as telephone cabinets as they are often used in a conference room specifically to hold a telephone. Generally, these units have hinged doors. A few styles may have sliding doors. Some units have a top drawer with shorter doors.

Taller units may combine several functions, with lateral files at the bottom and hinged doors on top. Hinged doors may conceal shelving, a coat rod, or be divided with shelving on one side and a short rod on the other side.

FILING AND STORAGE

In the United States, most business papers are stored in filing cabinets, generally by first placing the papers in a manila folder and then placing that folder in a hanging folder that fits or hangs inside the file cabinet (Fig. 4.4).

In other countries, particularly in Europe, papers tend to be different sizes than those used by US corporations. Corporations outside of the US also use different filing methods, such as oversized three-ring binders that are stored on shelves. When the designer is responsible for a project outside of the United States, it is important to verify the method of filing the client uses.

FIGURE 4.2 U-shaped desk, bridge, and credenza

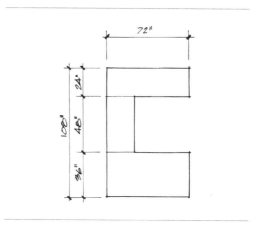

FIGURE 4.3 Bookcase

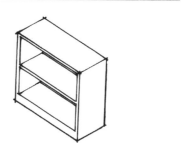

FIGURE 4.4 Filing procedure using manila and hanging folders

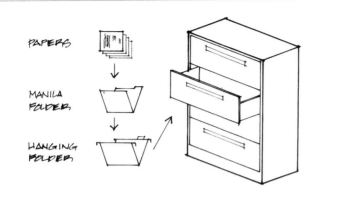

PAPERS

MANILA FOLDER

HANGING FOLDER

Paper Size

When specifying file cabinets, the designer must base the cabinet size and quantity of cabinets on the size of papers to be filed as well as the method of filing. In the United States, two basic sizes of paper are used for documentation: letter (8½ × 11) and legal (8½ × 14). Letter size is the most widely used (Table 4.1). A third paper size, ledger (11 × 17), is used mostly for graphic illustrations. In some situations, a few clients use other paper sizes, particularly those clients who use various forms on a regular basis. For a client with this particular storage need, the designer should verify the method of desired storage.

Finishes

The vast majority of file and storage cabinets are constructed of metal and then electrostatically painted. As with metal casegoods, cabinet paint colors can be selected from the manufacturers' standard color lines or be custom colored for an upcharge. Some manufacturers offer wood file cabinets, which are very expensive, in their casegood lines. To reduce costs, some manufacturers offer optional wood drawer fronts for their metal cabinets when clients want wood finishes.

Optional Features

For the final design, designers will need to select and specify options that include the type of drawer pull or handle, locks, drawer-front style, and so on. Most manufacturers offer options that coordinate among their various lines. Sometimes it is also possible to coordinate selected features between different manufacturers so the designer can, for example, select files from one manufacturer and peds from another.

Lateral Files

The term *file cabinet* is often shortened to and used interchangeably with *file*. There are two types of file cabinets, lateral and vertical; lateral files are the most commonly used in today's offices. Both files can accommodate either letter- or legal-size documents, but generally not within the same drawer. For the most efficient filing space, it is best to use separate cabinets, one for letter filing and another for legal filing.

Size

Freestanding lateral files come in only three widths: 30, 36, and 42 in. (Fig. 4.5). This is an industry standard accepted by all manufacturers. The standard file depth is 18 in., although some manufacturers have come out with a slightly deeper file of 19–20 in.

Height

Unless an exact height is required for a specific reason, file cabinet heights are usually listed by the number of drawers (dr), such as 2-dr, 3-dr, 4-dr, or 5-dr cabinets, instead of giving an actual dimension. A file that is 36"w and has four drawers is described as a 4-dr 36"w lateral file.

Overall heights vary between manufacturers. Although most construct their drawers at about 12"h, the base and top caps will vary in height. Some manufacturers offer only one base and top-cap heights while other manufacturers offer several heights. Bases can vary from 1–3 in. high, while top caps may be from three-quarter to 2 in. This allows a designer to select a height that will fit within the design scheme. A four-drawer file could be as low as 49¾ in. or as high as 53 in.

TABLE 4.1 Paper Sizes and Filing System		
	PAPER	**MANILA FOLDER**
Letter	8½ × 11	9½ × 11¾
Legal	8½ × 14	9½ × 14¾
Ledger	11 × 17	Either size—fold papers

Number of Drawers

The specified number of drawers in files should be based first on storage requirements but also on function and location. Files along a wall or in separate file rooms are usually four or five drawers high to use as much vertical space as possible. When functioning as room dividers (see Fig. 5.1b), three-drawer-high files are often used to allow people to see over the files and to use the tops for additional workspace.

Regardless of the number of drawers specified, the amount of required floor space remains the same for files of the same width. For example, a 36-in.-wide file with any number of drawers always requires 4.5 square feet (SF) of floor space (3 × 1.5 = 4.5) (see Appendix E.12).

Five-drawer files are a bit misleading because the fifth or top "drawer" is not actually a drawer, but rather a flip-up door with a shelf that may be fixed in place or rolled out. This drawer or shelf can be used for storage of supplies, small boxes, and so on, but it cannot be used as a regular file drawer. At approximately 62 in. above the floor, the drawer is too high for the average person to look into for finding file folders. Unless this shelf is needed for additional storage or the client requests five-drawer files, it is better to specify four-drawer files and save the client some money.

Filing Inches

Occasionally, people refer to the number of filing inches instead of the number of drawers (Fig. 4.6). Total actual filing inches can vary by 1–15 in. per drawer depending on file depth, method of filing, and paper size.

The actual number of filing inches is most important when clients have a lot of files and a limited amount of floor space. Then it is important to make every filing inch count. In most cases, though, it is easier to talk about the number of drawers and simply add another file when the amount of storage is in question.

Method of Filing

There are two methods of filing: front-to-back and side-to-side in the drawer (see Fig. 4.6). Both methods are acceptable, and all lateral files can accommodate either method. The method of filing is achieved by use of metal bars within each

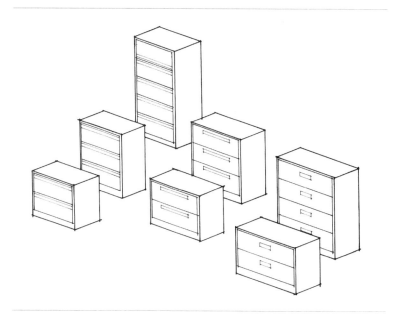

drawer. The desired method of filing should be specified at the time of ordering the file so the correct bars can be placed in the drawers. However, if a client starts out using one method and then wishes to change, new bars can be ordered from the manufacturer and inserted into the cabinets on the job site.

Vertical Files

The second type of file cabinet, called a vertical file, is an older style (Fig. 4.7). It is rarely specified in today's market, but it is still widely used by clients who have been in business for more than 15 or 20 years. Because files are expensive, when clients already have these files in their existing space, they often wish to reuse them in their new office space. This file requires a greater amount of circulation space in front of the file and is more awkward to use than a lateral file due to its depth (see Appendix E.9 and E.10).

Size

Vertical files come in two widths: 15 or 18 in., corresponding to letter- or legal-size filing. Except for some smaller two-drawer files purchased in stationery supply stores or through office supply catalogs, standard vertical files are 26½" or 28"d. Manufacturers offer one depth or the other, but very seldom both depths.

FIGURE 4.6 Methods of filing letter- or legal-size papers in lateral files

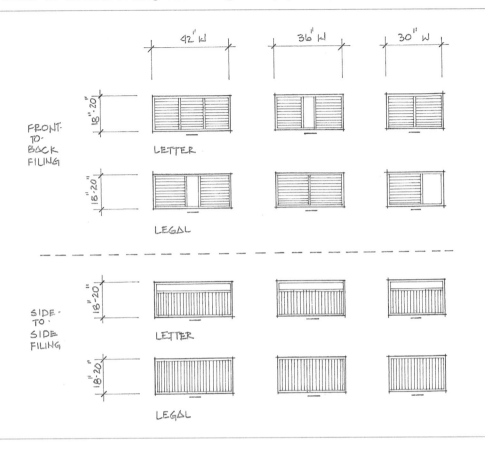

FIGURE 4.7 Vertical files

In overall height, five-drawer vertical files tend to be a little shorter than five-drawer lateral files; thus the fifth drawer is used as an actual drawer for filing and therefore, it is usually specified on a regular basis when this file is to be purchased. However, the actual overall file height can still vary from one manufacturer to another.

Method of Filing

With vertical files, there is only one method of filing: front-to-back. Legal- and letter-size files cannot be mixed within a drawer or within a file cabinet. The width of the file cabinet must be selected based on the size of documents to be filed.

Other Storage

Besides filing, many other types of storage requirements exist. Clients need to store 3 × 5 cards, disks, microfiche tapes, three-ring binders,

Height

As with lateral files, the height of vertical files is also based on the number of drawers. Descriptions of the file size are shown as 4-dr vertical file, letter or legal; or 5-dr vertical file, letter or legal.

product samples, and the like. Some items are small and take up shallow spaces. Other items are bulky and need extra room. To satisfy these varied needs, some manufacturers offer other methods of storage that can be combined within lateral file cabinets or added above a lateral file (Fig. 4.8). These methods include drawer heights of 3, 6, 9, 13, and 15 in., flip doors, inserts for hanging printouts or tapes, stack-on cabinets with sliding doors, and so on. The designer should always check with the manufacturer for available options. These options are not available for vertical files.

Pedestals

Pedestals in this section refer to freestanding, suspended, or mobile peds (Fig. 4.9). They have the same basic appearances, function, and drawer options as the integral pedestals discussed in "Executive Desks." However, these pedestals are ordered as separate items of furniture and installed in the field on the job site, often in panel system workstations or under millwork counters, and occasionally as truly freestanding peds. Except in some wood panel systems, these pedestals are constructed of metal and painted with manufacturers' standard colors.

Width

Most pedestals are 15–16 in. wide and set up to hold letter-size folders front-to-back in the file drawer. The drawer can be adapted to file legal folders side-to-side. Only a very few manufacturers make a legal size or 18"w pedestal for filing legal folders front-to-back.

■ FIGURE 4.8 Other storage units

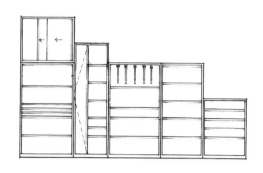

Depth

The exact pedestal depth may vary slightly, but most manufacturers offer three depths: 18–20 in., 22–24 in., and 28–30 in. To allow clearance space between the back of the pedestal and the wall or panel for electrical cords, many peds are nearly 2 in. shorter than the worksurface under which they sit. When the pedestal sits below a worksurface, the depth is usually shown as the same depth as the worksurface, no matter if it is exactly the same or slightly less (see Illustrated Table 7.3), unless a much smaller depth is used. Then it is best to show the exact depth.

Height

All pedestals are made to fit below a worksurface of 29–30 in. high. The specific height depends on the type of pedestals selected and the base and top heights offered by each manufacturer.

■ FIGURE 4.9 Pedestals

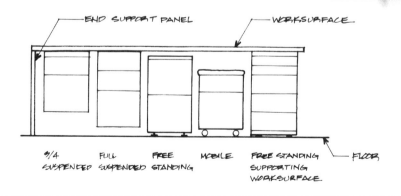

Suspended Pedestals

Suspended pedestals can be three-quarter or full-height pedestals. The top of the pedestal is attached to the underside of the worksurface so that the pedestal is actually hanging from the worksurface. Because these pedestals normally do not have a top piece, the inside of the top drawer is visible before the ped is hung. Once the pedestal is installed, the open top is covered by the worksurface.

Freestanding Pedestals

Freestanding pedestals are fully enclosed and have a finished top. These pedestals sit on the floor; they can be put under a work counter, left freestanding, or serve as end supports for holding a countertop.

Mobile Pedestals

Mobile pedestals come with casters, which may be either visible or hidden under a higher base. Because the casters tend to require more height than typical bases, the overall mobile pedestal height is reduced by one box drawer, resulting in a shorter ped, in order to fit below a worksurface. Many manufacturers now offer padded cushions for the tops of these pedestals, allowing for a place to sit during spontaneous collaboration within small workstations or other work areas that do not contain guest seating.

Drawer Options

The two drawer sizes used most often are the 6"h box and 12"h file drawers, creating bx/bx/file, bx/bx/bx/bx, and double file pedestals as standard products for most manufacturers. Other drawer sizes include 3"h personal and 15"h electronic data processing (EDP) drawers, which enable the designer to specify pedestals that satisfy a diversity of client needs by combining drawers, usually equaling 18"h or 24"h. For example, the designer could write, "1 personal/1 EDP drawer for an 18"h ped," or "2 personal/3 box drawers for a 24"h ped."

Storage Cabinets

Storage cabinets, as opposed to wood storage units under casegoods, are constructed of metal and painted. They are usually 30"w × 18" or 24"d or 36"w × 18" or 24"d. Numerous heights are available, usually in 6-in. increments from 36–78 in. As always, the designer should check with the desired manufacturer for specific sizes. Cabinets are generally used as wardrobe closets or with adjustable shelving. Some manufacturers offer combination storage of wardrobe and shelving.

Lockers

Although lockers are and have been prevalent in junior, middle, and high schools and many manufacturing or other blue-collar workplaces for decades, lockers are a fairly new phenomena in commercial office planning and layouts. In the past, there was normally sufficient storage space within private offices or workstations for personnel to store personal items in addition to regular work items and filing needs. With current average square feet per person going down (see Chapter 2), resulting in smaller typical office and workstation footprints, and with desk sharing becoming more common (see Chapter 7), firms have resorted to providing lockers to accommodate the personal needs of their personnel (see Chapter 11).

Vertical Lockers

Commercial vertical lockers are roughly the same size as high school lockers (Table 4.2), accommodating an upper shelf and either a coat hook or rod, and sometimes a lower shelf above a boot pan. However, doors are customarily upgraded as frameless doors vs. framed doors (see Chapter 10), offered with the options of metal or plastic laminate finishes and the vented air slots have been eliminated. Doors can generally be specified either right or left hinged.

Specific locker sizes and selections are based on several criteria including:

- Light or heavy coat usage, depending on climate zones
- Permanent or daily assignment of lockers
- Storage of laptop bags, or not
- Storage of personal items, or not
- Available floor space

Vertical lockers can also be specified as split lockers with a top and bottom locker when the criteria and personnel needs are slight in nature. This saves considerably on floor space as there are now two lockers in the same floor space as a single tall locker.

Taller lockers tend to be top heavy, creating possibilities for toppling, and a 12 in. by 18 or 24 in. does not provide much latitude for leveling the locker. Therefore, during installation, lockers are often ganged together from side-to-side or to the back wall.

Lateral Lockers

When more horizontal storage is desired and hanging coat storage is not a requirement, a lateral locker can be specified. In essence, these are lateral file cabinets turned into lockers when the manufacturer installs a security shelf between each drawer so that there is no access from one drawer to the next as in the lateral file cabinets.

Locking Capabilities

There are two basic methods for locking both the vertical and horizontal lockers—standard key or electronic lock. Standard key locks are much less expensive than electronic locks; in fact, standard key locks often come at no additional cost to the locker price. On the other hand, electronic locks may add up to $100 or more per lock per door or drawer.

When lockers are assigned on a permanent basis to a single staff, standard key locks may be the best solution. Each person receives a key for his or her locker. If the person is also assigned to a permanent workstation, and the storage in the workstation is from the same manufacturer as the locker storage, it is feasible for the manufacturer to key the locks alike for all storage for each person's "territory" so that each person will then have a single key to open all storage items, including lockers, pedestals, lateral files, overheads, etc.

For lockers that are available on a daily or other short-term basis, it is a better idea for the client to consider electronic locks. Even though these locks are more expensive, each day a different person can access and secure any given locker without having to first locate a key.

Numbering Lockers

At the time of specifying lockers, it is a wise idea to request that lockers receive either permanent numbers attached by the manufacturer or small holders, also attached at the factory, whereby the client can print their own numbered labels. In most cases, for permanent numbers, clients are able to select or designate a starting number or a desired numbering system that will work with the client's room and workstation numbering system. Without some type of numbering, the client and their staff are left with rows of lockers and a guessing game to find a particular locker.

TABLE 4.2 Locker Styles and Sizes			
STYLE	WIDTH	DEPTH	HEIGHT
Vertical	10"–18"	16"–24"	51"–66"
Vertical - split	10"–18"	16"–24"	25"–33" each x 2 = 51"–66" o.a.
Horizontal	30"–36"	18"–20"	2-, 3- or 4-dr

PANEL SYSTEMS

Panel systems are referred to by several names: *panel systems, workstations, cubicles, cubicals, furniture systems, systems furniture, open-office furniture,* and *landscape furniture* (Fig. 4.10a and b). In general, these terms are interchangeable, all relating to work areas made up and arranged by combining various components designed for such an application; assembled on site, also known as "in the field," by furniture installers. Components consist of worksurfaces, storage units, and accessories that are either freestanding or hung from or surrounded by panels. Although there are standard sizes for individual panels and components within each manufacturer's system lines, the designer can combine and configure the parts to achieve many sizes of finished work areas, which allows a great deal of flexibility in the overall space plan (see Chapter 7).

Panels

In general, a single panel cannot stand by itself unless specifically designed as a freestanding, mobile panel. To stand, at least two panels must be connected at 90-degree angles, or at 120-degree angles when a manufacturer provides that connector option. A single panel may be used if it is attached to a wall or other solid support by a wall bracket (Illustrated Table 4.4a and b).

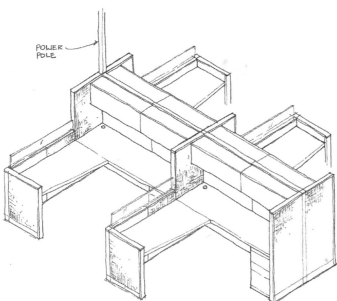

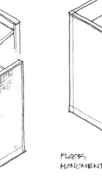

a. Cubicles with varying panel heights and power pole

b. Cubicles with high panels and doghouse floor monument

Thickness (Depth)

Because panels are so narrow in depth, the depth dimension is normally referred to as the panel thickness, which can vary from 1½–6 in. depending on the manufacturer or system selected. Until a specific panel system has been selected, it is wise to use 3 in., currently the most common thickness, as a standard panel thickness for initial space planning purposes. However, once a specific system has been chosen, the designer must remember to go back and review the workstation layouts to verify that all dimensions fit within the floor space.

Width

The five most common panel widths are 18, 24, 30, 36, and 42 in. These standard sizes should be used when initially space planning a workstation layout. A few manufacturers offer other sizes of 12, 48, 60, and 72 in. Twelve-inch panels are very expensive and serve little practical purpose except to fill in special conditions. Although a 60 or 72 in. panel is less expensive than two 30 in. or two 36 in. panels, two installers are required to handle these wider panels and they provide limited flexibility for future reconfigurations.

A few manufacturers offer very unusual panel widths of 25, 35, and 45 in., or 32 and 38 in. If one of these manufacturers has been selected for the project, the final drawing should be based on these sizes. However, until such systems are selected, it is best to plan with the standard panel sizes.

Height

Panel heights are less standard than other areas of furniture. There are five to seven panel heights, which inexplicably vary slightly from one manufacturer to the next. Occasionally, a manufacturer may agree to provide a custom panel height if the project is large enough. But, in general, the designer must select from the standard heights offered by each manufacturer. Panel heights correspond naturally to applicable uses (Illustrated Table 4.5).

Connectors

Panels are connected via hinges, universal connectors, or specified connectors. Manufacturers

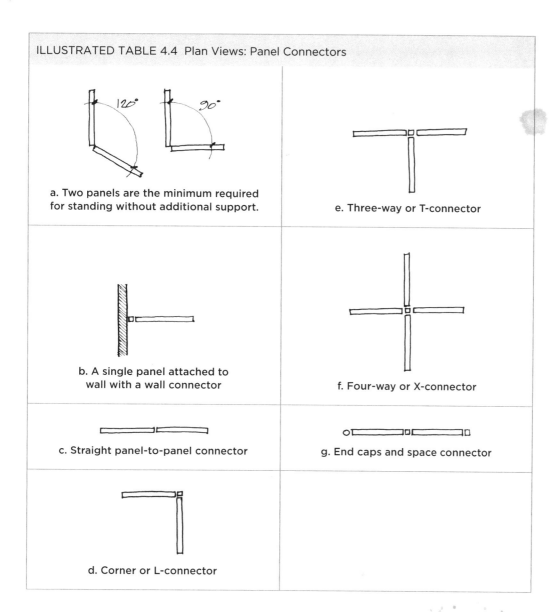

ILLUSTRATED TABLE 4.4 Plan Views: Panel Connectors

a. Two panels are the minimum required for standing without additional support.

b. A single panel attached to wall with a wall connector

c. Straight panel-to-panel connector

d. Corner or L-connector

e. Three-way or T-connector

f. Four-way or X-connector

g. End caps and space connector

offer the type of connector that best suits their individual systems. Connectors generally differ slightly from one manufacturer to another and are not interchangeable.

Hinged connectors are an integral part of each panel. There is a "female" and "male" or "up" and "down" part for every hinge that must be fitted together in the field when the panels are being installed. Generally, hinges protrude from the panel about ½ in.

Universal connectors are usually ½-in.-wide flexible vinyl or metal strips that are inserted into slots along panel ends to connect panels to each other. Often these connectors are shipped automatically with each panel, as the same

strip is used for all connections: straight, L, T, X, or angled. For the L and T connection, there is a "void" at the juncture of panels (Illustrated Table 4.4a), which many designers and clients found unpleasing, particularly in the early days of planning when many aspects of the entire project were neatly aligned throughout. Many manufacturers then offered, for aesthetic purposes only, filler posts that could be installed where desired to fill in the gaps. Although these posts may add to the design statement of the project, it is wise to remember that they are also adding extra dollars to the project. In today's market, with a medley of materials and finishes, juxtaposition of architectural features, and

ILLUSTRATED TABLE 4.5 Panel Systems: Panel Heights and Usage

PANEL HEIGHTS	PANEL USES	PANEL CROSS-SECTIONS
36 in.	Rarely used in older systems; only 6 in. above worksurface height. In newer systems: use to support 6 or 12 in. glass screens	36" H
38–43 in.	Reception and LEED recommended height; easy to see over panel when seated	38"–42" H
48–54 in.	Provides visual privacy when seated	48"–54" H
60–62 in.	Most people can see over panels when standing	CEILING FLOOR 60"–62" H 64"–67" H

mixtures of work areas, this connector, without filler posts, is making a comeback in updated forms as it is the least expensive connection and it does not need to be specified because it automatically comes with each panel.

For systems that use a post as a structural connection, connectors are dependent on the type of connection required. Thus, all connectors or posts must be specified for each type of connection: a straight panel-to-panel

PANEL HEIGHTS	PANEL USES	PANEL ELEVATIONS
64–67 in.	Required for overhead units	
69–72 in.	Few people can see over panels when standing	
84 in.	Required to install doors	
96–112 in.	Floor-to-ceiling demountable or moveable walls	

connector, a corner or L-connector, a three-way or T-connector, a four-way or X-connector, a Hi-Low connector, and end caps (see Illustrated Table 4.4c–g). Although these connectors typically add cost to the system, they tend to provide a cleaner overall appearance that many designers prefer.

Finishes and Materials

Traditional panels are usually covered in a loose-weave fabric over an acoustic and/or tackable surface, but there are numerous other finishes available from most manufacturers. Occasionally, the panel is finished with a wood veneer. While a wood finish is aesthetically pleasing, it is expensive and eliminates both the acoustic properties and tackable capabilities. Other materials include perforated metal, glass or colored acrylic inserts, all of which also eliminate acoustic properties. Some panels are designed with a thin metal trim along the edges to hold or support the finish materials; other panels are designed to allow the finish materials to go from edge-to-edge.

Base, Top, and End Caps

Panels are customarily finished with base plates, a top cap, and end caps where applicable (Fig. 4.11). However, some contemporary systems are now designed to go to the floor without a base or be finished on top and at the ends so as to not require caps. When used, bases are typically vinyl or painted metal plates ranging in height from 4–6 in. They generally come with the panel, although the designer may still need to specify some details (e.g., non-electrical or electrical as well as outlet knockout locations). Some bases snap into place with clips; other bases are attached with screws.

Top and end caps often need to be specified separately because they usually have more options. They will vary from ½–2 in. high and are made from natural metal, painted metal, wood, or laminated materials. The edges may be square, eased, beveled, or rounded.

Electrical Capabilities

A significant benefit of the panel system is the capacity to run electrical power, telephone lines, and data cables within the panels to individual workstations. With new technology, many firms now carry digital telephone connections through their data lines, thus eliminating that third wire or cable line. Most panels provide this option in the base, and in many cases also through the top cap or at the midsection of the panel. Outlets are installed either in the base or at the midsection as specified (see Fig. 4.11).

Panel Standards, Channels, and Brackets

Conventional panels have full-length standards on both the front and backsides along each end. Standards have vertical slots, at 1-in. intervals; this allows for some height adjustment of the components. The teeth of a component bracket are inserted into the slots for hanging. Some newer systems provide horizontal channels in place of vertical standards for hanging worksurfaces and other components. Channel heights are predetermined at the factory and, therefore, are not adjustable in the field (Fig. 4.12).

Panel Joints

Although panel joints are always visible to some degree, standards are fairly inconspicuous once the panels are connected. Some panel systems allow two side-by-side panels to share a common standard; other systems require individual standards for each panel. Channels may or may not be visible, depending on the system design.

■ **FIGURE 4.11 Panel elements: Base, top cap, foot levelers, and electrical knockouts**

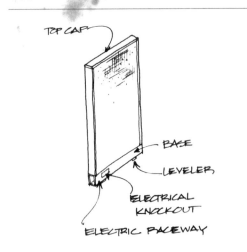

TOP CAP

BASE

LEVELER

ELECTRICAL KNOCKOUT

ELECTRIC RACEWAY

Hanging Methods or Brackets

Depending on the system design, several methods or types of brackets are used to support or hang worksurfaces and other components from the panels. Brackets are generally concealed on the underside of the worksurface or behind an overhead component (Fig 4.15), and thus, not visible.

Cantilever Brackets

Cantilevering is achieved by placing brackets below the outer edges of the worksurface and then hanging those brackets at the corners from panels along the backside of the worksurface (Fig. 4.13). Because the worksurface is supported mainly along the backside, the front edge of the worksurface may sag when excessive weight is placed along the front edge. For this reason, it is good design to install a panel on each end of the worksurface for additional support.

With cantilever brackets, panels on either end of the worksurface may or may not be the same width as the worksurface depth. However, the panel or panels along the backside of the worksurface must be the same width as the worksurface, known as a modular system, in order to insert the brackets into the standards. For example, if the worksurface is 60"w, the panels behind it could be:

- One 60"w panel
- Two 30"w panels
- One 24"w and one 36"w panel

Side Brackets

For better overall support, the worksurface can be hung with side brackets, either in standards or in channels. Now the worksurface is supported at all four corners. In this situation, the side panels must also equal the depth of the worksurface.

Horizontal Channels: Back Brackets

Systems with channels provide continuous or intermittent support along the backside of the worksurface using either cantilever or hanging brackets. Some manufacturers' systems allow the worksurface, and components, to be placed anywhere along a panel run without having to be the same width as the back panels, known as

FIGURE 4.12 Elevations: Panels

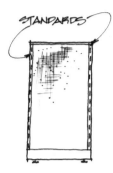
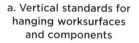
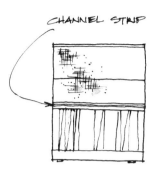

a. Vertical standards for hanging worksurfaces and components

b. Horizontal channels for hanging worksurfaces and components

a non-modular system. Other manufacturers' systems function much like conventional modular panel systems in that the worksurface width must correspond to the panel widths. Many systems that use a horizontal channel also offer the option of installing a leg at the front corner of the worksurface for additional support.

End-Panel Supports

Occasionally, such as when space is tight or the occupant requires greater visibility, it may be functionally or aesthetically desirable to eliminate a panel along one end of a worksurface. Although a cantilevered bracket can be used, it does not provide good support for that end of the worksurface.

In this situation, it is better to use an end panel for support instead of a bracket (see Fig. 4.13). This panel can look like the side of

FIGURE 4.13 Full end-panel support

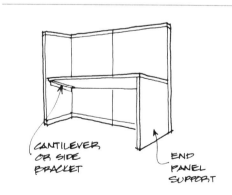

CANTILEVER OR SIDE BRACKET

END PANEL SUPPORT

a desk. In more contemporary systems, the end panel is often an open, tubular leg (see Fig. 7.15b). Whether open or closed, an end panel is installed below the worksurface, which saves the thickness of a structural panel in tight spaces. End panels are approximately 1 in. thick and are generally the same depth as the worksurface.

Worksurfaces

Typically, worksurfaces are hung from panels at 29–30 in. above the floor by means of brackets, or in some cases by using support legs or end panels. Recently, manufacturers started offering freestanding work area tables, either stationary or on casters, and work tables that can be raised and lowered to allow people to stand while working.

Historically, panel system manufacturers offered two basic worksurface styles—rectangular and corner units. Starting in the mid-to-late 1990s, manufacturers began offering additional options for curved, radii, oblique, obtuse, and many other worksurface shapes. Some shapes are unique to a particular manufacturer, and other shapes have become universal for all manufacturers. Many of these shapes add a great benefit to the cubicle layouts by increasing usable space and reducing back-corner, nonusable spaces (see Fig. 7.22).

Width

Standard worksurface widths along the backside for both rectangular and non-rectangular surfaces correspond to single or multiple panel widths. The smallest worksurface width is 30 in. Other widths include 36, 42, 48, 60, 66, 72, and 84 in. Manufacturers with odd panel widths of 35 and 45 in. have corresponding worksurface widths of 35, 45, and 70 in.

Occasionally when laying out clusters of cubicles, the designer may find it necessary to span a T-connection with a worksurface (Fig. 4.14a). The T-panel adds one panel thickness, approximately 2½ or 3 in., to the overall width of the worksurface. Most manufacturers are willing to make a custom-width worksurface in these cases, even for only one worksurface. It is important to notate this custom width when specifying the product. Custom

worksurfaces are priced at the next-larger worksurface size.

Depth

Rectangular worksurface depths include 21, 24, 30 and 36 in.; 24 and 30 in. are the most common. Manufacturers with odd-sized panel widths offer corresponding worksurface depths. For unusually shaped worksurfaces, the designer should consult the selected manufacturer's catalog for specific sizes and depths.

Thickness

Most worksurfaces are 1¼ or 1½ in. thick. A few manufacturers offer other thicknesses.

Corner Units

When two worksurfaces are placed at right angles to form an L-shaped work area (Fig. 4.14b), the far back corner is fairly inaccessible. Some clients prefer to install a corner worksurface to use as the site for the computer terminal (Fig. 4.14c). This design allows free workspace on either side of the seated person.

Corner units can be specified either with a straight or curved front edge (see Illustrated Table 7.3). Units with straight front edges are basically squares offered in three sizes: 36 × 36, 42 × 42, and 48 × 48 (42 × 42 is the most commonly specified size). Both return sides of the unit will be the same depth, normally 24 or 30 in. deep, and the front edge or angle will be 17 or 25 in. wide, depending on the corner unit selected.

Curved-front corner units generally include one return side as an integral part of the corner worksurface and range in size from 42 or 48 × 72, 78, or 84 in. This design is known as a right- or left-handed corner unit.

There are advantages and disadvantages of each unit, depending on its application. The large, 48 × 48 corners are great for large terminals but a waste of back corner space if the occupant uses a laptop or flat screen. Curved units provide a smooth, continuous surface on one side without a joint, but they are less flexible for future redesign and space planning due to the handed side. These options should be discussed with the client before specifying the corner unit to be used.

FIGURE 4.14 Plan views

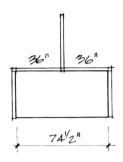

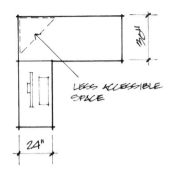
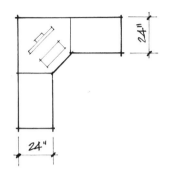

a. Custom-width worksurface spanning T-connection

b. L-shaped work area

c. Corner unit work area

Finishes

Plastic laminate is specified most often for worksurfaces. Manufacturers normally offer four to eight standard color options in several neutral tones. Manufacturers seldom allow the designer to specify a custom laminate. Edges can be specified as quarter round or with some type of edge banding such as metal, wood, or vinyl, although with the advent of *green design* many manufacturers are phasing out vinyl edgings.

A new finish offered by many manufacturers is powder coating, which is produced under a vacuum system. Any particles that do not adhere to the worksurface during the coating process are sucked into a vacuum for reuse in other applications. Powder coating offers a durable, sleek finish and is available in many colors. Worksurface edges can be formed in various profiles similar to those found on table edges (see Illustrated Table 4.7a).

Many manufacturers also offer several wood finishes as a standard option. As with casegoods, if another wood finish is desired, the manufacturer may do a custom finish at an upcharge price.

Any of the worksurface finishes can be used with any panel finishes, for example, laminate surfaces with wood top caps, wood surfaces with metal trim, etc. Selections should be based on the overall project design, the client's wishes, and the budget.

Overhead Storage

An advantage of using panel systems is the capacity for vertical storage above the worksurface in the form of shelving (Fig. 4.15a) or enclosed storage, called binder bins (Fig. 4.15b and c). Overheads can normally be reached by a seated person, so there is no need to get up and walk somewhere. Less floor space is used, which

FIGURE 4.15 Overhead storage

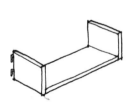

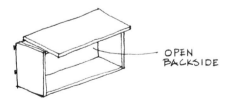

a. Overhead shelf

b. Door flips into bin

c. Door flips over or above bin

helps reduce required overall square footages and thus decreases rental cost. Initial costs are also reduced because most overhead units, as opposed to freestanding storage units, do not have backs and therefore cost less.

Size

Like worksurfaces, shelving and bins are hung onto panels with brackets. Therefore, it follows that component widths are standardized to match panel widths of 30, 36, 60, and 72 in. The 60- and 72-in. bins are single units with two compartments that appear as 30"w or 36"w single units. Most shelves and bins are 12–14 in. deep and 14–17 in. high, so they can accommodate three-ring binders.

Finishes

Most overhead storage units are made of painted metal. Wood systems may offer all-wood units as well as metal units with wood doors. A few systems offer plastic laminate shelves or binder bins with fabric-covered or acrylic doors.

Door Options

Some wood systems offer double-hinged doors, but most binder bins have a single door that flips into or over the bin (Fig. 4.15b and c). A few newer systems are now offering sliding doors. Some manufacturers offer only one door style; others offer several choices.

Under-Worksurface Storage

Under-worksurface storage consists primarily of pedestals and two-drawer lateral files, specified either from the selected panel system line or from another product line. There is no correlation between the storage unit widths and panels or worksurface widths.

Keyboard Tray

Whether computers are placed on a desk, desk return, or worksurface, keyboarding is of great ergonomic concern. Keyboards should be placed low enough to prevent the employee from developing carpal tunnel syndrome or other repetitive motion injuries. For some people, 29 or 30 in. is a bit high. In this case, a keyboard tray can be attached to the underside of the desk, return, or worksurface (Fig. 4.16).

■ **FIGURE 4.16 Keyboard tray**

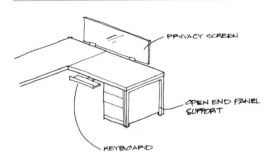

To save costs, some manufacturers have lowered the overall desk and return heights to 28½ in., which seems to be a good height for many users, so that a keyboard tray is not required. For panel systems that allow worksurface heights to be adjusted, the keyboard tray may not be required in this case either, but the designer must verify pedestal heights if they are to be installed below lowered worksurfaces.

Accessories

Most manufacturers offer at least one line of accessories, or *work tools* as they are now known, to be used with panel systems. Items may include but not be limited to tackboards, whiteboards, desk lamps, letter trays, file holders, pencil holders, signage, and visual dividers. Some items are designed to hang directly on panels or off panel rail tiles; other items are made to sit on worksurfaces.

Occasionally designers become involved in specifying these items. At other times, a furniture dealer assists the client in selecting various items once the furniture system is installed.

TABLES

Tables come in many shapes, sizes, styles, and finishes. Although the same table is occasionally used to serve different functions, such as when a training class is held in a conference room, many tables are made to serve a primary function.

Table Shapes

Conference tables periodically come in various shapes, but most tables are either round, rectangular, or square (Illustrated Table 4.6).

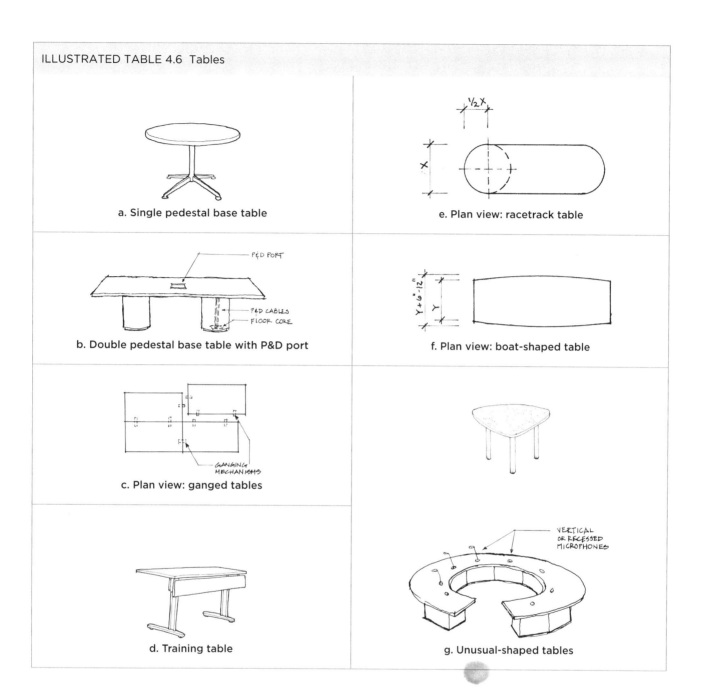

a. Single pedestal base table

b. Double pedestal base table with P&D port

c. Plan view: ganged tables

d. Training table

e. Plan view: racetrack table

f. Plan view: boat-shaped table

g. Unusual-shaped tables

Round

A round table is convenient and somewhat intimate for three to six people seated at an appropriately sized table. Round tables slightly reduce the amount of required circulation, which can be an important criterion when laying out large cafeterias or meeting areas within small rooms, 95 SF for a 48 in. diameter table vs. 100 SF for a 48" x 48" square table (see Appendix E).

Standard table sizes include diameters of 30, 36, 42, 48, and 60 in. Custom tables can be made in sizes of 9'-0", 10'-0", 11'-0" diameters, and larger. However, it is not possible to hand something across these large tables to a person seated opposite. One person must get up and walk around the table, or items must be passed around from person to person.

Except for banquet tables that have legs at the outer edges for ease of folding and storage, most round tables have a pedestal base that allows for greater leg movement. Larger tables will require two or three pedestals for proper stability (Illustrated Table 4.6a and b).

Round tables can be called *round* when referring to the style. When referring to the size or dimension, the table is said to be a 36-in.-diameter table, not a 36-in.-round table.

Rectangular

Rectangular tables are used extensively in training and conference rooms, although the finish, style, and size of tables for each use are different. Depending on the intended function, rectangular tables may have solid or splayed pedestal bases, straight legs either at each of the four corners or offset from the edges, C-channel bases, or another style (see Illustrated Table 4.6).

Square

Square tables, 30" × 30" or 36" × 36", are probably used most often in lunchrooms and other food rooms; but occasionally larger sizes can also be found in conference or other rooms. As with round and rectangular tables, the finishes, styles, and bases of square tables depend on how they are to be used.

Ganged Tables

As multi-functionality becomes a way of life, manufacturers introduced a new group of tables that can "grow" in size when needed and then made smaller again. By the method known as ganging (Illustrated Table 4.6c), individual tables are locked together with a connector on the underside of the tabletops to form a larger-sized, single table. Both the individual tables and the ganged table may be square, rectangular, or trapezoid. When not in use, tables can be stored or set along the side walls of the room.

Training Tables

Training room tables are usually 60"w × 24" to 30"d or 72"w × 24" to 30"d. Seventy-two inches allows two people to sit side-by-side, whereas 60 in. is a bit cramped for two people. Table depth is generally based on preference and the size of the room. These tables typically have plastic laminate tops, and the frames and legs are either natural finish or painted metal with the legs often off-set towards the front of the table to allow more clear space for chairs on the user

side. Normally, these tables come with some type of folding table top and casters so they can be nested and stored. Most manufacturers also offer a removable modesty panel at the front of table (see Illustrated Table 4.6d).

Informal Meeting and Lunchroom Tables

Informal meeting and lunchroom tables are often round or square with natural or painted metal pedestal bases, although other shapes can always be used. Standard tabletop finishes are customarily plastic laminate, but they may also be resin or metal.

Conference Tables

Conference tables are often among the most expensive pieces of furniture found in the office space. They are constructed of single materials or in combinations of wood, metal, marble, granite, glass, leather, and all other types of exotic construction materials. Many manufacturers offer standard sizes of 6'-0", 8'-0", 10'-0", and 12'-0" in length by 42", 48", and 60" in depth or width. Large tables of 15'-0", 20'-0", 24'-0" or longer are custom pieces provided by either a furniture manufacturer or a wood millwork shop based on the designer's drawings and specifications. In addition to typical shapes listed earlier, conference tables are often shaped to suit the needs of the room and the intended design.

Racetrack

Because many tables are so large, rounding the table ends can soften their overall appearance within the room. This can be achieved by using a racetrack table, the contract equivalent of a residential oval table, where each end of the table is one-half of a circle with a radius equal to one-half the width of the table (see Illustrated Table 4.6e).

Boat-Shaped

The boat-shape is another contract table equivalent to the residential oval table. This shape allows for a wider visual sight line of all people seated. There is approximately a 6–12-in. difference between the narrower ends and wider middle (see Illustrated Table 4.6f).

Custom Sizes and Shapes

Conference rooms, along with the reception rooms, are generally the two showcase areas for many companies. It is not unusual for both of these areas to receive custom-designed furniture pieces.

Custom-designed tables can be any size, dimension, or shape to meet the client and design criteria. Several custom sizes have already been mentioned. Other tables are as large as 35'-0", 45'-0", or 50'-0" long or 25'-0" in diameter. However, when designing these huge tables, the designer must keep two things in mind:

1. Large tables cannot be made and installed as one piece. Joints and seams need to be considered in the overall design of the table.

2. For tables installed on upper floors, the table parts need to be transported via the elevator to the appropriate floor. It is important to verify the elevator door width and interior cab carrying capacity.

With consent from the client, the designer may wish to design an unusual-shaped table. Before much time is spent designing such a table, the designer should be sure that the table is practical and that the client will approve it (see Illustrated Table 4.6g).

Corners, Edge Details, and Base Supports

Whether the table is a standard product or custom, the designer must select the edge detail and base support (Illustrated Table 4.7). The base, legs, pedestals, or other type of support used to hold up the table is critical. For more information on base support, the designer should consult with a manufacturer's representative or millworker.

There are many edge details. By considering this detail as seen from the top view of the table as well as the profile, the designer can achieve different visual aspects. The hardwood edge may have either the same color or stain as the rest of the table or a contrasting finish.

Finally, the designer should consider the corner detail for rectangular, square, boat-shaped, and other tables. On custom tables, the designer will have full control in specifying the option for corner detailing. Many standard products also come with similar edge detail options.

Electrical and Data Capabilities

As more and more firms replace desktop computers with laptops, employees bring those laptops to meetings as do guests and visitors. Although laptop batteries are often used for short terms, many people still prefer to plug in their laptops whenever possible. To alleviate cords running from the table, alongside seated persons, and to outlets in the walls behind (thus causing tripping hazards and chairs rolling over those cords), manufacturers now offer the option of installing power and data (P&D) jacks within port stations in the table top for all types of tables including conference, training, and coffee tables (Illustrated Table 4.6b).

Depending on each manufacturer's options, port stations can be troughs recessed into the table surface or elevated pop-ups from the surface. Ports generally include two or four single electrical outlets and two or four data jacks. When more outlets or jacks are required, additional ports can be installed. Again, depending on each manufacturer, on the underside of the table, the ports may come with standard cords and plugs, or they may require hardwired connections. In either case, the designer will want to specify a floor core and box, similar to workstation floor outlets (Illustrated Table 4.6b). Generally, one core is sufficient to service three to four ports as the wires and cables can be daisy-chained together below the table top. Even though floor cores are shown on the construction drawings, the exact core location is regularly coordinated in the field at the time of construction to ensure proper placement directly below a table base as the cords will run up to the underside of the table via a base.

A/V Equipment

With teleconferencing, speakers, microphones, and other equipment will need to be considered in each conference room layout, planned by the

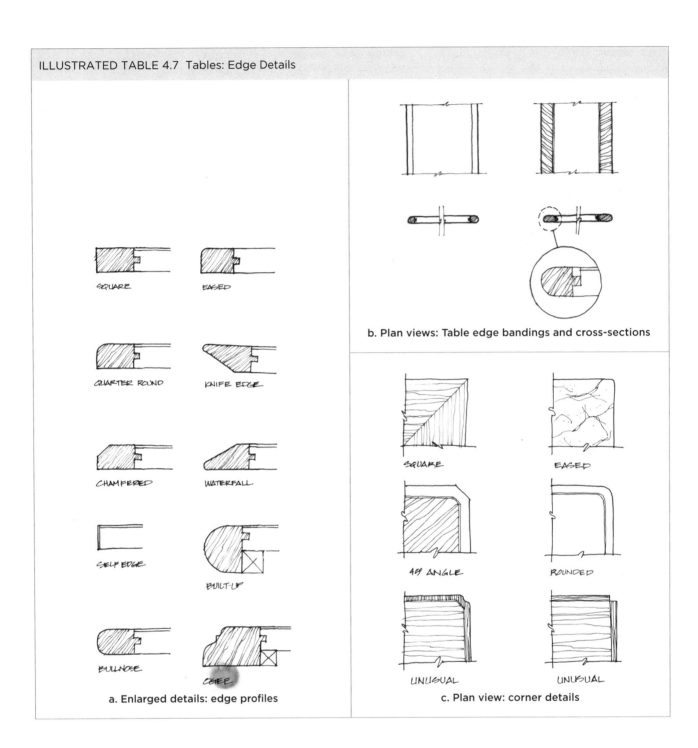

b. Plan views: Table edge bandings and cross-sections

a. Enlarged details: edge profiles

c. Plan view: corner details

A/V vendor and coordinated with the designer (see Chapter 8). For tables specifically, the item to consider may be microphones, which can be installed into the table top, fully recessed or slightly raised, in separate locations from the P&D ports (Illustrated Table 4.6g), or be movable, either wired or wireless, items that sit on the table surface. When microphones are planned for the table, recessed or movable, rather than in the ceiling, A/V cabling and connections will need to be added to the power ports and floor cores.

SEATING

Many office tasks are performed while seated, from talking on the telephone to keyboarding to eating. Many of these tasks are also performed under various levels of stress and in a range of posture positions:

- Relaxing to tense
- Comfortable to nervous
- Leaning back to leaning forward
- Continuous movement to limited movement
- Up, down, and up again to sitting and sitting and sitting

No one chair or seat can do everything or allow the designer to meet all of the above demands. *Seating*, as a universal term, covers a broad range of chairs and other types of furniture pieces such as benches, stools, and sofas. Some seating—such as guest or pull-up chairs, lounge chairs or benches—may be selected for its aesthetic appeal. Other chairs for the office and cubicle work areas should be selected based on their ergonomic ability to meet the users' functional requirements.

There are many criteria for selecting chairs and other seating pieces. Regardless of its aesthetic or functional importance, seating is generally one of the last items selected in the design process. There are so many styles and versions of each type of seating that the designer can develop the overall design scheme and then select from this wide range of offerings for the chair or seat to best fit the overall requirements.

Colors, Finishes, and Fabrics

Most manufacturers offer a wide range of standard colors, finishes, fabrics, and leathers for their seating. This is one of the easiest areas to bring in bright colors, patterns, and variety to the office design. Depending on the style of chair or seating, exposed frames will be constructed of wood, natural metal, painted metal, or plastic resins. Fabrics are often custom colored, customer's own material (COM), or customer's own leather (COL). All of these choices give the designer a great deal of latitude in pulling together the final design.

Size

Unlike other contract furniture, there are no standard sizes for seating. Many similar styles or types of seating are similar in size, but each type varies slightly from one manufacturer to the next.

Templates

When hand-drafting a floor plan, it is best for the designer to use a template for chairs and most seating. Many manufacturers provide plastic templates with cutouts for several of their chair styles and selections. Art stores have various generic chair templates that can also be used.

Most CAD programs have a library of chair templates that can be inserted into the floor plan in a manner similar to manual drafting.

Task Seating

General office seating is typically called task seating, as employees use it when performing various tasks such as data entry, keyboarding, research, lab work, other computer work, sales calls, receptionist duties, and so on. Employee jobs using task chairs range from mailroom clerks to data entry people to research analysts to mid-level managers to CEOs. Oftentimes the same chair must be adjustable to meet the various tasks performed, the size of person using the chair, and the status requirements of the person using the chair. For example, both a clerk and a paralegal may work extensively at the computer. Both need the same type of back, seat, leg, and arm support. Conceivably, the same chair could satisfy both employees. However, it is often perceived that a paralegal with a college degree has a higher status than a clerk and that this should be reflected by the finish, size, and decorative appearances of each person's chair. To meet the many demands of their occupants, most task chairs include six to seven ergonomic adjustments and other options to fit the chair to the person for the best performance (see Illustrated Table 4.8).

Ergonomics and Chairs

One of the first considerations for selecting task seating is its ergonomic capabilities—a very important feature. In actuality, the same chair cannot satisfy every use or need. According to one leading chair manufacturer,

> First of all, ergonomic does not mean adjustable. Ergonomic design involves a whole range of features that fit environments to people and the tasks they perform. Adjustability may be just one feature on an ergonomically designed chair.

a. Task chairs with and without arms

b. High-, medium-, and low-back task chairs

c. Executive seating

d. Ergonomic executive seating

[C]hoosing the right chair depends on a number of criteria: size, postural support, task, workstation design, personal preference, and even organizational culture. Certainly there are constants, features that are essential to all ergonomic seating. But much depends on the person using the chair, the tasks being performed, and the environment in which the chair is used.[1]

It is essential for the designer to understand ergonomics in order to assist clients in selecting the best chairs for their office needs. Designers should read brochures, talk with manufacturers' representatives, and attend seminars to gain a fuller understanding of ergonomics and its importance in today's office setting.

Arms or Without Arms

Most task chairs can be ordered either with or without arms. Many people find arms to be a comfortable benefit. However, arms add about 5 to 6 in. to the overall width of the chair and 5 to 10 percent to the cost. Therefore, in tight spaces or with a tight budget, it may be advantageous to order a chair without arms (see Illustrated Table 4.8a).

When specified, many arms come with the ability to be raised or lowered, swivel in and out, move in and out, or forward and backward. Some chairs can be retrofitted in the field to add or remove arms, but this option must be verified with the manufacturer for each chair style.

Back Size and Adjustments

To meet physical requirements or status level of various employees, manufacturers offer several back heights for the same chair. These are called high-, medium-, or low-back chairs. Some manufacturers may offer all three heights, while others may offer only two heights. High, medium, and low are descriptions, not specific sizes. A low-back chair, or high or medium, from one manufacturer will probably be a different height than a low-, high-, or medium-back chair from another manufacturer (see Illustrated Table 4.8b).

Seat Height and Chair Size

Task chairs customarily come with the ability to raise or lower the seat height through use of an adjustable pneumatic lift in the column base.

Known as a cylinder base, this two-part metal tube allows one part to slide in and out of the other part by means of gas within the tube. By activating a lever under the seat, a person can lower the seat while sitting in the chair. To raise the seat, the person must stand up and activate the lever so the gases can rise.

In addition to the height adjustments, most manufacturers offer other ergonomic features that may affect the overall chair size. Because chairs are highly mobile, and not required to *fit* within given dimensions, designers are fairly safe to use generic chair templates on furniture plans (Table 4.3).

TABLE 4.3 Chair Sizes and Dimensions			
TASK CHAIRS			
	HEIGHT	**WIDTH**	**DEPTH**
WITH ARMS			
Low-back	22–24″	24–27″	24–25″
Medium-back	24–29″	24–27″	24–25″
High-back	34–39″	24–27″	24–25″
WITHOUT ARMS			
Low-back	22–24″	18–20″	24–25″
Medium-back	24–29″	18–20″	24–25″
High-back	34–39″	18–20″	24–25″
EXECUTIVE CHAIRS			
	HEIGHT	**WIDTH**	**DEPTH**
High-back	39–47″	25–27″	26–27″
Medium-back	36–42″	25–27″	26–27″
CONFERENCE CHAIRS			
	HEIGHT	**WIDTH**	**DEPTH**
High-back	38–42″	26–32″	27–29″
Medium-back	28–32″	26–32″	26–29″

Casters

It stands to reason that a chair wheel (or caster, as it is called in the design industry) will roll differently on a hard floor than it rolls on carpet. Because most offices are carpeted, many manufacturers automatically ship chairs with carpet or hard-ball casters. But, if the chair is to be used on a hard floor such as wood, vinyl composite tile (VCT), and the like, the designer must specify soft-ball casters. At the time of ordering, the type of caster generally makes no difference in the chair price. However, if this detail is overlooked and the chair is shipped with the wrong casters, first the client will be unhappy because the chair does not roll properly; and second, someone will need to pay for new casters and labor costs to change them.

5-Star Base

Today all desk seating is made with a pedestal base having five feet or prongs. This is typically called a 5-star base, and it prevents the chair from tipping over. The prongs are short; they do not extend beyond the seat.

Executive Seating

There is customarily a distinct difference between the seating used by most general office workers and the upper management. Since executives tend to perform fewer repetitive tasks, many of them still prefer large, executive chairs (Illustrated Table 4.8c). To provide these status symbols as well as ergonomic seating for all levels of employees, many of the same properties discussed earlier for task seating are now being applied to the executive chair (Illustrated Table 4.8d).

Conference Seating

Conference seating often looks similar to task or executive seating. However, these chairs tend to have fewer ergonomic features, primarily because most meetings are at most one hour in duration, with few tasks performed during the meetings. With fewer adjustable parts, costs are more easily controlled. Many conference chairs are covered in leather, which then increases the chair cost.

Guest or Pull-Up Chairs

Guest or pull-up chairs are also known as occasional or side chairs. They are found primarily in individual private offices and the reception area. They can also be placed in large workstations, featured as a decorative piece in large corridors and public rooms, located next to credenzas in conference rooms, or positioned anywhere within the office that requires such a chair for either functional or aesthetic reasons.

Of all the pieces of contract furniture, this chair comes in the widest variety of styles. It can be contemporary, traditional, or transitional; ornate or simple; small, medium, or large in scale; have straight, curved, cabriole, or tapered legs; be ordered with or without arms, upholstered or nonupholstered, and the list goes on (Illustrated Table 4.9a).

Finish and Style

The frame and legs of these chairs can be either wood or metal. To some extent, the choice of material determines the final chair style and design. Chairs typically have four legs, but sometimes the front and back legs are joined along the floor in a continuous manner. This chair style, called a sled base, is used for many casual and lunchroom chairs. Another style, called cantilever, has only two front legs that are joined in a continuous U-shape along the floor.

Size

Most of these chairs are from 20–24 in. wide by 22–26 in. deep. Since they usually sit freely in open space, the exact sizes are generally not so important. If an exact size is required for a particular project, the designer should always check with the manufacturer or measure an existing chair to be reused.

Sofas

Due to space constraints and comfort level, sofas are seldom used in office settings. In individual or private offices, if the occupant remains seated behind the desk, the visitor will be at a lower eye level when seated on the sofa (a perceived imbalance in power). In reception areas, visitors tend to stand up while waiting rather than sit with an

a. Guest and pull-up chairs

b. Boxy and square lounge seating

c. Curved and soft lounge seating

d. Multiple seating

e. Stack chairs with a sled base

f. Collaborative seating

g. Other types of seating; stools, benches

unknown person on a sofa, especially if only the middle position remains open on a three-seat sofa.

Occasionally, though, sofas are used in reception areas (particularly those with traditional designs) or in law firm partner offices, which tend to be larger than in other types of businesses. In this case, the designer can draw on knowledge of residential sofas when space planning. However, for final selections and specifications, it is always best to use contract furniture.

Lounge Chairs

In large reception areas, pull-up chairs can look undersized or a bit too formal and uninviting. Because sofas are not recommended, it works well to use one or two pairs of club or lounge chairs, or *soft seating*, the new term that has evolved in commercial applications. These chairs tend to be fully upholstered, large in scale, and inviting looking. Styles can be boxy and square or curved with softer lines (see Illustrated Table 4.9b and c).

Finishes
Leather is probably the most frequently selected material for this type of seating, especially in reception areas. When a fabric is used, heavy-duty upholstery should be selected to ensure good wearability against the constant use the chair will receive.

Size

For initial planning, the designer should assume a minimum size of 30"w × 30"d, perhaps even 34"w × 34"d, for lounge seating. Most templates do not provide cutouts for chairs this large. Therefore, these chairs should be drawn to scale on the plan. As soon as these chairs have been selected, the designer should always verify their exact size and then redraw them to scale in the furniture plan. This step is needed to ensure they will actually fit as envisioned, because some lounge chairs can be as large as 42"w × 36"d. For design balance and visual scale, these larger chairs proportionally need more area, which may require that more space be allocated to the reception area.

Collaborative Seating

With more people teleworking, mobility and touch-down areas, both seating and workstations, have popped up in many interior office layouts. Numerous firms even encourage permanent workers to be mobile within the organization. To satisfy both the seating and work area requirements, manufacturers have added small table tops, or tablet arms, to lounge chairs (Illustrated Table 4.9f). As mentioned above, lounge seating is often large scaled. Therefore, to reduce space requirements, many of these chairs can be specified as armless.

Like lounge seating above, collaborative chairs may be specified in various textiles, finishes, and styles. Some of the chairs will come with casters, either in all four positions or just at the front of the chair, which reduces unwanted shifting, and handles on the back of the chair for easy movement. Most manufacturers offer the tablet arm to be specified on either the left or right side of the chair.

Multiple Seating

Ranging in size between pull-up chairs and lounge seating, multiple seating or waiting area chairs can be used to accommodate large numbers of people in reception areas. Chairs can vary in size from 24"w × 26"d up to 35"w × 31"d (see Illustrated Table 4.9d).

Lunchroom Seating

Most lunchroom chairs are armless and stackable; they are also slightly smaller in scale and size than guest chairs. Lighter-scale chairs are easier to move in-and-out and around the table. They can also be scooted closer together, allowing one more person to squeeze in and join the group for lunch (see Illustrated Table 4.9e).

Materials and Finishes
Fabric is seldom used on lunchroom chairs; the client is looking for easy maintenance. The body of these chairs is often made of a less expensive formed resin or hard plastic, or wood or metal. All of these materials are easy to wipe clean. When the seat or back is upholstered, the best material to use is vinyl or fabrics that have been

vinylized, again for ease in wiping clean. Frames may be metal, resin, or wood.

Other Types of Seating

Occasionally, the designer has the opportunity to use other types of seating (stools, benches, tandem seating, auditorium seating, modular seating, etc.). When these situations arise, the designer should check with various manufacturers of the desired type of seating for all the particulars required to design, lay out, and specify such seating (Illustrated Table 4.9g).

SHELVING

Every office or design project calls for some amount of shelving. All kinds of things can be stored on shelves, and many—if not most—of these items are not accessed or used often. When they are, it is for only a short time. No matter how infrequent their use, it is necessary to provide storage space for all items. Shelving is usually placed in out-of-the way areas or in separate storage rooms.

To meet the requirements of these umpteen different items and sizes, shelving comes in umpteen different sizes. It is generally constructed of a heavy-gauge metal and put together like an erector set. The designer or client will figure out the shelf size, the number of shelves, and how high each shelf unit needs to be. All of the parts are ordered individually and shipped individually. This is called knockdown (KD) shelving. When all the parts arrive at the site, an installer assembles them into a shelving unit or units (Illustrated Table 4.10a).

Finishes

Since this shelving is ordinarily planned for out-of-the-way rooms, it is typically painted some shade of gray. However, manufacturers generally offer several other paint colors at a slight upcharge.

Shelves

Most shelves come in a standard metal gauge (18 ga.) that holds up under a great deal of weight. When very heavy items are to be stored, it is wise to order a heavier gauge (22 ga.) shelf. Units of many sizes can be created and used in the same room. All shelves in any single unit must be the same size, but they can be installed at various heights.

Size

Shelf widths increase by 3-in. increments from 30–48 in. Depths also increase in 3-in. increments from 12–42 in.

Posts or Supports

To hold up the shelves, posts or supports are needed at all four corners of the shelving unit. The supports are also the means of providing the height for the unit. After determining the number of shelves to be used and the distance between each shelf, the height of the support can be calculated.

Height

Supports can be ordered in 6-in. increments from 30–108 in. Supports can be cut down in the field if they are too high. A layout should be planned before ordering the supports to determine the number of T- or X-connectors required for side-to-side or back-to-back units.

Single or Shared Side-to-Side Supports

When two units are the same depth and sitting side-by-side, they can be joined by sharing a common support, or T-connector. This setup cuts down on the cost and increases the stability of both units.

Back-to-Back Units

In the same way that two side-by-side units can share side supports, two units can be placed back-to-back and then share the same back supports. This setup can be used when there are several rows of shelving, known as stacks, with aisles between each row.

Shelving Restrictions

There are few restrictions for planning and laying out most shelving units and stacks. The designer should keep in mind, though, that shelves wider than 36 in. can sag or bow under excessive weight. This problem can be addressed by using deeper shelves or heavier gauge metal. Twelve-inch-deep shelving is not structurally sound enough to stand alone. It

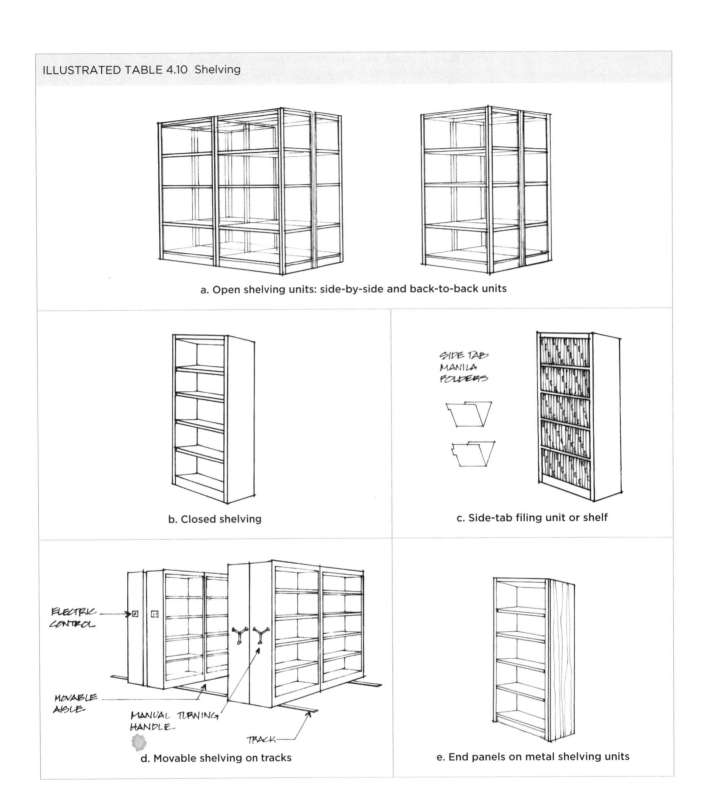

a. Open shelving units: side-by-side and back-to-back units

b. Closed shelving

c. Side-tab filing unit or shelf

d. Movable shelving on tracks

e. End panels on metal shelving units

must be placed against the wall, or back-to-back with another unit.

Open or Closed Shelving

Shelving discussed thus far is called open shelving because it has open sides, backs, and fronts. Stored items could overhang or stick out beyond the actual shelf. Normally, this is not a problem when the shelving is in a storage room and not seen by the general public. Open shelving is less expensive than closed shelving.

Sometimes, though, it is better to have closed shelving that fully separates units by providing backs and/or sides on the units. This may be done for security reasons, inventory control of small items, or visual aesthetics, such as with library stacks. Backs and sides, generally of metal, give the shelving a less institutional look (see Illustrated Table 4.10b).

Movable Shelving and Filing Systems

Corporations that have excessive filing or limited floor space may want to consider an alternate form of filing, called side-tab filing on shelving (Illustrated Table 4.10c), which provides greater density or more filing inches than the top-tab filing used in freestanding file cabinets. Although used extensively in doctors' offices, this form of filing is a bit unconventional in commercial offices unless the shelving is mounted on a movable system.

To conserve room and floor space, shelving can be installed on rollers over a track system to allow easy back-and-forth movement of the shelving (Illustrated Table 4.10d). Moving shelf units eliminate the need for aisle space between each stack of filing. The aisle is shifted and reused as another shelf unit is rolled out of the way (see Chapter 11).

End Panels

When shelving—whether open, closed, or movable—is used as library stacks, in public areas, or at the client's discretion, end panels can be installed over the metal sides. End panels give shelving units a completely different look that is rather handsome and much more inviting and friendly. Once books or DVDs are organized along the shelves, the metal parts and institutional look almost disappear; the public sees only the end panels. It must be kept in mind, though, that backs, sides, and end panels all add to the shelving costs (see Illustrated Table 4.10e).

Finishes

Often end panels are constructed of wood in any style or finish as desired. They can also be plastic laminate, fabric covered, resin, perforated metal, or designer's choice.

CUSTOM FURNITURE

Custom furniture generally refers to items that are fabricated in a millwork shop or furniture factory, designed and specified for an exclusive client or job site. Items are custom designed for various reasons:

- The designer may wish to match the exact finish or style of other standard items used throughout the design project.
- The designer may wish to *make a statement* by showcasing an item radically different from typical furniture styles.
- A size or dimension other than standard furniture sizes may be required for the space.
- Delivery time for a custom item may be less than for a similar standard item of furniture.
- Costs of a custom item may be less than those of a similar standard item.

Though a custom item *may* occasionally cost less than a standard item, most custom pieces of furniture are ordinarily more expensive than standard furniture items. Therefore, it is absolutely necessary to discuss the budget with each client. The designer and the client must understand the reasons and implications of custom designing one or more pieces of furniture for the project.

Although any item can be custom designed, the items most often custom designed are conference tables, reception desks, high-end executive desks, and some seating. Custom designing items in the other categories may be technically complicated or cost prohibitive. For instance, tables consist of the top surface and leg supports, generally constructed in part or totally of wood, a very workable material. File cabinets, on the other hand, are typically constructed, at least in part, of metal sheets that need to be formed, movable parts fitting inside of a cavity, and a locking mechanism. Designers will want to consider where to expend the most or least amount of energy and budget when and if they decide to custom design selected items.

Custom-designed items are drawn up by the designer in a manner similar to construction drawings: they include plan views, elevations, sections, enlarged details, dimensions, specifications, general notes, and any other information as required. Fabrication can be bid by several sources or given to a selected source.

Although many designers fully understand technical drawings, are skilled at detailing, and *know* exactly how they want the end product to look, fabricators often build items slightly different in the joinery areas from those shown in the drawings supplied by the designer. Each shop is set up a bit differently, may have different machines, and does construction in its own manner. Thus, before constructing the custom-designed items, it is important for a fabricator to provide the designer with shop drawings for review and approval. This way, the designer and fabricator can work together to achieve the desired results.

ACCESSORIES

In most cases, the selection and purchase of various non-panel system accessories (e.g., wastebaskets, office supplies, coat hangers, etc.) is handled by the client after move-in. Although the designer may not be responsible for selecting and specifying accessories, there is still the need to plan for these items.

When the designer has the opportunity to select accessories, plants, and artwork, it should always be done under a separate contract after completing the primary space planning and architectural design contract. These items are not part of space planning and design and are not typically included in the design fees.

Office Supplies

Accessories such as bulletin boards, letter trays, wastebaskets, trash cans, vases, rolling carts, and the like are normally considered office supplies (along with pencils, paper, tape, etc.).

It is important for the designer to plan storage space for these various items. Shelving is needed for small supplies, and floor space is essential for boxes of paper. Rolling carts are typically housed in a closet or separate room when not in use.

Plants

To add a human dimension to an otherwise linear presentation, designers customarily show several plants on furniture plans. But in most cases, the client handles the plant selections with a plant company after moving into the space.

Occasionally, designers select and specify planters, especially in highly visible public areas like the reception and conference rooms. But in general, planters are supplied by the plant company along with the plants.

Artwork

Artwork is usually treated in the same manner as plants. The designer plans specific locations, lighting, niches, and focal points for at least some of the artwork. But the client often hires a separate art consultant to help with selecting the actual pieces of art to be purchased—especially poster art, which tends to make up the bulk of wall art in offices.

Even though the designer does not specifically select these items, the client often refers to the plan to see where the designer suggested placing these items. The client may also ask for the designer's input on style and color selections for these items, but as mentioned above, it should be under a separate contract.

EQUIPMENT

Equipment is not selected, specified, or recommended by the designer. Equipment is not the designer's responsibility. The client should always deal directly with a sales person representing the manufacturer for the piece of equipment desired. However, the designer should be aware of the various types of equipment that can be found in an office in order to plan adequate floor or counter space, height clearances, electrical or data outlets, and other requirements.

Most offices will have at least one or more of the following pieces of equipment: copiers, printers, fax machine, postage machines, binding machines, and so forth. There are many styles and sizes available for each piece of equipment, such as a large- (Fig. 4.17) or medium-size copier (see Fig. 11.1). For the final plan, it is the designer's responsibility to measure and inventory each piece of equipment to be reused or ask the client for cut sheets of new equipment and then plan for adequate space. (See Appendix E.37.)

OTHER

Besides all of the furniture and equipment already discussed, there will always be other items to consider in a design project. Some clients will request light tables, drafting tables, coat racks, overhead or slide projectors, mobile marker boards, TV and video equipment, mailroom pigeon slots, bursters, recycle bins, and so on.

Furniture-related items, such as marker boards, will regularly be specified by the designer while other items may be purchased by the client from various supply stores or equipment vendors. No matter the source, it is important to remember that if the item takes up floor or counter space, the designer will need to plan for the item or items.

EXISTING FURNITURE, FURNISHINGS, AND EQUIPMENT

Many, many clients reuse at least some furniture or equipment from their existing location. First, it is very expensive to purchase everything new. Second, some of the existing items may be recent purchases that clients want to reuse. Third, clients may have a personal affection for a particular item. Fourth, new items may look and function exactly like existing items and thus need not be repurchased. Finally, by reusing existing items, the project may earn credits toward Leadership in Energy and Environmental Design (LEED) certification (Box 4.1).

Designers should determine the items to be reused; do a physical walk-through of each

FIGURE 4.17 Large floor copier

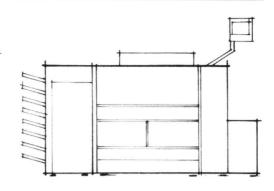

client's existing space; survey, measure, and inventory all items, typical or atypical, including furniture, furnishings, equipment, and appliances that could be incorporated into the new project design; and plan accordingly. Recording of inventoried items can be done manually and then input into an electronic document or electronically in the field, at the client's existing location, using forms similar to those found in Appendix F. It is always beneficial to take photographs for later reference. It is the designer's responsibility to account for all items to be located in the client's new space and make sure all items will fit and function within the allotted areas.

BOX 4.1 LEED CI Reuse of Existing Furniture[2]

Material and Resources Credit

INTERIORS LIFE-CYCLE IMPACT REDUCTION
MR Credit (1–4 points) Commercial Interiors

INTENT
To encourage adaptive reuse and optimize the environmental performance of products and materials.

REQUIREMENTS
Option 1. Interior reuse (2 points)
Reuse or salvage interior non-structural elements for at least 50% of the surface area. Hazardous materials that are remediated as a part of the project must be excluded from the calculation.

AND/OR

Option 2. Furniture reuse (1 point)
Reuse, salvage, or refurbish furniture and furnishings for at least 30% of the total furniture and furnishings cost.

FURNITURE LIBRARIES

Although many manufacturers now put their product lines, brochures, specifications and price lists online, countless design firms and design colleges still maintain libraries of furniture catalogs and finish samples displaying much of the furniture just discussed. Each manufacturer provides its own catalog, generally a three-ring binder containing brochures and price lists. Finish samples include boxes of paint chips, wood blocks or metal squares, 8" × 8" fabric memos or 3" × 3" fabric cards, edge details, 12" × 12" marble squares, 4" × 4" etched glass, 2" × 3" laminate colors, and so on.

When the designer is familiar with a piece of furniture or a particular finish sample, library brochures and samples are a great resource for pulling together an initial design concept. A furniture library can also save time, energy, and money by providing product and samples at hand for presentation boards. However, for the richest experience—for the fullest concepts and knowledge, for a hands-on approach, for complete resources of information—there is nothing like visiting, walking through, sitting on, and touching the real product in various manufacturers' showrooms.

PROJECTS

Project #1: Field trip to a furniture mart, design center, or furniture dealer in place of class meeting

Understanding furniture used for planning spaces and laying out floor plans is essential for achieving functional, efficient, and exciting space plans. Much of the furniture just described is used in creating typical room or area layouts (see Chapters 6–11), which are attached to both the Programming Questionnaire and the Program Report. Occasionally, individual items of furniture are used directly in the Program Report (see Fig. 12.5).

1. As a group, students should visit nearby furniture showrooms to view several manufacturers' product lines.
   a. If possible, it is a good idea to visit three-to-five different showrooms.
   b. Arrange to view no more than one or two categories of furniture at each showroom in order to stay focused on the category of furniture at hand.
2. Ask if each student can receive one or two furniture brochures to take in order to analyze the displayed products.

Project #2: Write a 3–4 paragraph essay

1. Describe how visual impressions of actual furniture items relate to written descriptions of the furniture in this textbook and the brochures received during showrooms visits.
2. Discuss similarities and differences among the same items—such as executive desks, files, and tables—from several manufacturers.

Project #3: Select three furniture items to draw

Designers often draw or sketch ideas in front of the client during meetings and presentations. It is a talent to accurately free-hand items in correct scale when making suggestions to clients.

1. Hand draft and dimension plan views of items at both $\frac{1}{8}$" and $\frac{1}{4}$" scale.
   a. Select three furniture groupings, such as
      1. Desk—chair—credenza
      2. Table—chairs
      3. Lounge chairs—coffee table
2. Practice free-hand drawing the items at each scale.
3. Free-hand-draw isometrics (axonometric) of the items to scale (Illustrated Table 4.1a, b, c and Fig. 4.5).

5

CIRCULATION AND CLEARANCES

People need clear, uninhibited floor space to walk on; to open cabinet doors and drawers; to sit in chairs at a table, desk, or work counter; to stand at copiers, scanners, and printers; and to move carts and other mobile items around. It is also nice to have some open space to provide visual relief in an office setting otherwise filled with rooms and workstations. Known as circulation, this type of space is planned adjacent to individual furniture items and equipment, within rooms, and in the overall floor plan as needed, based on intuition, industry standards, manufacturers' recommendations for servicing their equipment, and code requirements.

CODES AND CODE REQUIREMENTS

Though many codes—including fire protection, electrical, and mechanical—govern the design and construction of all buildings and interior build-outs, there are two primary code sources to be consulted during space planning: the relevant building codes and Americans with Disabilities Act (ADA) codes.

Building Codes

Building codes are used for the purpose of :

regulating and governing the conditions and maintenance of all property, buildings and structures; by providing the standards for supplied utilities and facilities and other physical things and conditions essential to ensure that structures are safe, sanitary and fit for occupation and use; and. . . providing for the issuance of permits and. . .[1]

In other words, code requirements provide for the health, safety, and welfare of the people who use and occupy buildings by providing guidelines for constructing spaces under various conditions. Building codes are not a federal mandate; "Jurisdictions *wishing* to adopt the 2015 International Building Code as an enforceable regulation governing structures and premises . . ."[1] *Wishing!* It is up to each governing body (state, county, city, or municipality) to adopt and use nationally recognized building codes; or they may elect to write their own codes that incorporate some or all of the points covered in another set of codes. Most of the points, topics, sections, and articles covered in each set of codes are the same, similar, or related to points, topics, sections, and articles covered in other sets of codes. Some very small, rural jurisdictions may not use codes at all. Each jurisdiction decides on the course of action it wishes to follow.

Although many code requirements become second nature to the designer, it is still the designer's responsibility to verify the codes in use for the location and jurisdiction of the project being space planned (Box 5.1), particularly when the project is located outside of the designer's normal location of planning, because some code requirements vary slightly. For example, most codes allow office suites to have a single means of egress when the occupied space is below a certain amount of square footage, but the square footage can vary from state to state or jurisdiction to jurisdiction. Under the IBC, an office suite that has only one exit is allowed to have a maximum of only 49 occupants and a maximum of 75 ft. of common path of egress travel distance (see Chapter 13).[2] This generally translates into a space of less than 5,000 square feet (SF) for office suites. For one project in a Midwest city that amended standard codes to meet their desired requirements, office suites needed to be less than 1,800 SF for a single exit. Upfront research can save a lot of time, hassle, plan revisions, and credibility down the road.

Americans with Disabilities Act (ADA) Codes

On January 26, 1992, the third part, Title III—*public accommodations and commercial facilities*—of the Americans with Disabilities Act (ADA) went into effect as a national code representing regulations codified by the Department of Justice.

> *This rule implements Title III of the Americans with Disabilities Act, Public Law 101–336, which prohibits discrimination on the basis of disability by private entities in places of public accommodation, requires that all new places of public accommodation and commercial facilities be designed and constructed so as to be readily accessible to and usable by persons with disabilities, and requires that examinations or courses related to licensing or certification for professional and trade purposes be accessible to persons with disabilities.*[3]

The entire Act, including Title I—*employment*, Title II—*public entities and public transportation*, Title III—*public accommodations and commercial facilities*, Title IV—*telecommunications*, and Title V—*miscellaneous provisions*, was signed into law on July 26, 1990, by President George H. W. Bush. In effect, the Act "*provides comprehensive civil rights protections to individuals with disabilities in the areas of employment, public accommodations, State and local government services, and telecommunications.*"[4]

BOX 5.1 Building Codes

Before 2000, there were four nationally recognized building code organizations. Each group wrote its own building codes, which generally included the same or similar aspects for many individual code requirements. In 1997, three of the organizations joined forces to write a single combined code called International Building Code (IBC). Through collaboration and urging from other organizations such as AIA, several other code agencies eventually joined with IBC to write a comprehensive family of approximately fifteen International codes, including some listed below. States or jurisdictions that previously used the older codes adopted either the new set of codes, kept their existing codes, or they wrote their own state or city codes.

1. **IBC   International Building Code**
   First developed and published in 2000 to replace many of the previously existing code agencies
2. **IRC   International Residential Code**
   Residential codes split off from commercial codes
3. **IEBC   International Existing Building Code**
   Addresses repair, alteration, addition, or change of occupancy in existing buildings
4. **IgCC   International Green Construction Code**
   Provides a framework for green construction and sustainability measures
5. **UBC   Uniform Building Code**
   Used primarily in western and central portions of the United States; replaced by the IBC
6. **BOCA Building Officials and Code Administrators**
   Used primarily in northeastern and central portions of the United States; replaced by the IBC
7. **SBC   Southern Building Code**
   Used primarily in the southeastern part of the United States; replaced by the IBC
8. **NBC   National Building Code of Canada**
   Used primarily in Canada

Unlike building codes, which are updated every three years, ADA codes have been updated only once since inception. On September 15, 2010:

The Department of Justice published revised regulations for Titles II and III of the Americans with Disabilities Act of 1990 "ADA"... These regulations adopted revised, enforceable accessibility standards called the 2010 ADA Standards for Accessible Design "2010 Standards" or "Standards". The 2010 Standards set minimum requirements—both scoping and technical—for newly designed and constructed or altered State and local government facilities, public accommodations, and commercial facilities to be readily accessible to and usable by individuals with disabilities.[5]

There is only one set of ADA code requirements, which apply to all governing bodies, buildings, and services. In general, the federal government has said that jurisdictions may build their buildings in any manner desired and with any building codes as desired, so long as the buildings are deemed safe. However, when it comes to using or accessing any part of the building, outside or inside, then the federal government dictates via ADA codes that all entities must meet or provide standards that allow all persons to "easily" or readily use the building or any part of that building; "State and Local government facilities *must follow* the requirements of the 2010 Standards, . . . Public accommodations and commercial facilities must follow the requirements of the 2010 Standards, . . ."[6] *Must Follow!* For example, public telephones are not required; but when they are installed, then at least one telephone must meet those ADA accessibility requirements (see ADA Standards Sections 217 and 704 Telephones).[7]

When there is a conflict between building codes and ADA codes, or any other codes used on a project, the more stringent code requirement will prevail.

TYPES OF CIRCULATION

According to the IBC definition, circulation or circulation paths are, "*An exterior or interior way of passage from one place to another for*

pedestrians."[8] Although initial interpretation of this definition may seem to refer to hallways, aisles, and corridors, when we consider a broader definition or perspective, then circulation does indeed include all open floor areas that are not specifically dedicated to a room, an object, a piece of furniture, equipment, appliance, or any other item that takes up actual floor space. After all, people need a "way of passage" to walk around within a room, walk from one piece of furniture or equipment to another piece of furniture or equipment, a way of passage to pull chairs away from a table to sit down, and a way of passage to stand at the copier.

Thus, there are two parts to circulation: main pedestrian passageways, generally part of the means of egress (see Chapter 13), and secondary passageways to facilitate the general flow of life. For the means of egress, all minimum required clearances and widths per building and/or ADA codes must be met. Most other areas of circulation are arbitrary, and while deviations can be made from recommended clearances, the designer should be practical in planning the final layout.

Assigning Circulation

Circulation is both quantitative for meeting required clearances and qualitative because many industry-accepted or recommended clearances can be adjusted up or down to meet particular planning opportunities or limitations. Typically, circulation is incorporated into the Program Report in two areas; first, as predetermined square-foot amounts added to individual items of furniture or an area (see Appendix E.11 and E.37 and Fig. 12.6, lines 18 and 19) and then as a percentage of overall square footages to account for pedestrian passageways. This last point will be further discussed in Chapter 12. During space planning, designers use these initial square footages as a starting point and then make adjustments as necessary.

Circulation space can be assigned to the following areas:

- Walking space
- Standing space
- Sitting space
- Space to open doors and drawers
- Space to move items
- Leftover or unusual space

FIGURE 5.1 Plan views

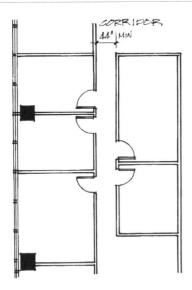

a. Corridor between offices

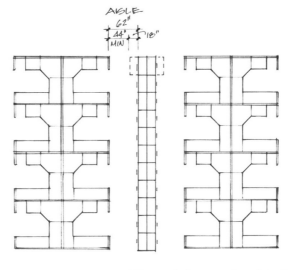

b. Aisles between banks of files and clusters of workstations

---

BOX 5.2 IBC Minimum Corridor Widths⁹

SECTION 1020 CORRIDORS
1020.2 Width and capacity. The required capacity of *corridors* shall be determined as specified in Section 1005.1 [see Box 13.4], but the minimum width shall be not less than that specified in Table 1020.2.

TABLE 1020.2 Minimum Corridor Width⁹	
OCCUPANCY	**MINIMUM WIDTH (INCHES)**
Any facilities not listed below	44
Access to and utilization of mechanical, plumbing or electrical systems or equipment	24
With an occupant load of less than 50	36
Within a *dwelling unit*	36
In Group E with a *corridor* having an occupant load of 100 or more	72
In *corridors* and areas serving stretcher traffic in ambulatory care facilities	72
Group I-2 in areas where required for bed movement	96

For SI: 1 inch = 25.4 mm.

Walking Space

In office settings, walking space is referred to as corridors and aisles rather than hallways. Corridors are defined as relatively enclosed passageways with doors that open into rooms or offices along the walls (Fig. 5.1a). Aisles tend to be more open walkways between workstations, files, shelving stacks, and so on (Fig. 5.1b). Whether the designer is planning hallways, aisles, corridors, or passageways, codes treat them as one entity with stipulated minimum widths, heights, and lengths; illumination; security access; protruding objects; floor-surface finishes; and change in elevation levels, to name a few conditions. For space planning, widths are addressed in this chapter and lengths in Chapters 13 and 14.

Building Code Minimum Corridor Widths

As a rule of thumb, in commercial office spaces, aisles and corridors need to be a minimum of 44 in. wide. They may be wider if desired, or required due to higher occupancy loads, but in all situations and plans, aisles and corridors must meet the required width of 44 in. or as stipulated for other occupancy groups (Box 5.2).

Building Code Exceptions to Minimum Corridor Width Requirements

Although corridors generally must be of a minimum width, most codes also allow for exceptions. Under the IBC, when an office space serves less than 50 business occupants (see Box 5.2, third line of the Table), or occupies less than 5,000 SF (see Table 13.1 for area allowances per occupant), corridors may be reduced to 36 in. wide and still be within code constraints.

In some situations, the code reviewer at the permit office may also allow certain aisles between workstations and shelving stacks to be reduced to 36 in. wide when that particular aisle is serving less than 50 occupants (even though the balance of the office space has more than 50 occupants). Although it is always best to plan for the stated code requirements, these exceptions can be beneficial in reducing the total square footages for small office spaces, or when the plan includes a great number of workstations or shelving stacks. However, this last exception is not a given; it is at the discretion of the plan reviewer.

Practical or Wider Corridor Widths

For each space plan, the designer must always ask, "Is the minimum corridor width desirable and practical? Or is there a better (wider) width that would be more aesthetically pleasing or functional, and still meet the client's budget and design criteria?"

In commercial office spaces, most designers plan primary corridor widths at approximately 60 in. wide. There are several reasons for increasing primary corridor widths from the minimum standard.

- Ambience: wider corridors provide a slightly more gracious *feel*.
- Practical: carts and other mobile objects can be transported more freely in wider corridors.
- Spatial: it is more comfortable for one person carrying items or two people walking abreast in wider corridors (Fig. 5.2).

By considering spatial standards for humans, we see that a corridor width of 44 in. may not be the most practical or desirable. Two people walking abreast need 54 in., or 10 in. more than the minimum width. Even one

FIGURE 5.2 Spatial standards for humans[10]

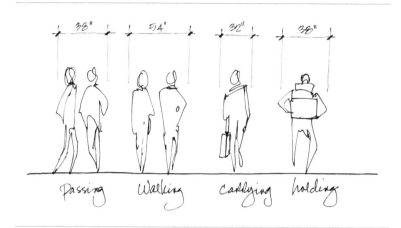

person carrying a stack of papers or other items needs 38 in., or almost the entire minimum width, which leaves no room for another person to pass by within that corridor unless both people turn sideways. Thus, a wider corridor more easily accommodates activities found or performed within it.

For highly visible, corporate executive floors, corridors are often planned at even greater widths of 7–9 ft. Wider corridors give a spacious feel of great luxury. However, on normal or average floors, overly wide corridors would be deemed impractical and a waste of space.

ADA Code Minimum Corridor Widths

While building codes look at corridor widths based on the greatest number of people to use any given corridor at any one time, ADA codes view corridor widths from the use of a single wheelchair in a corridor. With this in mind, ADA codes state that a corridor need be only 36 in. wide for a wheelchair-bound person to traverse them (Box 5.3).

Conflict of Code Requirements

Where there is a conflict between ADA and local code requirements, the more restrictive code supersedes the other code. In the case of corridors, building code minimum width requirements of 44 in. are more stringent than the ADA minimum width of 36 in. Therefore, building codes will apply, meaning that office corridors must be a minimum width of 44 in.

BOX 5.3 ADA Minimum Corridor Widths[11]

ACCESSIBLE ROUTES

403 WALKING SURFACES

403.5.1 Clear Width. Except as provided in 403.5.2 and 403.5.3, the clear width of walking surfaces shall be 36 inches (915 mm) minimum.

> **EXCEPTION:** The clear width shall be permitted to be reduced to 32 inches (815 mm) minimum for a length of 24 inches (610 mm) maximum provided that reduced width segments are separated by segments that are 48 inches (1220 mm) long minimum and 36 inches (915 mm) wide minimum.

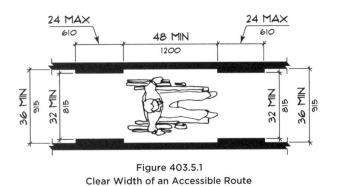

**Figure 403.5.1
Clear Width of an Accessible Route**

However, where there may be a column or other obstruction protruding into the corridor or aisle, the ADA code is more restrictive so that the designer can plan a 32-in.-wide walkway for a maximum of 24 in. long before the corridor must go back to 44 in. again (Fig. 5.3).

Standing Space

Shelving, printers, and other items, whether freestanding or sitting on a counter, require open floor space along their leading or front edge

■ **FIGURE 5.3 Plan view: Combining building code and ADA code requirements for minimum corridor widths**

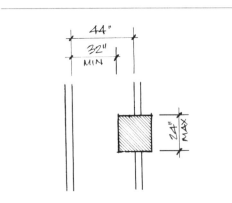

where a person can stand to access them (Illustrated Table 5.1a). Often this standing space is immediately adjacent to an aisle or corridor, but it cannot be part of the aisle or corridor (Box 5.4). Aisles shall be kept continuously clear. This means that the standing space is in addition to the required 44 in. of aisle space. Suggested clearances or overall widths for an aisle plus standing floor space are 62–80 in. (Table 5.1).

Sitting Space

Many times, users need to sit while performing tasks or operating equipment. In today's market, where most office employees have computers at their desk or workstation, this sitting space is planned and included in the layout of individual work areas (see Chapters 6 and 7).

In places where various people occasionally share pieces of equipment or counter space, such as kiosk computers for filling out applications in a permit office and surfaces for laptops in an airport, sitting space needs to be planned as an adjacent floor area. As with shelving and files, it is convenient to plan this area immediately off of or next to an aisle for direct access (Illustrated Table 5.1b). Like standing space, the sitting space must be in addition to and not part of the clear aisle width. It is important to remember that the sitting space requires the physical area for the chair as well as room to move the chair. Suggested clearances or overall widths for an aisle plus sitting floor space are 68–108 in. (Table 5.1).

Space to Open Doors and Drawers

To open doors and drawers, there must be sufficient clear floor space along the front of files, storage cabinets and lockers (Illustrated Table 5.1 c and d). Additional floor space is required as standing space for the user. This means the designer must plan "double" spaces for these areas. As with the two spaces just discussed, this space is supplemental to any required aisle widths. For files along only one side of an aisle, suggested overall widths range from 80–96 in. (Table 5.1).

Double-Loaded Aisles

When planning files along both sides of an aisle, even when using minimum widths, the overall widths can add up to 116 in. or 9'-8" between the

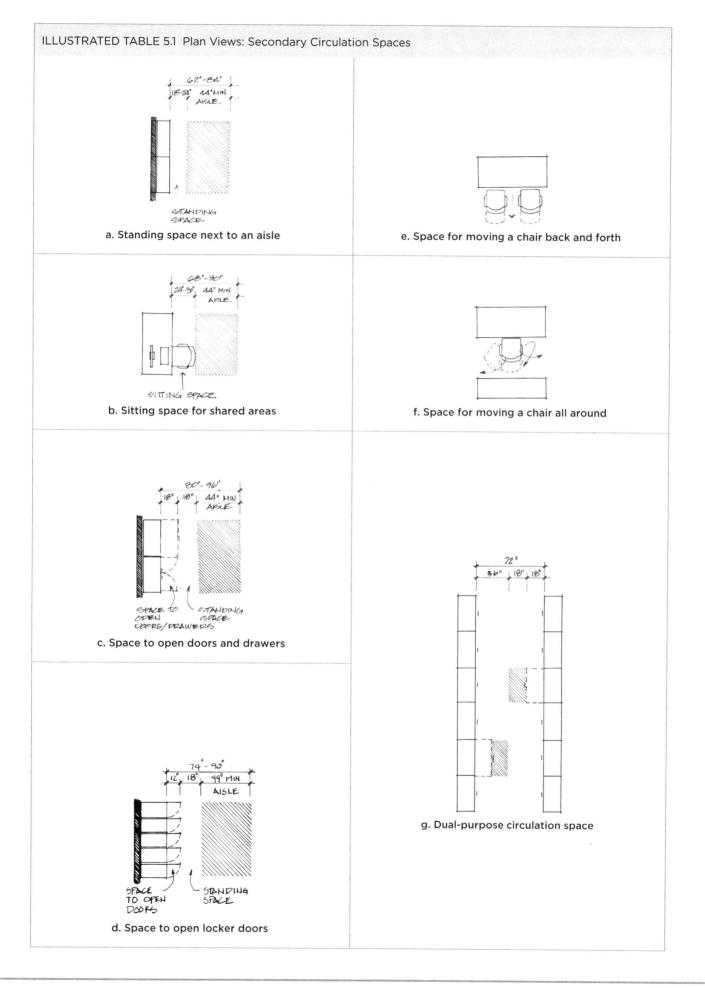

a. Standing space next to an aisle

b. Sitting space for shared areas

c. Space to open doors and drawers

d. Space to open locker doors

e. Space for moving a chair back and forth

f. Space for moving a chair all around

g. Dual-purpose circulation space

TABLE 5.1 Circulation along Aisles for Standing Space, Sitting Space, Door/Drawer Space

STANDING SPACE					
Shelving along Aisles					
	Aisle		One Side		Both Sides	Total Clearance
Minimum	44 in.	+	18 in.			=	62 in.
	44 in.	+	18 in.	+	18 in.	=	80 in.
Desirable	60 in.	+	18 in.			=	78 in.
	44 in.	+	24 in.			=	68 in.

SITTING SPACE					
Shared Worksurfaces along Aisles					
	Aisle		One Side		Both Sides	Total Clearance
Minimum	44 in.	+	24 in.			=	68 in.
	44 in.	+	24 in.	+	24 in.	=	92 in.
Desirable	60 in.	+	30 in.			=	90 in.
	60 in.	+	24 in.	+	24 in.	=	108 in.

DOOR / DRAWER SPACE					
Files and Cabinets along one side of an Aisle					
	Aisle		Open Drawer		Standing Space	Total Clearance
Minimum	44 in.	+	18 in.	+	18 in.	=	80 in.
Desirable	60 in.	+	18 in.	+	18 in.	=	96 in.

files. This is a really wide aisle. When multiple rows of files are required, most clients will not want to allocate so much floor space to aisles.

To conserve floor space along double-loaded aisles, the designer can consider several options when laying out the space. First, if these rows of files are not on a main corridor but rather located in a file room or open area where fewer than 50 persons regularly access them, it is conceivable to reduce the aisle width from 44 to 36 in. (see Box 5.2).

Second, the likelihood of consistently accessing both files directly opposite each other at the same time is small. Therefore, it is plausible for the aisle and door/drawer spaces to serve dual purposes by switching them back and forth; when one drawer is opened, there is a minimum aisle width plus both standing and open drawer floor space. This would reduce the overall clearance to a minimum of 72 in., an easier amount of space to accommodate within the plan (Illustrated Table 5.1g).

Space to Move Items Around

Circulation and floor space for chairs, video equipment carts, mobile files, easels, and so on are somewhat ambiguous. As with door and drawer space, there are two types of spaces to consider. The designer must allocate floor space to accommodate the item and then allocate a reasonable amount of space for movement or arbitrary placement of the item. But, what is a reasonable amount of space?

A "reasonable amount" depends on the intended use of an item. For instance, a chair at a table is moved mainly in and out, or back and forth (Illustrated Table 5.1e). When a chair is used at a counter, it may also go sideways or be turned around (Illustrated Table 5.1f). Answers to questions about type of use will guide the designer to provide appropriate amounts of circulation—not always the same amount, but an amount that meets the users' requirements.

Leftover, Unusual, or Angled Spaces

Buildings come in all shapes and sizes. Client requirements vary greatly. Very seldom do the client requirements fit perfectly within the building floor space. There are bound to be unusual or leftover spaces, particularly if the space plan is in an angled building or rotated within the floor plate. These areas become part of the overall circulation space, which the designer can plan or utilize in many effective ways:

- Wider aisles or corridors
- Larger rooms or offices
- Larger workstations
- Smaller, but more rooms, offices, or workstations
- The perfect spot for artwork, sculpture, or occasional chair
- Central gathering spots for employees
- Impromptu meeting areas
- General "breathing" space to provide relief from the maze of corridors and rooms

How this "extra" or "leftover" space is incorporated within the layout must meet with the client's approval, but it offers a great opportunity to test one's creative thinking, space planning, and overall design concepts.

CIRCULATION PLAN VIEWS

Circulation plan views displayed in Appendix E show recommended circulations and clearances for many of the furniture items discussed in Chapter 4. The combined square footages of the furniture or equipment items and associated circulation square footages are used when creating typical layouts (Chapters 6–11) and the Program Report (Chapter 12). Square footages and circulation are based on the floor area occupied by an item; not the height of the item. For example, when two items are the same width and depth, but different heights, such as a 36-in.-wide two-drawer file and a 36-in.-wide five-drawer file, they both require the same amount of square footage, in this case 14 SF (see Appendix E.12).

When combining several items, the designer should be able to use good judgment to calculate recommended clearances and circulations to achieve a well-defined space plan.

PROJECTS

Project #1: Site-measure and draft existing spaces to address circulation

While it is known that circulation and clearances are required in spaces, these factors are somewhat fluid; they are often "squeezed" by both designers and clients. To ensure adequate circulation in the final layouts, it is important to start with appropriate circulation patterns during space planning.

1. Select several rooms in the classroom building to analyze for circulation patterns.
   a. Rooms may include a classroom, library, lunchroom, and administrative office.
2. Measure the rooms including doors, windows, and any other architectural features.
   a. Draft the rooms to scale, either manually or electronically. Add overall dimensions, plan titles, and other sheet title information as appropriate.
3. In conjunction with measuring the rooms, inventory all existing items within the rooms. See Project #2 below.
   a. Once the rooms are drafted to scale, draft all existing furniture, equipment, appliances, and other items occupying floor space into the floor plans.
4. Draw dashed lines on the plan to show existing circulation spaces.
5. Label each space as walking, standing, sitting, or other circulation.

Project #2: Inventory existing furniture

1. As furniture, equipment, and appliances are measured for Project #1 above, the information should be recorded on an inventory form.
2. Some of this existing furniture and equipment is requested by the clients in Appendix A to be reused in their new office spaces.
3. See Appendix F for inventory forms.

Project #3: Write a 3–4 paragraph explanation

1. Analyze existing furniture and equipment conditions in the site-measured rooms.
2. Discuss the appropriateness or deficiencies of the existing circulation patterns.
3. Discuss how existing conditions could or should be changed to meet the minimum circulation and clearance requirements.

Project #4: Revise and redraw each room

1. Revise existing layouts to provide suitable amounts of circulation to improve or meet minimum circulation requirements.
2. Draw dashed lines on the plan to show newly recommended circulation spaces.

6

ROOM ENVELOPES AND TYPICAL PRIVATE OFFICE LAYOUTS

To plan or layout private offices, and rooms in general, designers must understand the *envelope* of the room (the walls, floor, and ceiling) and know what furniture will be used in it. Unlike some institutions and industries—such as schools, convention centers, and hospitals—that plan, design, and construct their buildings around program requirements that call for specific rooms and room sizes, office buildings are often built as *core and shell* buildings (unfinished on the inside) in which office spaces are planned, laid out, and in many cases, adjusted to fit within the architecture of the building. Designers need to understand how the building architecture might affect room sizes or layouts and be aware of the interior construction and detailing of wall partitions that make up the room envelope.

BUILDING ARCHITECTURE

For private offices and other rooms located on perimeter window walls, the width of the room may be determined by the building construction. Many office buildings are built using structural steel or concrete framing with *continuous*

windows. Although the windows may appear continuous from a distance, they actually consist of preassembled mullion and glazing panel units that are attached to the structural frame of the building to form a non-load-bearing exterior skin, known as a *curtain wall*.

Glazing is the most popular infill for curtain wall facades, but other materials commonly include spandrel units, metal panels, stone veneer, louvers, operable windows, and vents. These materials tend to give buildings a horizontal or vertical band effect (see Appendix B.1).

Other office buildings have a solid facade with load-bearing walls made from materials that range from 2 × 4 wood framing for light commercial construction to any type of masonry wall, such as solid brick, brick veneer, concrete, and concrete masonry units (CMU). Window and door "holes" are punched into these solid exterior walls, either at regular intervals or as needed (see Appendix B.1).

Plan views and cross-sections for curtain and solid perimeter walls vary greatly in design. When drawing typical layouts, or a building floorplate, designers should verify the type of building construction in order to draw the

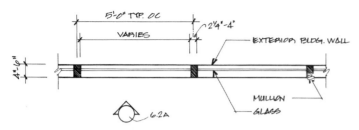

a. Curtain wall with floor-to-ceiling glazing and mullion panel units

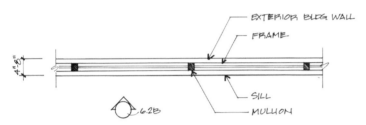

b. Curtain wall with glazing and mullion panel units above drywall skirt

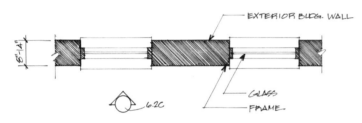

c. Solid facade, load-bearing perimeter wall with "punched" (inset) windows

correct profile (Fig. 6.1a–c). Curtain walls may be as thin as 4 inches (in.) but generally vary in depth from 6–12 in., and solid walls are typically 8–14 in. thick. Glazing may be centered or offset front-to-back within the mullions and window frames, providing a narrower or deeper windowsill.

Curtain Wall Facade

From the interior, curtain walls may provide continuous floor-to-ceiling windows (Fig. 6.2a) or may have a solid skirt approximately 24–42 in. high along the floor with continuous glazing above (Fig. 6.2b).

When the specific building and perimeter details are known, it is always best to draw layouts with the correct exterior wall dimensions.

If designers do not have building and perimeter details, they may use a generic cross-section or plan view (Fig. 6.1b). Regardless of curtain wall style, mullions are approximately 2½–4 in. wide by 4–6 in. deep. The top and bottom of the frame are the same depth as the mullion so that it aligns with the front and back mullion edges. Glass for these windows is generally double pane, roughly 1 in. thick. Eight inches serves as a good depth for a generic curtain wall.

Glazing and Mullion Window Widths

Many curtain-walled buildings use a 30 or 60 in. on center (OC) glass and mullion unit assembly, which means that the dimension from the centerline of one mullion to the centerline of the next is 5'-0". Therefore, the glass itself will be approximately 4'-8" to 4'-9½" wide between mullions, and the overall assembly unit will be approximately 5'-2½" to 5'-4" wide, depending on the specific mullion or its manufacturer. Thus, due to these variances, the dimension is measured from centerline to centerline of the mullions to achieve a consistent dimension, generally 5'-0" OC (Fig. 6.1a).

Window Width Variations

Although 5'-0" OC is the most commonly used width for window unit assemblies, it is not the only width available. Other common widths include 4'-9" OC, 4'-6" OC, and 4'-0" OC. For typical private office planning purposes, 4'-9" units can probably replace 5'-0" units with little or no difference because a room planned with two unit widths is reduced by only 6", from 10'-0" OC to 9'-6" OC. Generally, 4'-6" units can also replace 5'-0" units, creating a room width of 9'-0" OC. However, designers should double-check the intended furniture layouts within this narrower room. To maintain desired clearances, it may be necessary to either substitute a larger desk with a slightly smaller desk or provide an alternate layout.

On the other hand, using two 4'-0" OC units creates a room with a width of only 8'-0" OC. This is narrow for an office and is probably not acceptable. In this case, three mullions must be used, creating an office width of 12'-0" OC. This width does not lend itself to the more typical office layouts discussed later in this chapter.

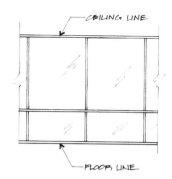

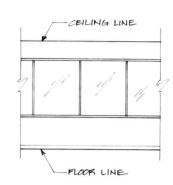

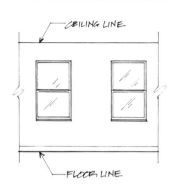

a. Curtain wall with floor-to-ceiling glazing

b. Curtain wall with solid drywall skirt at the floor line with continuous glazing above

c. Solid facade wall with punched (inset) windows

When this situation arises, designers should discuss with their clients whether a different layout may be required.

Drafting Curtain Wall Perimeters

To facilitate drafting accurate window dimensions and plans, here is a basic guideline. Window units should be drafted in 5'-0" widths or the stated on center width rather than with measurements of individual parts: mullion, glass inset, mullion, glass inset, and so on. Consider drawing a partial curtain wall of five mullions with glass insets. Using a 5'-0" window with a 2½" mullion, the overall dimension will be 20'-2½". Using either hand drafting or CAD, if the designer first draws a 2½" mullion, moves the scale or cursor to draw a 4'-9½" glass, then a 2½" mullion, a 4'-9½" glass, a 2½" mullion, etc., it is very easy for the individual measurements to "creep," thus creating an overall dimension greater or smaller than it should be (Fig. 6.3a). Soon, an overall measurement of 20'-2½" may become 20'-4½" or greater or smaller.

When drafted as an overall unit instead of individual parts, the drawing will be accurate even if some of the parts are slightly smaller or larger than they should be. For hand drafting without moving the scale, designers should mark off tick marks every 5'-0" for the total number of mullions and then draw the mullions off these pre-marked ticks. Even if the mullions are drawn slightly off the tick marks and are larger or smaller than 2½" or the actual mullion width,

the overall dimension will not be affected; it will be 20'-2½" (Fig. 6.3b). For CAD drafting, designers should draw one mullion and then use the copy Array command with a specific typed-in dimension to achieve an overall accurate dimension.

Perimeter and Interior Columns

Curtain wall buildings use strategically placed columns, both along the perimeter and within the interior of the building, for vertical support.

■ **FIGURE 6.3 Plan views**

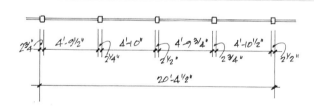

a. Drafting individual items causes "creeping" dimensions

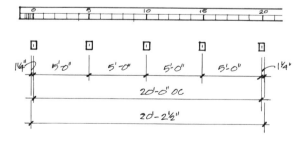

b. Drafting items as overall units provides precise dimensions

Columns may be square and as small as 12" × 12"; they may be rectangular or custom shaped and as large as 30" × 36" or more. Designers have no say over the location, number, or size of columns (although many a designer has jokingly or negligently eliminated or moved many of those columns on paper, but to no avail!). Columns are there to stay. Designers are responsible for including all columns and, further, incorporating those columns in their plans to the best advantage possible.

Depending on the structural design of the column grid as determined by the building architect, the width of windows next to a column may be reduced compared to the width of other windows when a consistent module is used across the building (Fig. 6.4a). When the architect deems it desirable to keep all windows the same width, then the column placement creates a non-continuous module across the building (Fig. 6.4b). In this building design, typical rooms incorporating perimeter columns may be slightly larger or smaller than other similar typical rooms. Many design firms use the building module congruently throughout their space plans. Other firms may use the module when convenient, but may also deviate from it when the module and program requirements do not meld well.

Solid Wall Facade

In a solid-facade building, windows may be of any size and quantity as determined by the building architect (Fig. 6.2c). Although the size of windows is generally consistent on any given floor, their widths, heights, and quantities may vary from one floor to another. Floor-to-ceiling windows may also be used in solid-facade buildings, but they are more commonly used in curtain wall buildings.

■ **FIGURE 6.4 Plan view**

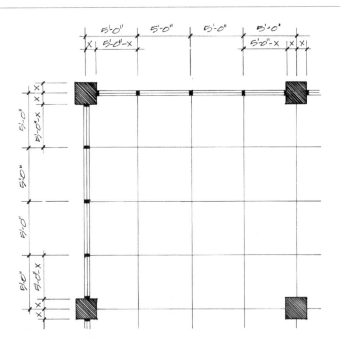

a. Columns on a consistent building module

ROOM AND OFFICE ENVELOPES

Although the actual room or office envelope consists of six planes—two side walls, a front and back wall, and the floor and ceiling—a typical layout normally includes only the four walls (Fig. 6.5). Occasionally, a floor covering or ceiling soffit is suggested on a presentation plan (see Chapter 15), but for initial layouts the focus is on room size, function, and furniture layouts. Ceiling and floor patterns are not shown on these plans.

Back Wall

When rooms or private offices are planned along the window or perimeter wall, this wall is considered to be the back wall of the office. The width of this wall, determined by the side walls, depends on the mullion spacing in curtain wall buildings or at the designer's discretion on solid-facade buildings.

For offices placed in interior locations, the back wall is likely constructed of standard drywall. Technically, interior offices, like perimeter offices in solid-facade buildings, can be any width desired because there are no mullions to determine the width. However, because many office buildings are curtain wall buildings, interior office widths tend to be standardized, based on typical mullion spacings.

Side Walls

With rare exceptions, interior walls, known as partitions, are not built up to the glazing. Partitions must attach to another partition, a solid part of the exterior wall, or a window mullion, but not to the glass itself.

Partitions off Window Mullions

Once the curtain wall and mullions are drawn, designers may extend partitions off the mullions to create rooms. After the first partition is

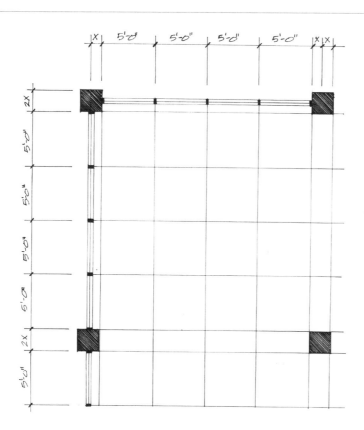

b. Columns on an alternately spaced building module

ML DESIGN

Client Name

- (1) 36 × 72 desk
- (1) 24 × 72 credenza
- (2) 36-wide low bookcases
- (1) desk chair
- (2) guest chairs
- (1) plant

PO-2   DEPARTMENT HEAD
OPTION B   225 SF

SCALE: ¼″ = 1′-0′
DATE:

BOX 6.1 IBC Minimum Room Widths[1]

SECTION 1208

INTERIOR SPACE DIMENSIONS

12.01 Minimum room widths. *Habitable spaces*, other than a kitchen, shall be not less than 7 feet (2134 mm) in any plan dimension. Kitchens shall have a clear passageway of not less than 3 feet (914 mm) between counter fronts and appliances or counter fronts and walls.

located on the first mullion, the second partition can be placed on the next mullion, the third mullion, or even the tenth mullion. Partition locations are based on the desired width of the room being created. Very rarely is a 5-ft-wide room acceptable or practical. In fact, under the latest IBC code, 5 ft is no longer acceptable (Box 6.1); rooms must now be at least 7 ft wide. Therefore, the next partition must be at least two mullions away, creating a minimum room width of 10 ft OC, or two window unit widths, depending on the window unit dimension (Fig. 6.6a). With 5 ft OC window units, room widths will be in multiples of 5 ft to create room widths of 10 ft, 15 ft, 20 ft OC, etc.

Partitions off Perimeter Columns

Partitions may be attached at any point along the column face or mullion on either side of the column (Fig. 6.6b). The exact partition location affects room widths on either side, which can be advantageous when a slightly larger room or office is required in the layout.

Partitions off Solid-Facade Buildings

In solid-facade buildings, partitions may attach anywhere along the perimeter wall (Fig. 6.6c). Every office could be a different size and width; however, due to corporate staff structures and any office politics that may result, it is best to standardize several office sizes and then plan a layout using those sizes as much as possible.

Perpendicular Partition Attachments

With a solid-facade building, the sidewall partitions abut the back perimeter wall and are finished using drywall construction much like any perpendicular partition. In curtain wall construction, a unique detail evolves regarding partitions that abut mullions. First, the partition may be thicker than the mullion width (Fig. 6.7). Second, as an integral part of the building envelope, mullions must not be compromised by attaching screws or nails. Instead, studs are secured to the

FIGURE 6.6 Plan views

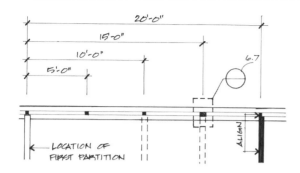

a. Partitions off window mullions

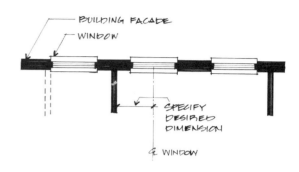

c. Partitions at solid facades

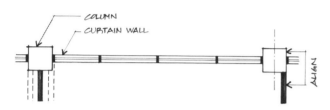

b. Partitions at columns

floor and deck above, and sealant fills any air gaps between the studs and mullions. Finally, when there is a drywall skirt below the window and mullion units, the partition will need to jog slightly over the lower skirt to fit as tightly as possible to both the lower and upper parts of the curtain wall.

Front Wall

For offices along perimeter walls, the front wall is ordinarily the wall opposite the windows. For interior offices, the front wall is generally the partition along an interior corridor. In most offices, the room door is usually located in the front wall. The position of this wall or the depth of the room may depend on various factors, some of which designers can control during space planning and some of which are predetermined by the building architecture. These factors include the following:

- Furniture layout
- Amount of furniture
- Client standards
- Building module (column placements)
- Overall floor plan

FIGURE 6.7 Enlarged detail: Partition at mullion

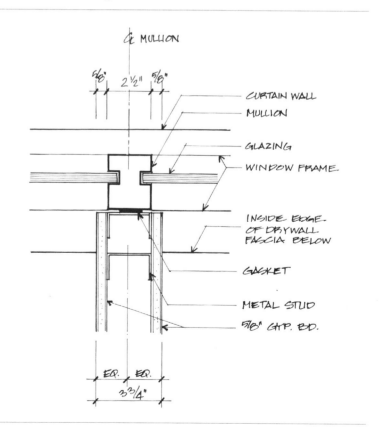

- Door placement
- Perimeter wall to core distance

Of the four envelope walls for any room, the front partition can best provide designers with an opportunity to create unique design statements. The front partition, like sidewalls, can be built as standard drywall; however, for both perimeter and interior offices, the front wall is often a full or partial glass partition. The glazing can be either framed or frameless, or sidelights can be installed adjacent to doors. Sometimes the front wall is canted, angled, or even stopped short of the ceiling as a partial-height wall. Many systems furniture manufacturers provide full-height panels that appear to be part of the construction rather than furniture (see Figure 7.7b). Other materials that can be used for front partition walls include metal, acrylic, and even fabrics or rice papers.

Doors

Doors complete the office envelope by providing access into the interior space. Except for exterior or exit doors that must open out in the direction of travel to comply with egress codes (see Box 13.10), the majority of hinged doors open into the room for which the door is intended. All door openings are required to have a minimum clearance of 32 inches (Box 6.2), which dictates an actual minimum door width of 33–34 in. so that the door extends about ½ in. on either side of the doorstops (Fig. 6.8a).

In older buildings and building interiors constructed before the Americans with Disabilities Act (ADA) was in effect, designers often find doors of varying widths. With the passage of the ADA, commercial doors were regulated to a standard 36-in. width; however, in tight situations the door width may be

FIGURE 6.8 Enlarged plans

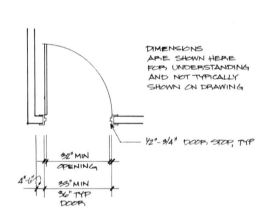

a. Typical commercial door opening at 90 degrees

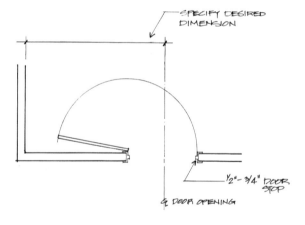

b. Door fully opened at 165 degrees

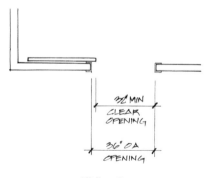

c. Sliding Door

BOX 6.2 ADA Code Door Clearances[2]

ACCESSIBLE ROUTES

404 DOORS, DOORWAYS, AND GATES

404.2.3 Clear Width. Door openings shall provide a clear width of 32 inches (815 mm) minimum. Clear openings of doorways with swinging doors shall be measured between the face of the door and the stop, with the door open 90 degrees. . . .

404.2.4 Maneuvering Clearances. Minimum maneuvering clearances at doors and gates shall comply with 404.2.4.

404.2.4.1 Swinging Doors and Gates. Swinging doors and gates shall have Maneuvering clearance complying with [Figure] 404.2.4.1.

404.2.4.2 Doorways without Doors or Gates, Sliding Doors, and Folding Doors. Doorways less than 36 inches (915 mm) wide without doors or gates, sliding doors, or folding doors shall have Maneuvering clearances complying with [Figure] 404.2.4.2.

Figure 404.2.4.1
Maneuvering clearances at manual swinging doors and gates

Front Approach — Swinging Doors

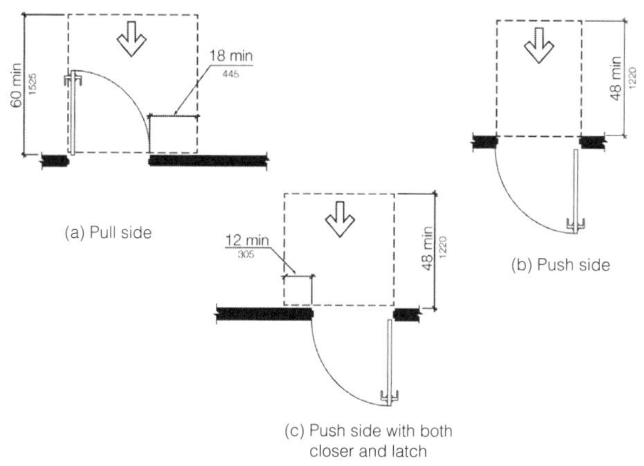

Figure 404.2.4.2
Maneuvering clearances at doorways without doors, sliding doors, gates, and folding doors

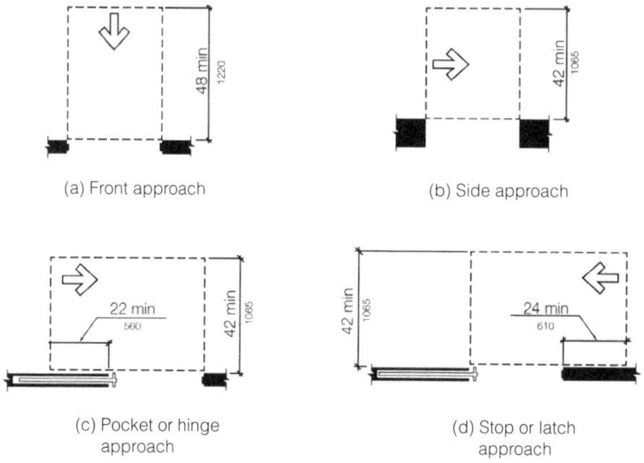

Hinge Side Approach — Swinging Doors

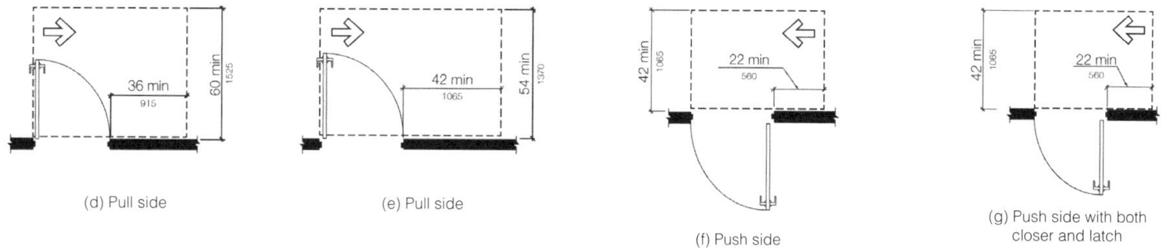

Latch Side Approach — Swinging Doors

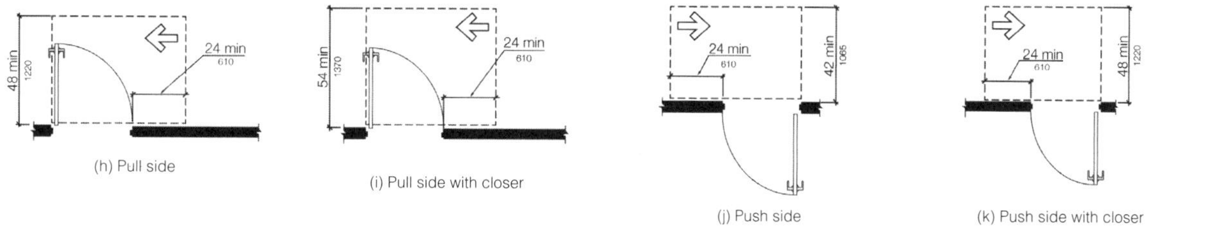

reduced slightly to 34 in. and still meet the 32 in. clearance.

Although most furniture dimensions are stated in inches, most architectural elements are stated in feet and inches. The correct terminology for this door is 3'-0", often pronounced as *three-O*. When a 30-in.-wide door (2'-6") is used for a coat closet, it is called a *two-six door*.

Door Location

Doors are drawn on floor plans and installed on-site about 4–6 in. from the corner of the nearest perpendicular partition. This is an approximate dimension for both designers and contractors because it is rarely scaled on plans or measured on the job site. Typically, it is not necessary to use the exact door dimension on plans unless there is a specific reason, such as an extra wide (perhaps 6 in.) traditional door casing that will require 8–10 in. or a door is located somewhere other than the corner of the room. In cases such as these, it is wise to dimension from the middle of the door opening rather than from either side, thus alleviating any confusion as to whether the measurement is to the casing, door frame, doorstop, door edge, etc. (Fig. 6.8b).

Maneuvering Clearances at Doors

To facilitate the opening of doors for everyone, people need clear floor space in which to maneuver when pulling or pushing a door open. According to ADA code requirements, the amount of maneuvering space depends on whether the door is being pulled or pushed open as well as on the direction of approach to the door (Box 6.2).

In general, designers should provide a 60-in. square area of clear floor space around each door. This includes 24 in. of clear floor space at the end of the door in an open position, 18 in. of clear space adjacent to the strike side of the door on the pull side, and 12 in. of clear space on the push side. When it is not possible to provide 24 in. of space at the end of the open door, the clear space along the strike side must be increased from 18 to 24 in. All doors must meet these maneuvering clearance requirements.

Sliding Doors

To conserve floor space, designers may recommend that clients consider using sliding doors in place of hinged doors, especially when the front walls of the offices are built using furniture panels. Most manufacturers that offer this type of wall also offer sliding doors that have been engineered to hang from the panel walls. Sliding doors reduce the required floor space inside the room from a 60 in. clearance to a 42 in. clearance (Box 6.2a and f), resulting in a floor area savings of 7.5 SF per door, down from 25 SF per door to 17.5 SF per door.

These doors must also provide a 32-in. clear opening according to the code (Fig. 6.8c). Because the door must overlap the opening about 3–4 in. to accommodate the inside handle, the door itself is roughly 37–38 in. wide.

Drafting Doors

Hinged doors leading into a room are regularly drawn in an open position at 90 degrees to the partition, even though most doors actually open to about 105 degrees. When a door is not installed at the corner of a room and the intention is for the door to fully open back against the wall, the door should be drawn at 165 degrees from the hinge side of the door (Fig. 6.8b). In this case, the door location must be dimensioned. For closet doors and other doors that are normally kept in a closed position, these doors should be drawn at 25 or 30 degrees open (see Figure 9.6a).

In manual drafting, doors have tended to be drawn as heavy single lines at 1/8-in. scale, and double lines capped at each end at 1/4-in. scale. Since most drawings are now produced on the computer, the door typically is a standard double-line door symbol that is discernible at larger scales and compacted at smaller scales. It is customary to include an imaginary door swing line on all doors. This line should be one of the lightest weight lines on the drawing. It can extend beyond the end of the door; however, the door should never extend beyond the swing line.

PARTITION CONSTRUCTION

For the majority of floor plans, especially in a set of construction drawings, partitions are drawn as two parallel lines (see Fig. 3.1). However, for typical layouts and presentation plans, it is customary to poché (to fill in, often by cross-hatching or using solid black) the walls for added punch on these drawings (Fig. 6.5). In either situation, walls should be drawn at their appropriate thickness based on the material sizes that make up their cross-sections.

Partition Cross-Sections

Interior office walls or partitions are normally made up of two products, studs and gypsum board. Studs for erecting walls and partitions can either be wood or metal. Generally speaking, wood studs are used in residential construction and metal studs are used in commercial construction. A cross-section for both a wood stud wall and metal stud partition shows the similarity between the two systems, with the primary difference being the overall thickness of the finished walls (see Appendix D). Wood stud walls are typically $4\frac{1}{2}$ in. thick, and metal stud partitions vary in thicknesses, but are usually $3\frac{3}{4}$ or $4\frac{7}{8}$ in.

Wood Studs

Wood studs and other lumber are listed in nominal sizes, such as a 2 × 4 stud or a 1 × 6 board. Nominal size refers to the rough dimension of lumber when it is sawn from a log. Rough-cut lumber is then sent through a planer for a finished size, thus having an actual size that is smaller than the listed size. Lumber is sold in standard lengths of 8, 10, 14 and 16 feet (ft). There are many sizes of boards and lumber, but 2 × 4s are the most commonly used size for wall studs (Table 6.1).

Metal Studs

Metal studs, also sold in lengths of 8, 10, 14 and 16 ft, are pre-machined with cutouts near the tops and bottoms to allow wires, pipes, and other construction items to pass easily through the studs and interior wall cavity (see Appendix D). As with wood studs, there are several sizes. However, with metal studs, the sizes listed are actual sizes (Table 6.1).

Depending on the area of the country, ceiling heights, the type of building, and the preference of the architect or building owner, both the stud size and drywall thickness can vary. For ceiling heights up to 9 ft, it is sufficient to use $2\frac{1}{2}$-in. studs, which is the size used throughout this book unless otherwise noted (UON). When ceiling heights are greater than 9 or 10 ft, heavier gauge or wider metal studs are required to negate vertical deflection. Larger studs are also used for plumbing walls and as sturdier bracing when many items, shelving, or workstation

TABLE 6.1 Wood and metal studs	
WOOD STUDS	
NOMINAL SIZE	**ACTUAL SIZE**
2 × 4 (51 × 102 mm)	$1\frac{1}{2} \times 3\frac{1}{2}$ (38 × 89 mm)
2 × 6 (51 × 152 mm)	$1\frac{1}{2} \times 6\frac{1}{2}$ (38 × 140 mm)
4 × 4 (102 × 102 mm)	$3\frac{1}{2} \times 3\frac{1}{2}$ (89 × 89 mm)
METAL STUDS (ACTUAL SIZE)	
$1\frac{1}{2} \times 2\frac{1}{2}$	
$1\frac{1}{2} \times 3\frac{1}{2}$	
$1\frac{5}{8} \times 3\frac{5}{8}$	
$1\frac{5}{8} \times 6$	

brackets will be mounted on walls. Obviously, larger studs generate thicker walls.

Drywall, Gypsum Board, and Sheetrock

Although the terms *drywall*, *gypsum board (GYP BD)*, and *Sheetrock* have slightly different meanings, these terms are used interchangeably by both the design industry and much of the general public. Drywall is technically the finished wall, whereas GYP BD and Sheetrock are the products used to construct the wall.

There are several types of gyp board or Sheetrock, which are selected and specified based on their intended usage and location (Box 6.3). After gyp boards are installed, drywall tape or mesh is adhered over each joint. Then two or three layers of compound are applied over the tape, allowed to dry, and sanded between each coat to achieve a smooth, finished appearance that is ready to receive paint.

Drafting Partitions

For each project, it is important to carefully consider the end use of the wall system and then to specify the appropriate stud type and size and gyp board type. Commercial wall systems typically use $2\frac{1}{2}$ or $3\frac{5}{8}$ in. metal studs with $\frac{5}{8}$ in.

1. Standard gypsum board
    - Available in $1/4''$–$5/8''$
    - Most common are $3/8''$ and $1/2''$
    - Used for residential building
    - Used for commercial ceilings
2. Type X or fire-rated (FR) gypsum board
    - Fire-rated for 1 hour
    - Available in $5/8''$
    - Used in commercial building
    - Used to separate units in residential buildings
3. Type C core gypsum board
    - Exceeds type X for fire ratings
    - Available in $1/2''$ and $5/8''$
    - Most common is $1/2''$
    - Used in commercial building
4. Green board or WR gypsum board
    - Waterproof
    - Paper surface tinted green
    - Available in $1/2''$ and $5/8''$
    - Most common is $1/2''$
    - Used in bathrooms, kitchens, and other moist areas
5. Blue board gypsum board
    - Paper surface tinted blue
    - Available in $1/2''$ and $5/8''$
    - New construction uses $1/2''$
    - Used under applied veneer finishes such as plaster finishes
6. Foil-backed gypsum board
    - Acts as vapor barrier
    - Aluminum foil replaces paper
    - Provides thermal insulation with proper installation
7. Decorative gypsum board
    - Used with prefinished vinyl siding
    - Used as a finished wall
8. Mold-resistant gypsum board
    - Has a textured surface
    - Available in $1/2''$ and $5/8''$
    - Some are also fire resistant
    - Used in basements and other high-moisture areas

the project being worked on, particularly when the project is located in a locale other than the designer's normal area of practice or the client's preferences.

When plans are hand-drawn at $1/4$ or $1/8$ in. scale, it is often hard to precisely indicate fractions. However, designers should always strive for accuracy; to the trained eye of a design professional, even slight variances jump out as glaring mistakes. For large-scale drawings, section details, and computer-generated drawings, all items should be drawn accurately to size. Walls may be two lines or a solid poched line, depending on the drawing application.

ROOM DIMENSIONS

When space planning, drafting construction drawings, and for on-site construction, all rooms need to be dimensioned. Depending on the desired outcome, building conditions, or code requirements, there are several methods for dimensioning rooms, areas, and partitions on a plan.

- Centerline (℄)
- On center (OC)
- Clear dimension (CLEAR)
- Outside or overall dimension (OA)
- Minimum dimension (MIN)
- Verify in field (VIF)
- Hold dimension (HOLD)

Centerline

Centerline dimensions are used when indicating placement of items such as partitions in new construction; when positioning items in relation to existing construction, such as mullions or columns; when exact dimensions of items are not known; or when dimensions involve fractions or other complicated figures. In these situations, it is easier to tell the contractor to center one item on another item rather than *guess* the dimensions and be wrong.

When partitions are constructed off mullions, it is ordinarily assumed that the middle or centerline of the partitions will align with the centerline of the mullions. Even so, on construction plans it is customary to label partition and mullion conditions as CL mullion (Fig. 6.7).

type-X, fire-rated gyp board in many regions of the country, resulting in $3\frac{3}{4}$ or $4\frac{7}{8}$ in. thick walls. Along the East Coast, it is more common to use $1/2$ in. type-C, fire-rated gyp board, thus reducing the wall thickness to $3\frac{1}{2}$ in. when using a $2\frac{1}{2}$-in. metal stud. Commercial plumbing walls, which customarily use 6 in. studs to accommodate 3- or 4 in. pipes, then result in $7\frac{1}{4}$ in. or 7 in. thick walls, depending on the gyp board used on the project. As with code requirements and other aspects of the project, designers need to verify the general practices in use for the area of

FIGURE 6.9 Plan views

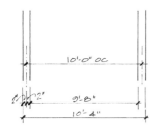

a. On center partition dimension*

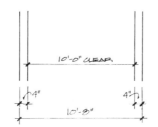

b. CLEAR partition dimensions*

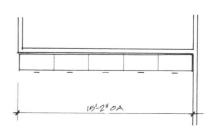

c. Outside or overall dimensions

*Dimensions across the bottom of the drawings in Figs. 6.9a and 6.9b are shown for information only. Actual drawings for construction will show only the 10'-0" OC or CLEAR dimension.

All conditions and locations are labeled, or the word *typical* (TYP) can be used (e.g., write CL mullion—TYP at a few locations when there are many partitions and rooms along the curtain wall).

Occasionally, a partition will be offset by aligning one side of the partition with one side of the mullion to create a slightly larger room. When an offset is desired, it should be clearly stated using both the alignment symbol and a note (Fig 6.6a).

On Center

Whereas the use of the symbol ℄ usually denotes the position of a single item, *on center* means that the room, partitions, mullions, etc., are measured from the middle or centerline of one partition or object to the middle or center-line of the next partition or object (Fig. 6.9a). Items should be dimensioned only once, using the most appropriate method. For instance, when partitions off mullions are dimensioned using the CL method, it would be redundant to use OC dimensions. OC dimensions are often used for placing or locating a series of interior rooms and partitions (see Fig. 14.3a).

When using OC dimensions, actual inside room widths are reduced by the amount of one-half the wall thickness on each side of the room for a total of one wall thickness. Normally, the loss of one wall thickness, approximately 4", will not make a big difference in an office or room layout, and thus nominal dimensions are used. Offices are simply listed as 10'-0", 15'-0", etc., rather than 9'-8¼" or 14'-8¼" (Table 6.2).

Clear Dimensions

Clear dimensions are measured from the inside or face of a wall to the inside or face of the next wall (Fig. 6.9b). Clear dimensions are true; thus the stated dimension is the actual dimension. Clear dimensions are used when the finished space must be large enough to accept a piece of furniture or equipment (see Figure 11.9d) or for partitions off existing building elements, such as a front office wall off a perimeter wall. Gener-ally, if the space plan and the on-site conditions allow, the constructed dimension may be slightly greater (by ¼–1 in.) than the stated clear dimen-sion. However, the final dimension cannot be less than the requested clear dimension.

It is acceptable to use either OC or clear dimensions for partitions; however, it is best to use only one method in a set of drawings. Designers should clearly state the method used

TABLE 6.2 Typical office widths using on center dimensions

ON CENTER WIDTH	INSIDE NOMINAL	INSIDE ACTUAL*
10'-0"	9'-8"	9'-8¼"
15'-0"	14'-8"	14'-8¼"
20'-0"	19'-8"	19'-8¼"

*Because the partition is actually 3¾" rather than 4", the actual clear inside dimension size is ¼" larger than the nominal size. However, in most cases the nominal size is acceptable. Adjust the size when using a 3⅝" stud.

in the general notes section of their drawings and indicate exceptions only where applicable.

For example, when the clear dimensions method has been noted as that used to dimension rooms for a plan, all dimensions will simply state 9'-0", 11'-6", etc., without writing CLEAR after each dimension. If, for some reason, it is necessary to dimension a particular room using OC, then OC will be written after that dimension (e.g., 12'-3" OC). The reverse is true when OC is the selected method. All dimensions will be written as 5'-9", 15'-0", etc., and only those that are clear dimensions will have the word CLEAR written after them (e.g., 13'-6" CLEAR).

Although there are no hard rules, interior design firms generally tend to use the clear method for dimensioning plans whereas architectural firms tend to use the OC method.

Outside or Overall Dimensions

Occasionally, an outside wall dimension is more important than the interior room dimension, such as when a row of workstations or bank of files is planned along the outside wall of a room. It would be unsightly for these items to stick out beyond the end of the wall. In this situation, the outside or overall (OA) dimension is an important factor and takes precedence over the interior dimension. The word OVERALL or *OA* should be written after the dimension (e.g., 15'-2" OA; Fig. 6.9c).

Minimum Dimensions

There may be times when a slightly larger dimension is desirable or acceptable, but at the very least, an absolute minimum dimension is required. Because designers do not know the actual site measurements when drawing the plans, designers communicate these tolerances to contractors by writing *minimum* after the dimension (e.g., 12'-1" MIN; see Figure 11.9c).

Verify in Field

Space plans are created on a base building drawing or file, normally provided by the building architect. In a perfect world, a hard copy of the floor plan, a computer drawing, and the actual space will all have the same dimensions, whether for new construction to be built or the existing space to be remodeled. In the real world,

this is often not the case. When feasible, it is a good idea for designers to go to each project site before starting a space plan to verify that all applicable dimensions on the base building drawing are accurate (see Appendix D). When this is not feasible, it may be desirable to have certain dimensions verified in the field by the contractor prior to installing planned items. Discrepancies between the drawing and actual site dimensions can be discussed and resolved between contractors and designers so that construction can proceed. Such requests are designated by adding *verify in field* (VIF) after the dimension on the floor plan (e.g., 30'-0" VIF; see Figure 11.6).

Hold Dimensions

Under certain circumstances, an exact finished dimension, such as the amount of space needed to install a set of double doors, is critical. Designers should note this on the construction documents by adding the word HOLD after the dimension (e.g., 8'-0" HOLD; see Figure 11.6).

TYPICAL PRIVATE OFFICE LAYOUTS

Once designers have laid out the private office envelope, they can plan the furniture based on function, ambience, according to their clients' standards, or as desired.

Keep in mind that there are no absolutes, no definite rights and wrongs. Furniture layouts should be pleasing and acceptable for each individual occupant. Options for office layouts include the position of the desk, such as the front up against a wall, facing toward the door, facing toward the windows or on an angle; using systems furniture instead of a desk and credenza; or using no desk at all. Many firms select one of these options to standardize private office layouts and then allow the other variations as specific requests made by an individual occupant.

Office Sizes

Although specific furniture layouts and office sizes depend on various factors, because of the mullion spacings, office sizes and layouts have gravitated toward three basic sizes, which have become industry standards.

1. Small: 10 × 15 or 10 × 12

   More people, staff, supervisors, managers, and special personnel sit in this small-size office than any other office size.

2. Medium: 15 × 15

   Generally, there are fewer medium-size offices than small offices except in law firms, accounting firms, and other businesses with partners who share an equal ownership in the firm. This medium-size office typically houses middle to upper management and partners.

3. Large: 15 × 20

   Large-size offices, occupied by the president, owner, or other senior management staff, are few in number. They are often positioned at the outside corners of the floor plate with two window walls.

Typical Office Layouts

Obviously, the size of an office will determine the amount of furniture that can be used. Conversely, the amount of furniture required will determine the size of office needed. For traditional layouts, offices start with four primary pieces of furniture. Optional furniture is added when required for functional reasons, when status plays a role, or as the office size allows (Box 6.4).

BOX 6.4 Private Office Furniture

Primary Furniture in a Private Office
- Desk
- Credenza
- Desk chair
- Guest chair(s)

Optional Furniture in a Private Office
- Bridge or return
- File cabinet(s)
- Bookcase(s)
- Storage cabinet(s)
- Round table with chairs
- Sofa
- Lounge chair(s)
- Occasional table(s)
- Marker board
- Plant(s)

FIGURE 6.10 Enlarged plan: Typical office furniture layout

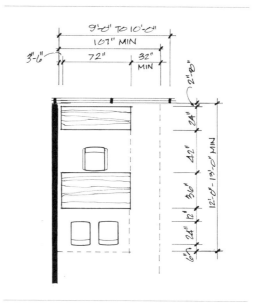

Designers should start a basic layout in any size office by placing the credenza in front of and parallel to the back wall, probably the most common layout. Leave a few inches between the credenza and the side and back walls. Not only is it visually pleasing to see a little white space between furniture and the walls on a plan view, in actuality, furniture is not jammed against the wall anyway. Rather it is offset from the wall to allow for cords dropping over the sides (Fig. 6.10). When the back wall has windows, allow about 8 in. of space for draperies or blinds that might go to the floor. Next, leave 42–48 in. of circulation in front of the credenza for the desk chair, and then place the desk directly in front of the credenza, also parallel with the back wall and offset from the sidewall. Guest chairs are placed in front of the desk, facing the windows or back wall. These chairs need some circulation space both in front and in back. This completes the basic front-to-back layout for a majority of private offices. When offices are 15 ft or wider, the desk and credenza layout may be rotated 90 degrees so they are perpendicular to the windows (Fig. 6.11d and e).

At the other end of the desk, a minimum of 32 in. is required for passageway between the desk and wall to the desk chair. Depending on

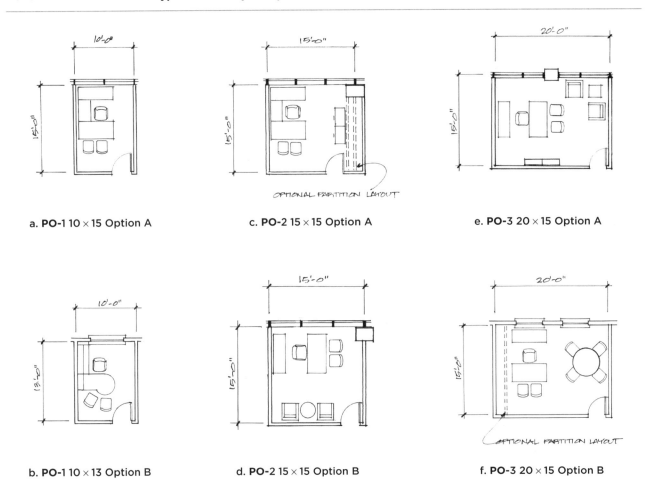

a. **PO-1** 10 × 15 Option A   c. **PO-2** 15 × 15 Option A   e. **PO-3** 20 × 15 Option A

b. **PO-1** 10 × 13 Option B   d. **PO-2** 15 × 15 Option B   f. **PO-3** 20 × 15 Option B

the office width, there may or may not be extra space in addition to the required 32 in. When additional space exists, it can be combined with the passageway for greater clearance; used to lay out optional furniture items, such as a 12 in. deep bookcase; or be taken up by a wider desk.

Office Depth

If no other furniture is required beyond the primary furniture, the front wall can be placed immediately behind the guest chairs for an inside office depth of 12'-2" to 12'-10", adjusted to 12'-0" or 13'-0". At 120 SF to 130 SF, these are generally the smallest size private offices requested by firms.

Because many people require some amount of storage by way of shelving, bookcases, or files,

office depths are frequently increased by 2–3 ft beyond the minimum depth, which allows some items to be placed behind the guest chairs. The specific depth may depend on preexisting client standards, the building module, or the overall building interior dimensions, with 15 ft generally being the maximum depth for most offices. Greater depths simply add more circulation space around the desk or chairs, which is unnecessary.

In the past, 10 × 15 was considered the normal office size. With high real estate costs and corporate downsizing, in today's market a 10 × 12 office is becoming the norm. With this smaller-size office, many firms are also requesting alternate layouts using systems furniture that can provide upper storage in place of files on the floor (Fig. 6.11b).

Optional Furniture and Layouts

Once office sizes have been determined for a given client and the primary furniture has been planned within the room, optional furniture items can be included in the layouts as required. Furniture should be drawn at industry-accepted standard sizes (see Chapter 4), unless the specific furniture has already been selected or the client is reusing existing furniture that varies from industry-standard sizes. If so, then furniture should be drawn at its actual size.

Several options should be drawn for each office size (Fig. 6.11). Options provide choices and points of discussion for clients. Some options may vary only slightly, such as adding a bridge between the desk and credenza or substituting a bookcase for a file. Other options may be completely different, such as reorienting the desk and credenza or substituting a table and chairs in place of a sofa and occasional table.

All layout options are agreed upon and approved by clients prior to the programming phase or space planning.

Door Position

Primary furniture is generally positioned off the sidewall opposite the door opening and not directly in front of the door. This position provides clearance for the door to swing open. Also, when furniture is placed in this location, there are no obstacles between the door and the guest chairs or path of travel.

When designers provide optional furniture layouts for typical offices, the door should be in the same location for all drawings. The door serves as a point of reference. As clients review the options, they can focus on the different furniture layouts without having to first consider the room layouts (see Fig. 14.1). For the actual floor plan, furniture layouts are normally mirrored when an office door is on the opposite side of the room.

DRAFTING TYPICAL PRIVATE OFFICE LAYOUTS

There is no industry standard format for a typical work area page layout. Layouts will vary from designer to designer and the layouts may vary from project to project, but the information included on the page layout is generally the same.

1. Typical layouts are usually presented on 8½ × 11 bond paper.
    a. Page layouts may be portrait or landscape.
        i. It is a good idea to pre-plan the questionnaire, layouts, and final report (see Chapter 12) to coordinate items together as one package.
    b. Typical layouts are normally attached to the program questionnaire.
2. Work area footprints should be drawn at ¼-in. scale.
3. Typical work areas often display a bit of pizzazz.
    a. Walls may be pochéd.
    b. Wood graining can be added to desks and credenzas.
    c. Line weights vary in thickness based on item importance.
    d. One or two plants provide visual interest.
4. Each page layout should include identifying information.
    a. Client name
    b. Office type or label and option number
    c. Size, square footage, and dimensions
    d. Scale and date
    e. Design firm name
5. For many clients, it is helpful when designers list the furniture specifications as part of the page layout (Fig. 6.5).
    a. 36 x 72 Desk
    b. 24 x 72 Credenza
    c. Executive desk chair
    d. Guest Chairs – 2
    e. Other

Layouts may be drafted manually or drawn on the computer in CAD files. Layouts created by either method should follow a similar format as listed above. Clients should receive only photocopies of hand-drawn plans, never the original drawings, so that changes can be made to the original vellum or Mylar drawings or on the computer. Revised copies can then be resubmitted for approval.

Visual Impact

Drafting is an art form. Many clients do not know how to read a scale or floor plan and cannot draft a layout. When viewing a blueprint or plan, especially for the first time, clients are impressed by something they cannot do themselves. It is important for designers to remember that these drawings create a visual impact for clients.

Negative Impact

All information may be correct and accurate on the drawing, but if the drafting is sloppy, the page layout is unbalanced, or the line work is "flat," then the client may be unimpressed and ignore the accurate information.

On the other hand, it benefits no one to produce pretty drawings that are inaccurate. When clients first see such drawings, they may be impressed, but when they discover incorrect information, their opinion of you, the designer, and then possibly of all designers, may erode.

Positive Impact

While drafting is an art form, it also provides technical information. Plan the entire page layout to accommodate all of the required information, and then, using various line weights, draft a good plan in a visually attractive manner.

PROJECT

Draft typical private office layouts

Layouts should be based on the client profile selected from Appendix A for Chapter 2 projects. These layouts will become part of the students' portfolios and be attached to the Program Report in Chapter 12.

1. Provide at least two optional layouts for all offices requested by the selected client.
2. Layouts may be drafted manually or electronically in CAD files.
3. Only photocopies of hand-drawn plans, never the original drawings, should be submitted for grading so that changes can be made to the original vellum or Mylar drawings.
4. Graded copies can be revised and then resubmitted for additional credit.

7

TYPICAL WORKSTATION LAYOUTS

Many office workers sit in workstations or cubicles, which, like private office layouts, are generally typical throughout the workspace (Fig. 7.1). And, just as the work area mix undulates over time between more or fewer offices and workstations, the philosophy behind workstations and their physical makeup also evolves for many businesses.

Following World War II, increasing numbers of people joined the white-collar work force. Many of these people filled staff positions not considered worthy of window offices. To accommodate the many positions and tasks, rows of desks were laid out in large rooms. Some tasks, such as bookkeeping and drafting, were quiet tasks presenting little problem for this mass layout. Other tasks such as typing and telephone conversations were often distracting for coworkers. In any case, there was no personal privacy.

During the early to mid-1960s, several manufacturers had the innovative idea to develop *freestanding walls* that could surround and separate individual desks. Early walls were originally constructed of lumber and were quite heavy. They could stand individually on their own with feet supports that typically extended

about 1 foot (ft) from the walls. These walls did not need to be very high—just high enough to conceal a seated person, thus providing some privacy for the workers. Walls could be arranged and rearranged as people and desks were added or removed from a room or open area. In addition, by covering these walls, or *panels*, as they later became known, with carpet or other thick fabric, some acoustic qualities could also be realized.

EVOLUTION OF PANEL SYSTEMS

Today, it is doubtful that any of those original panel walls are still used. Instead, early systems evolved first as monolithic panels that were connected together, with the ability to hang worksurfaces and overhead storage from the panels as modular units. As technology and work methods change over time, manufacturers continue to update existing panel systems and systems furniture product lines to accommodate current needs and desires and to introduce new, innovative lines. In many situations, work areas have gone back to freestanding panels and

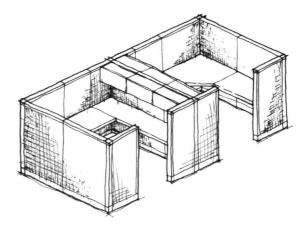

worksurfaces, albeit as a contemporary version of freestanding panels (Fig. 7.17).

Dozens of manufacturers offer their own versions of panel systems furniture. Many features are similar from one manufacturer to the next. Yet, each manufacturer incorporates its own unique features into its products. Most manufacturers conform to standard size components and design (Illustrated Table 7.1), while some manufacturers offer radically different sizes and versions of panel systems by using a post and horizontal beam system or vertical stanchions (Fig. 7.16 and 7.18) or full glass panels (Fig. 7.3).

TYPICAL WORKSTATIONS AND WORK AREAS

Unlike freestanding furniture and private offices, there are no typical industry-accepted standard workstation sizes or layouts, also known as *footprints*, for either conventional workstations (Fig. 7.2) or contemporary work areas (see Figs. 7.17b and 7.21b). Components, which are standard sizes (see Chapter 4), can be combined in various configurations to produce countless workstation and work area sizes and layouts.

Based on each client's individual requests, the designer lays out one or more work areas with components and panels or privacy screens, creating various footprint sizes that meet the client's needs. Many firms regularly select two or three layouts and sizes—conventional, contemporary, or a combination of the two—as typical

workstations based on their average employee needs.

In general conversations, particularly during the discovery process when a project first begins, many designers refer to typical 8 × 8 stations or work areas. However, an 8 × 8 station is not a universally accepted standard size. It is a generic term used to connote what will become a specific workstation size and layout that revolves around and is unique for each individual firm. One firm may actually use 8 × 8 stations, whereas the next firm may have smaller or larger stations, such as 7'-6" × 8' or 8' × 8'-6" stations.

Granted, many corporations end up with workstation footprints similar to those of other corporations, both in terms of L- or U-shaped layouts and overall size, roughly 6 × 6 up to 8 × 8. On paper, many two-dimensional layouts appear very similar. However, there actually may be more or fewer panels, panel heights may vary, there may be more or fewer storage units, worksurfaces may be straight or at angles, and two or three worksurfaces may be used in place of a single worksurface. There are no standard rules. Each company's workstation layout is planned and designed based on specific needs of that company and, ultimately, the chosen manufacturer and product line.

Assigning Workstation Layouts to Staff

In theory, the size and layout of individual workstations should be based on the functional requirements of each user or user's job

FIGURE 7.2 Handout: Typical workstation layout

ML DESIGN

Client Name

- (1) 42 × 42 corner worksurface
- (1) 30 × 30 return
- (1) 30 × 48 return
- (1) 24 × 90 worksurface
- (3) 30" overheads
- (1) bx/bx/file ped
- (1) 36" 2-drawer lateral file
- (2) task lights

WS-1   STAFF WORKSTATION
OPTION A   60 SF

SCALE: ¼" = 1'–0"
DATE:

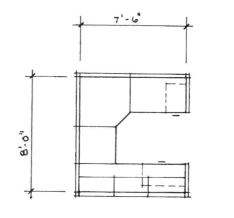

FIGURE 7.3 Panel systems (circa 2007)

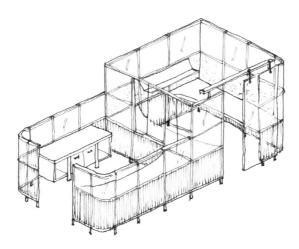

in a company. However, companies often have numerous employee jobs, and if each workstation were planned to function for only one job position, there would be many, many different layouts. This can add a great deal of confusion and frustration for the designer trying to plan the overall space and to lay out each unique workstation, as well as for the company's furniture inventory control, for the specifier, and finally, for the installers. Therefore, it is best to have typical workstations based on two or three diverse needs.

Even though functions may differ, it is amazing how many functions have the same basic worksurface and storage requirements. Consider job descriptions of people who customarily sit in workstations: secretaries, data-entry staff, office administrators, human resource staff, underwriters, accountants, auditors, consultants, technicians, supervisors, architects, interior designers, information systems specialists, and low-level managers.

These positions represent a wide range of tasks, status, education, and talent. Yet, especially in a paperless office, although they may be doing dissimilar types of work, many people are working in the same basic manner; they are sitting in front of a computer inputting or receiving data and information. They need a worksurface on which to place a monitor or laptop, space for a few papers, and a chair. Conceivably, they could all occupy the same typical workstation, whatever that typical workstation might be.

The difficulty that frequently arises when using the same workstation for all of these job positions occurs when status and education are considered. Even worse is when a lower-level position, such as a data-entry clerk, requires more worksurface area than a higher-level position, such as a supervisor. This can create a dilemma for the designer and client.

What should the designer do?

1. Give the same amount of space to everyone regardless of status, position, or education?
2. Give more space to the lower-level person, as needed and risk complaints from higher-level persons?
3. Give less space to the lower-level person and force that person to work in inadequate space?

Layout and Finish Variations

Unfortunately, logical aspects of establishing typical layouts do not always satisfy people's feelings. Many people are very concerned with where they are in the company hierarchy or the amount of square footage their work area occupies. To provide a successful design, in addition to aesthetics and workflow, the designer must also be able to meet the client's psychological expectations. Special situations, however, should not and do not have to create new workstation

sizes or layouts. Instead, distinguishing factors can be incorporated into typical workstation footprints for many diverse positions of people to achieve a philosophical or emotional objective without sacrificing the functional needs or actual size and layout of the typical workstation.

Panel Height Variations

By varying the panel heights, a clear distinction can be made between positions even though the workstations may be the same size, have the same component layouts, and look the same on a two-dimensional plan. Workstations with lower panel heights of 36–48 in. (inches) are generally viewed as lower-status cubicles because they do not afford the greater amount of privacy provided by higher panels. For those people sitting in a cubicle with high panels, their workstation feels like it has greater status than those workstations with low panels, where the occupants can easily be seen by everyone. For this reason, higher panels are often used for managerial workstations and lower panels are used for administrative assistant or data-entry positions (Illustrated Table 7.1a and b).

Material and Finish Variations

The feel of status variation can also be achieved by the type of material applied to the panels or worksurfaces. Wood surfaces or wood trim give a richer feel and thus a higher level of status compared with workstations with fabric, painted trim, and plastic laminate. Glass panels provide a psychological barrier and status between the cubicle occupant and general population, but at the same time glass panels leave the occupant visible in the same manner as low panels. Another variation is to select a few panels to receive a special finish and serve as accents, thus providing the occupant with another type of special treatment (Illustrated Table 7.1).

Layout Variations

Occasionally, the overall cubicle size is adequate, but the typical layout is not appropriate. For instance, the human resource position will most likely require more filing space than a consultant. In these situations, the typical layout within the cubicle can be adjusted by replacing a portion of the worksurface with a file while leaving

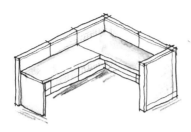

a. Cubicles with low panels and standard finishes

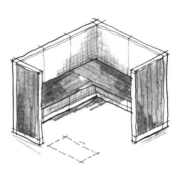

b. Cubicles with high panels and upgraded wood finishes

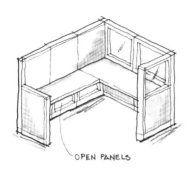

c. Cubicles with non-monolithic panels accepting glass or other finish tiles, or left open without any tiles

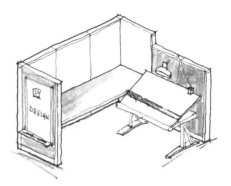

d. Non-typical workstation with special finishes on selected panels

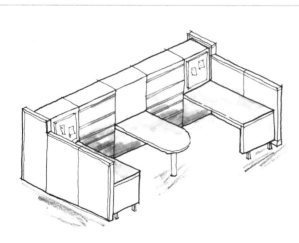

e. Double-shared workstation

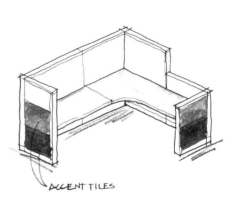

f. Optional layout with a curved corner and accent tiles

the overall basic layout and size the same as all other typical workstations (Illustrated Table 7.2c and d).

At other times, the designer must provide exclusive workstation sizes for certain positions within a firm. These are often one-of-a-kind positions that are unique within a firm, such as a graphic designer within a real estate firm. Brokers, while customarily more highly compensated than a designer, require average work areas, whereas the designer will need a larger worksurface to lay out mock-ups and other print materials. These situations do not typically create adverse employee morale, as those positions are generally known to be unique.

Non-Typical Workstations

Normally, a unique or non-typical workstation is one in which one or two employees perform specialized tasks. Requirements for truly unique, special, or non-typical workstations are often voiced at the beginning of a project because it is understood by upper management that these jobs do indeed have unique requirements, such as a shared station for two people who work closely together in accounts receivable (Illustrated Table 7.1e).

On the other hand, at some firms all of the employees require layouts other than the three or four basic layouts used by people working at computers. Such is the case for interior designers who may still use drafting boards, which are generally freestanding and deeper than average worksurfaces. Additionally, all interior designers need larger worksurface areas on which to lay out drawings, thus, creating a larger, non-typical workstation (Illustrated Table 7.1d).

Typical Workstation Layouts

After interviewing key client personnel, after touring existing facilities to observe work patterns, and after considering functions to be performed, the designer is ready to plan typical layouts for the client. Many people can work comfortably within one of the basic layouts shown in this chapter; however, designers should not try to force a basic layout on a firm when that layout is not a solution that will best meet the client's daily needs. By no means have all possible layouts been shown. Use the layouts that meet client requirements, and change, modify, or adapt the layouts that are close, but not quite right. Use panel height and finish variations to achieve status differentiation when just changing the worksurface layout or size will not work.

Even when the designer believes that one typical layout will work for all personnel at a firm, it is best to provide optional layouts within the typical cubicle size (see Isometrics in Illustrated Table 7.1b and f and corresponding layouts in Illustrated Table 7.2c and Illustrated Table 7.3d). The client likes to feel involved in the selection and decision-making process.

CONVENTIONAL WORKSTATION LAYOUTS

Many firms and organizations have invested a great deal of capital in conventional panel systems. They will continue to use and purchase these panel systems for many years to come. To stay at least semi-current for existing customers and end-users, manufacturers also continue to design new parts and pieces, panels, attachments, and components to work with existing systems to meet contemporary desires and aesthetics. Occasionally, some companies still surround freestanding desks with panels, but for the most part, these workstations are comprised of panels with attached worksurfaces and components.

Workstation Dimensions

Like other furniture categories, individual worksurface, panel, and component sizes are always listed in inches: 36-in. panels, 24" × 72" worksurfaces, 30-in. storage bins, etc. However, once the components are configured into a workstation layout, the overall workstation size is then stated in feet and inches: 6' × 8', 7'-6" × 7'-6", 8' × 8', etc.

Because it is well known that workstations are listed as feet, it is common practice to drop the reference to feet and inches during verbal conversation and simply say, *six by eight*. These marks are also generally dropped in typed information when specifically referring to workstation sizes: 6 × 8, 7-6 × 7-6, 8 × 8, etc.

For typical drawing layouts, however, it is customary to continue using the feet and inch marks as would be shown on any architectural drawing.

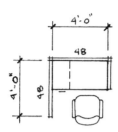

a. Small workstation layout: Option A—16 NSF

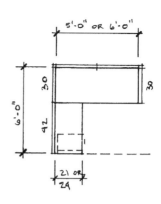

b. Basic workstation layout: Option B—36 NSF

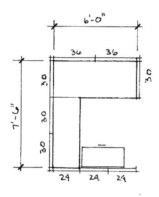

c. Basic layout: Option A with another
worksurface and file—45 NSF

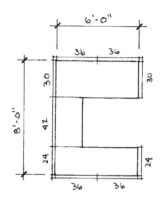

d. Basic layout: Option B with one additional
worksurface—48 NSF

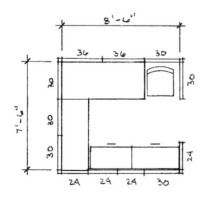

e. Basic layout: Option A—with another worksurface,
two files and guest seating—64 NSF

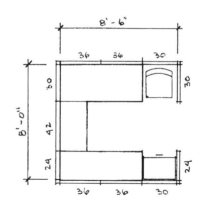

f. Basic layout: Option B with another worksurface,
file, and guest seating—68 NSF

Workstation Layouts

Design or planning of workstations generally starts with the selection of primary and secondary worksurfaces. When space allows or functions dictate, additional worksurfaces can be included in the layout. Next, overhead components and lower storage units are added as needed or as allowed by the budget. Finally, panels are drawn on two, three, or four sides of the worksurface layout, with an opening for access into the work area.

Basic Layouts

For some companies, such as a call center, a typical workstation may consist of a narrow, single worksurface with a pedestal below, given that many customer service people have little need for extensive work areas or storage. Duties typically consist of light computer data entry, telephone calls, maintaining a dozen active and tickler files, and meeting with their supervisor. For the most part, employees need a place to sit and make calls. These are very small workstations that generally serve a niche market (Illustrated Table 7.2a).

Most companies, for their average employees, provide L-shaped or U-shaped layouts similar to a desk and return or desk, return, and credenza, using the same basic sizes as those of standard desks and returns. With an L-shaped layout, a pedestal can easily be installed below a 72-in.-wide primary surface using either a 21-in. or 24-in.-wide side surface, but space for leg room is limited with a 60-in. surface. For this reason, many companies have tended to opt for the wider 72-in. primary surface over the 60-in. surface. In either case, a secondary surface is regularly included in this workstation because most occupants need worksurface space for both a monitor and laptop, or even two monitors and laptop, and a writing surface. If there are no other needs for this person, such as storage, filing, or work area, the workstation is now complete. The smallest cubicle layout will be a basic 6 × 6 or 36 net square foot (NSF) workstation (Illustrated Table 7.2b).

Basic Layouts with Additional Components

A 6 × 6 cubicle does not provide much storage area. When additional filing and worksurfaces are needed, these items can be added along the back side of the basic layout. The cubicle now increases in size to 6 × 7-6 (45 NSF) or 6 × 8 (48 NSF). Depending on the specific manufacturer or system selected, some worksurfaces and panels may need to change in size or width from the basic layout in order to meet the overall requirements and to function in the best capacity (Illustrated Table 7.2c and d).

Additional worksurfaces can be added to the basic layout, as can storage units or guest chairs, as desired. All such additions will adjust the amount of square feet and configuration. This new cubicle is now 8-6 × 7-6 (64 NSF) or 8-6 × 8 (68 NSF). Worksurfaces and other components can be added, removed, rearranged, and changed to any size (Illustrated Table 7.2e and f).

Basic Layout Alternates

For layouts considered thus far, the primary and secondary surfaces are arranged based on traditional desk and return layouts where one end of the secondary surface is placed along the width or face of the primary surface. Although not feasible with desks and returns, another layout that can be considered with panel systems is to place the secondary surface on one or both ends of the primary worksurface (Fig. 7.4a).

The same add-on concept that has just been discussed for the first basic layout would also be applied to this layout. Start with two surfaces creating a 7 × 6 workstation layout and build it up to a 7 × 8 station or any size desired (Fig. 7.4b).

Corner Worksurfaces

Angled or curved corner worksurfaces provided extra deep space for the larger, older, desktop monitors. Though most firms have gravitated to flat-screen monitors, many people still prefer corner units for a softer transition between all surfaces. Although it is not mandatory, it is typical to add a worksurface on each side of the corner unit. Side surfaces should be wide enough to accommodate both a pedestal and legroom. A side surface that is 30 in. wide allows only 14 in. of clear legroom between the pedestal and corner surface and very little worksurface space. This layout is for a heavy computer user only as it is not feasible to do much paperwork on the side surfaces (Illustrated Table 7.3a).

FIGURE 7.4 Plan views: Alternate workstation layouts

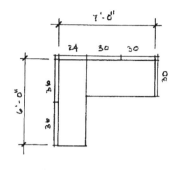

a. Alternate basic workstation Option C—42 NSF

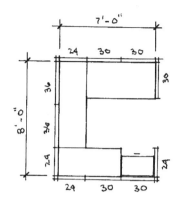

b. Alternate basic workstation
Option C with add-ons—54 NSF

ILLUSTRATED Table 7.3 Plan views: Corner worksurface layouts

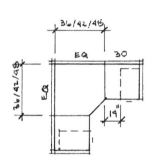

a. Corner worksurface layout with short returns

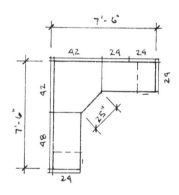

b. Corner worksurface with equal side returns

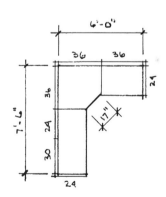

c. Corner worksurface with unequal side returns

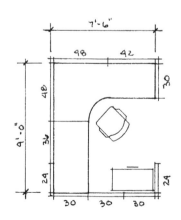

d. Corner workstation with a curved worksurface and
add-ons

When daily tasks are divided equally between the computer and paperwork, the side worksurfaces must be increased to a minimum of 36 in. wide and preferably 42 in., 48 in., or 54 in. wide to allow for more legroom. Side surfaces can be of equal or varying lengths. Layouts using corner units are built up in the same manner as described for straight surfaces. Designers start with a corner and add other worksurfaces, storage, or space as desired (Illustrated Table 7.3b–d).

The primary disadvantage of a corner unit cubicle over a straight worksurface cubicle is that people are typically sitting with their back toward the aisle. This is not necessarily a disadvantage, but in this position cubicle occupants may not see or be aware of visitors entering their cubicle. It may be wise to consider using glass or lower panels along one or more sides of these cubicles (Illustrated Table 7.1c and f).

Office-Style Workstations

Workstations discussed thus far are representative of cubicles occupied by the bulk of office staff. Increasingly, workstations are also being planned for middle to upper management (see Chapter 2). These employees may accept the logic of systems furniture, but in return they desire more office-style layouts than typical staff cubicles. They want or need their privacy and status.

Using tall panels, stations can be laid out to look like real offices with a "desk and credenza." Doors can be installed and locked. Space can be provided for one, two, or more guest chairs. Panel walls can even go all the way up to the ceiling, if need be (Fig. 7.7b).

Many managerial workstations start with a 9 ft or 10 ft length across the back of the station and then build forward in the same manner as discussed for setting up traditional offices in Chapter 6. Very few manufacturers make a 10-ft-long worksurface. Therefore, the back wall of this station will be laid out with two shorter worksurfaces or one worksurface and a storage unit (Fig. 7.5). A 48-in. return or side surface provides a nice spacious feel. It also ensures adequate chair circulation since it is not possible to push the "desk" slightly forward as in a conventional office.

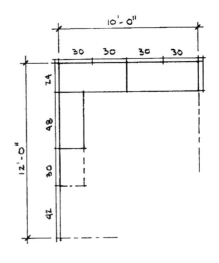

Most manufacturers offer several desk or primary worksurface options, either 30 or 36 in. deep (Fig. 7.6). These primary worksurfaces are freestanding on one end and attached directly to either a panel or another worksurface on the other end. Some units accommodate front modesty panels and pedestals and other units are open below and in front to more closely resemble a table. In some situations, a freestanding table unit is used in place of an attached worksurface (Fig. 7.7a).

Space is provided in front of the primary unit to allow room for guest chairs. Panels can be installed along the very front of this workstation for a more enclosed area or left off for a more open area. Customarily, the panels around these workstations will be 84 in. high. Some manufacturers also offer a line of panels (known as demountable walls) that can be installed full height to the ceiling. Although these layouts are panel systems, they give a very strong impression of being a real office (Fig. 7.7b). In fact, occupants in managerial workstations habitually end up with more work area and storage than a traditional office set-up of standard size desks and credenzas. By using panel systems to create offices, if desired, footprints can easily be reduced to 10 ft × 12 ft, or 120 NSF, down from 150 NSF for conventional drywall offices. A net savings of 30 NSF per office not only reduces

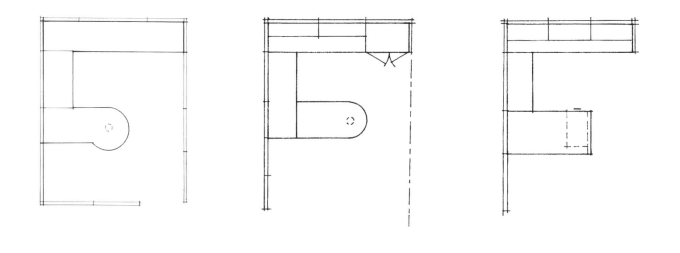

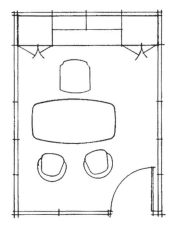

a. Plan view: freestanding desk or primary worksurface option

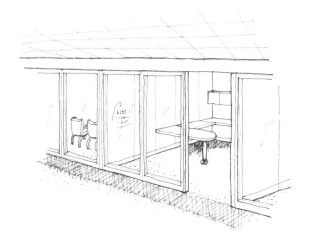

b. Perspective: panel system walls often look like permanent construction

the total required leased space, but as furniture, it can be written off on income tax returns more quickly than hard construction items (see Chapter 2).

Overhead Units

Overhead units may be hung above any one or more worksurfaces (Fig. 7.8a and b, and see also Fig. 4.10a and b). For systems using traditional panels with vertical standards (Figs. 7.8a and b and 7.15b, and see also Fig. 4.12a), overheads must be the same width as the panel on which they are hung, known as a modular system. Many, but not all, systems with horizontal channels allow overheads to be positioned anywhere along the panel run, often staggered across panel connections (Figs. 7.8c and 7.15a, and see also Fig. 4.12b). As a word of caution, unless the designer absolutely knows the selected system has channels for off-modularity, during preliminary space planning it is best to assume that the overheads need to align with the panels. Later, once the actual manufacturer and panel system are selected, overheads can then be repositioned as allowed.

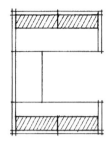

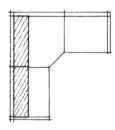

a. Modular panels with overhead components along the front and back of the workstation

b. Modular panels with overhead components along the side of the workstation

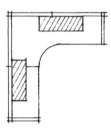

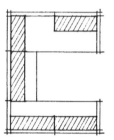

c. Off-modular panels with offset overhead components

d. Overhead components do not fully meet when placed at right angles in panel systems.

BOX 7.1 LEED CI Light Controls for Adjustable Usage[1]

Indoor Environmental Quality Credit

INTERIOR LIGHTING
EQ Credit (1–2 points) Commercial Interiors

Intent
To promote occupants' productivity, comfort, and well-being by providing high-quality lighting.

Requirements
Option 1. Lighting Control (1 point)
For at least 90% of individual occupant spaces, provide individual lighting controls that enable occupants to adjust the lighting to suit their individual tasks and preferences, with at least three lighting levels or scenes (on, off, midlevel). Midlevel is 30% to 70% of the maximum illumination level (not including daylight contributions).

For all shared multioccupant spaces, meet all of the following requirements.

- Have in place multizone control systems that enable occupants to adjust the lighting to meet group needs and preferences, with at least three lighting levels or scenes (on, off, midlevel).
- Lighting for any presentation or projection wall must be separately controlled.
- Switches or manual controls must be located in the same space as the controlled luminaires. A person operating the controls must have a direct line of sight to the controlled luminaires.

Overheads are designed to be placed side-by-side either along the spine or on panels perpendicular to the spine. They are not designed to be placed at right angles in the corner of a workstation. Doing so will result in a void or gap created by the differences in the unit depths and end panel widths in modular systems or an overlap in non-modular systems (Fig. 7.8d). Incidentally, very seldom are more than two or three overheads placed in a station. When that much storage is required, the designer may want to consider including a file cabinet in the typical layout (Illustrated Table 7.2c).

A task light is often added below one or more overheads. Depending on the manufacturer, lights may be installed in a permanent position or be repositioned as desired by the cubicle occupant. Some manufacturers also offer free-standing or desktop fixtures (Fig. 7.23). Either way, since the occupant controls the on/off switch, including task lights can assist with achieving LEED credits (Box 7.1).

Pedestals and Lower Storage

Pedestals and lower storage units do not need to conform to panel widths. In many cases, lower storage units are freestanding and thus can be positioned anywhere below a worksurface. Even when pedestals are suspended from a worksurface, they do not necessarily align with panels.

Technically speaking, pedestals can hang from a worksurface at any position on the underside of the surface, but most worksurfaces come automatically predrilled to accommodate pedestals at each end of the worksurface. *Predrilled* is a term used for the starter holes on the underside of worksurfaces that are drilled during manufacturing to make it easier for the installers to attach the pedestals in the field.

Accessories

With rare exception, accessories are not drawn on a full space plan. A few accessories, such as letter trays, pencil cups, or file holders, may be drawn on a typical ¼ in. scale layout for the client to consider a fully coordinated design approach. However, specific accessories are generally chosen during the design development phase, not the conceptual space planning phase.

Panel Surrounds

In planning typical layouts, panels are added after the worksurfaces are laid out. First, all worksurfaces and other items such as files or guest chairs are laid out for a typical workstation to establish the standard footprint and size. The panels are then added around the footprint, corresponding with the worksurface or component sizes. Normally, there are several panel widths that can work with any given layout; it is up to the designer to determine the most appropriate panel widths to use (Fig. 7.9a and b).

Standardized Panel Widths

Most manufacturers offer between six and nine panel widths. It is conceivable that the designer may select and use every panel width offered. However, for practical reasons it is wise to minimize the number of panel widths specified on any one project. Panel systems are designed for reconfigurations in the future. More panel widths mean more inventory control, sometimes fewer options for future reconfiguration, and probably greater up-front costs as narrower panels tend to cost almost as much as wider panels and installers will need to spend more time sorting out the various panel widths. In an attempt to standardize on a few panel widths throughout the project, it is common practice for the designer to employ the same panel widths for each typical footprint used for a particular client, although there are times when it is necessary to adjust panel widths for certain workstations to accommodate items on the other side of that workstation.

FIGURE 7.9 Panel surrounds

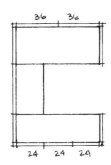

a. Assigning panel widths to workstation layouts

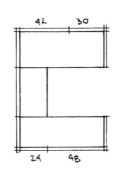

b. Panels may be equal or unequal widths

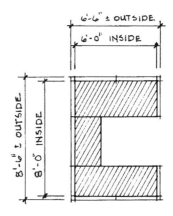

c. Nominal and actual workstation sizes for 6 × 8 cubicle

Panel Installation

During installation, the process is reversed; installing the panels precedes the worksurfaces and other components. Installers will stand, connect, arrange, and position all panels first. When all panels are up, like little empty rooms, the installers go back to hang the worksurfaces and components. If it is necessary to reconfigure a few workstations for special needs that arise after the initial design concept, the time to do that is during the panel installation prior to hanging the worksurfaces, not after the client moves in.

Drawing Symbol

When drawing single workstations, it is customary to use heavier line weights for the worksurfaces and lighter lines for the panels, as shown in these illustrations. When hand-drafting workstations, it is also common practice to extend or overlap the dividing panel lines beyond the 2–3 in. panel thickness. As a full space plan is drawn, panel line weights tend to become obscure when workstations share common panels.

Stated vs. Actual Cubicle Size

There is a difference between the stated or nominal cubicle size, 6 × 8, and the actual cubicle size. Typical workstation sizes refer to the inside panel dimensions, or generally speaking, the overall worksurface sizes and layouts (Fig. 7.9c). Panel thicknesses are normally not included in stated workstation sizes. When these thicknesses are added to the workstation size, the actual overall size for a 6 × 8 station is really 6-5± × 8-5±, depending on the selected manufacturer. The ± refers to an approximate thickness or size of the panel, which may or may not have been selected at this time.

Several reasons for not incorporating panel thicknesses into the stated typical workstation size include the following:

1. Worksurface sizes, and thus inside panel dimensions, remain consistent from one manufacturer to the next, whereas panel thicknesses vary from one manufacturer to the next.
2. Once space planning begins, cubicles regularly share panels with other cubicles that are beside, in front of, or behind a given cubicle. This would result in giving half-panel thicknesses, often fractions, to the typical workstation size.
3. Many people prefer to deal with feet and half feet or whole numbers, rather than with inches and fractions, which would be the result if panel thicknesses were added to the workstation sizes.

PLANNING MANY WORKSTATIONS

For a final space plan, workstations are normally planned in clusters or rows, although occasionally there will be one or two stand-alone stations. During space planning, there are several concepts to keep in mind.

Sharing Panels

Systems are designed to share panels. If panels were not shared, then panels would needlessly be placed back-to-back. More square footage would be required, and furniture costs would increase (Fig. 7.10a). Assuming the panels are 3 in. thick and the cubicles are 8 × 8, then 17 ft would be required across this cluster of eight individual cubicles and 34 ft along the length, for a total of 578 NSF (Table 7.1).

This plan leaves out an important consideration: components can be hung on both sides of a panel. In this plan, the back sides of panels have been ignored. Many panels are backed against other panels, resulting in double rows of panels.

To achieve a more efficient and economical plan, both sides of any and all panels that lend themselves to such an application should be used. This would eliminate all double rows of panels, thus reducing both the amount of square footage required and overall furniture costs (Fig. 7.10b).

Using the same 3" thick panels and 8 × 8 cubicles, only 16'-9" is required across a cluster of eight cubicles and 33'-3" along the length when panels are shared. This cluster of cubicles requires only 557 NSF, or 21 less square feet of floor space and 24 fewer panels than when panels are not shared (Table 7.1).

FIGURE 7.10 Plan views: Planning for many workstations

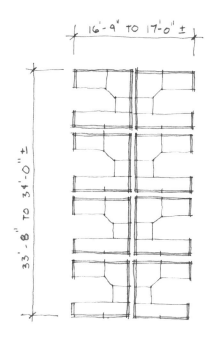

a. Cluster of individual typical workstations

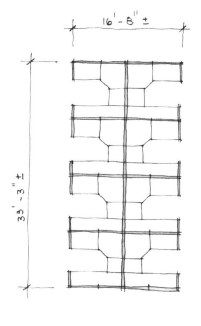

b. Planned cluster of typical workstations sharing panels

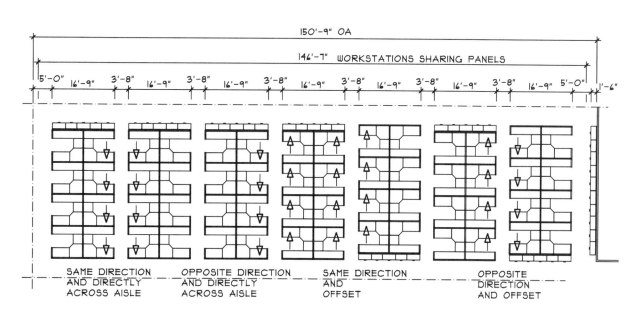

c. Space planning multiple clusters of typical workstations

TABLE 7.1 Workstations

	WORKSTATIONS WITH NON-SHARED PANELS	WORKSTATIONS THAT SHARE PANELS
Panels	3″ thick	3″ thick
Workstations	8′ x 8′	8′ x 8′
Width across	3″ + 8′ + 3″ + 3″ + 8′ + 3″ = 17′-0″	3″ + 8′ + 3″ + 8′ + 3″ = 16′-9″
Length down	(3″ + 8′ + 3″) x 4 = 34′-0″	((3″ + 8′) x 4) + 3″ = 33′-3″
Overall size	17′-0″ x 34′-0″ = 578 NSF	16′-9″ x 33′-3″ = 557 NSF
Panel counts	16 end panels + 24 spine panels + 8 front and back panels + 24 cross panels 72 Total Panels	16 end panels + 12 spine panels + 8 front and back panels + 12 cross panels 48 Total Panels

Although the inches and square feet may be incidental for a small layout, on large floor plates with hundreds of workstations, these small inches add up to many feet. Consider a plan requiring 56 typical cubicles. Using the same cluster of eight stations, depending on the final space plan, 3 linear inches per cluster, or up to 1'-9" overall, will be saved across the layout when panels are shared between workstations. This saved floor space can provide the client with a rent savings by reducing the amount of required square footage, or the floor space can be used for other items, such as a bank of files (Fig. 7.10c).

Panel Creep

Unlike stated sizes for typical offices where the slight variation in inches between nominal and actual sizes due to wall thicknesses does not overly affect the furniture layouts and the overall space plan, with workstations those inches do matter. Although typical workstation layouts are stated in nominal sizes, when planning clusters of workstations, the designer must plan these inches, known as *panel creep*, into the overall layout.

During initial planning stages, it is often customary to use a blank box or square (see Fig. 14.4b) to represent a typical workstation rather than a fully drawn and laid out cubicle. Using only the stated dimensions of a typical 8 × 8 workstation, a cluster of eight stations creates an overall planning box of 16 × 32. When the panel thicknesses are added, the dimensions increase to 16'-9" × 33'-3", almost a foot more in one direction and more than a foot in the other direction (Fig. 7.11a). These added inches definitely affect the overall space plan. Unplanned panel thicknesses create a great deal of frustration during installation. Workstation runs may not align as intended, the aisles may not be wide enough, or there may not be enough space in some situations. For this example of seven clusters of workstations (Fig. 7.11a), the actual overall width required is 139'-3", or 5'-3" more than if the designer had used the nominal size for each workstation.

Non-Typical Workstations Sharing Panels

When cubicle layouts are typical or configured using the same panel widths, it is very easy to share panels by mirroring them from side-to-side or front-to-back. On the other hand, when workstations vary in size, layout, or panel widths, it may take a little more planning and ingenuity on the designer's part to use shared panels. Nevertheless, as many panels as feasible should be shared to capture both floor space and cost savings. With the exception of one custom-width

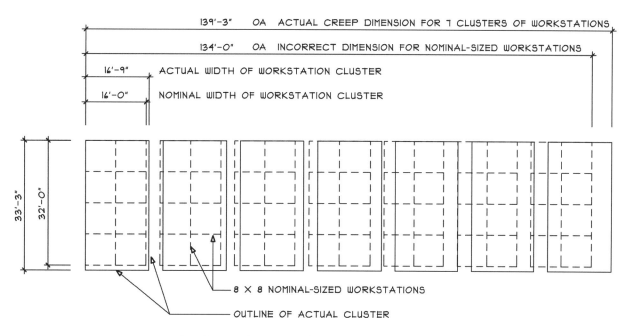

a. Panel creep due to actual workstation sizes vs. nominal sizes

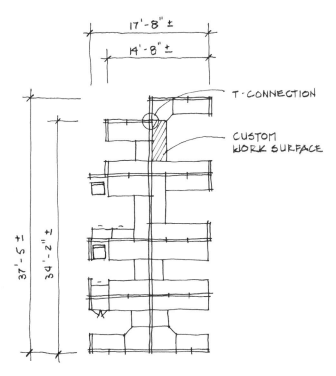

b. Combining non-typical workstation layouts

worksurface to span a T-intersection, all other product is standard in this cluster of eight non-typical, individually planned workstations (Fig. 7.11b).

Cubicle Access across Aisles

Together with planning the physical cubicles, shared panels, and space plan layout, the designer must also consider the human element. Assuming everyone will receive the same typical cubicle and layout, will all cubicles be oriented in the same direction, opposite directions, or be offset from one another?

In other words, for two cubicles on either side of an aisle, will people sit directly across from each other so that each person's activities are undoubtedly observed by the person in the cubicle directly opposite? Or, should the cubicles be positioned and planned to lessen intrusion by other people wherever possible (Fig. 7.10c)?

Answers to these two questions will be determined in part by the actual floor plate plan, the available space, the typical cubicle layout and components, other furniture requirements, and the overall space plan to reflect the client's needs and corporate culture. Other determinants for cubicle arrangement will be the type of work being performed by the cubicle occupants and their need for confidentiality or reduced noise level, company philosophy, and collaborative or non-collaborative work efforts between the various cubicle occupants.

Existing work habits and flow, which can be repeated in a new location, become apparent during the programming phase. However, moving to a new location is also an ideal time to implement new ideas and work habits where and if the client desires to do so. The designer will want to discuss various notions, concepts, potential layouts, and case studies with the client prior to actual space planning.

Electrical and Data Outlets

Providing power to workstations is an integral part of space planning. During initial planning stages, the designer should discuss power requirements with the client. In turn, the designer can then discuss these requirements with the sales representative when selecting and determining the system to be specified.

Power within Workstations

Electrical and data power can be supplied via designated channels or *raceways*, as they are known, through the inside of panels to outlets positioned at strategic locations within the panels. The two sources, electrical and data, must be physically separated from each other, often by a simple dividing strip of metal or plastic, which then allows these sources to generally share the same raceway for reaching the workstations. In most cases, manufacturers install UL-approved power strips, raceways, and outlets directly in the panels at the factory and ship the panels pre-wired with power capabilities. Furniture installers can then install panel-to-panel connectors on the job site to complete the power supply.

Pre-wired panel raceways and connectors save the cost of having an electrician install electrical wires through the raceways, offer a clean solution for bringing power to each outlet in a workstation, and provide outlets that are easily accessible. Pre-wired panels also provide a simple means for reconfiguration of cubicles in the future. First, the panel-to-panel connectors are disconnected, panels are configured according to the new layout, and the connectors are reconnected between panels, all by a furniture installer.

For the majority of municipalities, pre-wired panels are an acceptable solution. However, as with many building code requirements, it is important to verify or research intended solutions for the locale in which workstations are being installed. Some cities, such as Chicago, do not allow factory-installed power strips. Chicago requires that conduit be installed in the panel systems by licensed electricians on the job site, and then the electrical wires are pulled through the conduit. This precise code requirement does not particularly change or affect the actual space plan, but it does affect furniture specifications, coordination of the installation, installation costs, and future reconfigurations.

Although power and raceways can be added to panels in the field, either by using power strips or being installed by an electrician, it is best to specify which panels should be powered when initially placing an order with the factory. Most panels are shipped with a base cap; non-powered panels receive a straight, solid cap over an empty base and powered panels receive a raceway base with knock-outs to accommodate electrical, data, or telephone outlets (see Fig. 4.11). Many panels can also have the outlets installed at midsection just below or above the worksurface height. When the panels are ordered with power, these items are factory installed, thus saving labor costs to install these items on the job site. If electrical components are ordered after the fact, then costs include the items themselves and the additional cost of the on-site installation.

Panels to Power

Typically, power is run down the center spine on a row of workstations (Fig. 7.12). Although the wiring, either power strips or conduit, can make a 90-degree turn for installation through the cross panels of a workstation, this is seldom done unless the user has high electrical requirements. Powered panels cost more than non-powered panels, so it is prudent to put power only where it is required. To control furniture costs, telephones and equipment can be methodically placed along the spine portion of the workstation layout, thus saving the need to power all panels.

Power and Data Connections to Workstations

Generally, we think of electrical and data outlets as being located in walls—plug and unplug—click and unclick. However, even when factory-installed power strips are specified as part of the panel system, a licensed electrician and data cabling installer must provide hardwired connections from the sources of power to the workstations via a length of furniture manufacturer supplied conduit (1 in. diameter, 6–18 in. long) called a whip (Fig. 7.12). Depending on the amount of power usage required by occupants, each whip can serve between six and ten workstations.

There are three ways to bring the sources of electrical power and data (P&D), to workstations for hardwired connections to the furniture whip: from the wall, up through the floor, or down from the ceiling.

When workstations are positioned next to a wall, panels to the floor usually prevent easy

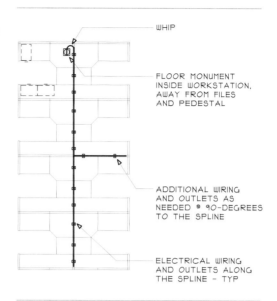

FIGURE 7.12 Plan view: Electrical provisions in workstations

WHIP

FLOOR MONUMENT INSIDE WORKSTATION, AWAY FROM FILES AND PEDESTAL

ADDITIONAL WIRING AND OUTLETS AS NEEDED @ 90-DEGREES TO THE SPLINE

ELECTRICAL WIRING AND OUTLETS ALONG THE SPLINE - TYP

access to any wall connections. Even systems with removable or open tiles (Illustrated Table 7.1c), are not always practical. A whip cannot be easily cut, and it requires a 2–3 in. projection when bent to make a 90-degree turn from the wall to a panel connection. Depending on the layout, workstations may need to be pulled away from the wall to accommodate a whip behind the panels or the whip may be visible along the outside of the first or last station in a row.

When clusters of workstations are located in the middle of the room, this creates an obstacle for connecting power to wall sources. Obviously, it is not desirable to have cords or conduits running across aisles where people walk. Traditionally, designers have preferred to bring power up through floor junction boxes rather than down from the ceiling via power poles. The floor boxes are usually hidden below worksurfaces, where they are out of sight (Fig. 7.12). Sometimes the junction boxes are fully recessed into the floor, leaving a smooth, clean appearance. At other times, 2-in.-high monuments, or *doghouses*, as they are called, are used because these junction boxes are less expensive than fully recessed boxes (Fig. 4.10b). In either case, careful coordination is needed during construction to make sure the boxes are in the corner of a workstation area and not in the aisle, task chair seating area, or under a panel or pedestal location. Power in the boxes is then connected to power in the panels via a whip (Fig. 7.12). Up through the floor is the most expensive alternative because the contractor will need to drill a hole through the floor, called a *floor core* or *core drill*, and then install wiring from below, often through another tenant's ceiling or plenum space. A second, and possibly third, core drill will also be required below the electrical closet and/or LAN room to bring the wiring back to the original sources of power (see Fig. 11.5).

The least expensive method for bringing power to workstations is to run it down from the ceiling through a hollow pole, called a power pole. In the past, 4 in. × 4 in. white power poles extending from the ceiling to the floor were the primary solution for connecting power to the workstation panels (see Fig. 4.10a). These poles were functional and inexpensive, but not very aesthetic. In recent years manufacturers have come out with many innovative ways to improve the appearance of power poles. Poles now come in colors to blend in or contrast with other workstation finishes. Some poles are very high-tech with vertical sides that may be convex or canted; circular, hexagonal, or rectangular; or visually open. Poles may be constructed of various materials, including perforated metals or other finishes. Poles are now integrated as part of the overall system rather than added as an appendage as with earlier poles.

Finally, some systems allow, and designers are designing, high-tech solutions in which wiring from the ceiling is completely visible as an exposed element in the space. In these situations, hanging straps or ladder trays (see Chapter 3, opening photograph), are used to support the wiring.

Because floor space is often tight, where the budget allows, particularly in buildings of steel beam and metal pan construction (skyscrapers and other high-risers), designers tend to specify floor cores for all stations, including those along walls when there are other clusters of stations already receiving floor cores. This provides a cleaner installation, and the amount of money saved on one or two wall connections does not amount to much in the overall project costs. In buildings with reinforced concrete flooring systems, a bit more planning and coordination in the field may be required in order to avoid

drilling holes through the thicker portions of the concrete system. Finally, in buildings constructed in the near early 20th century, using structural clay tile floor systems, it may not be possible to use core drills at all, in which case, designers will need to plan for wall or power pole connections.

Acoustics

Acoustics are of great concern throughout much of the designed spaces, especially in areas where many people are congregated. For years, high panels, with their acoustic properties, were "the answer" in large, open work areas. But, with the advent of lower panels or no panels (see next section), some people are concerned that large, open areas may become too noisy. There is a right to be concerned, but just as panel systems are changing, so too, are other aspects of life. Keyboarding is not nearly as loud as it was when typing on a typewriter. Rather than talk on the telephone, more and more people are sending emails, text messages, and other forms of modern communication, which reduces much verbal noise. And, ubiquitous earbuds and headphones drown out most remaining distractions.

Where concern still remains, especially for those workers who do not use earbuds, acoustic ceiling tiles with high noise reduction coefficients (NRC) are often used to absorb as much sound as possible. But, the same high NRC tiles should not be used in a private office because too much sound would be absorbed in such a small area, thus creating a muffled atmosphere. Hence, manufacturers make tiles with various NRC, yet have the same appearances so as to provide a consistent look throughout the space.

If concern still remains, another method for diminishing sound and unwanted noises is to reduce the number of hard surfaces that reflect sound and increase soft surfaces that absorb sound. Examples include fabric in place of leather, perforated feature walls that allow sound to pass through the holes, additional lounge and collaborative seating, baffles, fabric covered wall panels, openings in place of glass, on the list goes.

Finally, rather than congregating all workstations in the same large, open area, break up and separate workstations into pods with rooms, soft seating, open staircases, file cabinets, or break rooms between groupings of workstations. Not only is there an actual separation, but the psychological separation will mentally reduce distractions that are not seen across the way.

CONTEMPORARY WORK AREAS, WORKPLACES, AND WORKSPACES

The way many people work today, their needs and desires, both in terms of actual work requirements and personal satisfaction, and their requests for greater attention to green practices is constantly changing. Even the lexicon for typical workstations and cubicles is changing. New terminology has gravitated toward names such as *work areas*, *workspaces*, and *workplaces*.

For much of today's work, people tend to function better where there is a more open environment rather than when surrounded by high panels. They want more collaboration with other employees, more eye contact, more natural light.

In these office environments, when some privacy or separation is required, divider screens can be attached to the leading edge of a worksurface (Fig. 7.13). Businesses in Europe have been using this type of freestanding furniture for some time. Only recently has the American worker begun to accept this more contemporary style of furniture and openness. Both manufacturers and designers have embraced the new openness concepts in several ways to bring natural light and collaboration to the everyday workplace.

Modifying Existing Systems

Manufacturers have responded to the evolving needs of the modern workplace by expanding or retooling existing systems, intertwining existing systems, or introducing new systems that can often be incorporated with existing systems. They have also expanded the ways in which systems furniture can be laid out, planned, and connected. For instance, when a need for large amounts of paper storage exists, is it really necessary to first specify panels between workstations and then place files in front of the panels? Rather, modified files can also separate two cubicles, thus reducing furniture costs by eliminating one or more panels per station (Illustrated Table 7.2e and Fig. 7.14). In addition, floor space per occupant is reduced from 64 SF in the conventional layout down to 60 SF with this modified layout.

Other modifications, horizontal hanging channels and off-modular panel systems (see Chapter 4), allow greater flexibility for configuring non-typical workstations in a cluster. It is easier to span T-connections without having to order a custom-sized worksurface since surfaces can be placed anywhere and panels can be wider, which can provide both a more monolithic appearance and help reduce overall costs (Figs. 7.8c and 7.15a).

Finally, manufacturers have updated the product styling to reflect the open environment concept. Panels that once went all the way to the floor are now raised 4–6 in. above the floor (Fig. 7.15b). Fully enclosed end-support panels

FIGURE 7.13 Freestanding systems furniture

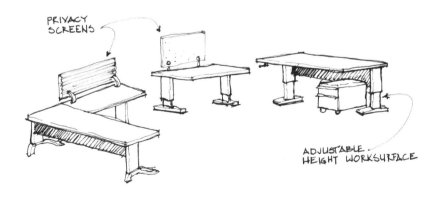

FIGURE 7.14 Furniture units, such as files, used in place of panels

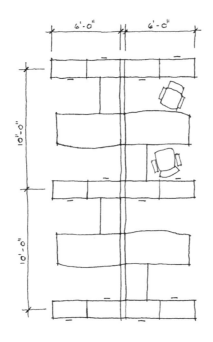

have been redesigned as open frames. Opaque, translucent, rippled, colored, or laminated glass have been added to panels either as an option to the clear glass inserts or as screens that can be attached to worksurfaces or tops of panels, providing some privacy yet allowing natural light to penetrate all work areas. In some cases,

this sharing of natural daylight can help achieve credits toward LEED certification (see Box 14.2).

Electrical Updates

Along with more collaboration and interactive communication, today's employees tend to have greater electrical requirements than in the past. Where once people plugged in a pencil sharpener and calculator, the list of equipment that needs outlets has been greatly expanded: one or more PCs or laptops, monitors, printers, desk telephones, cellphones, chargers, iPods, and more. Plus, these items tend to be plugged in and removed more frequently than equipment in the past, so the outlets need to be readily accessible.

Over the years, manufacturers made great strides to accommodate vast amounts of electrical wiring by adding channels at mid-level of panels or by making the entire interior cavities of panels open to carry bundles of wiring. But with the advent of lower or even no panels, an alternate wire management solution was needed. Manufacturers introduced post and beam systems to carry even greater bundles of wiring through the hollow cavities (Fig. 7.16a). Worksurfaces are supported from the beam in a manner similar to panel systems with horizontal channels. Another option for carrying wiring and cabling is to add open troughs below worksurfaces (Fig. 7.16b).

FIGURE 7.15 Modifying existing systems

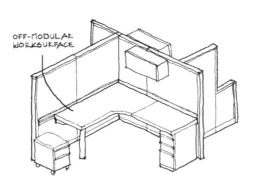

a. Off-modular panel systems and horizontal hanging channels provide greater flexibility for planning non-typical layouts or T-connections

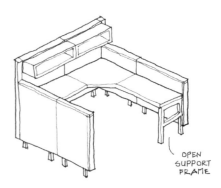

b. Contemporary panels, open-end panels, and overhead units

FIGURE 7.16 Wire and cable management solutions

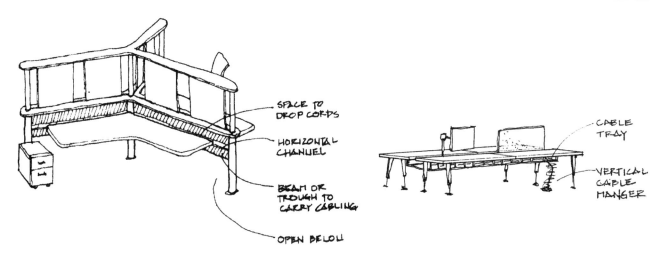

a. Post and beam systems provide great capacity
for electrical wiring through beams

b. Cable troughs below worksurfaces

Freestanding and Mobile Systems

Some clients require flexibility in their systems because the number of collaborative and team participants can increase or decrease with each new project or phase of a project. Obviously, as more people join a team, more work areas or places are needed. And the reverse is the same; as a project winds down, people go on to other projects, so fewer work areas are required.

Although conventional panel systems were designed to be reconfigured as needed, reconfiguring is still a task that takes time to disassemble and then reassemble the various panels and components. It is also a task generally performed by furniture installers. In reality, conventional workstations are fairly fixed and do not lend themselves to quick, spontaneous regroupings.

For truly flexible work areas, people, firms, and manufacturers have gravitated toward freestanding and mobile furniture. Rather than attaching the primary worksurface to the spine, worksurfaces can now be detached tables, either with or without casters. These tables are generally not much larger than 48 in. wide for easy movement. Tables may be oval, round, rectangular, or trapezoidal to abut another person's table. They can be moved to another work area for collaboration

and team projects or rotated within a work area to suit individual tastes (Fig. 7.17a).

In the past, mobile files or pedestals were specified on a limited basis as they are more expensive and have less filing storage than typical two-drawer pedestals. Plus, they were seldom moved. Now that more work is mobile, these mobile pedestals are more commonly used in offices even though they are still expensive. An added benefit is that many of these files now come with a seat cushion to double as a chair for guest seating (Fig. 7.15a).

Many panels are once again freestanding or mobile. These panels can be used for additional privacy at individual work areas or in groupings, much as folding screens were used years ago to isolate certain activities (Fig. 7.17a).

Radically New Systems

Every few years some manufacturers will bring out an "off-the-wall" system to display in their showrooms. These systems are usually on the leading edge of technology and work methods, far beyond the average workplace (Fig. 7.3 and Fig. 7.18a).

These radical systems are generally bought and used by leading firms, particularly those firms pioneering new concepts. More often these systems inspire new ideas for ways of working, associating with coworkers, and designing new spaces. It is always important for the designer to stay abreast of new trends, even if they are not immediately practical.

Current Trends

When companies relocate to new space and they have decided to purchase all new furniture, a completely contemporary approach to open work areas with all low panels and glass inserts (Fig. 7.19) and freestanding furniture is realistic, if this represents the client's requests and mode of operation. Companies often like the idea of openness, but wish to take a slightly more conservative approach somewhere between conventional cubicles and completely open, freestanding furniture. Openness and collaborative work areas can be achieved by lowering the height of some panels; eliminating end panels where possible; laying out double, triple, and quadruple work areas rather than individual

■ FIGURE 7.17 Freestanding and mobile systems

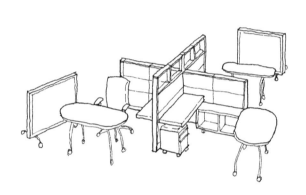

a. Isometric: detached primary worksurface and mobile panels

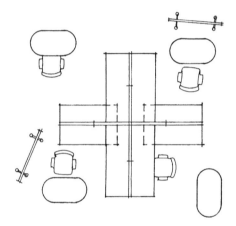

b. Plan view: typical layout using mobile worksurface and panel units

■ FIGURE 7.18 Leading-edge panel systems

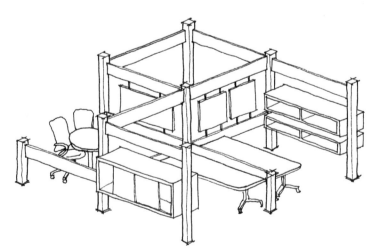

a. Isometric: post and beam system

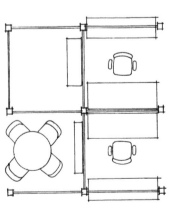

b. Plan view: typical layout using post and beam system

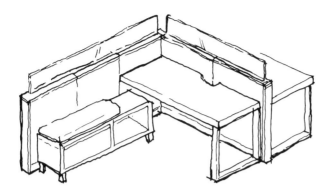

workstations; and using mobile furniture to save space or double its usage.

Even when remodeling spaces for companies with existing workstations, it is possible to incorporate new product and contemporary concepts by replacing and supplementing existing panels with lower panels or panels with some type of glazing. Panels can be eliminated and individual workstations can be rotated to achieve team work areas rather than keep individual cubicles (Fig. 7.20 and Illustrated Table 7.1e).

Overhead and Accessory Units

One of the advantages for using panel systems has been the ability to provide vertical storage or overheads above worksurfaces within easy reach of the seated occupant. Now, even though people may no longer want high panels, they are not willing to give up their convenient storage.

Manufacturers developed new vertical standards called *stanchions* or *rails* that attach to low panels, a beam, or the worksurface. Overhead bins, shelving, and paper-flow accessories are then installed onto the stanchions as desired, generally leaving open space between the worksurface and underside of the overhead unit. People can still communicate across work areas. Task lights can still be added below most overheads. Even privacy screens can be attached to the desk unit in those situations where complete openness is not desirable (Fig. 7.21a).

Planning Open Work Areas

Planning for open, freestanding, or semi-detached systems furniture proceeds in a similar manner as that for planning for conventional panel systems. First, the designer determines the functions of the work area occupants and

■ **FIGURE 7.20 Combining new concepts with existing or new contemporary panel systems**

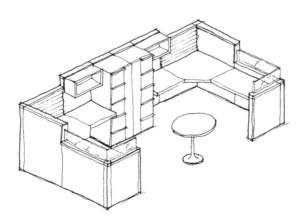

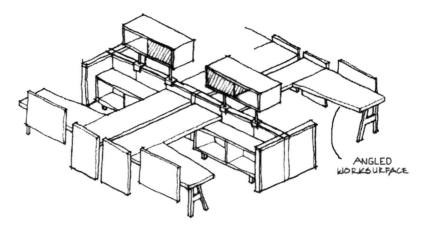

a. Overhead components on stanchions provide greater visibility

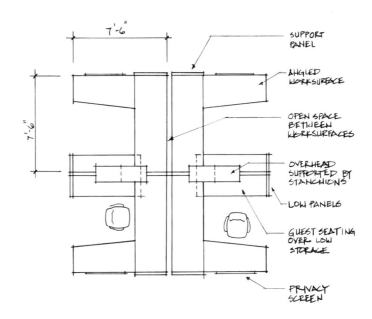

b. Plan view: typical layout using contemporary work area components

the basic square footage to be assigned to those functions. The designer then starts with the worksurface units and builds a footprint based on occupant needs. If the primary worksurface is a mobile table, the designer allows an appropriate amount of circulation space around it and then adds storage or other units in a manner similar to laying out conventional workstations (Fig. 7.17b). If a post and beam system is used, the designer should verify the length of the beam to be selected and then add components as desired (Fig. 7.18b). If all items are freestanding or

semi-detached, the designer selects and arranges the items in a suitable layout.

In most cases, footprints for contemporary systems furniture will look analogous to conventional workstation layouts (Figs. 7.21b and 7.10b). There is a primary worksurface; there is space for the occupant's chair; there may be a secondary worksurface; and there will be some type of storage, either overhead or on the floor. Even the sizes for most components of the newer systems will be the same as those of conventional systems, with the possible exception of worksurfaces. For instance, the contemporary workstation in Figure 7.19 is based on the very same footprint, IT 7.2c, as the workstations in IT 7.1a-c.

Worksurfaces

When seated at a linear worksurface, the outside edges and back corners are less accessible and not within arm's reach (Figs 4.14b and c). By "wrapping" the worksurface around the user, the outer edges become more accessible. In the interest of ergonomics, manufacturers offer numerous worksurface layouts. Even though these worksurfaces may look different on the user side, the straight-edge sides used for attaching the worksurface to the panel system conform to standard sizes. It is just the leading edges that have been curved, canted, or otherwise angled (Fig. 7.22).

HOTELING, JIT, FREE-ADDRESS, AND MOBILITY WORK AREA STYLES

In today's market, many employees are very mobile. They travel between the company office and their clients' offices. In fact, some workers spend more time on the road or in their clients' offices than in their own office space. Other people, following the US government's alternative work schedule (AWS), are working 10-hour days, four-day week schedules, or working one day a week at an alternate suburban office rather than commuting to downtown main offices. Another route offered by the US government is a true mobility work policy that allows federal workers to work remotely up to eight days in every pay period or two weeks. Still other employees spend a great deal of time in the airport, their cars, their homes, other job sites, showrooms, and convention centers—any place except their own office or workstation. Sometimes they do not see their offices for days or weeks at a time. Some firms and government agencies even encourage their on-site staff to be mobile within the office floor plate. After all, when you are connected via phone, wireless, scanning, computer network, automatic paycheck deposit, etc., there is less and less reason to actually go to the office at all or even have a permanent work area within the office space!

With a mobile workforce, to conserve floor space, companies may request that some of their staff share a station—not a double station, but

■ **FIGURE 7.22 New contemporary worksurface shapes**

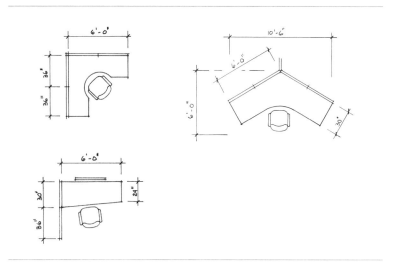

a single, unassigned station that any employee could occupy when that employee happens to be in the main office. Consider if person **A** is in the office only 25 percent of the time and person **B** is in the office 35 percent of the time, which means that any given work area is sitting empty for at least 65–75 percent of the time. Average 70 percent vacancy is a lot of rent to pay for empty space.

In theory, **A** and **B** should be able to share or use the same station, especially if **A** is in the office on Monday and Tuesday and **B** is in the office on Thursday and Friday. The key to this scenario is that the 25 percent and 35 percent time frames do not overlap—that both **A** and **B** are not in the office on the same day.

When there are a small number of employees or when employees are in the office more than 60 percent of the time, this concept of sharing cubicles is difficult due to the low ratio of total workstations. When there is a large group or whole department of people who are in the office on an average of no more than 35–60 percent of the time, then a ratio of workstations to people can be calculated to provide enough stations to handle peak times of office occupants. Depending on the total number of mobile workers and the amount of time spent out of and in the office, a ratio of work areas to people will be somewhere between one work area for every 1.5-to-3 people.

Up until approximately 2010, the primary way to assure a mobile worker that there would be a workstation available upon arriving at the office on any selected day was for the person to call into the office and talk with a live "concierge" responsible for assigning work areas. Now more and more firms are implementing reservation or booking systems whereby the worker uses a laptop or mobile app to view available work areas, make a selection for a specific seat, and then reserve the space for a day, a week, as needed or allowed by the firm. Firms may set their own guidelines as to who (departments, teams, etc.) may sit where and the longevity of the bookable time. They will also determine the specific work areas to be incorporated under the reservation system, including workstations, offices, collaborative rooms, or other areas. Guidelines will vary from firm to firm, perhaps floor to floor or from season to season, all according to each firm's designations.

Unassigned, shared workstations began to appear in the mid to late 1980s when accounting firms first realized that their auditors were spending three-to-six months off-site at client locations, then returning for a month or two in between assignments before they moved onto the next client site location. Various terms were coined or borrowed to define this alternative style of sharing work areas. At one time, *hoteling* was the term used most often, but it was not the only term. Now that many workers are more mobile, coming and going on a daily or weekly basis rather than just between assignments, the current term is *mobile workstation*.

1. **Mobile workstation**: Employees use an app to locate and reserve a work area, anywhere from a week to as little as one hour ahead of time. People either bring their laptop each time or they may be able to store it in their locker. The firm generally provides appropriate supplies, such as paper, staplers, tape, scissors, etc., in a centrally located copy/printer room.

2. **Hoteling**: Each employee checked-in with a "concierge" ahead of time to make a reservation for a work area. The concierge assigned a work area to that employee and made sure all necessary items, including files, paper, computer, etc., were placed in the assigned workstation on the day of check-in. This arrangement provided the greatest degree of control as to who was where on any given day. For firms without an electronic booking system, this may

still be a viable method for reserving work areas for their mobile workers.

3. **JIT**: JIT, or just-in-time, is an alternate term for hoteling. JIT is a concept that originated in factories in Asian countries where parts and pieces are delivered just in time, as they are needed, to avoid the costs of maintaining inventories. So too— work areas are delivered just-in-time on the day of need.

4. **Free-address**: Employees sit where they like on a first-come, first-served basis. This can be an incentive for people to get to work early, but it can also create confusion because it is difficult to find people.

5. **Airport lounge**: This term really refers to two types of layouts, both of which are found in airport club-member lounges. The first layout is a bank of telephones along a wall, now largely replaced by benching units (Fig. 7.23), that is used as a series of touch-down stations for employees to get messages, return calls, and plug in laptops. The second layout is lounge seating where employees can casually sit to discuss strategic planning ideas, now largely known as collaborative rooms and areas.

6. **Benching or touch-down stations**: Benching is similar to the bank of telephones in that there is a row of countertops or worksurfaces where anyone can sit down to make telephone calls or plug in a laptop. Yet, while telephone stations have traditionally been compact and up against a wall, bench or touch-down stations are larger and typically freestanding opposite another row of benches or stations. Benches can be assigned as in mobility and hoteling or first-come, first-served, as in the free-address style (Figure 7.23).

Planning Mobile Work Areas

Because mobile workstations are generally occupied on a short time basis, perhaps only an hour, perhaps the entire day, maybe even two days, but not on a permanent everyday basis by the same person, many firms have reduced the size of this work area to a 6 × 6 station with limited amounts of storage. After all, how much "stuff" can one person need for a day?

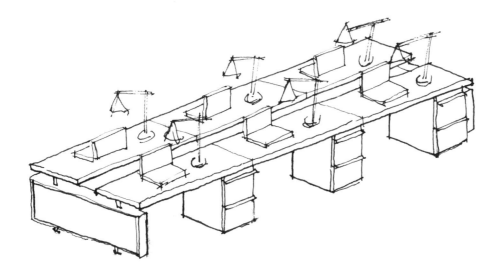

Quite often these workstations face each other (Fig. 7.24), as benching first came on the market as very long worksurfaces, approx. 30 in. by up to 10 ft. A single structural beam was able to support one worksurface on either side, appearing somewhat like tables pushed together (Fig. 7.16b). Beams could be connected to then provide worksurfaces that appeared to be 20 ft or 30 ft long, allowing at least 5 ft per seated area. These early benching systems were truly touch-down stations for sales reps and other early mobile people to come into the office, meet and greet, and have a place to make telephone calls.

Table benching is still very popular, but other methods and systems have evolved to provide similar solutions. Work areas can be very open (Figs. 7.23 and 7.24a) where worksurfaces are supported along the back and by pedestals or they can be supported by a panel system (Figs. 7.19 and 7.24b). Worksurfaces can be "divided" from the worksurfaces opposite with privacy screens or nothing at all. Storage, what storage there might be, can be fixed, as with the supporting pedestals, mobile, movable as with free-standing lateral file and cushion cabinets, or no storage at all.

Once the mobile workstation footprint is determined, planning proceeds as with other conventional or contemporary workstation planning. Some of these alternate work style concepts use the same types and sizes of workstations, either conventional or contemporary, already discussed. Others downsize or vary the station, or completely eliminate it. Space plans may or may not look different from conventional plans. It depends on the clients' needs and the type of alternative office style they feel will work best for their firm.

NEW WORK AREA FUNCTIONS

With the methodically reduced size of mobile work areas and the more open atmosphere, three new phenomena have crept into the work place and space plan:

- Collaborative or focus rooms and areas
- Lockers
- Protocols

Collaborative or Focus Rooms and Areas

For all the collaboration that workers may be demanding, people still need "alone" time. In fact, in order to collaborate, people need time to think of new ideas to share, they need time to de-stress from too much noise and stimulation, and they need time to complete and organize the items agreed to during the collaborative sessions or newly thought up ideas for the next collaborative meeting. New rooms, collaborative

■ FIGURE 7.24 Plan view: Mobile workstation layouts

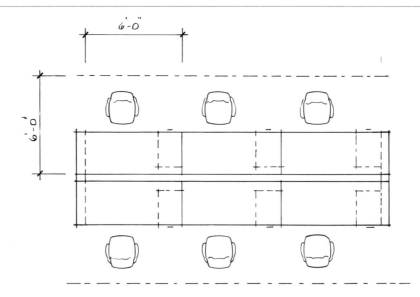

a. Touch-down stations using a beam support system – 36 NSF

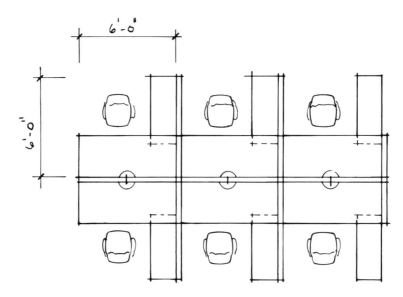

b. Touch-down stations using panel systems – 36 NSF

and quiet rooms, are now being added to new space plans (see Chapter 11).

Lockers

Even though workers may come into the office only one or two days every week or so, they need a place to hang their coat or jacket, a place to store a purse or items carried for the day, a place for personal items they might not want to bring every time they come into the office, such as a tissue box, a few snacks or an extra pair of shoes. Some of these items can easily be stored in the pedestal found in the mobile workstation, but it is not easy to hang a coat in that file drawer! Vertical lockers are a new answer for storage (see Chapter 11).

Protocols

Do I really want to sit at a workstation where two other people, who I may not even know, sat at this station yesterday and the day before? Do I really need to listen to someone talking over my head to another person behind me, even though those people can see each other and are only about 12 ft apart? Will there be enough workstations for me to find a good place to sit when I do come in? Will my manager be happy with my work when I do not come in?

Protocols will need to be established for new mobility work areas. Guidelines such as talking and quiet zones, cleaning up after oneself each day, and the ability to sit or not sit in the same workplace more than one day at a time, are essential for mobility workplace success. Each firm will need to come up with and implement their own protocols. Designers may offer ideas as to what other firms are doing, but designers do not set the rules. It is for each firm to decide how much additional work the cleaning people will need to provide with wiping down workstations each night, or the firm may decide to provide stands with "wipes." Where will you, the designer, plan the stands into the new space plan? The firm may decide to assign a locker to each staff member on a permanent basis, or lockers may be used on a daily basis only; *too bad, bring whatever you need each day that you come into the office!* Lockers may be a first come, take your pick, or the lockers may be reserved in the same manner as a work area. Each firm must decide the new protocols to install, not the designer. The designer only needs to plan the various areas based on direction from the client.

DRAFTING TYPICAL WORKSTATION LAYOUTS

Drawing *typical workstation layouts* is done in much the same way as drawing typical private office layouts (see Chapter 6). The designer must discuss with the client the amount of square footage to be assigned to employees who will occupy workstations or workstations that will function for mobility workers. In addition, it is important for the client to understand what components and storage can be accommodated within a given amount of square footage. Workstation sizes and configurations can be changed, revised, enlarged, and rotated very easily when looking at one or two typical layouts as opposed to many different layouts on a finished space plan (Fig. 7.2). As with the office typical layouts, typical workstation layouts will be included as part of the program questionnaire, and later as part of the Program Report (Chapter 12).

PROJECTS

Project #1: Draft typical workstation layouts

Layouts should continue to be based on the client profile selected for previous projects. These layouts will become part of the students' portfolios and the Program Report in Chapter 12.

1. Format information should follow the typical office drawings to provide a consistent presentation package to the client (see Chapter 6).
2. Workstation layouts may be drawn either manually or on the computer.
3. Present at least two options for each requested workstation size.
4. Graded copies can be revised and then resubmitted for additional credit.

Project #2: Draft a cluster of workstations

1. Combine 4–6 typical layouts in a cluster by sharing panels.
2. Combine two different workstation layouts into a cluster of 4–6 workstations.

8

CONFERENCE ROOMS

Conference rooms are typical in that they generally contain the same four types of items: table, chairs, credenza or other side surface, and some type of audio/visual or other communication equipment like a podium or easel. Beyond these four items, the rooms will vary widely. Many conference rooms are positioned along perimeter window walls, but they are just as likely to be found in interior locations. Conference rooms differ in formality and size, ranging from small meeting rooms that seat four to six people up to large, elaborate boardrooms that seat 30–50 people. Rooms may use different finishes or furniture depending on where each room is located within the floor plan, or rooms may be duplicated throughout the space.

Therefore, as similar as conference rooms might appear to be, they are never truly typical for various reasons:

1. Except for large multi-floor corporations that duplicate rooms from one floor to the next, many firms have a single main conference room.
2. Two to four various-sized conference rooms are added, as needed, to satisfy a mixture of requirements.

3. Beyond the basic four furniture and equipment items, additional items and amenities can vary greatly from one firm's conference rooms to the next firm's rooms or even from one conference room to the next within a given firm.

ITEMS IN A CONFERENCE ROOM

Occasionally some conference rooms will be of an informal nature or reflect a cultural difference best suited to sofas, chairs, and other types of lounge seating. One such famous meeting room is the Oval Office in the White House where the president meets with visiting dignitaries or cabinet members while sitting in an open circle of sofas and side chairs. Although soft seating is becoming more prevalent as companies move towards innovative collaborative settings, as a general rule of thumb, most US conference rooms contain a table with chairs and some type of A/V and teleconferencing equipment.

General conference room items meet the basic needs of perhaps 50 percent of a company's meetings. Other meetings may require additional items for more sophisticated presentations (Box 8.1). Based on their individual needs, each firm should have at least one conference room equipped with some or all of the optional items that meet today's technological demands. However, what works for one firm may not meet the needs of other firms.

SIZING THE ROOM

Conference rooms are "sized" around the table, or rather the number of people to be seated around the table and within the room. Most clients do not know the actual room or table size that they will need, thus it is customary for designers to ask clients how many people will attend an average meeting conducted within a given conference room (Box 8.2).

For most firms, an average of 6 to 14 people attend the majority of meetings. Therefore, many firms request two conference room sizes, a main conference room to hold 12 to 18 people and one or more smaller rooms to hold 6 to 10 people. When there are a few more people in either one of these meeting rooms, extra chairs can be brought in and squeezed around the table or placed along the walls.

In the past, meetings consisting of only two or three people were regularly held in someone's office or cubicle unless there was a reason to establish neutrality, in which case the meeting could be held in any available conference room regardless of room size. While many meetings are still held in personal work areas, as firms now provide any number of quiet rooms and collaborative areas (see Chapter 11), small group meetings are being scheduled or sought out on spontaneous occasions for these smaller areas. On rare occasions when more than 25 people attend a meeting, people are either required to stand in a crowded room or the meeting may be taken off-site. Depending on the meeting's purpose and agenda, it is often possible to rent a room at another location equipped to handle large meetings, such as a local hotel, convention center, or other organization that specializes in providing meeting or conferencing rooms for just such occasions. On the other hand, if a company consistently conducts large meetings, then a large enough room should be designed within their office space.

Table Size

The length or diameter of a table is based on the number of people to be seated around it. Although the average meeting size is stated as a range of attendees (i.e., 8 to 12 people), a table seats a specific number—8, 10, or 12 people. Unless the design calls for ganged tables, conference tables do not come in an adjustable size; they cannot be pulled apart to add leaves or extensions. Designers must make a decision to size the table for a specific number of people.

SIZING A TABLE BASED ON THE NUMBER OF PEOPLE TO BE SEATED

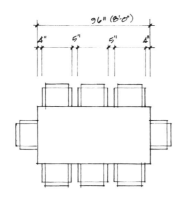

a. An 8'-0" table to seat 8 people

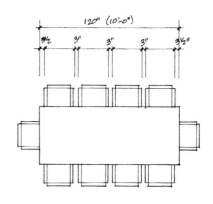

b. A 10'-0" table to seat 10 people

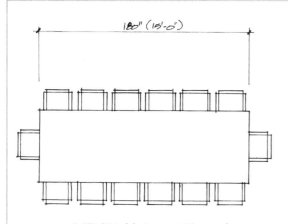

c. A 15'-0" table to seat 14 people

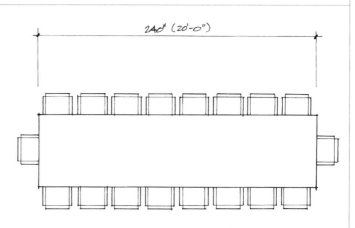

d. A 20'-0" table to seat 18 people

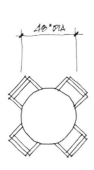

e. A 4'-0" diameter table to seat 4 people

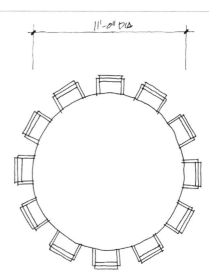

f. An 11'-0" diameter table to seat 12 people

In most situations, it is best to provide a table that will seat the greater number of people. If the range is 6 to 8, select a table to seat 8 people. If the range is 20 to 25, then select a table to seat 24 or 26 people. With round tables, it may be possible to seat an odd number of people, but a square or rectangular table will always seat an even number of people.

To some extent, the length or diameter of the table in feet equates to the number of people to be seated. For instance, a 10-foot (ft) table will effectively seat 10 people and a 48-inch (in.), or 4-ft-diameter table, will easily seat four people. As the number of people to be seated increases over 12 or 14 people, table sizes must be adjusted upward to comfortably accommodate everyone (Illustrated Table 8.1 and Boxes 8.3 and 8.4).

When selecting a table size, in addition to considering the number of people to be seated, designers must also consider the size of the chair that will be used. (See Table 4.3.) Obviously, wider chairs will require more space, and thus a longer table may be needed to provide capacity for those chairs. When the room size is limited due to building architecture or is smaller than desired due to remodeling of an existing space, thus requiring a table smaller than otherwise preferred, it may be necessary to specify smaller chairs to adequately seat the desired number of people.

Circulation

Once the table has been sized and the chairs laid out, circulation space must be added around the table. Be sure to allow space for both chair circulation and walking circulation around all four sides of the table. Approximately 30 in. should be allowed for chairs and 24–36 in. for walking (Fig. 8.1a). Sixty inches (5 ft 0 in.) overall is ideal, and 42 in. (3 ft 6 in.) is the minimum (Fig. 8.1b). As the table and room increase in size, the circulation should also increase to provide a more balanced proportion.

Other Items in the Room

Before establishing the final room size, designers should locate and place into the layout all other items that will be in the room, including separate lounge seating, credenzas, and equipment. Specific sizes and locations of these items will affect the overall room size. For example, credenzas can be located on either an end or side wall of the room, which dictate two distinct shapes and sizes of rooms (Fig. 8.2a and b). When a credenza is placed on an end wall with a 10 ft table, the room will be rectangular, approximately 22' × 14', whereas the room will be more square, 20' × 16', when the credenza is placed on a side wall (Table 8.1).

Either layout is perfectly acceptable. The selected layout will depend on the personal preference of the client or designer, the building configuration, the overall space plan, location of the conference room within the plan, and internal or external adjacency requirements of the room. When two credenzas are required, they can be planned side-by-side and probably not affect the room size, especially if they are placed on the side wall, which ordinarily has more lineal

FIGURE 8.1 Circulation

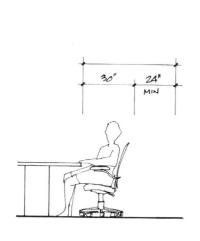

a. A seated person at a table with walking circulation behind

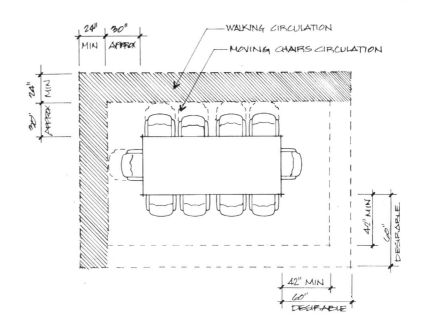

b. Plan view: chair and walking circulation

FIGURE 8.2 Plan views

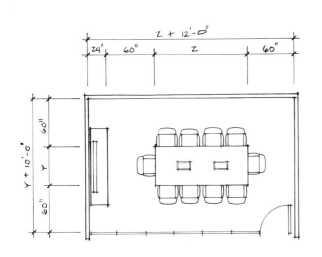

a. Adding a credenza to the conference room—end wall

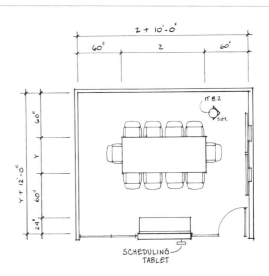

b. Adding a credenza to the conference room—side wall

TABLE 8.1 Table and room size	
10'-0" × 4'-0" TABLE AND A 24" × 72" CREDENZA	**20'-0" × 4'-0" TABLE AND A 24" × 72" CREDENZA**
A. Credenza on end wall Rm A = [Z + 12'] × [Y + 10'] Rm A = [10' + 12'] × [4' + 10'] **Room A = 22'-0" × 14'-0"**	A. Credenza on end wall Rm A = [Z + 12'] × [Y + 10'] Rm A = [20' + 12'] × [4' + 10'] **Room A = 32'-0" × 14'-0"**
B. Credenza on side wall Rm B = [Z + 10'] × [Y + 12'] Rm B = [10' + 10'] × [4' + 12'] **Room B = 20'-0" × 16'-0"**	B. Credenza on side wall Rm B = [Z + 10'] × [Y + 12'] Rm B = [20' + 10'] × [4' + 12'] **Room B = 30'-0" × 16'-0"**

Legend:
Z - Table Length
Y - Table Width

space. On the other hand, if one credenza is placed on an end wall and the other credenza is placed on the opposite end wall or a side wall, then the room size will need to be adjusted in width, length, or both width and length to properly accommodate the second credenza.

Equipment

Equipment in a conference room may range from a single telephone, generally a speakerphone that is left on the table or housed on a credenza unit until needed and then brought to the table, to the most complex videoconferencing equipment, with multiple screens, cameras, and electronic marker boards. Designers may recommend that clients consider advanced technology for one or more conference rooms, but designers do not select or specify any of the equipment. Normally, clients will work with a separate equipment vendor or audio/visual (A/V) designer, who will coordinate the equipment and equipment requirements, including power and data (P&D) and architectural elements, with the space planner.

Electrical, Data, and A/V Requirements

All equipment requires some type of electrical connection, via a standard plug into a duplex outlet, a special plug into a specially designated outlet, or a hardwire connection that permanently connects the wires to the equipment. Much of today's equipment also requires some type of data connection. Like electrical

connections, data cabling may be permanent or removable connections. Unlike electrical, which still requires some type of physical wire connection, many firms are installing wireless access points to eliminate actual data cabling connections. When cable TV is required, coax cabling will need to be installed. Additionally, there will be cabling for A/V equipment.

Often these outlets and connections are hidden within or behind architectural elements such as a junction box above the ceiling for connecting a ceiling-mounted projector. Other outlets and connections may need to be brought forward through built-in wall units or the wiring may be brought up through the floor to be connected to P&D ports within tables (see Illustrated Table 4.6b). In all cases, it is the designer's responsibility to locate the proper symbols on the P&D plan, add height requirements to locate the outlets higher than the standard 18" AFF, and any special notes such as the need for the millworker to cut a hole in the back of a cabinet to accommodate junction boxes.

Room Scheduler and Tablet

To aid with scheduling conference rooms for meeting requests, many firms have adopted an electronic system that allows employees to use either their laptop or mobile app to schedule or book designated rooms for preferred periods of time. Some systems allow the scheduling person to select from various floor plan layouts when two or more configurations of furniture are available for a given room. Generally, these systems also include a small tablet to be installed on a wall outside of each conference room door (Fig. 8.2b and 8.5a). Once a meeting is ready to start, someone, usually the person who booked the room, can key into the tablet that the room is now booked and unavailable for other meetings until such and such a time. As systems vary in their P&D requirements, some require an actual 120v duplex while others bring low-voltage electrical power through the data cabling, the designer will need to verify specific requirements with the vendor and then add the appropriate information to the construction documents.

Wall Units

As optional items are added or moved around the room at will, the conference room may begin to look disorganized and unplanned. For instance, there could be an easel in one corner, a flat-screen and audio equipment in another corner, a projector on the table, marker boards with all kinds of scribbles hanging on a wall, cords running across the floor or onto the table such as for the speakerphone, or carts placed everywhere. When these various items are shared between several conference rooms or when a particular room is in constant use, this free-will planning may be the best solution.

When the room is more formal, is seen frequently by visitors, is the only room to use the equipment, or must have a specific layout, designers may consider housing some of the movable items in a standard credenza or a built-in wall unit similar to a home entertainment center. Most commercial units are custom designed by the designer and then built by a millwork contractor using the materials specified, such as wood, plastic laminate, granite, marble, metal, etc.

Unit Size

Wall units may appear to be a single unit, but they are normally composed of several units brought to the job site and then installed to look like a single unit. Individual units can be different sizes, heights, widths, and depths, yet when installation is complete, all units should appear as a unified whole.

During initial planning stages, designers should use 24–30 in. as a good unit depth. As design development proceeds and specific equipment or other items to be housed within the units are identified, adjustments can be made as necessary. In particular, the designer will want to coordinate A/V equipment requirements with the A/V vendor. Depending on the final A/V and teleconferencing design, there can be numerous pieces of equipment such as a receiver, amplifier, or recorder, possibly over-sized, and there will be temperature control requirements, as A/V equipment tends to produce a lot of heat. Cut-outs may be required along the toe kick or back of the unit to provide ventilation, or a fan may need to be installed within the unit to cool the equipment when in use.

Built-In Units

When the wall unit is built within the room, designers must increase the room size in a manner similar to the method used to plan space for credenzas. Wall units may fill the entire length of one wall (Fig. 8.3), fill part of a wall, fill a niche (Fig. 8.4), create a niche, project into the room, etc. Some or all of the unit may be full height or credenza height; be partially or totally enclosed with hinged, bi-fold, sliding, or receding doors; have open shelving, closed shelving, or any combination as desired; include drawers that are either visible at all times or hidden behind doors; incorporate a floating ledge; etc. Because these units are custom designed, they can take any form as desired to fit the clients' requirements.

Concealed Wall Units

Although some wall units may look like entertainment centers, other wall units may be part of the wall construction or housed within a closet or room next to the conference room. Slide projectors, flat-panel screens, etc., can be set on a table or counter in an adjacent room with doors or sliding panels to cover cutouts in the common wall (Fig. 8.5). When the equipment is in use, the doors can be opened; otherwise, the doors are left closed to provide a finished look for the conference room.

This type of layout will not affect the conference room size, but designers must remember to allow space in the final plan for the equipment

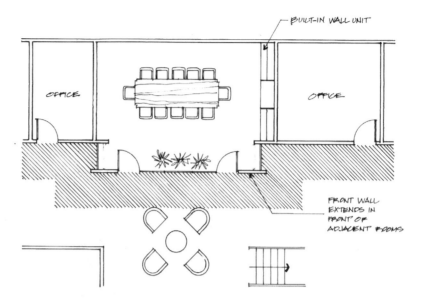

**Built-in wall unit in conference room and front glass
wall protrudes in front of adjacent room walls[1]**

room, which can be located at either end of
the conference room. There is no specific size
requirement for the room, but it is generally
about 7 ft deep. It may run along the entire width
of the conference room wall or only along a portion, as required. There may be one or two doors
into this room directly from the conference
room, the corridor, or another room.

TYPES OF CONFERENCE ROOMS

Many employees feel that there are never
enough conference rooms within their firm's
space. Yet numerous clients are reluctant to
allocate more rooms than absolutely necessary
to this function. After all, a conference room may
sit empty a good portion or all day long on any
given day. Therefore, it is essential to discuss
conferencing needs with clients and then offer
options for various types of conference rooms.

Boardrooms

Major corporations generally include a boardroom in their requirements. This room, a very
large conference room often seating anywhere
from 20 to 50 people, is usually spacious,

■ **FIGURE 8.4 Plan view**

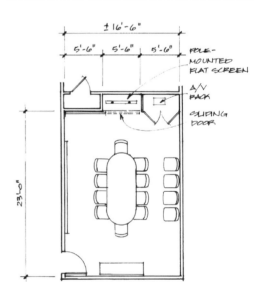

**Built-in wall unit in niche
inside conference room**

generously proportioned, and designed in great
detail, incorporating most of the optional items
found within conference rooms (Fig. 8.6).

Some corporations allow this room to be used
extensively by all employees as needed, while

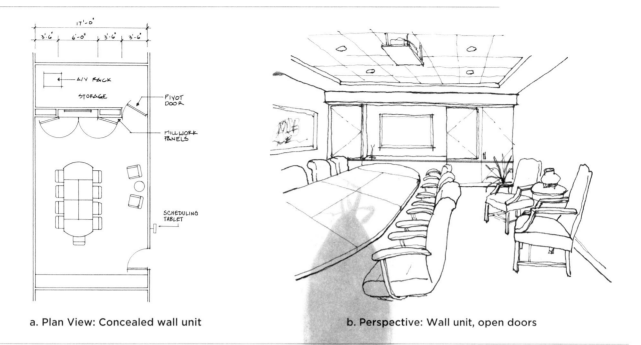

a. Plan View: Concealed wall unit   b. Perspective: Wall unit, open doors

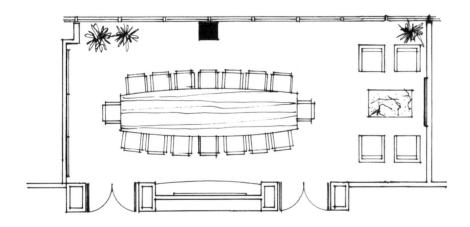

Boardrooms are generally enhanced conference rooms with high-end finishes

other companies reserve this room strictly for board and other top executive meetings, leaving it empty the rest of the time. The firm may, when this room is available for firm-wide use, require users to reserve the room in order to maintain some control over its use.

Main Conference Room

For firms and organization that do not require a huge boardroom, the main conference room is customarily placed adjacent to the reception area for several reasons. First, this is a neutral location, which tends to prevent the room from being claimed by any one group or department. Second, this location provides easy access for visitors, rather than having them walk through the office. Finally, when required, the receptionist can be used as overseer to track activities within the room.

Like the boardroom, main conference rooms often receive special design attention and detail. After all, this room is a major showcase to visitors attending meetings on site. This room is generally scheduled for major meetings or meetings planned well in advance. In some cases, firms allow this room to be used on a spontaneous basis when it is not being used for a scheduled meeting.

General Conference Rooms

It is advantageous for a firm to have several general conference rooms strategically placed throughout the space. Some of these rooms may be devoted exclusively to a given group or department if it has heavy conferencing needs, or the rooms may be available for anyone within the firm to use. Some companies always require scheduling these rooms in advance for any meeting, but with tablets at each door, often these rooms are available on a first-come, first-served basis when they are not already booked (Fig. 8.7).

Videoconferencing Rooms

As recently as 2010, videoconferencing rooms were specialized and costly rooms set up by only a handful of firms who were either on the leading edge of technology or large, multi-location firms. Now, in some form or other, videoconferencing has become the norm, moving into most conference rooms, from boardrooms down to 2 to 4-person collaborative rooms. There are basically two different options—video telepresence and video teleconferencing.

Video Telepresence

Under this scenario, rooms are designed for participants within each room to feel like they are within the very same room as participants in other rooms joined to these video conferencing meetings. Each room to be connected for participation in scheduled meetings is designed, laid out, and furnished in the exact same manner as all other rooms within the concept. A

single room can cost anywhere from $300,000 to $1 million to equip with the necessary flat-screens (often as large as the wall itself), cameras, microphones, speakers, air conditioning, lighting, room finishes, furniture, internet cabling, electrical wiring, and other interactive equipment, such as copier marker boards, desktop tablets, and ceiling copiers. Then, to use the room, clients need to provide a similar room and costs at one or more of their branch locations.

Video Teleconferencing (VTC)

A less costly but similar concept to telepresence is VTC. These rooms will also be equipped with one or more flat-screen monitors, cameras, microphones, speakers, air conditioning, lighting, furniture, internet cabling, electrical wiring, and other items as desired. The difference is that no one is trying to believe or imitate that all participants are in the same room. Cameras easily display differences in the backgrounds and furniture from one room to the next. The flat-screens may be large, or there may even be two screens, but the screens are not taking up the entire wall as to give the illusion of life size form "within" the same room. Under this scenario, many telecommuting personnel are able to participate from home or elsewhere using their laptops.

Clients will want some form of videoconferencing within their newly designed floor plan; it may be stationary within a room or rooms, or they may want flat-screens on mobile carts that can be used in collaborative seating groups. Designers will need to work with the client's vendor of choice to set up these rooms.

Training Rooms

Occasionally, smaller companies will use a conference room for training purposes when a dedicated training room does not exist. Depending on the setup of the conference room, trainees will sit around a large table or tables can be reconfigured as allowed (see Illustrated Table 4.6c). Larger firms, on the other hand, will regularly plan for separate training rooms (see Chapter 11).

Focus and Collaborative Rooms

By including several small focus or collaborative rooms within a floor plan (see Chapter 11),

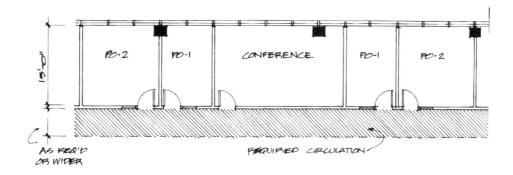

a. Perimeter window wall conference room layout in line with adjacent offices

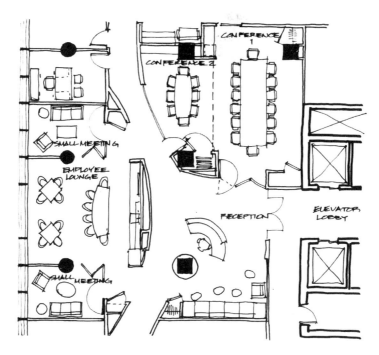

b. Conference room layout as an unusual shape[2]

firms are able to provide more meeting spaces as requested by employees yet keep unused, large conferencing spaces to a minimum. This is a new type of room that should be explained to and explored with the client.

CONFERENCE ROOM LAYOUTS

As with any room, office, or area, conference rooms can be positioned along a window wall or in the interior space. There are opposing views about which location is best.

Window Location

To position a conference room along a window wall is to "solicit" comments from most visitors as they enter the room, even when the view from the windows is only mediocre. Windows act like magnets in their ability to automatically draw people to them. Employees also enjoy stepping into the conference room from time to time to gaze out the windows.

Windows provide natural daylight, which can be very welcoming in a room full of people or for people who otherwise occupy interior space. Windows also provide an open, relaxed atmosphere.

Room Width

When positioned along window walls, all of the same guidelines and restrictions discussed in Chapter 6 regarding room envelopes apply to the conference room. In curtain wall buildings, based on window mullion widths of 5 ft OC, the width or length of a conference room will be 15 ft, 20 ft, 25 ft, etc. In solid-wall facade construction, conference rooms can be any width that works with the window spacings and overall floor plan.

Room Depth

The room depth for window wall conference rooms will often be the same depth as adjacent office depths (Fig. 8.7a). This provides a clean line along the front walls to form a straight corridor or aisle. However, as with every aspect of design, designers should not restrict the layout to conform to general guidelines when there is an opportunity to provide a better or more interesting layout (Fig. 8.3 and 8.7b).

Blackout or Added Light Provisions

A potential drawback for placing conference rooms on the window wall is the need to darken a room when videoconferencing or when videos, overheads, slides, or other electronic media are used. Lights can be turned off, but rooms receiving natural daylight will often not be dark enough. Design solutions are available in the form of blackout draperies or other heavy window treatments. Some options can be expensive, in which case, clients may use normal draperies that can darken a room but not provide complete blackout. In other situations, clients will request complete blackout provisions, which can include black-lined draperies, shutters, rolling screens, or shades. This is an opportunity for designers to put their creative ideas in play.

Conversely, under the new green construction codes (see Box 14.3), for all rooms along

perimeter window walls, the lights will automatically be dimmed based on the amount of daylight streaming into the space. Currently, conference rooms are not listed under the exception provisions; thus, designers will need to seek a variance to install light control overrides in order to turn light fixtures on at 100 percent brightness when needed for visual presentations.

Interior Location

When conference rooms are planned within the interior space, they can be any size and shape that meet clients' needs (Fig. 8.7b). Of course, certain building restrictions such as interior columns or core-to-window depth must be taken into consideration; otherwise, interior conference rooms can be sized and located within the plan as desired. Interior locations can also provide complete blackout conditions or full light fixture brightness for visual presentations without the added costs of providing special provisions as windowed conference rooms.

Another means for reducing costs in interior rooms is to install motion sensors for light fixtures. As long as the room remains unoccupied, light fixtures remain off, but turn on immediately, based on motion, once someone enters the room. After the meeting has ended, with no persons any longer in the room, or lack of motion, the light fixtures will automatically turn off, based on a pre-set time delay. Although this is not a green energy code requirement, IgCC requires motion sensors only in stairwells, storage rooms, and parking garages (Box 14.3). GSA compels all government owned and leased spaces to install motion sensors for sporadically used rooms, such as conference, copy, and file rooms. Many commercial firms are also implementing this practice.

Interior Glazing Walls

Regardless of whether a conference room is located on the window wall or is an interior room, many conference rooms have at least one or part of one interior glazed wall. Glazing may be clear, sandblasted, etched, silk screened, framed, frameless, full height, partial height, or any myriad of combinations as designed by the designer. This architectural touch provides a feeling of accessibility and openness. Additionally, potential users of the room can see if the room is occupied without having to open the door, which can be distracting to those meeting in the room. Finally, natural daylight can pass through the glazing into the balance of the space when the room is located on a perimeter wall or into the room when it is in an interior position.

Doors

Although doors customarily open into the room, when the room occupancy load exceeds 50 occupants (see Box 13.10), then the doors must swing out in the direction of egress travel. Using the SF floor area for assembly table and chairs (see Table 13.1), 15 SF times 50 occupants, when a conference room is larger than 750 SF (approx. 35 ft. by 21.5 ft., 38 ft. by 20 ft., or similar dimensions), consideration should be given as to how best to meet the out-swinging door requirement (Fig, 8.6).

Per code, there is also a requirement for at least two doors when the occupant load exceeds 49 occupants (see Box 13.3). When there are fewer than 49 occupants, only one door is required and it may swing in or out. However, based on the design of the room layout, if there are two or more doors, it may be possible to make one of these doors sliding, but both doors cannot be sliding when the room occupancy load exceeds 10 occupants (see Box 13.10).

Flat-Screen Monitor Walls

Screen sizes, 70 in., 90 in., refer to the diagonal dimension, yet when planning, designers need to concern themselves with the actual width and height of the screen along with the depth of the both the screen and the bracket for mounting the screen on the wall (Table 8.2). Exact dimensions need to be verified with the A/V vendor, but, for instance, two side-by-side 60 in. monitors require between 9-to-10 lineal feet of wall space. If the room door opens against the same wall, to avoid conflict of door and screen, another four to five feet of wall space is needed, thus requiring a room to be at least 14-to-15 ft deep. Additionally, the monitors will be offset with the center of the room. The offset may not be an issue when a credenza is planned along a side wall (Fig. 8.2b), but during

TABLE 8.2 Flat-Screen Monitor Dimensions

STYLE (DIAGONAL)	WIDTH	HEIGHT	DEPTH
60"	54"–55"	32"–33"	2"–3"
70"	62"–64"	36"–38"	3"–4"
80"	73"–75"	44"–45"	3"–4"
90"	81"–84"	47"–50"	4"–5"

DD the ceiling will also need to be designed offset in order to align the light fixtures above the table. To prevent this scenario, whenever possible, it may be better to lay out the room with the door located on a wall opposite the monitor wall (Fig. 8.2a).

Installation of Flat-Screen Monitors

Some screens are as thin as two or three inches, but mounting brackets often add another two to three inches for an overall depth of at least five inches. According to code (see Box 5.4), except for handrails, no other objects may protrude four or more inches from the wall. Thus, even under the thinnest of conditions, flat-screens cannot be mounted on a wall without some type of designed treatment.

1. Recess the mounting brackets into the wall (Illustrated Table 8.2a, b and c). This option will probably entail a thicker wall using 4–6 in. stubs vs. the typical 2½ in. studs.
2. Build a low wall along the face of the monitor wall (Illustrated Table 8.2d, e, and f). This option may still use a thicker monitor wall to house recessed brackets, or the low wall may be thick enough to accommodate the overall depth of the monitor plus the brackets.
3. Build a double wall with a cutout in the front wall to frame the monitor, and recess or mount the brackets in the back wall (Illustrated Table 8.2g, h, and i).
4. Permanently place a credenza or built-in counter, with the lower edge no more than 27 in. above the floor (see Box 5.4), on the

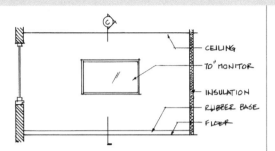

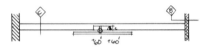

a. ELEVATION: Flat-screen monitor with recessed bracket box in wall behind

b. PLAN VIEW: Flat-screen monitor with recessed bracket box in 5" wall behind

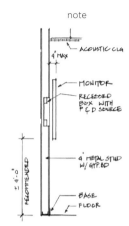

c. Cross-section: 5" thick wall with recessed bracket box

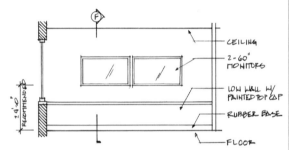

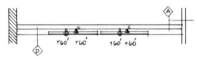

d. ELEVATION: Two flat-screen monitors with low wall below

e. PLAN VIEW: Two flat-screen monitors with low wall below

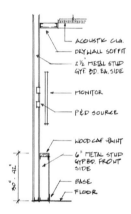

f. Cross-section: Typical wall with low wall in front

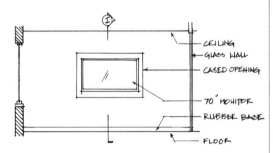

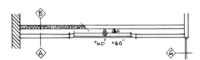

g. ELEVATION: Flat-screen monitor recessed in double wall

h. PLAN VIEW: Flat-screen monitor recessed in double wall

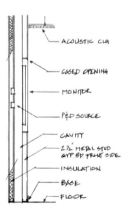

i. Cross-section: Double wall with cased opening in front wall

ILLUSTRATED Table 8.2 Wall Details for Flat-Screen Monitor Installations, *continued*

LEGEND

Ⓐ	A. 2½" metal stud with gyp bd. on each side	⊕	Duplex Outlet
Ⓑ	B. 2½" metal stud with insulation and gyp bd. on each side	⊕	Quadraplex Outlet
Ⓒ	C. 4" metal stud with gyp bd. on each side	◄	Data jack
Ⓓ	D. 6" metal stud for low wall with wood cap	◄ᶜ	Data jack with coax cable
Ⓖ	G. ½" clear tempered glass	▯ᴬⱽ	2-gang box for AV outlets

wall below any monitor that protrudes more than 4 in. from the wall (Fig. 8.2a).

Acoustics

It is important to plan for and address acoustical aspects within conference rooms. There may be numerous people, sometimes talking at the same time, people on dial-in (with speech coming through speakers), microphone amplification, TV and other A/V sounds, also coming through speakers and general movement of bodies and chairs. All of this sound either travels through walls and ceilings or is reflected back into the room, depending on the materials composing the walls and ceilings of the room. Glass, drywall and other hard surfaces such as marker boards, wood, and leather reflect sound back into the room, while acoustic ceiling tiles, fabric textiles, and insulation absorb sound. Openings within walls or ceiling transmit sound into the next room. Designers should plan to utilize a combination of materials to balance the amount of sound within each room. The quality and type of A/V equipment can also affect the sound quality.

Drywall ceilings provide a "more expensive look," but when too much sound is reflected back into the room, dial-in callers may experience noise distortions through the microphones. A combination of drywall soffits and some acoustic tiles will provide both the desired "look" and acoustic properties for absorbing noise.

Although drywall reflects sound, noise easily travels through openings cut in the walls for outlets and bracket boxes, and up-and-over walls that are installed to the underside of ceilings where acoustic tiles are installed over the top of the wall, thus potentially creating unwanted distractions for people occupying work areas adjacent to conference rooms. To reduce some of this travel noise, electricians can caulk around outlet boxes to seal open spaces, insulation can be installed within wall cavities, or the walls can be constructed to go through the ceiling so that the ceiling stops within the room (see Illustrated Table 8.2c and i).

Finishes

Because smaller, 6- to 10-person conference rooms are customarily used for informal or interoffice meetings, these smaller rooms will probably use manufacturers' standard products and be finished in lower- to medium-priced materials (Chapter 4).

As conference rooms increase in size and public visibility, their overall appearances tend be more elaborate; the rooms are more spacious, and finishes are often upgraded. Main conference rooms frequently serve as a focal point, clearly visible to visitors as they enter the reception area (Fig. 8.7b). Tables larger than 12 ft long may be custom designed, and much attention is given to all details of the room, table, chairs, fabrics, finishes, flooring, walls, etc. This room presents a valuable opportunity for design creativity and usually becomes part of the designer's showcase for the project.

DRAFTING CONFERENCE ROOM LAYOUTS

To many people, conference rooms are the second most important part of the total office space after their own work area or office. Even though there are no truly typical conference rooms, and the room size or layout may easily change in the final space plan, it is often beneficial to include one or two "typical" conference room layouts (Fig. 8.8) in the typical office and workstation layout package given to the client at the time of distributing the program questionnaires.

▪ FIGURE 8.8 Handout: Typical conference room layout

ML DESIGN

Client Name

- (1) 48 × 72 table
- (6) chairs
- (1) 24 × 60 telephone cabinet
- (1) marker board
- (1) plant

C-1   CONFERENCE ROOM (6 people)
OPTION A   225 SF

SCALE: 1/4" = 1'-0"
DATE:

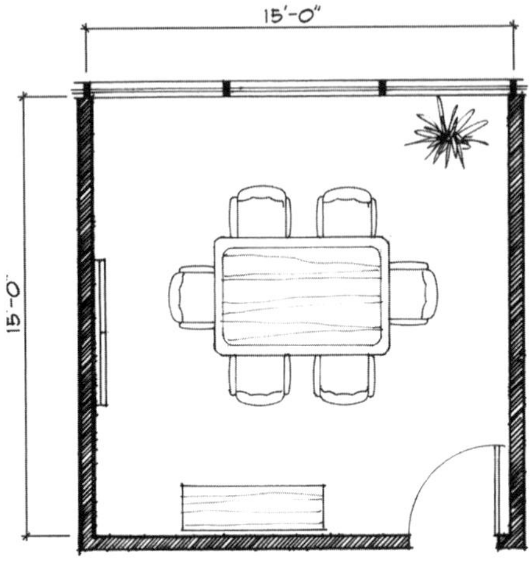

PROJECT

Project: Draft conference room layouts

Layouts should continue to be based on the client profile selected for previous projects. These layouts will be used in Chapter 12 to calculate parts of the Program Report.

1. Format the information to follow the typical office drawings to provide a consistent presentation package for the client (see Chapter 6, "Drafting Typical PO Layouts").

2. Conference room layouts may be drawn either manually or electronically.

3. Present at least two options for each requested conference room size.

4. Graded copies can be revised and then resubmitted for additional credit.

9

RECEPTION AREAS OR ROOMS

Each reception area is distinctive: it reflects the needs and personality of the firm for which it is designed. Businesses want to make a positive impression on new or prospective clients, the general public, and other personnel who cross their threshold. They want visitors to come back and feel that they will enjoy returning, to stay loyal, and to tell associates and others about this great firm. Customarily, this influence is created by the visual impact of the reception area or room, usually the first room most visitors enter when calling on a firm for the first time and each time they return. Thus, reception areas or rooms are not "typical."

Although each reception room may contain a receptionist as well as other similar items such as a desk or counter, guest or lounge seating, company logo or artwork, and a magazine table, each room will be unique in style, size, location, layout, furniture, and finishes (Box 9.1). Even when firms implement corporate-wide branding, the final layout of the reception room may still vary from one location to the next due to the building configuration, the area of the country in which the office is located, the program requirements of the specific location, and other variables. There are some useful similarities to consider and guidelines for laying out reception areas, but these are only guidelines. It is up to designers to apply their creative intuition, design knowledge, and experience to reflect understanding of their clients' public image desires—to make each reception area one of a kind.

RECEPTION ROOM SPATIAL QUALITIES

Firms have assorted visitor requirements, diverse natures of business, distinct philosophies, and individual financial assessments. They may have very few visitors, they may be able to adhere closely to their appointment schedules so that visitors will sit for only a minute or two and then go in for their appointment, leaving that seat available for the next visitor, or visitors may pile up in the reception area awaiting their appointments. For some firms, a smaller reception area may be sufficient, with *smaller* being a subjective term. Other firms have many visitors or long waiting periods, thus requiring more seating and a larger reception room. Some firms wish to provide a large, gracious reception area for a grand ambience even when there are only a few guest chairs, whereas other firms view this as a waste of space and rent money.

RECEPTION DESKS

For the majority of offices, it is customary to have a receptionist in the main entry, or reception area, into the office suite. When tenants occupy several floors, they may have a main receptionist on the primary visitor floor and one or more secondary receptionists on additional floors, as needed, for such departments as the office administration area. Should a firm occupy an entire building, this area may be in on the ground or main floor of the building, or the building lobby area, at which point it might be replaced with a security guard desk.

For first-time visitors, and even for returning visitors who may know the person to be visited and the location of that person's office, protocol is for the visitor to greet the receptionist and let the receptionist notify the staff member that a guest is in the reception area. Visitors will then either wait in the reception area until someone comes to escort them or they will proceed to the appropriate office when permission is given.

The receptionist or reception desk may be located anywhere within the room based on clients' preferences, the symmetrical or asymmetrical balance of the design, the shape of the room, the overall layout pattern for the entire plan, or any myriad of design concepts. Desks can be located directly in front of the entry door (Fig. 9.1a and b) or to one side or the other (Fig. 9.1c and d). The final desk location should work with the overall design and space plan and afford an easy view of the entry door.

Desk Styles

Desk styles can be traditional, transitional, or contemporary. Whether selecting a standard product or custom designing this piece of

FIGURE 9.1 Plan views: Reception rooms

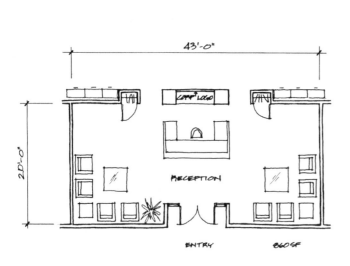

a. Symmetrical layout for reception room

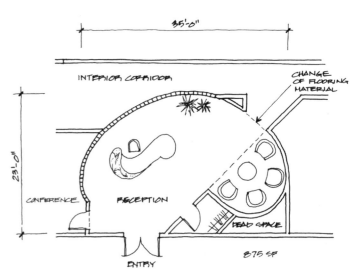

b. Unusually-shaped reception room layout

furniture, designers will want to ensure that it works with the rest of the firm's overall design, as this is often the first design item that visitors see when entering an office suite.

Desk Size

Reception desks are generally oversized or larger than standard office desks, partly because a larger desk will look proportionally better in a spacious reception room and partly because of the functional needs of the receptionist. Many receptionists serve as an additional administrative assistant, telephone operator, office manager, billing person, or any of the other positions within the firm. As such, they often need increased workspace for multitasking. Even when the receptionist serves solely as a receptionist, a computer, telephone console, message slots, etc., will still be needed, thus requiring plenty of worksurface. When a firm is quite large or has many visitors, it may have two receptionists sharing the desk. Although specific design details will vary, dimensions for reception desks are fairly consistent from one desk to the next desk (Table 9.1).

Desk Height

The worksurface is a standard desk height of 29–30 inches (in.), but the front and sides of the desk are customarily elevated above the worksurface to approximately 42 in. above finished floor (AFF) for several reasons:

1. Raised fronts obscure accessories such as staplers, tape dispensers, telephone, etc. from general view.
2. Raised fronts provide support for a standing height ledge, also known as a transaction shelf, used by visitors to sign in or for placement of special accessories, such as the firm's name plaque, flower bouquets, etc.

Desk Profile

When selecting reception desks, it is important to keep two conditions in mind. First, when people are standing, their toes protrude in front of their body. Because people (visitors) walk directly up to the desk, there should be either a natural toe kick or a durable material installed along the base of the desk front (Fig. 9.2 and Illustrated Table 9.1a).

Second, a portion of the desk front, ledge, or side needs to be lowered to standard desk height, or 34 in. maximum, to meet ADA code requirements for accessibility for a side approach (Fig. 9.3a and b).

Materials and Finishes

Reception desks are designed and constructed using many different materials and finishes,

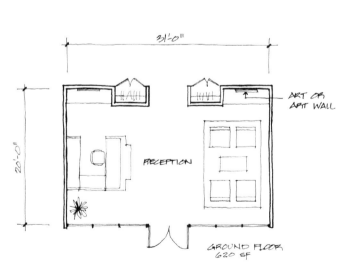

c. Asymmetrical layout for reception room on ground floor

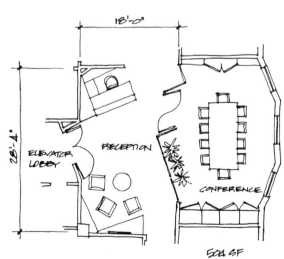

d. Angled reception room layout[1]

TABLE 9.1 Reception Desk Dimensions					
DEPTHS		**HEIGHTS**		**WIDTH**	
Ledge	9"–14"	Ledge	34" or 38"–44"	1 person	8'–10'
Worksurface	28"–30"	Worksurface	29"–30"	2 people	12'–15'
Overall	36"–42"				

often with several diverse materials used on the same desk. Some materials, such as metal, can be used as both the means of construction and the final finish, whereas other materials, such as fabric or leather, are applied over substrate construction. This provides designers with an opportunity to combine several design features. Popular desk finishes and materials include wood, metal, glass block, slate tile, Corian, marble, granite, plastic laminate, leather, fabric, and paint.

Manufacturers' Standard Desks

Many manufacturers provide several reception desk styles as companion pieces to their standard casegoods or private office desk lines. Credenzas, returns, or U-shapes can be added to the layout as needed.

Panel Systems

Another option for the receptionist's work area is to use panel systems. A unit can be dressed up with wood veneer, wood top caps, and custom-designed fabrics (Fig. 9.3a) or make a bold statement using stainless steel base caps and translucent resin privacy panels.

Custom Desks

Because reception desks are such highly visible pieces of furniture, many firms are willing to spend extra money to have a desk custom designed specifically for their office suites, even though a single desk can easily cost $10,000 or more. Custom designs allow designers to incorporate architectural details used throughout the space into the desk or to design an unusual or unique desk that will stand out within the design envelope (Fig. 9.3b).

As with conference tables, seaming, joints, and elevator sizes must be considered when designing a custom desk. Either a millwork shop or furniture manufacturer can fabricate the desk off-site and then bring it to the job site for installation. Sometimes the desk is secured firmly in place as if it was part of the architecture, or it can be freestanding and movable like other pieces of furniture. Alternatively, the desk can be built partially on-site using construction materials such as drywall or glass blocks as the structural support, and then a worksurface and other finishes and accoutrements can be installed.

Depending on the overall design concept, desk front elevations and cross-sections can be designed using several methods of construction. Four primary cross-sections include:

1. Flush front: The ledge hangs or cantilevers entirely over the worksurface. There is no toe kick, thus allowing the desk front to form a continuous straight line down to the floor. This will provide

■ FIGURE 9.2 Standing profile and toes

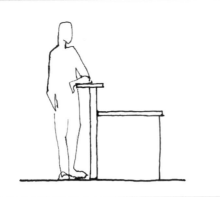

■ **FIGURE 9.3 Reception desks**

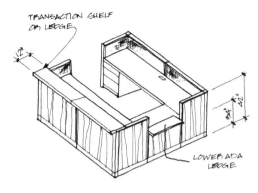

a. Panel systems reception desk
with transaction shelf

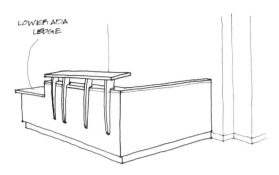

b. Custom-designed reception desk
with lower ADA accessibility ledge

a contemporary, sleek look (Illustrated Table 9.1a).

2. Overhang: The ledge straddles the vertical support with part of the ledge projecting over the worksurface and part of the ledge projecting over the desk front. An overhanging ledge provides a natural, albeit elevated, toe kick (Illustrated Table 9.1b).

3. Toe kick: A specific toe kick can be incorporated into the desk similar to a toe kick under kitchen cabinets. The ledge can be flush with the front of the desk or the inside edge, or it can straddle the vertical support. An advantage to this particular profile is the ability to run electrical wires through the cavity (Illustrated Table 9.1c).

4. Recessed: A recessed profile is similar to desks with recessed fronts. It requires the greatest depth to accommodate a ledge cantilevered in front of the worksurface (Illustrated Table 9.1d).

Desk Plan View

In plan view, many desk profiles look the same, with the primary difference being the actual scaled depth or shape of the desk (Illustrated Table 9.1e–h). For initial space planning when a desk will be custom designed, a general size and shape, such as a 36 × 96 desk, can be drawn. However, as soon as the desk has been designed and approved by the client, the actual size and shape of the desk should be drafted onto the space plan to ensure that it will fit into the area as planned.

Reception Counters

Occasionally, businesses need an exceptionally long reception counter, such as in a permit office where each discipline has a separate section along the desk or counter. Any reception desk option can easily be expanded or lengthened as needed to meet a business's particular requirements (Fig. 9.4a and b). Some organizations prefer fully built-in counters and others prefer panel systems or a combination of both.

SEATING

Seating serves both a practical and aesthetic purpose. Depending on the nature of the client's business, these attributes may be equally important or one may outweigh the other. Public service organizations, such as a permit office, are probably looking for durable materials and finishes, and a layout that maximizes the number of occupants that can be seated within the reception or waiting area. On the other hand, many private sector organizations may be looking for an aesthetic statement for seating that reflects the nature of their business.

Seating Selections

As already discussed in Chapter 4, sofas are seldom specified in commercial offices. Instead, either medium-sized, multiple-seating chairs or over-sized lounge chairs are specified for reception areas. There are many styles from which to choose the perfect chair for the designed space. Some lounge chairs are classics designed years

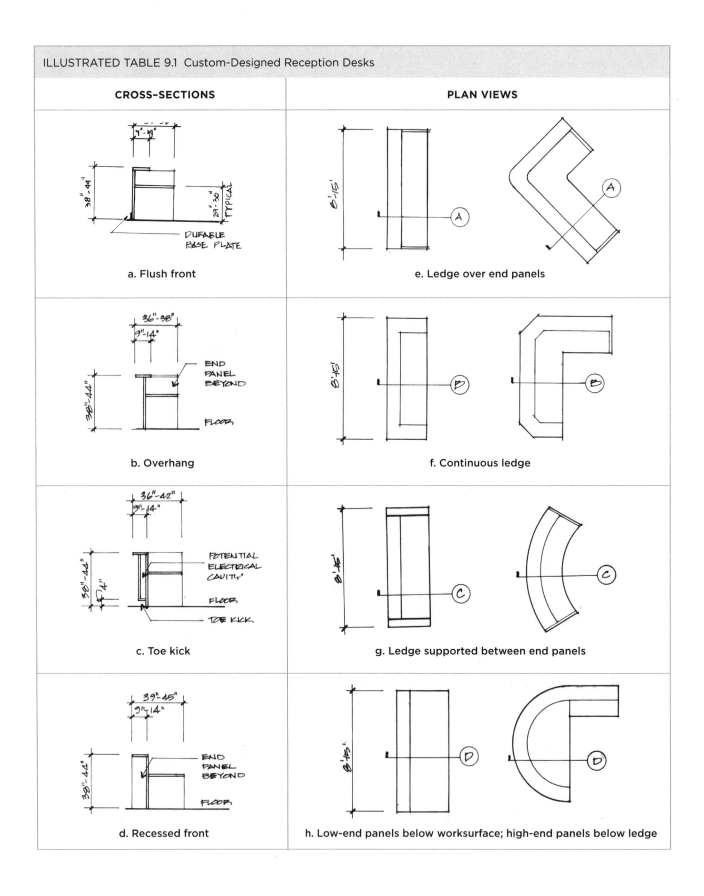

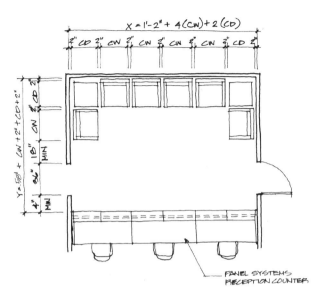

**a. Quantity and/or size of chairs
determines reception room size**

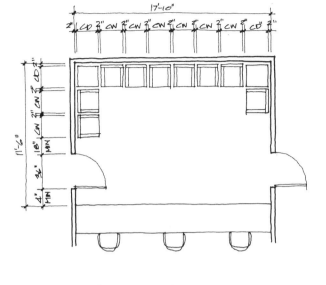

**b. Room size determines
quantity and/or size of chairs**

ago by such famed designers as Le Corbusier, Mies van der Rohe, and Eames. Naturally, these are some of the more expensive options. Because they are not affordable for many firms, over the years these classics have been "knocked-off" and sold at lower prices. It is up to each designer and client to assess the importance of practicality, design purity, and budget when deciding whether to use original or knock-off pieces of furniture or whether to choose something else entirely.

Besides the classics and their knock-offs, there are many other styles and selections for reception seating. Often, it is possible to find the right chair that visually reflects the architectural design. At other times, the chair may be selected first and then influence the office design.

Multiple-Seating Layouts

When multiple seating is required, chairs are systematically placed along the walls within a reception room to achieve greater density. There are two ways to plan room size and chair quantities:

1. The size and number of chairs will determine the room size.
2. An existing room size will determine the number or size of chairs.

When the quantity and type of seating is known, designers can draw a quick sketch for a furniture layout and then position walls and doors around the furniture, much like sizing conference rooms. Of course, when there are more chairs or if the chairs are larger, the room will be larger; and when there are fewer chairs or the chairs are smaller, the room can be smaller (Fig. 9.4a and Table 9.2).

For rooms that already exist, the number of chairs that can be arranged within the room depends on the size of the chair. Clearly, fewer chairs can be placed within the room when a large-sized chair is used (Fig. 9.4b). Each layout is based on the needs of the individual client (Table 9.3).

Corporate Reception Seating Layouts

Unless the firm and reception room are very large, most corporate reception rooms have between two and six chairs. Seating may be positioned anywhere within the reception area. A popular layout is a pair of chairs opposite another pair of chairs, with a coffee table between them (Fig. 9.5a). Another popular layout is an L-shape that may or may not include a coffee table (Fig. 9.5b). The designer may wish to soften the layout by using a round coffee table

TABLE 9.2 Room Size Based on Chair Size	

| CW = chair width |
| CD = chair depth |
| QW = quantity across |
| QD = quantity down |
| SP = space between chairs or wall |
| NSP = number of spaces |

Multiple Seating Chairs: Quantity—6
(See Chapter 4, Illustrated Table 4.9d)

room width = (CW × QW) + (CD × QD) + (SP × NSP)
room depth = Aisle width / door clearance + CW + CD + (SP × NSP)

Chair A:
Large lounge: 34-1/2"w × 31"d
17'-10" (214") = (34-1/2 × 4) + (31 × 2) + (2 × 7)
10'-9-1/2" (129-1/2") = 4" MIN + 36" + 18" MIN + 34-1/2
                                      + 31 + (2 × 2)

Room Size: **17'-10"w × 10'-9 1/2"d MIN**

Chair B:
Small lounge: 24"w × 26"d
13'-6" (162") = (24 × 4) + (26 × 2) + (2 × 7)
9'-6" (114") = 4" MIN + 36" + 18" MIN + 24 + 26 + (2 × 2)

Room Size: **13'-6"w × 9'-6"d MIN**

TABLE 9.3 Quantity of Chairs Based on Chair Size	
Room Size:	17'-10" × 11'-6"
Chair A:	
Large lounge:	34-1/2"w × 31"d
Quantity: 6	
Chair B:	
Small lounge:	24"w × 26"d
Quantity: 8	

with an X-layout (Fig. 9.5c). Although these layouts illustrate different chair types, all three layouts could use the same chair.

These seating layouts, or groupings, generally require generous amounts of open space around all sides (Fig. 9.1c). Groupings may fit in a corner or along one wall, but designers must envision the overall scale of the room. Visitors do not want to feel as though they are walking into a room of wall-to-wall furniture. Reception rooms are one of the few areas within the office suite for which firms may be willing to provide extra amounts of space, so designers should take advantage of the opportunity.

When the room does not allow for such generous layouts, the chairs may be split into smaller groups, such as a pair of wingbacks and an end table along one wall (Fig. 9.5d). Finally, although the majority of designers use large lounge seating, this is not an absolute. Smaller-scale lounge chairs or side chairs can also be used, either as the only selection of chairs or as seating in addition to the larger lounge pieces (Fig. 9.5e and Chapter 2 photo).

OTHER FURNITURE AND EQUIPMENT

Other furniture may be added to reception rooms as needed or desired. This includes all sorts of tables: coffee, end, side, corner, or console. It also includes hutches, credenzas, bookcases, display cases, curio cabinets, kiosks, and more. These items come in many sizes, finishes, colors, materials, and styles. Pieces may be arranged in any manner that is appropriate to the design, scale of the room, or overall layout.

A single large flat-screen TV or a group of multiple smaller-screen TVs is fast becoming a norm in many reception areas. Screens may simply be hung on any available wall. However, for a coordinated design look, it is better to incorporate the screens in wall niches, hanging bars, framing stand-off systems, freestanding kiosks, or shelving designed specifically for the flat-screen.

COMPANY LOGO AND NAME

Most companies display their name and/or logo at least once near the entry doors or in the reception area. As a rule, designers do not have any control over the style of the company name or logo. However, by planning for this display, designers can control the overall aesthetic appearance of the reception and entry areas. The name and logo may be displayed in several ways in areas including, but not limited to, the following:

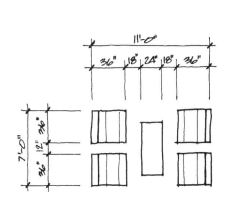

a. Two pairs of lounge chairs
opposite each other

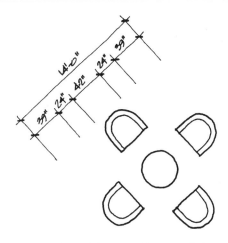

c. X-shaped layout of lounge chairs

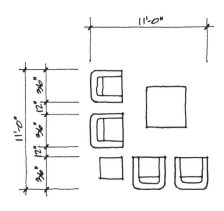

b. L-shaped layout of lounge chairs

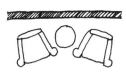

d. Pair of large chairs

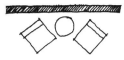

e. Pair of small chairs

- On the entry door(s) (see Illustrated Table 14.1b)
- To the left or right of the entry door (see Illustrated Table 14.1a)
- On a billboard outside the building
- On an exterior window
- On interior glazing
- In the elevator lobby
- On a reception room wall
- Behind the reception desk
- As a movable plaque
- As part of the floor material

Client Approval

Before actually incorporating a firm's name or logo into the design, designers must always inquire about the company's standards and regulations for using these items. Most companies have very specific standards.

Designers must always be considerate, respectful, and flexible in this area of design to meet each firm's requirements regarding the use of their name and logo. Once use, placement, and design of the name and logo have been discussed, reviewed, and approved by their client, designers should then ask for camera-ready artwork to be used for any final fabrication.

Materials and Finishes

As with all other items discussed thus far, many materials and finishes can be used for fabrication of signage for the company name or logo. Materials can serve as both the finished display or serve as a substrate, including metals, paints, silk screens, etched glass, vinyl appliqués, marble, granite, plastics, acrylics, wood, carpet, tile, and vinyl floorings.

COAT CLOSETS

Coat closets are an optional item in a reception area, depending on the location of the firm. When I moved to Los Angeles after having practiced design in Chicago for several years, some designers laughed at one of my initial space plans for a local client. They wanted to know what this thing was in the reception room. "Well, it's a coat closet. What does it look like?" Then they wanted to know what were people supposed to do with a coat closet in sunny southern California.

For another space plan, this time a Los Angeles branch office for a Chicago-based firm, the client contact, who traveled regularly to Los Angeles from Chicago, did not care if he was the only one who would use the coat closet. The company had coat closets in Chicago. Moreover, he wanted a place to hang his coat when he traveled to Los Angeles. Their branch office, in sunny southern California, would have a coat closet.

In all aspects of the design process, it is important for designers to know or learn the codes, habits, idiosyncrasies, accepted practices, etc. for the area, city, state, and country for which the design project is being done. It is the designers' responsibility to inquire about potential differences when designing in a location other than that with which they are most familiar.

Closet Depth

Some firms prefer a walk-in closet, but the majority of closets will open into the room (Fig. 9.6a). A 2-foot (ft) clear depth is required for coats to hang straight. Allow additional depth for the door in a closed position, for an overall minimum depth of 2'-6" from the face of the closet's front wall to the face of the closet's back wall.

Closet Width

Closets will vary in width depending on the room layout, the number of anticipated visitors, whether it is used exclusively by visitors or if it is shared with employees, and the geographic climate necessity for heavy or light coats. In northern climates with heavy coats, plan for 3–4 coats for every linear foot of closet width. Approximately 18–24 winter coats can hang in a 6-ft-wide closet. By contrast, in moderate climates, 4–6 lightweight coats can hang in every linear foot of closet width, or about 24–36 coats in a 6-ft-wide closet.

Closet Doors

Bi-fold doors are very seldom used in commercial offices, and in the past, neither were

FIGURE 9.6 Closets

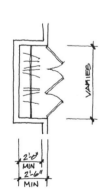

a. Plan view: Coat closet with non-paired doors

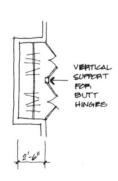

b. Plan view: Coat closet with two pairs of hinged doors

c. Plan view: Coat closet with two pairs of pivot doors

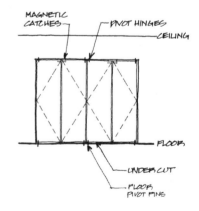

d. Elevation: Coat closet with two pairs of pivot doors

sliding doors. However, sliding door hardware and surface-mounted installations have changed and improved tremendously, so many designers are now specifying sliding doors to conserve on floor space.

Hinged doors, as either a single door or pair of doors, offer full visibility of the inside of the closet when in an open position. There are no preset closet door widths. Each individual door will be from 21–36 in. wide. A single door up to 3 ft wide can be used on smaller closets. For closets over 3 ft wide, doors should be paired, although occasionally it may be necessary to use an odd number of doors (Fig. 9.6a).

Once the closet exceeds 6 ft in width, thus requiring more than one pair of doors, the door type is often switched from hinged doors (Fig. 9.6b) to pivot doors, which allows the doors to abut without needing an intervening vertical support as with hinged doors (Fig. 9.6c).

Pivots, or small pins, placed on the top and bottom edges of the door, take the place of hinges along the side of the door. The pivots are then inserted into the overhead door jamb and floor, allowing the door to rotate or pivot along the vertical axis. Small magnets and catches are installed at the door top and overhead jamb to hold the door closed (Fig. 9.6d).

Drafting Coat Hangers

Adding hangers to the floor plan fully defines the closet. Hanger widths should not be confused with hanging coat widths of 2 ft. Remember, a coat is bigger and bulkier and hangs over the hanger.

- Metal hangers: 16 in. wide
- Wood hangers: 17 in. wide

In commercial offices, most closets are not crowded with hangers as in residential closets, so there should be fewer hangers drawn in the closet. In addition, hangers do not hang perfectly straight and parallel to the next hanger: they undulate this way and that. Draw the hangers at different angles.

Initially, draw guidelines 7 in. on either side of the coat rod. With practice, designers can estimate this distance. Then, using a straight edge, draw lines at various angles: draw about a half-dozen hangers for every 6 ft (Fig. 9.6b and c).

The hat shelf is usually not drawn on $1/8$ in. scale plans. It is optional on $1/4$ in. scale plans.

ARTWORK, PLANTS, AND ACCESSORIES

As discussed in Chapter 4, the actual selection of artwork, plants, and accessories is typically not included in the primary design contract. However, designers usually plan for the location of such items, particularly in the reception room, and indicate them on the plans to ensure the continuity of the overall design. With this knowledge, the client can later confer with the appropriate consultant or vendor for purchase of these items, thus realizing a designer's intent.

RECEPTION ROOM LAYOUTS

Because there are no typical reception room layouts, room sizes, or shapes, designers can lay out each reception area to fit the needs and desires of the client, space plan, design, and the building within which the room is to be located. Approximately 50 percent of all reception rooms are interior spaces, and the other 50 percent are located on a window wall.

Room Location

As a point of entry, the reception room should be conveniently located for direct access by both visitors and staff, with the specific location depending on whether the space is located on the ground floor or upper floor, in a high-rise or street-front building, and whether the space is on a single- or multi-tenant floor (see Chapter 13). The location of the floor or the type of building also influences whether the reception room is located as an interior room or on the window wall. Finally, when feasible, it is normally desirable for this room to be centrally located within the overall client space to eliminate the feeling of preferential treatment for one group over another.

Interior Locations

In large metropolitan areas, many businesses are located in high-rise or multi-story buildings. The reception area is accessed via the building lobby, an elevator, and possibly a public corridor to the entry door. In this situation, the reception room is generally an interior room without windows.

Interior locations offer the greatest opportunities for planning an irregularly shaped reception room. An important advantage is the ability to create a layout without having to conform to window mullion spacing, although some buildings have interior columns that may need to be incorporated (with inspiration) into the layout (see Fig. 8.7b).

Window Locations

Offices located on the ground level, a street front, or in an unusually shaped building often allow the reception room to be located along a window wall (Fig. 9.1c and 9.7a). Even in high-rise buildings, some clients wish to have reception rooms large enough to extend to a window wall (Fig. 9.7b).

Placing the reception room along a window wall can be both an opportunity and a challenge. Windows can provide lots of natural daylight and expansive views. Windows can also allow outsiders to look in. If the windows are floor to ceiling, careful thought must be given to furniture placement along those windows (Fig. 9.1c). When the building is of curtain wall construction, the reception room dimensions must conform to the window mullions.

Once the general location of the reception room has been established, either as an interior or window location, designers begin by blocking out an area and then laying out the selected furniture items; the size or location of the blocked area can be adjusted as needed. As with seating, generous amounts of circulation are planned around the entry door and desk. Without this additional space, the room can look and feel crowded, particularly when several visitors are waiting at the same time.

Room Size

Reception areas can easily range in size from 500–1,000 square feet and larger. When the room ends up smaller than desired due to building configuration, limited amount of leased space, or other program space requirements, the amount of furniture or the furniture sizes can be adjusted downward to provide a scaled décor. Construction elements such as glass walls, perforated metals, and other translucent materials can be incorporated to provide grander or expanded illusions beyond the immediate area.

Room Shape

Reception rooms, and perhaps lunchrooms, offer the most flexible areas for creating unusual and unique room shapes. These rooms provide an opportunity to create a hexagonal room, circular or angled room, or any other shape that might be deemed appropriate for the plan, building, or client (Fig. 9.1b and d). These unusual shapes can often create pizzazz and excitement more easily than can conventional shapes, particularly on a floor plan, but it is important to envision the built space to minimize disorienting perceptions or nonfunctional dead spaces (Fig. 9.1b).

Because many clients are more comfortable with straight lines rather than curves and angles, and less space is required to lay out most items into a straight plan as opposed to a non-straight plan, the reception room or area regularly evolves into a rectilinear shape. When this is the situation, designers can use other resources such as the overall room size, window views,

▉ FIGURE 9.7 Plan views: Reception rooms

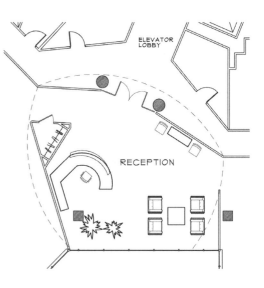

a. Reception room on window wall in oddly shaped building

construction materials, and other attributes to create a design impact.

Balance

One principle of design, *balance*, is consistently used in the reception room layout. Just as the balance of a wall can be achieved in one of two ways—*symmetrical* or *asymmetrical*—so too can the room layout be either symmetrical or asymmetrical.

Symmetrical

In a symmetrical layout, one side of the room mirrors or reflects the same layout as the other side of the room (Fig. 9.1a). These layouts usually convey a more formal ambience or structured approach. In many ways, this is an easy layout to achieve, but designers should not always take the easy way; designers must be sure the layout fits the needs of the client and the space.

Asymmetrical

With many rooms, it simply is not possible to plan an exact symmetrical layout. Asymmetrical layouts (Fig. 9.1c) can provide balanced rooms by "weighting" various items against the others. Although this layout may suggest a less rigid plan, traditional styles of furniture can still be used to achieve a traditional effect if desired by clients and designers.

Entry Door(s)

Entry door(s) are generally the first image seen when approaching a place of business. Therefore, to set the tone of desired ambience, entry doors will often be grander than other doors used throughout the office space. Options for setting entry doors apart include:

- Double doors
- A larger single door
- A door with glass sidelights
- Double doors with sidelights

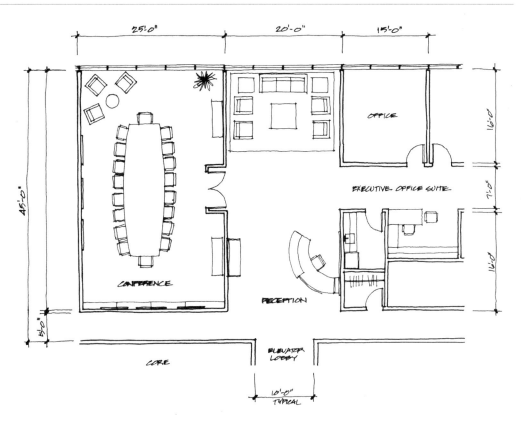

b. Large reception room on window wall in rectangular building

- Glass doors
- Metal doors
- Wrapped doors

As a rule, entry doors must swing out in the direction of travel to be in compliance with building codes (see Box 13.10). In some situations, when the office's total square footage is less than that required by code for the occupancy, egress doors may open into the space, but the codes for the amount of that square footage may vary depending on the local jurisdiction of the project and the codes being used (see Chapter 5). Designers must be familiar with or research the code requirements applicable for the locale under design in order to ensure that the main entry doors conform to code.

Security Options

Security and safety are big concerns for corporations and their employees. Corporations must pay attention to the physical safety of their employees and visitors as well as to the safety of their property and records. Depending on the nature of the business and the security needs, each company must decide on the level of security to provide for both the reception entry doors and doors within the office. Options include:

- Standard locks and keys
- Security guard
- Release/buzzer system
- Security card pass system
- Enhanced security system

Installing standard locks and keys is the primary method of securing most individual private offices and general storage rooms and constitutes the lowest level of security. A company may choose to post a guard in place of a receptionist, particularly in lobby settings, with provisions similar to those given to a typical receptionist. Or a company may choose more enhanced security systems that use cameras; monitors; voice-, hand-, or eye-recognition devices; speakers; and other paraphernalia. These systems must be coordinated between clients and a security vendor of their choice. Once clients have selected and agreed upon a system, the electrical information and device locations are given to designers for inclusion on the construction drawings.

Release or Buzzer System

With a release button, the entry door remains locked until someone inside the space releases or pushes a button that temporarily unlocks the door. This system relies on the receptionist observing the visitor before releasing the locked door. With this system, the entry door can be glass or have glass sidelights, or there may be a sliding window when the reception room is secured from the office space, such as in a record-keeping office. In situations where there is no receptionist or reception room, firms may use an audio or intercom system in place of a visual system. With either system, once the lock is released, it re-engages after the door closes or after a short time lapse. Electrical requirements for this system must be added to construction drawings.

Security Card Pass System

With a card system, visibility is not a requirement. Everyone with a security card can swipe or pass their card through the card reader, which then releases the locked door. Card readers are usually located on a wall adjacent to or near the door. Designers should preplan for the reader location during design development so that it does not interfere with the door swing. Electrical requirements are added to construction drawings.

A similar system, called a *cipher lock*, operates with a keypad instead of a card. In this case, the keypad is installed on the door near the lever. Employees do not need to carry a card. Rather, they must remember a code to punch into the pad.

Both systems allow employees to come and go at will. These systems are generally used for back-office entry doors, areas within an office space that have higher than normal security requirements, public restrooms in multi-tenant buildings, or in exit stairwells for employee convenience for tenants with offices on multiple floors. These systems are seldom used at the reception entry doors.

DRAFTING RECEPTION AREAS

In actual practice, a reception room layout is not drawn as a typical layout when the designer is producing other typical layouts. Customarily,

■ **FIGURE 9.8 Plan view: Building entry area lifted from final space plan to show to client during presentation on design development[2]**

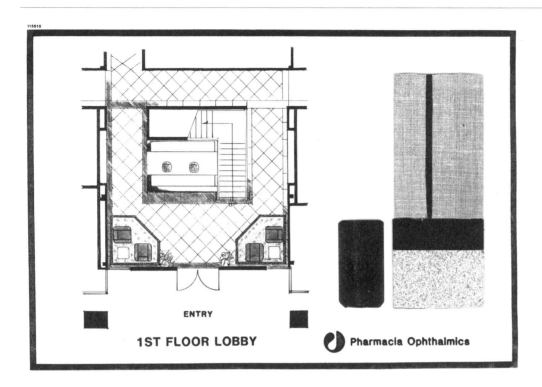

■ **FIGURE 9.8 Plan view: Building entry area lifted from final space plan to show to client during presentation on design development[2]**

ENTRY

1ST FLOOR LOBBY   **Pharmacia Ophthalmics**

reception areas are drawn only at the time of space planning the entire layout, which allows the designer to bring all kinds of concepts, skills, creativity, and knowledge into play for a coordinated and integrated whole space plan. Once the overall space has been planned and laid out, the reception area layout may be rendered and printed at a larger scale for use and display during the design development and presentation phases. This provides designers with a tool to use to explain the overall concept to the client (Fig. 9.8 and Fig. 15.5).

SIGNIFICANCE OF THE RECEPTION ROOM

Designers often lavish extra time and design effort on reception rooms. It is where a great deal of money is spent on furnishings, many aspects of the room are custom designed, and a greater amount of square footage is allotted. Even for cost-conscious clients, this is an area for which they are probably open to upgrades for the finishes and furniture.

Two ways for designers to expand their knowledge and inspire creative thought regarding reception areas are to read interior design magazines and to take field trips.

Magazine Photos

Reception areas are probably the most photographed area for all projects. Trade magazines and brochures abound with photographs of all types, sizes, colors, and layouts for reception areas. A floor plan is often included in the article. Designers should often take opportunities to study the photographs in conjunction with the floor plan to envision a two-dimensional plan and the resulting three-dimensional perspective. When doing so, observe the many details. Ask yourself whether the floor plan conveys the same spaciousness or intimacy as the finished photographed space. Do the details of the photographed space follow the visual impression received from the floor plan? Do the desk details respond to the architectural details of the room, or is the room designed as a backdrop for the artistic desk? Does the style of seating appear to belong in the room? What size is the seating? How does the seating relate to the desk or the rest of the room? How is one reception room similar to other photographed reception rooms? How are they different?

Field Trips

Naturally, it is always most beneficial to visit the real place. Whenever possible, go see business reception areas in person. Many local businesses are happy to arrange a tour of their offices.

PROJECTS

Project #1: Write a 3–4 paragraph essay

As the first point of entry into an office suite, reception rooms can create a very visual impact on visitors and employees. It is important to understand the type of ambience desired by the client.

1. Select two magazine articles displaying reception area photographs—one with a pleasing atmosphere and one with a less-than-desirable impression.

2. How are the projects similar; how are they different?

3. Why is one reception seen as pleasing while the other reception is not as exciting?

4. How can the less desirable reception area be changed for a better presentation?

Project #2: Draft reception area layouts

Even though reception area layouts are normally not included as part of the typical layout package attached to the program questionnaire, they are drawn here as part of a learning exercise. Layouts should continue to be based on the client profile selected for previous projects. These layouts will become part of the students' portfolios, and used in Chapter 12 to complete the questionnaire.

1. Format the information to follow the typical office drawings to provide a consistent presentation package for the client (see Chapter 6, "Drafting Typical PO Layouts").
2. Reception room layouts may be drawn either manually or electronically.
3. Present at least two options for a prototype reception room.
4. Include adjacent requested rooms such as a pantry or coat room as part of the layouts.
5. Graded copies can be revised and then resubmitted for additional credit.

Project #3: Field trip and short essay

Either individually or as a group, take a field trip to view two existing office spaces and reception rooms.

1. What impressions do the reception areas send out?
2. How are the two reception areas similar; how are they different?
3. Could or should one or both reception areas be changed? If yes, how and why?

10

COFFEE AND OTHER FOOD ROOMS

Recognizing employees' needs for food, casual interaction with coworkers, and breaks to renew personal energy, a majority of organizations provide some type of "food room" within their premises. Provisions for this room can range from the very simple solution of a counter with a coffeemaker to a fully supported cafeteria. Size and location of these rooms vary greatly based on the building location, size of the organization, and corporate philosophy. Each option naturally has its benefits and drawbacks. The final solution for any client's food room must take into account the company's goals and requirements and yet be within the client's financial means.

Kitchens

The term *kitchen* is very seldom used when referring to food rooms in commercial settings unless it is part of a restaurant or cafeteria. By definition, a kitchen is a place to prepare and cook food, generally using a stove, range, or oven, all of which are required by building codes to provide ventilation via an exhaust fan to the exterior of the building. In addition to a building permit, the local health department also requires a separate permit for kitchens. Therefore, food rooms are customarily referred to by other names when planned into commercial office settings.

Food Room Names

Names for food rooms vary based on size, provisions, and purpose of each room. Although they all serve the purpose of providing a place for food storage or consumption, each type of food room provides its own unique function. Clients will generally choose the types of rooms based upon their goals for its purpose. Typical food room names include:

- Pantry
- Coffee room
- Vending room
- Lunch/break room
- Employee/staff lounge
- Cafeteria

BUILDING LOCATION

The building location may greatly influence the need for a simple food room as opposed to a more elaborate food room within the firm's space. Firms who lease space in an office building located in a downtown environment with multiple food sources within easy walking distance may wish to provide a smaller food room than would a firm in a building located in a remote area. For buildings located along an interstate in rural areas or in industrial parks, the need for on-site food rooms is much greater. In these situations, firms may need to plan for a full cafeteria or adjoining restaurant within the complex when there is nothing else nearby.

SIZE OF AN ORGANIZATION

Like the building location, size of an organization can also influence the type of food room selected. Similar businesses tend to use the same food room terminology and to provide similar types of food rooms.

Firms with fewer than 10 employees will probably devote one small area in the corner of a copier or mailroom to place a coffeemaker, whereas a corporation with over 500 employees may have a dozen coffee rooms in addition to a large lunchroom. Factories usually have two separate food rooms. Often those rooms have different names: a break room for office workers and a lounge for the laborers. Schools and higher education facilities tend to request separate food rooms for students and staff. Private brokerage firms may provide full-blown cafeterias where they partially or fully finance employee lunches, but a publicly traded company is not likely to pay for employee lunches no matter the type of food room provided.

No Food Rooms

Sometimes firms decide not to provide any type of food room within their office floor plan. With a vast array of coffee houses, fast-food outlets, restaurants, food trucks, and street vendors nearby, a company does not always see the need to devote costly floor space to a food room that is occupied for only an hour or two each day. Nevertheless, rent must still be paid for the space, occupied or not.

Although eliminating a food room may save on the total space required and thus rent paid, there are at least two drawbacks to this option:

1. If employees bring their lunches, either from home or as take-out food, then they tend to eat at their desks where liquids

or food can spill on documents and equipment.
2. If employees go off-site for coffee or lunch, they may need a longer lunch hour or special break periods, resulting in lost work time.

In view of these consequences, most organizations do not rely solely on outside sources. More often than not, some type of food room is provided on the premises.

FOOD ROOM PROVISIONS

Most food rooms, although they may go by different names and serve various purposes, contain some or all of the following elements:

- Countertop
- Base cabinets
- Upper cabinets
- Sink
- Dishwasher
- Coffee brewer
- Microwave
- Refrigerator
- Filtered water
- Garbage containers
- Recyclable bins
- Table and chairs
- Vending machines
- Other options

Countertops

Although a freestanding table can be used as the primary counter, it is fairly standard practice to build the coffee counter similar to a counter in a home kitchen.

Size

Pantry countertops, typically 26 inches (in.) deep, will vary in width as desired or as space allows (Fig. 10.1a). At one time, all counters were 36 in. high (Fig. 10.1b); however, the Americans with Disabilities Act (ADA) code states that sinks must be no more than a maximum height of 34 in. AFF (above finished floor) (Box 10.1). Thus there are two options for counters with sinks: either the entire counter can be lowered to 34 in. (see Fig. 10.4a) or it can be 36 in. high and then dropped to 34 in. at the sink area (see Fig. 10.7b).

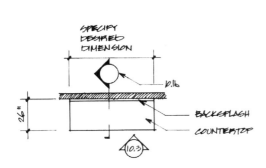

a. Plan view: Counter width

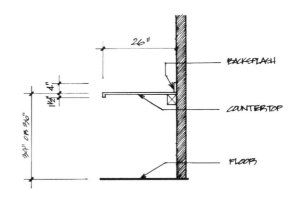

b. Cross-section: Counter height

Where water is present, customarily either a 4 in. backsplash is installed along the back and side walls of the counter (Fig. 10.4c) or a full splash is installed, extending from the counter-top to the underside of the upper cabinets (see Fig. 10.4b).

Finish Materials
Plastic laminate (PL) over ³/₄-in. plywood is probably the most common finish used for most countertops. Other finishes include Corian, granite, wood block, ceramic, and stainless steel.

Each finish can provide a different design ambi-ence and cost point. Designers should discuss both the finish and the budget with the client before making a final selection.

Edge Details
Depending on the material used, countertops can have different edge details. Corian and granite edges can be shaped similar to the table edges shown in Illustrated Table 4.7a. Stainless steel, regularly used in institutional kitchens, will have a self-rolled edge or a self-raised lip edge.

BOX 10.1 ADA Sink Heights and Clearances[1]

606 Lavatories and Sinks
606.2 Clear Floor Space. A clear floor *space* complying with 305, positioned for a forward approach, and knee and toe clearance comply-ing with 306 shall be provided.
606.3 Height. Lavatories and sinks shall be installed with the front of the higher of the rim or counter surface 34 in (865 mm) maximum above the finish floor or ground.

305 Floor or Ground Space
305.3 Size. The clear floor or ground space shall be 30 inches (760 mm) minimum by 48 inches (1220 mm) minimum.
305.4 Knee and Toe Clearance. Unless other-wise specified, clear floor or ground space shall be permitted to include knee and toe clearance complying with 306.

306 Knee and Toe Clearance
306.2 Toe Clearance
   306.2.3 Minimum Required Depth. Where toe clearance is required at an *element* as part of a clear floor *space*, the toe clearance shall extend 17 inches (430 mm) minimum under the *element*.
   306.2.5 Width. Toe clearance shall be 30 inches (760 mm) wide minimum.
306.3 Knee Clearance.
   306.3.3 Minimum Required Depth. Where knee clearance is required under an *element* as part of a clear floor space, the knee clearance shall be 11 inches (280 mm) deep minimum at 9 inches (230 mm) above the finish floor or ground, and 8 inches (205 mm) deep minimum at 27 inches (685 mm) above the finish floor or ground.
   306.3.5 Width. Knee clearance shall be 30 inches (760 mm) wide minimum.

Plastic laminate counters typically have a self-edge or a wood band (Fig. 10.2a and b). A quarter-round continuous PL edge is possible only if the laminate selected is specifically designed for such application (Fig. 10.2c).

Base Cabinets

Occasionally, firms provide just a countertop with open space below. More often, base cabinets with doors and/or drawers are included below the coffee counter. Cabinets are often "custom-designed" in that they are laid out to fit exactly within the space, drawn up on blueprints, and then fabricated by a millwork shop rather than purchased from a manufacturer. Although custom designed, the finished product will conceivably look similar to many manufacturers' standard products. The difference is that the custom cabinets are built for a specific project, often at non-standard dimensions. Recently, with so many new and better-built products on the market, many designers now specify standard cabinets from a local store (Table 10.1).

Framed Construction

There are two types of cabinet construction: framed and frameless. Framed construction (Fig. 10.3a) is used primarily in residential kitchens. With this type of construction, cabinets have a frame around each opening. Frames serve as drawer and door stops and as the basis for attaching door hinges, which are visible from the front of the cabinets. Drawers and doors sit in front of the frames, thus appearing raised. Although hinges are drawn on this example, they are normally not shown on elevation drawings.

Frameless Construction

Frameless construction is used more often for commercial cabinets and high-end residential kitchen cabinets. Because there are no frames, hinges are set on the backside of the doors and attached to the cabinet wall on the inside of the cabinet and thus are not visible until the door is opened. This type of construction allows the doors and drawers to abut with a minimum joint line (Fig. 10.3b).

■ **FIGURE 10.2 Details: Counter edges**

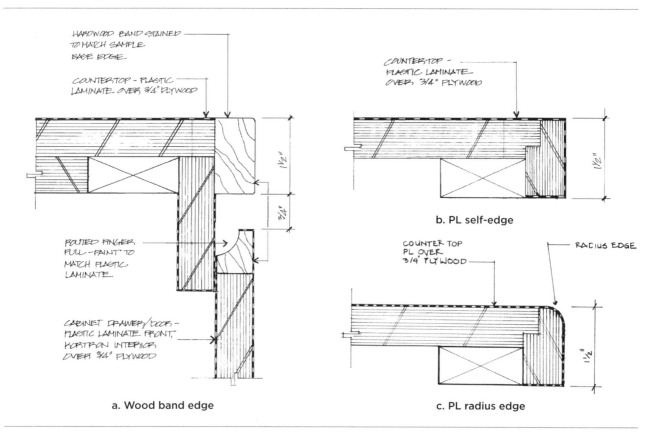

a. Wood band edge

b. PL self-edge

c. PL radius edge

TABLE 10.1 Base Cabinets and Upper Cabinets

	BASE CABINETS	UPPER CABINETS
CABINET	24″ or 25″ d	14″ d
DOORS	15″–21″ w 22″ or 28″ h for 34″ h counters 24″ or 30″ h for 36″ h counters	15″–21″ w 30″–42″ h
DRAWERS	15″–21″ w 6″, 9″, 12″ h ±	
	Toe Kick: 3″ d x 4″ h Sink Panel: 6″ h ±	Installed at 20″ above counter 24″ above coffee maker—verify 30″ above sink 68″ AFF at refrigerator—verify

FIGURE 10.3 Elevations: Base cabinets

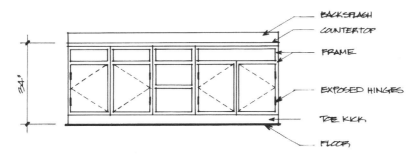

a. Cabinets using framed construction

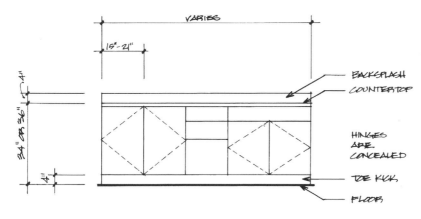

b. Cabinets using frameless construction

Specifications

Although both framed and frameless cabinets can be constructed to any size or width, the framed cabinets tend to be manufactured in predetermined set intervals, such as 15 in., 18 in., 21 in., etc., whereas the frameless cabinets are usually offered in more incremental widths that allow a better fit in a given space. The frameless style is a more expensive means of construction.

Cabinet manufacturers offer both types of cabinets, keeping some styles in stock with several drawer and door options. Millwork shops also make either type of cabinet based on designers' specifications, but the lead times are often up to twelve weeks.

Finish Materials

As with countertops, plastic laminate over $^3/_4$-in. plywood is the most common finish for base cabinets. Other finishes and options include wood, metal, or custom finishes, and selection of the hardware. To reduce costs, a thinner laminate or less-expensive material is often specified for the inside of the cabinets.

Upper Cabinets

Even though upper cabinets are fairly standard in residential kitchens, they are less prevalent in office settings where there are fewer items to store. Most firms supply some utensils and perhaps a few coffee mugs, but they seldom provide full sets of dinnerware and glasses. In addition, there is little need for pots, pans, bowls, and other dishes. Since cabinets are expensive, firms may opt to eliminate upper cabinets when there is adequate storage in the lower cabinets.

When upper cabinets are provided, their widths, methods of construction, and finishes normally match that of lower or base cabinets. It is important to ensure that these cabinets are installed high enough to clear items on the counters.

For visual purposes, it is aesthetically pleasing to align the upper cabinets with the base cabinets (Fig. 10.4a). Cross-sections should always accompany elevation drawings to provide a total picture (Fig. 10.4b). Drawings shown in these examples are basic cabinet drawings to illustrate the information discussed. For alternate concepts and specific design details,

■ FIGURE 10.4 Cabinets

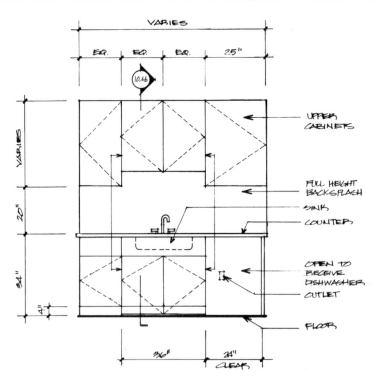

a. Elevation: Upper and lower cabinets

designers should refer to drafting books and detailing sources.

Sinks

Some clients or building managers consider a sink to be an optional item. A sink requires plumbing and drainage, an increase to build-out costs. However, when a sink is not provided, employees carry water from the restrooms through the office space to the area where a coffee pot is set up. Half-filled cups are left setting around during the day. At the end of the day, someone must bring the cups and coffee pot to the water source for cleaning and washing. Designers should explain that in the long run it is better and more efficient to pay the up-front costs to provide a sink.

Costs can be minimized by locating the sink and coffee room as close as possible to the building's water source. At least one clean or potable drinking water pipe runs vertically through a building, starting at the ground floor or lower level and continuing up through the top floors. This pipe is usually located next to one of the interior columns and is referred to as a "wet" column (see Figure 13.6a).

Size

Assuming there is adequate counter width, a double-bowl sink has distinct advantages; the two bowls allow independent washing and rinsing. However, if a single bowl sink is specified, it is better to select the larger size because the smaller bowl sink is very small. A double-bowl sink requires a 36-in.-wide base cabinet for installation (Fig. 10.4a), whereas the large single bowl can be installed in a base cabinet either 36 or 33 in. wide (Table 10.2).

TABLE 10.2 Sink Bowls	
Single bowl	15" w x 18" f-b x 6" d 30" w x 18" f-b x 7" d
Double bowl	33" w x 22" f-b x 7" d

f-b: the dimension from the front edge of the sink to the back edge
Sizes shown are typical industry sizes, which may vary slightly with each manufacturer's products.

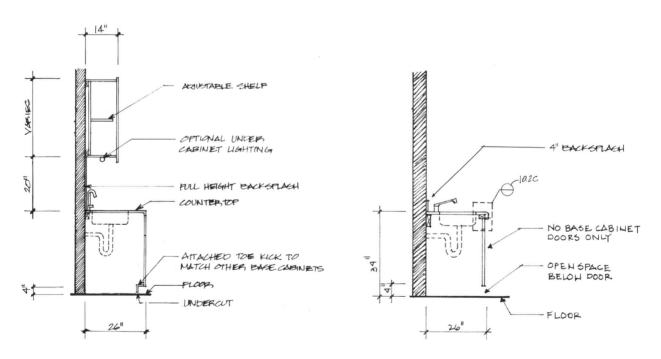

b. Cross-section: Upper and lower cabinets

c. Cross-section: Alternate sink cabinet door to meet ADA code

Sink Base Cabinet

To comply with ADA requirements, a base cabinet below a sink is not actually a cabinet but rather an opening that provides a 30 in. wide clear floor space when the doors are opened. Because there is no base platform, just the floor, when the doors are opened a wheelchair is able to pull up to the sink (see Box 10.1). The toe kick can be an open space (see Fig. 10.4c) or a simulated kick can be attached to the doors (Fig. 10.4b).

Finishes

Sinks come in two primary materials, stainless steel and ceramic. Stainless steel sinks are generally in stock for immediate delivery. They are typically less expensive than ceramic sinks and used more widely for commercial projects. Ceramic sinks are often stocked in white, with a wide selection of colors available on a short lead time. Although darker ceramic colors may have an aesthetic appeal to fit with the selected design scheme, it is ordinarily better to select lighter colors because the darker ceramic colors such as black or navy blue tend to show water spots.

Dishwashers

Installation of dishwashers often depends on the amount of dishware and glassware supplied and used by a firm. When a firm does not supply these items, or has a limited number of dirty cups, there is little need to install a dishwasher. If a firm supplies dishware or does a lot of entertaining, then a dishwasher is a great asset. It is best to install the dishwasher to be as close as possible to the sink. All brands of dishwashers require 24 in. of clear undercounter width and depth (Fig. 10.4a).

Coffee Brewers

It is best to plan for a commercial coffee brewer rather than home drip coffeemakers. Many commercial brewers have a second or third warming plate that allows people to use one pot of coffee while another pot is brewing. Some brewers also include an instant hot water tap for tea, instant soup, or hot chocolate. In recent years, many organizations have started to use larger, self-contained single-cup serving machines, which offer all types of options, including regular, decaffeinated, mild, and strong coffee as well as tea, hot cocoa, etc.

Size

Coffee brewers, including cappuccino machines, come in many styles and sizes. It is best to ask clients to consult with a local coffee service provider to select a brewer that will meet their needs. Since the service provider will probably also be contracted to provide monthly shipments of coffee, it is important for the client to feel comfortable with the provider. Once a selection is made, the client should give a cut-sheet (brochure) of the selected brewer to the designer for planning purposes.

Finishes

Because most brewers are stainless steel with brown, walnut grain, or black trim, there are generally limited color options for coffee brewers.

Planning Guidelines

Brewers are typically set on top of the counter. If upper cabinets are installed, it is important to plan the exact location of a brewer, as a higher clearance is usually required between the counter and underside of the upper cabinets. All cabinets can be raised slightly or just that portion of cabinet raised above the brewer (Fig. 10.5a). Another option includes lowering the base cabinet on which the brewer sits (Fig. 10.5b).

There are two options for transferring water to the brewer: fill the coffee pot with water at the sink faucet and then pour the water into the brewer or automatically dispense water into the brewer. No one seems to enjoy transferring water to the brewer, and water often drips all over the counter. It is much more convenient and less messy to connect a small water line directly to the brewer to automatically dispense water into the brewer at a push of a button on the machine. Provisions for a direct connection are made by adding a note on the appropriate construction drawing sheet stating:

Note: Contractor to install a 1/4" copper waterline to the coffee brewer.

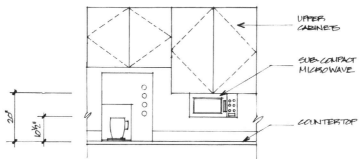

a. Counter with single-cup brewer, condiments,
and subcompact microwave

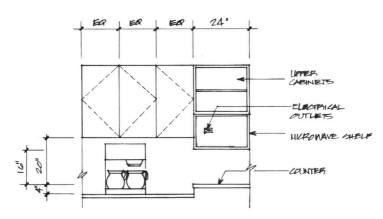

b. Counter with coffee brewer and shelf for
medium-sized microwave

Coffee Accessories and Condiments

With coffee come many accessories for which the designer must plan counter or cabinet space. This storage space should include items for both daily use and backup supplies. Items may include packages of both regular and decaffeinated coffees, filters, K-cups, sugars, artificial sweeteners, creamers, stir sticks, napkins, and cups. In addition, many firms also provide items such as teas, hot chocolate, salt and pepper, and soups.

The amount of required counter and cabinet space depends on clients' opinions regarding how many items may be visible at all times. For instance, coffee cups can sit on the counter or be placed in a cabinet above the counter. Tea bags and cappuccino packs often sit on the counter for easy selection, but they can just as easily be placed in a base cabinet drawer.

Besides the accessible items, there should be secured storage for supplies either in a locked closet adjacent to or within the food room or one or more base or upper cabinets specified with a lock. According to one coffee service vendor, "As a minimum, twelve (12) cubic feet of secured storage space are recommended per coffee brewer."[2]

Microwaves

Microwaves come in three basic sizes and several power combinations. As with coffee brewers, it is generally a good idea for clients to select and purchase a microwave that best suits their office needs (Table 10.3).

TABLE 10.3 Microwaves	
Large	30" w x 13" d x 16" h
Medium	23" w x 12" d x 11" h
Subcompact	18" w x 12" d x 10" h
Sizes shown are typical industry sizes, which may vary slightly with each manufacturer's products.	

In an office setting, a microwave is used primarily for reheating single portions of food rather than cooking a whole meal. Therefore, unless the client specifically requests the larger size, it is better to plan for a medium-size microwave, which requires less counter space. To further conserve space, it is possible to house a medium-size microwave on a shelf designed within the upper cabinets (Fig. 10.5b). Be sure to verify the microwave dimensions before finalizing the shelf design.

Most subcompact microwaves are designed to be installed hanging from the underside of an upper cabinet, generally leaving enough clearance between the counter and microwave to set condiments and other items (Fig. 10.5a). The major benefit of this size microwave is to conserve counter space, but clients should be informed that this is a very small microwave, only large enough to heat sandwiches or a cup of liquid.

Planning Guidelines

Intuition suggests placing the microwave near the refrigerator because many foods to be heated or reheated are stored in the refrigerator or freezer. Adjacent counter space is needed on which to set food both before and after heating. Because most microwave doors are hinged left, it is generally desirable to plan for more space on the right side of the microwave, since that is the side where the door opens.

Finishes

Microwaves normally come in basic colors only. Options may consist of black, white, off-white, stainless steel, or any combinations of these colors.

Power Selections

When purchasing a microwave, clients should be advised to select a model with at least 1,000 watts electrical input, the minimum amount of power necessary to microwave popcorn. Microwaves require a dedicated electrical outlet, which designers should note on the electrical plan.

Refrigerators

There are three basic types of refrigerators: undercounter, upright, and compact (Illustrated Table 10.1). Undercounter refrigerators are limited in size, but the other two types of refrigerators come in various sizes and combinations, with icemakers and/or water dispensers, as a combination refrigerator/freezer or just a plain refrigerator, with top and bottom doors or side-by-side doors. Therefore, it is important to determine the needs and wishes of each client in order to specify the right refrigerator. For instance, if the client already has filtered water service, then a water dispenser on the refrigerator is not necessary. On the other hand, floor or counter space could be conserved by having the water dispensed from the refrigerator rather than from a separate water cooler.

Undercounter Refrigerators

Undercounter refrigerators are small, intended for limited use only. There are several models: refrigerators only, freezers only, and a combination, all designed to be either freestanding or placed below a counter for a flush appearance. When planning for an undercounter model, care must be taken to coordinate the refrigerator and counter heights.

Upright Refrigerators

The most popular refrigerator used in office food rooms is the traditional style upright refrigerator with a freezer on top, ranging in storage capacity from 16–26 cubic feet. For firms employing between 30 and 70 people, a middle size of 18–22 cubic feet provides quite adequate storage space for daily brown-bag lunches or occasional party plates.

Compact Refrigerators

Upright refrigerators jut out in front of the counter a few inches. For this reason, some designers

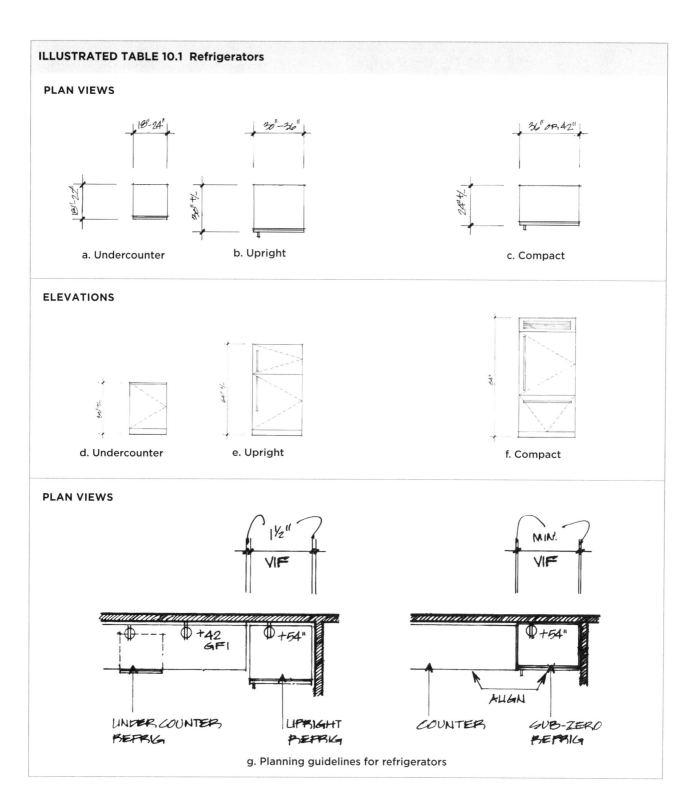

ILLUSTRATED TABLE 10.1 Refrigerators

PLAN VIEWS

a. Undercounter b. Upright c. Compact

ELEVATIONS

d. Undercounter e. Upright f. Compact

PLAN VIEWS

UNDER COUNTER REFRIG UPRIGHT REFRIG COUNTER SUB-ZERO REFRIG

g. Planning guidelines for refrigerators

and clients prefer the compact refrigerator, which is flush with the front of the base cabinets. However, the compact is much more expensive and much larger than an upright refrigerator. Be sure this is what the client wants when planning begins.

Sizes

The figures in Illustrated Table 10.1g show basic dimensions for initial planning. Before space planning and drawings are finalized, the designer should specify a new model or verify the size of the existing refrigerator to be reused.

Refrigerators are one of those pre-existing items that clients often bring from their old location to their new office space. When this is not the case, the general contractor normally purchases this item based on designer specifications.

Allow 1 to $1\frac{1}{2}$ in. of clearance around all three sides of the undercounter and upright refrigerators for air circulation, clearance for opening the door, and space for the cord in back. Compact refrigerators are designed to fit exactly within a space, so side and back clearances are not required.

Finishes

Uprights traditionally come in white. Other color options depend on the prevailing color schemes available for appliances at the time of purchase. For instance, available colors during the 1970s were olive, rust, and harvest gold in addition to white. During the 1990s, it was almond, white, and black. By the twenty-first century, stainless steel became a popular finish. Consumer trends dictate appliance colors.

Some undercounter refrigerators come in white, but brown and walnut-grain finish have been the predominant colors for the past 30 years. Compacts are designed to have plastic laminate or wood panels installed on the door fronts so that the refrigerator finish matches the cabinetry finish for a completely custom-designed look.

Filtered Water

Many firms provide some type of filtered water via freezer/refrigerator dispensers, chilled refrigerated containers, individual chilled water bottles, or sink-side or stand-alone dispensers.

In most cases, water dispensed through the freezer is not actually filtered water but rather chilled water. If the client desires this option, the designer must add to the construction drawings a note similar to that specified for the coffee brewer waterline, requesting that a $\frac{1}{4}$ in. copper line be connected to the freezer. This option must also be included on the freezer/refrigerator specification.

When a push-button container of water is to sit on a shelf within the refrigerator, a larger-size refrigerator may be required to ensure adequate room for the container, brown-bag lunches, and any other items stored in the refrigerator. The same is true if individual bottles of water are to be stored within the refrigerator for general usage, although this option is becoming passé with the rise of green consciousness.

Providing filtered water at the sink can be handled in one or two ways, either by attaching a small filter system to the faucet head or by installing another faucet (Fig. 10.7b) with a filtering system installed in the sink cabinet below. Both systems are economical and conserve floor space. The under-sink system may require careful planning for installation if other items such as a garbage disposal or waste collector are also installed. A chiller container for cold water is optional. Without the chiller, the water is filtered, but not cold.

A stand-alone dispenser/cooler provides both filtered and chilled water. It requires approximately 1 square foot (SF) of floor space with about 3–4 in. of space around all sides (see Appendix E.35). When a paper cup holder is attached to one side, provide an additional 4 in. of space on that side. Plan to include adjacent floor space for a small wastebasket. In addition to the water cooler, nearby storage space must be provided for both empty and full bottles. The bottles can be stored in either an upright position or be shelved on their sides.

Garbage Containers

Although it is true that clients generally purchase and place wastebaskets or trash bins for the majority of rooms within the space (see Chapter 4), for food rooms it is best for the designer to plan for the specific location and to specify the size of the garbage containers and recycle bins.

Proximity of the garbage container to the coffee brewer is an important consideration. As people dump wet coffee grounds, they often forget to hold a protective covering below the funnel, inevitably dripping water/coffee across the floor, along the counter, or wherever the path of travel goes between the brewer and garbage container.

Another point to consider is visibility of the containers. Sides and edges of containers get dirty and sticky and overflow with food, trash, and other sundry items, becoming very unsightly. With this in mind, either a larger container can be installed or sufficient space planned for two or three containers. Removable or flip lids can be added to most containers. However, this option is also messy and requires regular cleanup because discarded foods or liquids often leave spills and leftovers on the lid.

Alternative options are to place the garbage containers within cabinets using a flip door, similar to disposal stations seen in many fast-food chains, or on full-height, roll-out base drawers. These trash cabinets, regularly painted black on the inside, can be part of the main base cabinets (see Fig. 10.7b), stand alone, or be additional cabinets. As with the lids mentioned above, regular maintenance must be provided for cleaning the flip door and inside of the cabinet where food can miss the container and fall to the floor. When containers are included as part of the cabinets, base blocking to hold a container in place, flip door or open locations, and heights are designed and dimensioned based on the selected container to ensure a proper fit.

Recycle Bins

Building managers and their tenants (the clients) can (and in some situations, must) encourage employees to recycle items at work by providing separate bins or containers in addition to garbage containers. Recycling bins can be treated and planned for in a manner very similar to garbage containers. The bins or containers can be set along one wall of any designated room, many times a food room (see Fig. 10.7a and Fig. 10.11b), or be designed into cabinets see Fig. 10.8c). All bins should be clearly labeled for the items to be recycled: *cans*, *bottles*, *newspapers*.

For those clients considering Leadership in Energy and Environmental Design (LEED) certification, space provisions to accommodate recycling bins are a prerequisite under the "Materials and Resources" requirements. Floor space can be provided either by the building management or within the tenant space (Box 10.2).

Vending Machines

Vending machines come in many different sizes, with many different options. Types of dispensed items include but are not limited to cold drinks and sodas; hot drinks or coffee; tea and soup; sweets, cookies, and candy bars; refrigerated foods such as yogurts and sandwiches; and chips and crackers.

For basic planning purposes, a 39 in. × 27 in. rectangle can be used, but some machines are as small as 24 in. × 18 in. or as large as 42 in. × 30 in. It is best to have the client consult with a vending representative to make specific selections

---

BOX 10.2 LEED CI Recycling Procedures[3]

Material and Resources
Storage and Collection of Recyclables
MR Prerequisite

Intent
To reduce the waste that is generated by building occupants and hauled to and disposed of in landfills.

Requirements
Provide dedicated areas accessible to waste haulers and building occupants for the collection and storage of recyclable materials for the entire building. Collection and storage areas may be separate locations. Recyclable materials must include mixed paper, corrugated cardboard, glass, plastics, and metals. Take appropriate measures for the safe collection, storage, and disposal of two of the following: batteries, mercury-containing lamps, and electronic waste.

---

before much planning is done. Once the client has made their selections, the representative should provide exact dimensions and clearances required for each machine. Some clients also like to include an ATM machine in the vicinity of the vending machines.

Who will stock the machines, the client or the vendor? Will surplus items be stored on-site or be brought in each time the vendor stocks the machines? Will a separate room be needed to store attic stock? The designer must be sure to discuss all options with the client and to provide for them in the floor plan.

Tables and Chairs

The desire or need for tables and chairs varies greatly from company to company, even from one branch location to the next branch location for the same firm. There seems to be little consistency as to when or why some companies or branches choose to provide tables and chairs and other companies or branches do not. Provision of these items often comes down to available space, the designer's planning, or a request by the manager in charge. When tables and chairs are included in the layout, adequate space should be planned for circulation paths (Fig. 10.6a and b).

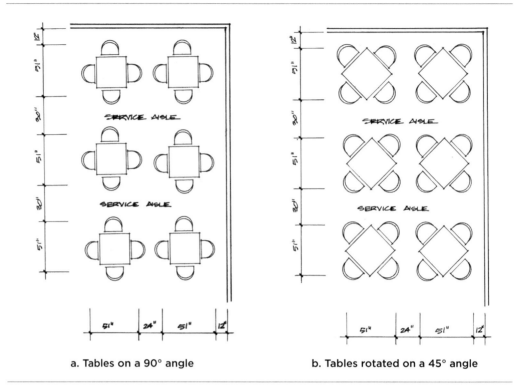

a. Tables on a 90° angle   b. Tables rotated on a 45° angle

Other Items

Many other items may be added or planned into a food room, such as a garbage disposal, trash compactor, electric can opener, paper towel dispenser, mop/broom closet, storeroom, ice-maker, or toaster. Clients may have any number of wishes to be included in their food room. For one project, a movie theater's corporate office required counter space for a commercial pop-corn popper and drawers to hold various kinds of unpopped corn. Each option selected should be considered and planned for in a manner simi-lar to the various provisions already discussed.

Electrical Requirements

It is essential to consider electrical requirements in food rooms. Several appliances, including the refrigerator, microwave, and coffee brewer require either dedicated or 240V/20A (voltage/amperage) outlets. Dedicated outlets provide a homerun or conduit directly back to the electri-cal panel without being daisy-chained to other outlets, while 240V outlets provide a higher volt-age than standard office outlets of 120V. Some vending machines, such as those with hot and cold drinks and refrigerated foods, need a stan-dard 120V/20A outlet. Also, many of the newer machines, refrigerated or not, that accept credit cards require electrical outlets.

Unless otherwise noted (UON), room outlets are typically installed at a standard height of 18 in. AFF to comply with ADA code requirements for height reaches while seated in a wheelchair. When drafting power plans, designers normally add a general note to the plan stating the typical outlet height of 18 in. and then insert the outlet symbol at all locations where outlets are needed without writing a height next to each symbol. For outlets to be installed at another height or over a counter, the designer must indicate the height of the outlet next to the outlet symbol on the power plan (Illustrated Table 10.1g).

In general, outlet plates are not drawn on most elevations. But when outlets are at various heights or in special locations, they are methodi-cally drawn as dashed rectangles and labeled on the elevation (Figs. 10.4a and 10.5b). All outlets in wet areas, especially along a sink counter, need to be specified as GFCI (ground fault cir-cuit interrupter).

Although designers are not responsible for electrical wiring, it is their responsibility to show all outlets on the power plan in a set of construction documents. Background plans showing this information are given to the electrical engineer, who then designs the electrical loads and wiring diagrams. Additionally, designers must provide cut-sheets and other specific information, including a list of appliances, model numbers, and quantities to the electrical engineer.

FOOD ROOM LAYOUTS

Food rooms probably come with the least number of stated requirements from clients than other areas. Clients simply want to be able to get their coffee, get their lunch, and perhaps take a minute or two to chat with coworkers who might be passing through the room at the same time. This leaves a lot of latitude for the designer to discern the best food room to provide, its location, its size, and its design finishes. There are no typical food rooms; each one is unique.

Room Location and Shape

When tables and seating are incorporated, it may be desirable to locate the food room along a window wall to take advantage of natural daylight. Room size, shape, and partition location are usually based on perimeter wall construction (see Chapter 6).

Because window walls are at a premium in many floor layouts, food rooms are often planned as interior rooms. This offers the designer opportunities to shape and size the room to accommodate a range of amenities or interject some design zest. Although the layout examples shown in this chapter are rectilinear, food rooms often provide opportunities for variously shaped rooms. Table and chairs can easily lay out in angled corners, along diagonal walls, around curved pathways, close together, far apart, and in different sizes to fit the space and appear cohesive within the plan. In general, it is a good idea to design straight counters, but these too can be angled or curved to fit the design.

Food Room Doors

For some reason, in commercial plans, it seems natural to show a door on food rooms. After all, most other rooms on the plan have a door, so we tend to automatically add a door to the food room. But, is a door really needed?

In reality, a food room door is very seldom closed. Therefore, the designer may suggest that money could be saved by not adding a door for this room (Fig. 10.7a). Then, the door opening, now a cased opening, can be widened, perhaps to 4 or 5 ft., to provide a more open feeling. With this open approach, it may be possible to incorporate the circulation space of the food room with an adjacent area circulation, thus reducing not only materials costs, but also floor space and rent costs.

Room Sizes

As with conference and reception rooms, the number of individual items, appliances, counters, tables and chairs, and layout will determine the overall size of the room. For example, when the client requests only an undercounter refrigerator and coffeemaker, the designer can plan a much smaller room than for a food room requested to accommodate a full-sized refrigerator, soda machine, and sink.

Finishes

Though this room is habitually thought of as a functional room, it also offers designers the opportunity to provide a little extra pizzazz. Many times companies wish to make this room a fun relief from the daily grind, a place for employees to relax and unwind. Designers should make the most of this opportunity.

Coffee Room

Even though many people prefer other beverages, *coffee* has predominated as the term used to identify the most basic of food rooms within an office setting. Coffee rooms generally contain these minimum provisions:

- Sink
- Counter
- Base cabinets
- Coffee brewer
- Microwave
- Refrigerator
- Garbage container(s)

Room Layout

Designers should start the layout by planning a counter along one wall and then logically add other items into the plan (Fig. 10.7a). When the refrigerator is a new upright, it can be placed at either end of the counter; designers must remember to specify the desired side for the door hinge, left or right. If the existing refrigerator will be reused, designers should check (field verify) on which side the door is hinged so that in the new location, designers can plan to locate the refrigerator on the end of the counter that allows the door to open away from the counter (Fig. 10.7a).

Designers should consider the plan in elevation to evaluate that the layout can spatially fit all items (Fig. 10.7b). Once the basic plan is achieved, it is easy to add other provisions as desired (Fig. 10.8a–c).

Duplicate Coffee Rooms

According to one coffee vendor, "As a guideline, satellite coffee areas should be provided to serve, at a maximum, every 50 employees within a work area."[5]

When more than one coffee room is planned within large tenant spaces, it is wise to plan all rooms to be as similar as possible, in both size and provisions, to minimize any favoritism or jealousy between groups. All employees should be made to feel that their group is as important as the next. An exception to this guideline would be for groups that are distinctly different in the nature of their work or position from

■ FIGURE 10.7 Coffee room and counter

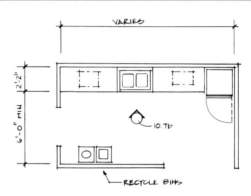

a. Plan view: basic coffee room with lower sink cabinet and cased openings in place of a door

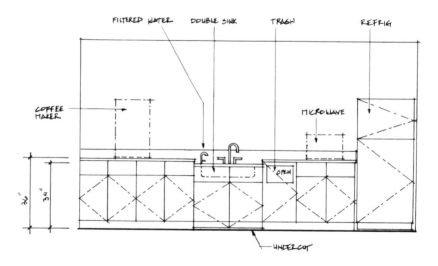

b. Elevation: counter at higher 36" height dropped to 34" at sink for ADA code

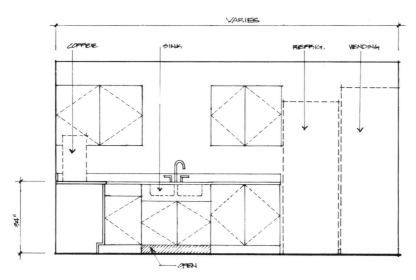

a. Elevation: Continuous counter
at required ADA 34″ height

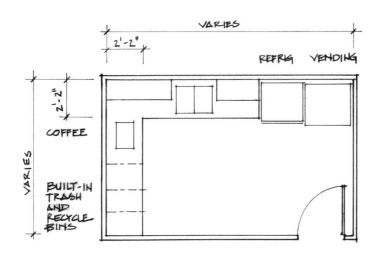

b. Plan view: Coffee room

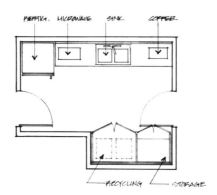

c. Plan view: Coffee room

other groups within the company. Examples include:

- Executive areas vs. general employee areas
- Specialty areas vs. general work areas
- Factory worker areas vs. factory office worker areas

Pantry

Specialty areas that may require a pantry include the reception and the main conference areas. It is common practice to offer visitors a cup of coffee or soda while they wait for their appointment. Many conference meetings, especially early morning meetings, include coffee and sometimes donuts. Meetings over the lunch hour and late afternoon gatherings may offer catered meals or finger foods.

Having a small coffee room or pantry in the reception or conference area alleviates people from trooping through the office space to the main coffee room. By using smaller sizes of each provision, a compact room can be designed to serve this area and the small number of people who may find it more convenient to use this pantry rather than the primary coffee room (Fig. 10.9a and b).

Vending Areas and Rooms

Sometimes it is easier, more convenient, and less messy to provide prepackaged goods.

Almost every kind of food can be packaged and sold through vending setups. These self-serve machines require little maintenance. This type of food service is great for public attractions such as theme parks, museums, train station terminals, and hospitals, but it can also be useful in a work setting, particularly where it is not convenient for people to bring their lunch each day or go out to a local restaurant.

A vending area can be contained in its own room or in niches along much-used aisles or corridors (Fig. 10.10). When planned along passageways, the designer must remember to plan for separate standing areas in front of the machines in addition to the minimum corridor width (see Chapter 5). Overall corridor widths can be increased to account for both minimum circulation requirements and standing areas, or the recessed niches can be planned at a greater depth to include both the vending machines and the standing areas. This allows the corridor to remain at the minimum width if necessary.

Roughly, 2–3 in. should be planned around each machine for air circulation and to easily move the machines forward for servicing. A soffit or fascia may be designed overhead, but some space or clearance is needed for air circulation. Electrical outlets, now required for most vending machines, are shown on the power plan. It is wise to include a storage room nearby when feasible.

■ **FIGURE 10.9 Pantry**

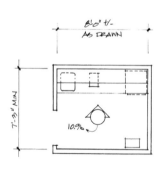

a. Plan view: Pantry

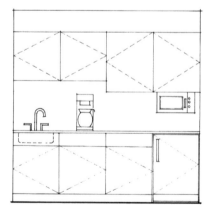

b. Elevation: Pantry

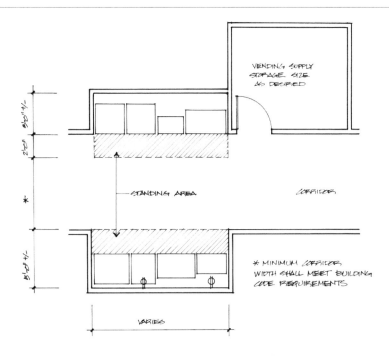

Break Rooms and Lunchrooms

Whereas coffee and vending rooms imply "coming and going," lunchrooms and break rooms invite sitting, relaxing, and eating on the spot. In many cases, these rooms are just an extension of the coffee or vending area, created by increasing the room size to include tables and chairs and other amenities as desired (Fig. 10.11a and b). Although there is no hard and fast rule, a room having a counter and base cabinets is customarily called a lunchroom, and a room that primarily includes vending machines is often called a break room.

Employee Lounge

A lounge customarily includes sofas, easy chairs, coffee and end tables, a flat-screen television, perhaps lockers, and any other items that may provide some short-term rest and relief of fatigue. Occasionally, employee lounges are referred to as lunchrooms or break rooms, even though they may contain soft seating. The room may have vending machines, a coffee counter, or just a refrigerator. There may be one unisex lounge or two separate lounges, one for men and one for women.

This type of room is found often in warehouses, factories, and other businesses where the employees are on their feet for much of the day or on shift lines where they cannot leave their position at will. A lounge setting allows employees to re-energize and get some much needed relaxation moments during their regulated break periods. It also provides a statement from management that the employees are important and that their health and well-being are of concern.

Other businesses and organizations that typically provide lounge settings include educational institutions, which have student and faculty lounges, transportation hubs with airport VIP and train first-class lounges, and executive lounges in hotels.

Smoke Room or Area

Some companies used to have a smokers' room. Since many buildings are now smoke-free, this room has generally been eliminated. However, in rare cases, company-owned buildings still provide this room on a limited basis. The designer must remember that the room needs to be separately ventilated to prevent secondhand smoke from mixing with the rest of the building air. LEED certification does not allow for this room. It stipulates that a designated exterior area must be at least 25 ft from all entries, outdoor air

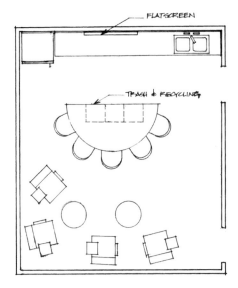

a. Lunchroom

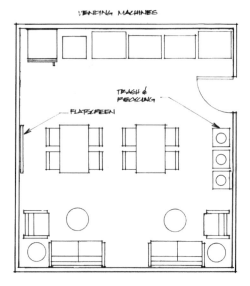

b. Break room

intakes, and operable windows.[6] This topic, if it arises, needs to be fully discussed with clients before appropriate planning is undertaken.

Cafeterias

Full-blown cafeterias look much like buffet restaurants. There is a serving line where employees move their tray along a rail and pick out the food desired. Hot meals may be cooked on-site or catered from off-site. Tables and chairs or booth seating may be laid out within the same area or in an adjacent room.

Any company, firm, or business can have a cafeteria designed into their office space or building. However, the practicality of doing this must be considered. Quite a bit of space is required to accommodate a kitchen, serving line, queuing line, and seating area. Approximately 1200–1500 SF is required for seating 75–100 people.

The amount of space required and costs to build out a cafeteria result in an expensive alternative to the other food rooms discussed. However, when large firms have over 500 employees,

are located in remote or rural areas, or have high profit margins, overall costs may be justified when compared to the costs of employees leaving the building, especially if they have short break periods, lack access to nearby food places, or work under a great deal of stress.

Should clients decide to proceed with a full cafeteria, they should retain a food service specialist or cafeteria designer for this portion of the design. In this scenario, even though the specialist designs the kitchen area and serving line, the designer still retains control over the project as a whole, first by identifying and blocking out the general area for a cafeteria on the floor plan, second by laying out the seating areas based on the specialist's plan, and finally by selecting the color schemes. Kitchen drawings are given to the design firm to include in the engineering package.

Other Food Considerations

Many firms use catering services throughout the year. Services range from supplying bagels and donuts every Friday morning to monthly luncheons to the company holiday party at the end of the year. This is not a primary topic considered during the programming phase, but it should be discussed with the client at some point.

Bagels and donuts are easy, as they are ordinarily delivered on large disposable platters wrapped with clear plastic and placed in the lunchroom on a counter or table. Employees help themselves at will, and when empty, the platters are thrown away. There is minimal cleanup.

Luncheons are normally set up in a conference room on a credenza or other horizontal surface that can hold two or three selections of hot or cold foods along with a variety of napkins, condiments, liquids, desserts, prizes, and so on. Firms may ask the caterers to stay for cleanup, or someone within the firm may dispose of used items and leftovers.

Holiday or company parties may occur only once a year or perhaps on a quarterly basis. These occasions are more elaborate, often with caterers circulating through the crowd. Most definitely, the caterers need an area, possibly the lunchroom for yearly occasions or a separate room for regular events, where they can set up shop from which to operate a successful event.

Catering requirements may or may not affect the overall space plan or individual rooms. Additional provisions often depend on the amount of catering done and the items already provided in other areas of the layout. Like many areas of the plan, it is best to address all food and party needs with the client.

DRAFTING FOOD ROOM LAYOUTS

Depending on the size of the project or philosophy of the client, a food room may or may not be drafted and presented as part of a typical room's package at the time of programming (see Chapter 3). When only one food room will be provided in the new space, a layout or plan is normally not included in the package unless clients specifically request otherwise, perhaps to give their employees an idea of what will be provided in the new space. For larger clients, when the room will be duplicated on multiple floors or for several departments, a layout is often included in the typical package to ensure heads of each department that their groups will receive the same amenities as the next department. Sometimes a suggestive food room layout is included in the Program Report (Chapter 12) to provide an example of the number of appliances and other items that can feasibly fit within a stated amount of square footage. In either case, the final layout of the food room or rooms will most likely adjust in size and shape depending on where it is positioned in the final space plan layout.

PROJECT

Draft lunchroom and pantry layouts

Layouts should continue to be based on the client profile selected for previous projects. These layouts will become part of the students' portfolios and included with the Program Report submitted in Chapter 12.

1. Format the information to follow the typical office drawings to provide a consistent presentation package for the client (see Chapter 6, "Drafting Typical PO Layouts").

2. Lunchroom and pantry layouts may be drawn either manually or electronically.

3. Present at least two options for a prototype lunchroom and pantry.

4. Include reused furniture and appliances that were inventoried in the Chapter 5 project as part of the layouts.

5. Graded copies can be revised and then resubmitted for additional credit.

11

SUPPORT ROOMS AND FUNCTIONS

Support rooms are often back area, out-of-sight, not for public display areas. With few exceptions, these rooms and areas are generally not top on anyone's priority list, neither for the client nor the designer. In fact, during initial planning stages, it can be very easy to forget completely about these areas or push them aside with the intention of fitting them in later wherever there might be extra space.

But heaven help the designer who actually forgets about these areas or locates them without thought to their intended function. When the client moves in and wants to send mail or make photocopies, if the proper area does not exist or is inconveniently located, the client may forever feel annoyed and frustrated with the designer. Therefore, to create a successful design project, designers need to address and plan for all necessary office functions for each client right from the beginning.

GENERAL SCOPE OF SUPPORT FUNCTIONS

In this book, space planning information is more general in scope for support rooms than for other rooms. First, it is impossible to cover every support room, function, and area because there are just too many different types. Second, support rooms, although common to many businesses, are unique on each individual floor plan. There are standard guidelines, but there are no typical support room layouts. Finally, by understanding other room layouts, most designers are sufficiently armed with planning technology to apply logic, intuition, and forethought in this final area of room layouts.

Defining Support Functions

As the name suggests, support rooms and areas house the functional tasks that help support the operations of a business. Some support functions, such as photocopying, are common to almost all types of businesses, including general offices, churches, banks, hospitals, and schools. Other support functions may be exclusive to a particular type of business, such as coat checkrooms in restaurants or safe-deposit box booths in banks. Finally, some businesses may require a room or area that is unique, created just for a particular firm. For example, on one project the head of human resources asked for a composure room where employees who had just been laid off could compose themselves in private, vent some anger, cry, make telephone calls, use a mirror and sink for washing their faces, and, in general, face the future without immediately encountering coworkers.

A support function may require an entire room and thus be named as such on a space plan. Functions can just as easily occupy a small corner within a larger room or sit out in an open area within the overall space plan and be referred to by the function name or as an area rather than as a room. For instance, there may be a *copy room* in large business offices or just *the copier* in a smaller office. Files may be stored in a secured room or serve as a dividing line between the accounting and administrative workstation areas. A library may fill niches along corridors, or it may occupy its own room off a corridor. In reality, functions, rooms, and areas are adapted to each floor plan and client to best fit the requirements at hand.

Importance of Support Functions

Without support rooms and areas, businesses could be handicapped in terms of time if documents must be sent out for photocopying, in terms of quality control if research must be conducted by outside laboratories, and in terms of satisfaction if self-parking is located two blocks away, etc.

Many of these areas are unmanned, unoccupied rooms that are accessible to all employees at all times. However, some areas, such as the computer or mailroom, may have a specific person assigned to the room for security reasons or to assist employees as needed. Most functions or rooms have individual requirements that may include larger amounts of floor space; special electrical and data outlets; additional air supply or exhaust; specialized construction, security, or equipment; custom millwork; and alternate flooring or lighting. When these rooms and requirements are identified prior to the start of space planning, they can be strategically placed within the floor plan along with the more highly aesthetic public areas.

Support functions can be divided into three groups.

1. Basic functions
2. Optional functions
3. Unique functions

BASIC FUNCTIONS

Basic functions, those common to most businesses, are usually accessed on a daily basis. General guidelines are used to plan each of these areas:

- Copier or workroom
- Mail and delivery room
- Supply room
- File room
- Storage room
- Technology room
- Shared equipment
- Public utility services

Copier or Workroom

Today's copiers have greatly expanded their capabilities from strictly copying documents to also include printing, scanning, and faxing documents. Though some businesses may have a desktop copier, most copiers take up floor space (see Fig. 4.17 and Appendix E.37). Copiers, along with printers, which usually sit on a counter, play a very vital part in the everyday life of the business world. There are numerous types of copies needed: black and white copies; color copies; letter, legal, or 11×17 sizes; single pages; multiple pages with stapling; sorted copies; single-sided; double-sided; copies on special paper; and so on. Some copiers can perform all tasks, but other copiers are limited in capabilities. Printers can generally handle various sizes and types of paper but are limited in performing other tasks just listed for copiers. Depending on each client's choice of equipment and needs, multiple copiers and printers may be scattered throughout the space plan, or several copiers and printers can be grouped together in a central area.

Customarily, the word *photocopier* is shortened to *copier* or *copy room* on floor plans. Stand-alone printer areas are generally called just that, *printer areas*, but copier rooms are still referred to as copier rooms even though there may be printers within that room. In addition to the actual copier, there are other provisions to consider in this area.

Collating Area and Counters

As copies are being made, a horizontal plane is needed on which to place both the copies and originals for sorting and collating. A table or bench can serve this purpose, but many times a millwork counter is built along one wall with some shelving above and/or below for storage (Fig. 11.1).

Various accessory items—including staplers, tape, paper clips, three-hole punches, and scissors—are normally found in collating areas. Other items frequently found in this area include a paper cutter and binding machine for making spiral booklets. The binder may actually be two machines, one to punch the holes and one to add the spiral.

Generally, for the average company, a 6-to-10-foot (ft) wide by 30-inch (in.) deep counter provides sufficient space for all of these activities. Be sure to verify the size and depth of any printers to set on this counter, as some large printers may need a slightly greater depth. Backsplashes are not required in non-wet areas.

Paper, Paper, and More Paper

There is no end to the various types of paper used for copying and printing. Packages of paper (500 sheets), called *reams*, are often purchased in bulk with twelve reams to a box, as this is less expensive than single reams. Because paper is used so quickly, it makes sense to buy it in bulk,

but there must be sufficient space to store several boxes of paper. A box of letter-size reams is 11½" × 17" × 12" high. A box of legal-size reams is 14" × 17" × 12" high.

Boxes can easily be stacked in any available space, including open floor space or in space below counters, which can help keep the balance of the area neat and orderly. Some companies prefer to break down the boxes and stack all reams of paper on a shelf, or open several reams and put some loose sheets of each type of paper in a sorter unit for quick use. Shelving can be part of the millwork counter, a bookcase, a metal unit, or a cabinet.

When copiers or printers are located in an open area of the office, it may be desirable to install cabinet doors below counters, but more often shelving is left open, without doors, especially when this area is within an actual room. Open shelving helps cut down on construction costs and provides easy access.

Recycle and Trash Bins

As with food rooms, it is wise to plan for both general trash bins and bins for recycling paper. The general trash bins can be smaller in the copier/work area, whereas the recycle bin should be larger because, unfortunately, there is much superfluous copying and printing that is simply thrown away. In addition, firms with high security

FIGURE 11.1 Elevation: Workroom counter

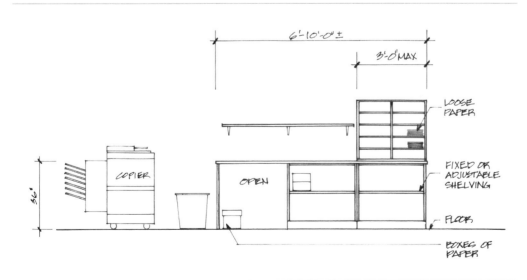

concerns may require a third, lockable bin for disposing secure information and documents. While daily trash and recycled items are typically removed by the building cleaning crew, separate arrangements are made by the client to have their secure documents removed and burned by a third party vendor on a regularly scheduled basis.

Workroom

Because this room may house other functions in addition to the copier, it is sometimes referred to as a workroom. Often, people actually work in this room: they make booklets, sort items, use the stapler, etc. To facilitate these functions, a desk may be included as part of the millwork or as a freestanding piece of furniture.

Room Layouts

Copy rooms can be large or small, placed in the interior space or on the window, have doors or open passageways with no doors. It is wise to locate this room or area centrally within the plan for convenient employee usage. Each room is tailor-made for each client (Fig. 11.2a and b).

■ **FIGURE 11.2 Plan views: Copy rooms**

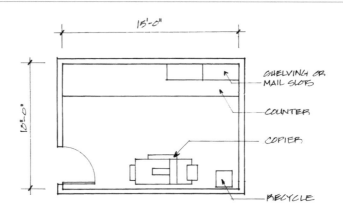

a. Small interior copier room

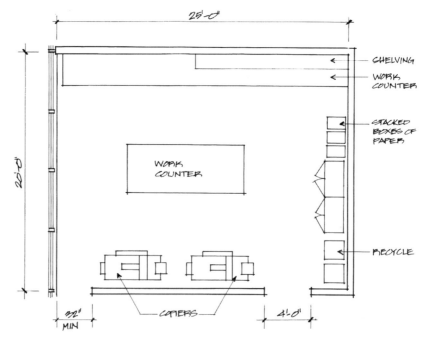

b. Large workroom on window wall

TABLE 11.1 Copier Power and Electrical Requirements[1]

POWER REQUIREMENTS—QUICK REFERENCE SHEET

MODELS	POWER REQUIREMENT			RECEPTACLE		
	VOLTAGE	AMPS	CYCLES	NEMA PART NO.	XEROX PART NO.	LOOKS LIKE
All Standard Products 4118/M118/M20 FaxCentre F110, F116, 2121, 2121L, 2218, 765 CC/WC/WCP 123/WCP128 CC/WC/WCP 232/238/245/255 WC5632/38/45/55 WC7328/35/45 Digital front ends (Fiery, Creo, Docusp, Splash)	115V	15A	60 Hz Single phase	5-15R	600S3704	
4110/4590/4595 4112/4127	208–240V	15A	50–60 Hz	6-15R		
WC5665/75/87 CC/WC/WCP 265/275 **WC7655/65** DocuColor 240/250 DocuColor 242/252/260 Docutech 75 MX Wide format 510 dp	115V	20A	60 Hz Single phase	5-20R	600S3703	
CC/WC/WCP 90	208–240V	20A	60 Hz Single or three phase	14-20R	604K05820	

Mechanical, Electrical, and Data Requirements

Copier rooms have special mechanical, electrical, and data requirements. First, rooms should be independently exhausted from the balance of the space because copies produce an off-gassing smell. Second, copier electrical cords have three-pronged plugs that require special outlets (Table 11.1). Third, in order to print to copiers and printers, or scan back to one's computer, there needs to be one or more data jacks for connecting cables from the equipment back to the computer room and then to individual computers or laptops. Fourth, when faxing is required, an analog connection is often required, though some firms have the ability to route this connection through their data servers, thus using a typical data jack rather than a separate telephone jack.

During the design development and construction document phases, engineers will design the specific mechanical and electrical requirements for each room or area, and an IT person will design the data requirements, but it is usually the designer's responsibility to ask clients to obtain specific information and cut sheets from the manufacturers who are supplying new equipment for their project or servicing the existing equipment to be reused. In turn, clients give the cut sheets to designers who then provide this information to the engineers and IT people. When cut sheets are no longer available for existing equipment, the designer will need to record the manufacturer and model number listed on the equipment and then provide this information to the engineers (see Appendix F).

Mail and Delivery Room

Although the internet has taken over a great deal of communication between people and companies, there is still a need for a mailroom and delivery room. Due to its unique requirements, this area is often handled as a separate entity under the programming effort (see Chapter 3). A list of guidelines furnished by one corporation covers the major aspects of mailrooms to consider during the planning and design phases:

Mailroom services include receiving and sending mail and packages from all carriers, and sorting. . . . Ideally the mailroom is located. . . directly across from the freight elevator. . . . This will provide the most direct route for incoming and outgoing deliveries and be the least disruptive to the building tenants. As this can be a noisy environment, its location should be away from conference rooms and business groups with high volumes of visiting customers.

Work flow should be the primary consideration in mailroom design and divided into three basic areas: staging, inbound, and outbound.

- *Staging . . . that accommodates the delivery of bulk . . . items.*
- *The inbound . . . mail (bags, tub, and/or trays) and overnight delivery items. . . .*
- *The outbound . . . mail and overnight deliveries of interoffice, metered and express mail. . . ."*[2]

Shipping and Receiving Room

Another term used for this area is *shipping and receiving room*, which covers all types of packages and items in addition to those delivered by the US postal service.

Other deliveries and shipments can include:

- United Parcel Service (UPS)
- World Wide Carrier Ltd.
- Federal Express (FedEx)
- DHL

- Local messengers and couriers
- Delivery trucks for supplies
- New furniture and equipment
- Catering services

Not only is space needed for packages, boxes, and other items, both inbound and outbound, but also there is generally separate equipment used for tracking and metering most of these items. The US mail will require both a stamp-metering machine and a scale that may sit on a counter; or, in some cases, one or both are large enough to take up floor space. Some delivery firms place their own computers in mailrooms with direct links back to their own central locations. All of this equipment requires various electrical outlets and other power and data link considerations.

Other Provisions

To prepare for shipping and receiving of items, it is necessary to have other provisions, such as envelopes in various sizes, boxes, packaging materials, forms, tape, scissors, etc. Not only should these accessories be provided, but they also must sit on counters or be stored. The amount of storage required, and the room in general, depends on the size and type of business for each client. An advertising company that does a lot of printing may need large open floor spaces to receive pallets of paper. Pallets are 4 ft×4 ft×4 in. high. A company that sends out a lot of promotional materials and gifts will need larger mail machines and shipping or pickup areas. A small company may have minimal needs.

Recycle and Trash Bins

Space plans should include generous-sized bins for both general trash and recycled paper. It is also wise to plan some open floor space in this area for bulk trash (such as outdated computers, broken-down boxes, discarded design samples, etc.) accumulated either from the mailroom itself or from the firm as a whole.

Room Requirements

Many people, items, carts, and activities regularly flow through the shipping/receiving mailroom. In addition to the ideal location near the elevators, there are several other considerations regarding the room's layout. There should be at least two doors into this room, one leading into the company space, which may be locked, and one leading directly to the exterior of the space, usually a public corridor. For large items or items delivered in bulk, it is wise to plan for double doors or a wider than normal door, perhaps 42 or 48 in. wide.

When a company is large and occupies several floors, it may be necessary to provide small, localized mail areas on each floor. Some companies may use a mobile cart to distribute mail to each individual, and other companies may ask for mail slots where employees or departments pick up their own daily mail. Depending on the company size, the mailroom may be included as part of the copier room, or it may be a separate room.

Room Layouts

There should be separate counter space for the mail-related equipment and another counter for sorting letters. One long counter can accommodate both types of tasks, but it is unreasonable to think that items can be moved around in order to perform both tasks on the same counter space. Some companies prefer custom-built millwork counters and cabinets in this room, whereas other companies prefer

metal furniture made specifically for mailrooms (Fig. 11.3).

Supply Room

A supply room must accommodate a variety of items. Many supplies are small, such as tape, staples, clips, pens, pencils, three-ring notebooks, tab dividers, notepads, manila folders, etc. These items are periodically purchased in bulk (packaged 12 to a box) and reordered when only a few items remain. A client may also store equipment such as hole-punches, tape dispensers, and staplers. Some companies even store an extra chair or two, filing cabinets, desks, and computers so that they have all items on hand when needed.

Depending on the size of the company, all supplies may be under lock and key and dispensed only through a requisition form, or the supplies may be in a general storeroom that is accessible to anyone at any time. Often there is a compromise in which furniture, computers, and bulk supplies are kept in a locked or remote room, and a small supply of disposables, such as pens, pencils, clips, etc., is made readily available to all personnel.

Shelf Storage

Because many items are small, it is sufficient to provide shelving on which to store these items,

■ **FIGURE 11.3 Plan view: Mailroom layout**

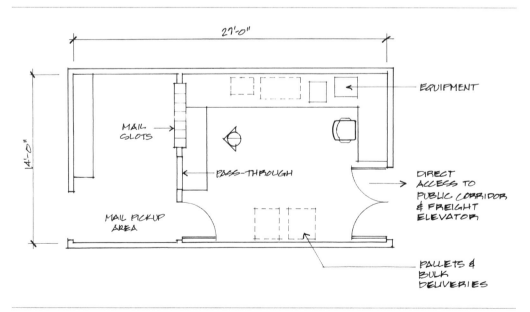

even in bulk. Metal shelving can be assembled in a separate storage room. Sometimes items are stored on shelving above the cabinets in the copier room or mailroom rather than in a separate storage room. Occasionally, supplies are stored in the fifth drawer of five-drawer lateral filing cabinets (this drawer is really a roll-out shelf behind a flipper door), or firms may use regular storage cabinets (see Chapter 4). There should also be adequate floor space for larger items.

File Rooms

Files can be located either in open areas of the office as a divider between groups of workstations (see Figure 5.1b), along walls (see Illustrated Table 5.1c), or in rooms used solely for the purpose of file storage (see Fig. 11.9a and b). There are advantages and disadvantages to each option. When located in open areas, files are usually closer to the employees, making access more convenient. With this design concept, it is normally desirable for all files to match in color and style for the best aesthetic appearance. However, files are expensive; some companies may not want to increase their furniture budget to buy matching files, especially if they wish to reuse what they already have. When existing files do not match, one option is to paint them, even if they are of various styles, to coordinate them with the new design scheme.

When three-drawer files are used as a divider, it is customary to install a continuous plastic laminate counter over the file tops to serve as practical workspace. If there is a security issue with access to proprietary information, individual files in open areas can be specified to have locks. Locks are normally an add-on cost.

For files located in a separate room, files do not need to lock if the room is locked for overall security. Moreover, mismatched files are less noticeable when housed in rooms rather than in the open. However, if employees access this room several times a day, they may complain about having to walk to another area, or they may leave the door unlocked rather than relocking it each time they go in and out of the room.

Circulation Square Footage

Regardless of whether the files are in a room, along walls or out in the open, it is important to remember that files require a lot of circulation space, and designers should plan accordingly (see Appendix E.9 to E.13). When there are few files in relation to the overall space, additional circulation is not a huge factor. However, for large or paper-intensive organizations, great numbers of files require a vast amount of circulation space, and thus greater amounts of rentable square footage. To reduce square footage, companies may wish to consider alternative ideas for filing options.

For example, a brokerage firm's headquarters required two additional floors of space to accommodate their lateral files and accompanying circulation. To conserve floor space, movable shelf filing was recommended on each floor, which meant central file locations on each floor where several groups were required to share the same file room. In this case, the cost savings was worth the risk that employees might complain.

Movable Shelving and Filing Systems

Although movable shelving systems save a considerable amount of floor space, clients must agree to this type of filing (see Illustrated Table 4.10d). First, movable shelving is even more expensive than conventional files. Second, the firm will need to convert from a top-tab filing system to a side-tab filing system (see Fig. 4.4 and Illustrated Table 4.10c). Third, paper is actually very heavy when concentrated in mass. An open metal shelf, 18d×42w×88h, stacked full of paper files can weigh as much as 760 pounds or 145 pounds per square foot (PSF).

Most contemporary buildings are designed to carry 80 or 100 PSF of live weight (the combined weight of interior construction, furniture, equipment, human beings, and paper). When greater amounts of weight, such as a movable filing systems, are anticipated on a floor, designers must always consult with a structural engineer regarding acceptable weight loads on the selected floor location. It may be necessary to add structural support to the floor for reinforcement to carry the added weight of this filing system. Reinforcement can be done on top of the floor, but it is more customary to install it from the underside of the floor. Costs for both the engineering fees and reinforcement are borne by the client.

For the brokerage firm project mentioned earlier, the firm was fortunate that the building they selected for their new office space had been designed with heavier floor construction to hold up to 150 PSF at each end of the building core (Fig. 11.4). By placing the movable shelf and high-density filing rooms in these specific locations, the firm was able to take advantage of saving floor space without having to spend money for additional floor reinforcement.

A Paperless World

As more and more firms rely on and take advantage of electronic document storage, there is less and less need for hardcopy filing storage, especially for new documents, and thus, a reduced need for file cabinets. When companies relocate or renovate, they often retain an outside vendor who specializes in scanning existing documents that can then be disposed of, which then helps reduce the need to keep existing file cabinets for reuse or to purchase new cabinets. The designer will want to be sure to address this issue during the programming phase.

There is an important side note to keep in mind when scanning existing documents, particularly for central filing documents shared by many personnel. A taxonomy, which aids with organizing, searching, and locating documents in the future, will need to be structured per each client's needs and organizational makeup. Generally, vendors who are capable of supplying the scanning services are also versed in setting up taxonomy outlines.

Storage Rooms

There is always something to store. Some companies do not think about storerooms during initial space planning or do not wish to spend money on such rooms. However, it is wise to provide some type of storage room, even if it is only a small room. Because storage areas can be messy and untidy, it is best to put a storage room behind closed doors.

Many firms are legally required to keep certain documents and records for a set number of years. For them, this storage room, which probably has a lockable door, may contain open metal

■ **FIGURE 11.4 Plan view: Potential movable shelf and high-density filing room locations**

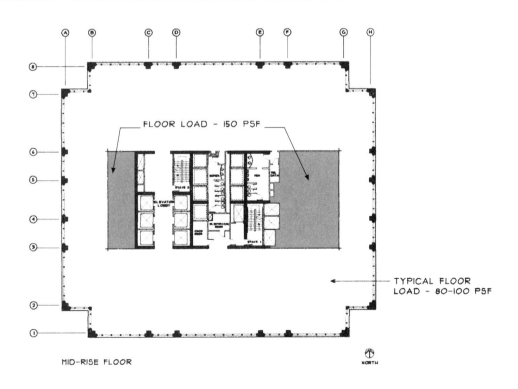

shelving for archiving file boxes. Banks and financial brokers may offer promotional gifts such as teddy bears and toasters for opening new accounts. They too may want a room with open shelving to store these items. Other company needs include space for A/V (audio/visual) carts, seminar materials, holiday decorations, umbrellas left behind, etc.

Technology Room

There are several names for this room or function, such as LAN room, computer room, and data room. Most companies run wires, cabling, or fiber back to this room, where each computer is then connected to a local server and telephone outlet, thus forming a local area network (LAN). Some firms also connect copiers, printers, A/V items, and other equipment to their network system. Another acronym, WAN (World Area Network), is used for the system that connects branch offices together in a manner similar to LAN.

Because this room has many technical requirements for equipment, clearances, electrical connections, and security, clients should retain an outside consultant or use their internal IT department to plan this room for size, final layout, and power requirements. For initial planning purposes, designers can start with an average room size of 10 ft × 15 ft, regardless of the size of company, unless the company is a trading or technology firm or has some other mega-computer usage. It is best to locate this room centrally within the space, as there is generally a maximum length of about 300 ft for cable runs. This length includes the vertical rise of the cable from the equipment rack up into the ceiling, the horizontal run out towards the edges of the office space, and the descent down to the piece of equipment itself. When there is more than one floor, a smaller room or large closet should be stacked directly above or below the main LAN room to allow for the vertical distribution of the cables. From this smaller room, the 300 ft runs start over for that floor.

Most LAN rooms require supplemental or 24-hour air conditioning to cool the equipment. Sometimes the ceiling is left open to the slab above to allow for the vertical rise of warm air.

The floor may remain as exposed concrete, have vinyl composite tile (VCT) or another hard surface, or use a raised platform system. When a raised floor system is used throughout the space,

the cabling and electrical wiring are distributed below the floor system, providing easier access to that wiring than when it is run through ceilings or walls. Some raised floor systems also provide the means for ventilating the conditioned air from below.

Because so many firms have moved from PCs or desktop computers to laptops, many spaces are being designed with wireless connection points in the ceilings. On the one hand, this change in technology does not particularly affect a space plan because a computer room is still needed, and the space plan is not yet at the point of ceiling design. On the other hand, mobility of laptops has given rise to open, spontaneous, collaborative work areas that may alter program requirements. As the conceptual plan moves into design development, though, the designer will want to track those connection points, which will compete for space in the ceiling along with light fixtures, exit signs, sprinkler heads, etc.

Shared Equipment

Of all support functions, shared equipment is more often located in an open area, typically adjacent to an aisle, rather than in a room. Shared equipment may include:

- Printers
- Scanners
- Copiers
- Plotters
- Fax machines
- Computers
- Typewriters

Some equipment will be in walk-up areas, and other items will be in sit-down areas. (See Chapter 5 for planning guidelines.) In the overall scheme, shared items require a small amount of space, but they are of great importance since many of them are accessed on a regular basis.

There may be a black-and-white printer for every four to ten employees, but only one color printer for the entire floor or firm. The copier, fax, and scanner may be an all-in-one with a printer or be stand-alones. Items may be grouped together as floor items or on the same counter, or each item may be placed in separate areas, such as near the reception desk or in a copier room. Sometimes a firm may have only one copy of a licensed program that is placed on

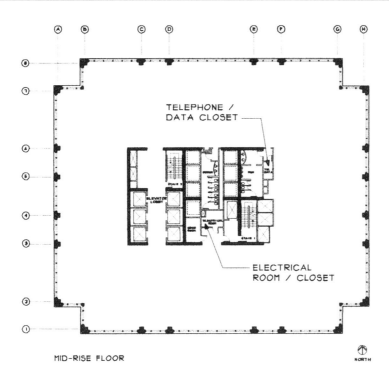

TELEPHONE / DATA CLOSET

ELECTRICAL ROOM / CLOSET

MID-RISE FLOOR

NORTH

a shared computer. Many companies still have one or two typewriters for filling out forms.

When employees have some of this equipment within their own work areas for their own exclusive use due to status, heavy usage, or just the nature of their business, the same planning guidelines apply.

Public Utility Services

Electrical, telephone, cable, and now fiber optic cable companies provide service to each building either by underground or overhead wire connections. Overhead wires are more prevalent in suburban and rural areas, whereas underground connections are more common in urban areas. The building provides a separate room, typically in the basement or other lower-level floor such as a parking level, to each utility company for its use and connection into the building. Each service is then distributed vertically onto each floor, usually into separate closets in the building core (Fig. 11.5). Finally, all services are distributed to each tenant's LAN room.

OPTIONAL FUNCTIONS

Optional functions, unlike basic functions used at will, are ordinarily used on a sporadic or scheduled basis. Such functions, common to many firms, include:

- Training rooms
- Project and team areas
- War rooms
- Libraries
- Sick room
- Lactation room
- Game room
- Telephone booths and quiet rooms
- Lockers

Training Rooms

Learning and training in corporations is an ongoing process. Employees must learn updated computer programs, new approaches for conducting business, new methods for accomplishing daily tasks, new ways of doing their jobs, and new knowledge about their work. Topics of training can cover many subjects, such as equipment training, public speaking, company policy, employee orientation, etc.

Room Layout

Furniture in a training room may include individual chairs with or without tablet arms (such as those found in high schools); individual work tables and chairs; long tables to be shared by two, three, or more individuals; or tables that can be ganged together to form larger tables for group seating (Fig. 11.6). Unless fixed seating is specifically requested, it is a good idea to provide versatile and mobile furniture to allow the room to be reconfirmed in a variety of layouts to achieve maximum or flexible styles of training. There may be computers and other equipment for each person, or items may be shared.

Room Size

Room size depends on the type of training, the furniture layout, and the number of people to be trained at any given time. If the training is strictly lecture style, with limited audience participation, the room can be a large one, long and narrow in shape, with the lecturer up front. A dais and podium can be included, if desired.

When the room is set up with tables for interaction between the trainer and trainees, it is best to limit the number of participants and provide a more horizontal layout, which allows for good eye contact between the trainer and participants.

Accessories

Accessories can be mobile and moved in and out of the room as needed or be permanently installed. Accessories may include projection screens, flat-screens, marker boards, easels, lecterns, microphone, A/V equipment, computers, etc. Clients must be carefully consulted about their specific needs for training areas.

Alternate Training Rooms

Large corporations often provide a separate room or suite of rooms devoted strictly to in-house training. Not all companies have this

■ **FIGURE 11.6 Plan view: Training room layout**

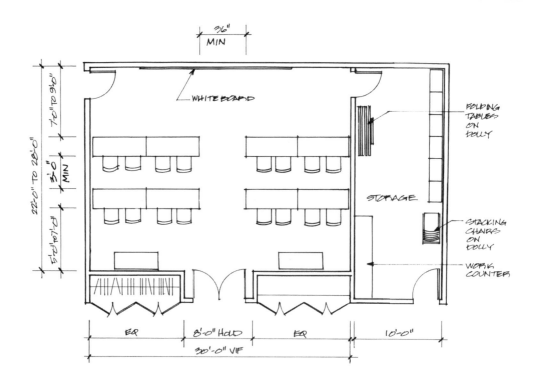

luxury though. Smaller companies may not be able to justify the cost of rent for such rooms even though they still need to provide some type of training from time to time.

Sometimes companies simply use their conference rooms for training (see Chapter 8). Many of the accessories generally needed in training rooms are also found in conference rooms. Since conference rooms are scheduled on an as-needed basis, it is a great use of space to have this single room serve a dual purpose.

There are also two other options for training rooms. First, rather than have the trainer come on-site to the company location, company employees can go to the training site. This saves space and rent for the client. Now, all of the guidelines and requirements for planning a training room are transferred to the trainer's space.

Finally, many companies rent space at a nearby hotel for occasional training. Hotels have created a great niche for such services. Hotels need large spaces for banquets and other evening social events, but those spaces often sit vacant during business hours. By renting out these spaces for training, hotels are able to generate money and businesses are able to save overall rent.

Lighting

Although lighting is very important in all aspects of the work environment, proper and flexible lighting is essential in training rooms. To make the room truly flexible, lighting options should include some combination of direct and indirect lighting; general, task, and accent lighting; visual and non-visual sources of light; and a combination of lamp types. To paraphrase several sources, lighting is both an art and a science.[3]

As a science, levels of light can be calculated and then provided for various tasks. A low level of light is needed for video screen presentations, but direct lighting is vital for viewing a white board at the front of the room. Indirect lighting is best for computer usage, yet the users also need sufficient task lighting to view paperwork.

As an art, multifaceted levels of light are desirable for social interaction of participants. Wall washing can highlight artwork or key presentation diagrams on sidewalls to give an expansive impression, even when the general lighting is low for large-screen presentations. Pendant fixtures can be prominently displayed for their beauty, or fixtures can be architectural, concealed behind moldings or below rails to emit a glow of lighting in an otherwise dark room.

All lighting sources should be controlled either through dimming capabilities or the number of lights that can be turned on or off at one time, as each training session requires. Either independent switches or master control boxes with multi-scene pre-set light levels can be installed to control light fixtures and lighting levels. It is popular to have three-way or four-way switching so that lights can be turned on at the point of entry into the room and at the front of the room during training. Finally, lighting control provisions can assist with LEED credits (see Box 7.1).

Storage

To meet all of the training needs, it is desirable to plan for storage space. Booklets and other training materials are stored between sessions; a staging area is essential to assemble those materials. A/V equipment, when not used for a training session, should be stored out of sight. When furniture is rearranged, a place is needed to store the items not in use.

Millwork, credenzas, or other furniture within the room can accommodate some items, but when feasible, it is a good idea to plan for a separate, lockable storage room, either adjacent to the main room or nearby. When the room is adjacent, one door can provide direct access from the storage room into the training room, and another door can lead from the storage room into the corridor.

Other Items

Because training can run from very simple to more complex instructions and involvement, there may be other items required within or near the training room. Such items may include videoconferencing equipment, interactive technical equipment, marker board photocopying, acoustical wallcoverings, wall or ceiling speakers, additional air conditioning and ventilation, copier, restrooms, food room, and more. Obviously, clients need to be consulted for direction on their specific training needs.

Project and Team Areas

Many jobs require people to work together in teams for part or all of the day. Teaming areas tend to be less formal than conference rooms either by providing smaller tables that can be ganged together for larger work areas or broken apart for smaller team areas, or in today's new workforce, teaming areas may be simply a sofa and lounge seating where people are seated comfortably while brainstorming ideas and informally discussing thoughts and concepts.

Sometimes team areas are in enclosed rooms. This provides wall space for hanging up visual representations of ideas and plans. But, these areas are just as commonly located in open spaces at the end of a workstation run or in angled corners. Open-area meeting spots help provide relief from large expanses of continuous workstations. They can also help create more relaxed settings for spontaneous or impromptu get-togethers (Figs. 11.7 and 14.9).

Collaborative Work Areas

With laptop mobility, terminology is evolving from *project team areas* to *collaborative work areas*. Large tables are not needed so much anymore because, technically, people can put their

"computer" on their lap. And because everyone is looking at the same thing on their own laptop, there is no need to lay out papers on the table. Perhaps just a comfortable lounge chair with a small, attached tablet arm (see Illustrated Table 4.9f) or a small, movable table (similar to the old-fashion TV trays) will suffice for the new mobile workforce. When required, mobile marker boards or flat-screens on mobile carts can be wheeled into this collaborative area. Now, more and more personnel work together or alongside of each other in just such settings, either in open areas or within small focus rooms (Fig. 11.8).

For planning purposes, many of the chairs used in these collaborative areas are similar in sizes to lounge seating used in reception areas; the primary difference is the addition of a tablet arm. The same spaciousness will need to be provided on the floor plan (see Fig. 9.5). When placed within enclosed rooms, designers often specify sliding doors to conserve on floor space (see Chapter 6), but it is important to be cognizant of the final room size. As a meeting or assembly area, the room moves from Group B for the overall office classification to Group A occupancy (see Chapter 2), where each occupant is calculated at 15 NSF (see Table 13.1). Then when

■ **FIGURE 11.7 Plan view: Spontaneous team areas, quiet rooms, and touchdown stations**

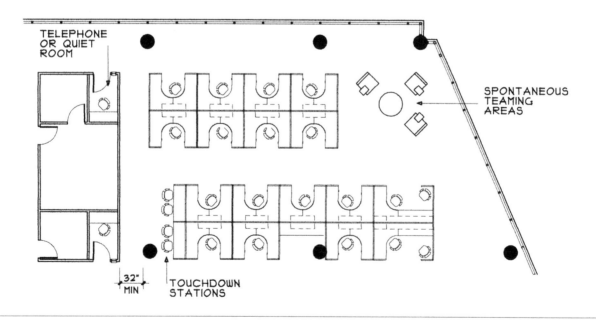

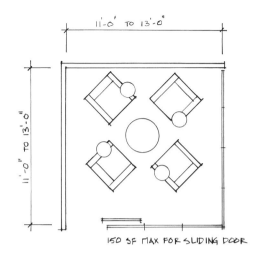

For example, there is the design library, which houses all kinds of samples such as plastic laminates, fabrics, carpets, marbles, and woods. There are catalogues, mock-ups, examples, and loaner displays. With this in mind, it is easy to see that a library may have many kinds of shelving, small drawers, large drawers, files, pegboards, hanging rods, and other storage requirements in addition to or instead of traditional library bookcases.

Other Provisions

As with other functions, there are always other provisions required in a library besides the primary aspects. Other items found in a library may include work areas, display areas, desks, shared spaces, telephones, computers, and special lighting.

Planning Guides

Most library shelving, or stacks, as they are known, can be planned with 36-in.-wide aisles (see Appendix E.1) because, normally, fewer than 50 occupants are served at one time. Typical planning guides and circulations should be used for the balance of items required in the library space. Depending on the nature of the company, the library may be regulated to an enclosed room, be housed in shelving along corridors, or be an open area wherever appropriate within the space plan.

looking at the IBC code regarding door swing (see Box. 13.10), we see that sliding doors are allowed only as an exception where the occupant load is 10 or less within the space. By calculating 10 occupants times 15 SF per occupant, a room with a sliding door can be no larger than 150 SF, approx. 12 ft by 12.5 ft, 10 ft by 15 ft or similar dimensions.

War Rooms

Originally used by the military for strategically planning battles, war rooms are a cross between conference and team rooms. Manufacturing companies adopted the term for rooms they use while planning new products. Ideas are presented and hashed out within these walls either loudly or quietly, while sitting, standing, or walking around, using back-up documentation, or off the cuff. A war room usually has a large table and many white boards and tackable surfaces on all four walls. Some firms still refer to *war rooms*, but in general the function and terminology for these rooms have evolved into the more sedate *team areas*.

Libraries

Traditionally, we think of a library as rows or stacks of bookshelves. Alternatively, if we think of it as a reference area, we understand that there are many types of libraries in the business world.

Sick Room

A sick room can be as simple as anterooms to the men's and women's restrooms or a unisex room with a cot, or it can be as elaborate as a whole sick bay, including a nurse. Some companies provide this room and some do not. There are some liabilities associated with this function, so each company must give designers clear direction in this area.

Lactation Room

More and more companies are providing dedicated lactation rooms for working mothers. According to one AIA source, "Mothers returning to the workplace after childbirth are incredibly driven to provide for their new babies but also to be productive members of the workforce. Companies that provide lactation rooms in the workplace help these employees achieve both of these goals."

Continuing on, the source states that at a minimum, "lactation rooms should provide a lockable door, a work surface and chair, a small utility-type sink, storage for cleaning supplies and paper towels; adequate HVAC service . . . and electrical outlets. Telephone service and network connections . . . are also recommended . . . along with a full-length mirror."[4]

Other considerations may include a small refrigerator, a coat rack, trash can, scheduler or bulletin board, and sound privacy. Rooms can be as small as 7 ft×7 ft, which allows a 5-foot turn radius in addition to a counter and chair. The room should be located within the space plan to consider both safety and privacy.

Game Room

In today's workforce, both the work itself and the job site have become a whole way of life. People often spend much more time beyond the traditional 9 to 5 at job locations. In the past, some companies provided small gyms or exercise rooms. This was often problematic due to costs involved to equip the rooms properly, the limited number of employees who used the rooms, and the amount of time they took to shower and change clothes. Some companies still provide small traditional exercise areas, but other companies feel it is important to provide a different type of "exercise" or "breakout" room, a type of room where everyone can enjoy some downtime, relief time, relaxation time, and fun time, even if for only 5- to 15-minute periods.

There are many names used to describe this concept or room: game rooms, decompression rooms, time-out rooms. This is an area where employees can socialize, read a book, or play games. Games may include pool, ping-pong, or foosball. There may be a TV, stereo, juice bar, cappuccino machine, lounge seating, and other amenities.

Like gyms, these rooms can also have special requirements and high budgets. But, unlike the gyms, these rooms cater to more in-and-out breaks as opposed to changing clothes and showering. Due to its uniqueness, it is important to get direction from clients for this room.

Telephone Booths and Quiet Rooms

Workstations and open-area panel systems provide very little telephone privacy. Even so, employees frequently need to make personal calls or have confidential conversations. There are also visitors and out-of-town staff who occasionally need to make general telephone calls.

Another purpose served by this room, and also by collaborative rooms, can be a *moment of sanctuary*, a counter to regular office noise and pull of the plugged-in atmosphere that many people work under on a daily basis. In actuality, most people, and some more than others, need quiet time, time alone, personal time, down time, whereby they can regroup, relax their minds and de-stress from the workday grind. Too much noise can over stimulate one's mind, so it is a good idea to take a time out every once in a while.

An empty office or conference room with a telephone, or cellphone reception access, can be used when available, but people cannot always count on these options. To address this issue, companies sometimes ask for one to three telephone booths or rooms that can be used by both employees and visitors (Fig. 11.7). These rooms tend to be smaller than the collaborative rooms as quiet rooms are more often used by only one or, at the most, two people. One room may be located near the reception or main conference room, and one or more rooms may be located within the employee working areas. At least one of the booths should have a closed door. In addition to a telephone or cellphone access, comfortable chair, and counter, it is a good idea to provide electrical and data outlets for laptop computers as well as some writing materials.

Lockers

With the advent of mobility and touch-down workstations, which generally provide limited storage within the workstation footprint (see Chapter 7), staff and other personnel customarily require some additional type of permanent or daily storage space in which to place personal items. Many firms now provide groupings of lockers, often adjacent to or very nearby workstations, to accommodate these storage needs. Depending on the locker style, lockers can be grouped along walls, in open work areas, or in separate rooms, in a similar manner to file cabinet layouts (see Illustrated Table 5.1c and d, Fig. 5.1b and Fig 11.9a similar). As with file cabinets, lockers require double circulation floor space in addition to any adjacent aisle or corridor floor space (Illustrated Table 5.1d).

Initial intuition may want to fight the added floor space and circulation overall square foot requirements, as available floor space is always precious during the planning stages. But, as typical workstation footprints go down from 48–68 SF (see Illustrated Table 7.2) to 36 SF in the new mobile workstations (see Fig. 7.24a and b), when locker square footages of 5–7 SF (see Appendix E.7 and E.8) are added to the new workstation square footage, the resulting square footage is maximum 43 SF or a minimum of 5 SF less per person than the previous 48 SF per person. When multiplied by 20, 100, or X-number of employees, the square foot savings can be extensive. As more and more firms provide lockers, this support function will probably move from the Optional Functions category to the Basic Functions category.

UNIQUE FUNCTIONS

Finally, it is important to know that at any time, any company may have a request for a special room or area that is unique to the firm or type of business, such as the composure room discussed at the beginning of the chapter or a bank headquarters that may want an actual vault within its office space. When these situations arise, designers must ask many questions. Sometimes designers may not be familiar with a particular room or function, especially when it is outside of their normal design expertise. In some cases, clients may not know exactly what it is that they want; they only know that they want something. They may have some ideas, or they may have seen something similar to what they want. When they have not actually seen such a room, it is usually hard for them to fully describe what they want.

This is an opportunity for designers to expand their communications skills. In addition to asking questions, designers can draw sketches in front of clients. They can make

analogies and comparisons. Designers can do research and bring the information to the next meeting. Designers can take field trips with clients to view spaces similar to those clients have mentioned. Most of all, designers should carry on a dialogue, ask questions, and offer suggestions until they are confident that they have a good grasp on what clients want.

Providing for client satisfaction is the basis for developing solid client relationships. When clients believe that a designer has their best interest at heart, they continue to use the same designer rather then look around for someone else.

SUPPORT ROOM LAYOUTS

Because there are no standard items or typical layouts for support rooms, it is up to designers to listen to clients, ask questions, and then provide the best room layouts based on personal experience and feedback from clients. Numerous configurations can work equally well to achieve the goal of providing adequate space and circulation for all items housed within a support room or area. Variations in the layout will produce a slightly more rectangular, square, or other geometrically shaped room, with the final layout and room size based on the location within the floor plan, the building floor plate, and the particular client's other program requirements.

Room Sizes

Room sizes depend on the type of support room and the items to be housed within the room. There are two methods for calculating the overall room size—size based on a layout or size based on square footage.

Size Based on a Layout

As with reception areas and food rooms, one approach for determining support room layouts and sizes is to do a quick sketch showing an arrangement of how the requested items could be laid out in a particular room. Walls can then be added if an open area is not desired. For programming calculations, an approximate room square footage can be determined based on this initial layout, which can be adapted later during space planning for the specific floor plan.

For example, a client may ask for these items to go into a file room:

- (7) Vertical letter files
- (3) Vertical legal files
- (6) 36 in. wide Lateral files
- 24×60 Table and chair
- 24×30 Supply cabinet

Plan or layout files in a linear fashion (Fig. 11.9a) or in rows (Fig. 11.9b). Add a door, when desired, and then draw walls around the items to achieve overall room sizes. Both plans provide well laid-out file rooms requiring approximately the same amount of square footage, 221–223 SF. Either layout or a combination of the two can be adapted to the final space plan depending on the room location within the final plan.

Size Based on Square Footage

An alternate method for calculating the room size for the Program Report, but without sketching something, is to add up the individual item's square footage, circulation, and clearance, which in this case yields 234 SF (see Table 11.2 and Fig. 12.5, Lines 9 to 13).

Actual room sizes will vary slightly based on the method of calculation or final room layout.

With the layout method, it is feasible to plan for some shared circulation areas, thus reducing the overall square footage slightly over the individual item calculations where there is no sharing of circulation. Clients may have additional ideas on what size certain support rooms should be. For instance, they may want a very generous space for a particular room, such as the library, even though calculated square footages may be less. The library can then be used as an alternate break area for those employees who prefer some quiet or solitude as opposed to the noisier game room.

Then again, the client may wish to reduce the amount of space normally required for certain functions, such as coat closets in hot climates. Sometimes designers will be able to persuade clients to accept the space plan with more or less space for each function, but ultimately it is best to listen to clients and try to meet their desires and wishes.

Creep

Like workstations, files and bookcases also creep. Unlike workstations that creep because of actual sizes vs. nominally stated sizes, files and cabinets creep due to a fraction of space that remains between the two items when placed side-by-side or back-to-back. By adding ⅛–¼ in. between each file cabinet and the next cabinet

■ **FIGURE 11.9 Plan views: File cabinets and rooms**

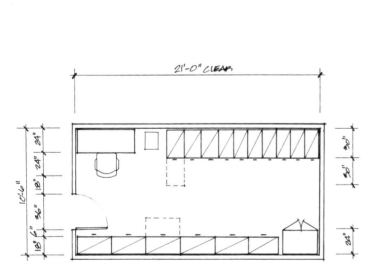

a. File Room—Rectangular layout—221 SF

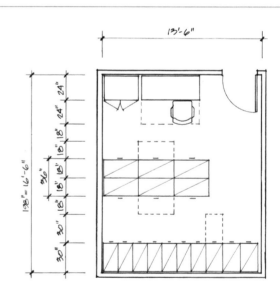

b. File Room—Slightly square layout—223 SF

and another ¼–½ in. at each end of a file run, the designer can design a room or niche to have a perfect fit (Fig. 11.9c). Without these added fractions of space, the files will not fit into a room or niche that is exactly the width of the files.

Another way to achieve a built-in look is to make a wall niche oversized and then plan for a spacer between each end of the file run and the wall (Fig. 11.9d). First, furniture installers position the files. Then the contractor or millworker installs vertical spacers and a countertop over the files to prevent papers and other items from falling behind them.

Location! Location! Location!

Oftentimes support rooms are placed in interior locations. After all, the prime real estate window areas are likely to be given over to private offices, perhaps a major conference room, or, under green building practices, the workstations. Interior locations allow the rooms to be any size and shape. Interior locations also provide four solid walls for vertical storage, millwork attachments, etc.; a much better solution than placing items in front of windows.

There are always exceptions to this general concept. Sometimes the configuration and size of the building footprint just do not provide enough interior space for all support rooms.

TABLE 11.2 File Room SF Calculations

QTY.	ITEM	UNIT SF	SUB-TOTAL SF
7	Letter files	8	56
3	Legal files	10	30
6	Lateral files	14	84
1	Table	25	25
1	Cabinet	14	14
1	Door	25	25
Total SF			234 SF

See Appendix E for specific or extrapolated SF. See Box 6.2 for door.

Sometimes there are not enough offices to fill the entire window length. Then there are times when a function may be located on the window wall to provide visual relief to the staff who work within the room, such as in a large mailroom or workroom (Fig. 11.2b).

When placing the support rooms within the plan, it is up to the designer to consider the givens—typical office standards and locations, semi-typical areas, or specific client direction—and

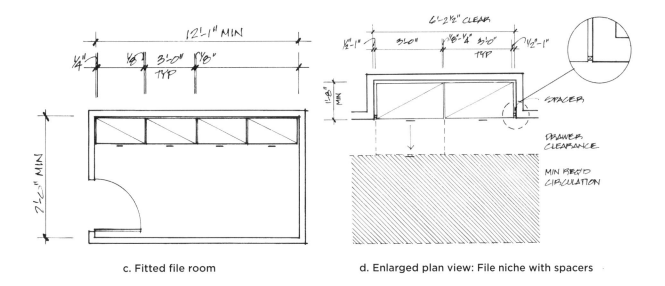

c. Fitted file room

d. Enlarged plan view: File niche with spacers

then plan for the support areas to achieve the best overall layout. Since there are many things to consider in space planning, it is a flowing and fluid effort to consider both individual rooms and the overall space plan.

Specific Locations

Although support rooms can be placed anywhere the layout allows, there are still certain thoughts to keep in mind for planning.

- Mailrooms and shipping/receiving rooms receive outside vendors and deliveries, so locate this area to be easily accessible to an exterior corridor or freight elevator.
- Copier, file, and storage rooms are used on a daily basis, so locate these areas central to the employee work areas.
- Libraries usually require quiet levels, whereas training rooms have a higher noise level, so do not locate these rooms near each other.
- Some functions can operate in either a room or open area, so options should be discussed with the client.

With careful thought and consideration, the designer will be able to produce a well-organized space plan that can be both enjoyable to look at and functional for the client.

DRAWING SUPPORT ROOM LAYOUTS

Because there are no typical support rooms, layouts for these rooms are normally not drawn as part of the typical layouts package presented for programming. However, like food rooms, periodically it is beneficial to provide selected support room layouts to show the client, even though the final layouts may change during space planning.

Some clients may want to know what a "telephone booth" looks like. Others may ask how much space would be needed and what it would look like if they provide a game room. As projects become larger, many more people are involved in the decision-making process. General staff look to mid-level managers for answers and assurances regarding the department area and daily functions. Managers look to upper management for the same answers. They also want to know what other departments are getting. Is everyone being treated fairly? In situations such as this, it is a good idea to draw up several basic support rooms, such as a copier or file room, along with an optional room, such as a training room, especially when these rooms will be duplicated on several floors or within several departments. This way, everyone knows what everyone else will receive.

Not only do these extra "typicals" provide an anticipated level of equality between departments, these drawings can also serve as talking points. Clients may request a separate training room, thinking that the room need be only 15 ft×15 ft for a total of 225 SF; then, as the company grows in size, they can convert the room into an office. A drawing based on this room size will quickly demonstrate the limitations of such a training room. By reviewing the drawing, clients can then make a more informed decision to enlarge the room, eliminate it, or keep it, knowing the limitations of that room size for training purposes.

As with food room layouts, either when specifically requested by clients or for clarity of a given room, suggestive layouts can be included with the other typical layouts in the final Program Report (Chapter 12).

PROJECT

Draft support room layouts

Although final layouts may change, as part of the overall design package, students should draw support room layouts for their selected client, which will be included with the Program Report in Chapter 12.

1. Format the information to follow the typical office drawings to provide a consistent presentation package for the client (see Chapter 6, "Drafting Typical PO Layouts").

2. Support room layouts may be drawn either manually or electronically.

3. Present at least two options for a prototype work room or other requested support areas.

4. Include reused furniture and equipment that were inventoried in the Chapter 5 project as part of the layouts.

5. Graded copies can be revised and then resubmitted for additional credit.

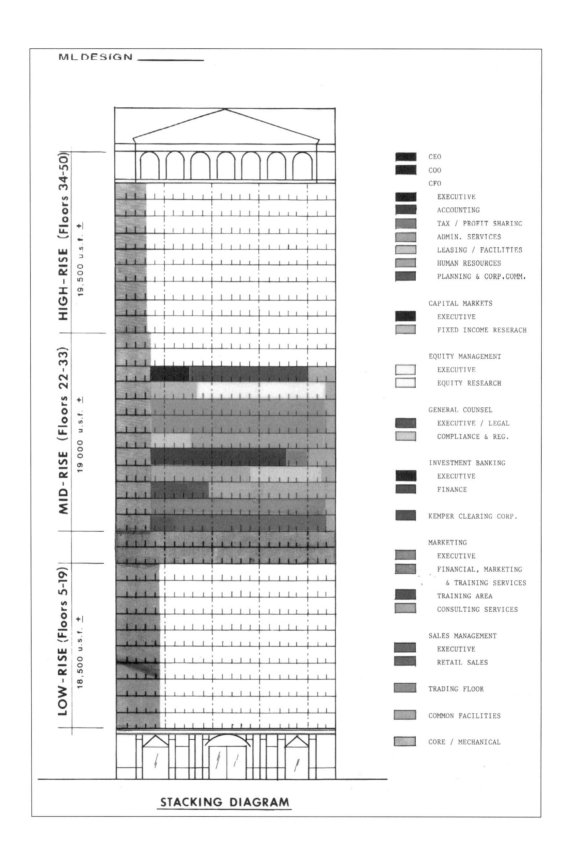

ML DESIGN

STACKING DIAGRAM

12

PROGRAM REPORT

A Program Report depicts a graphic and written summary of an idealized concept for a client's space requirements based on information obtained during the programming efforts, questionnaires, interviews, and typical work area layout assignments (see Chapter 3). As previously mentioned, once the information is culled from the questionnaires, the questionnaires are filed as backup information and are used as needed by the designer; questionnaires are ordinarily not shared with other parties unless there is a specific reason or request to do so. In their place, a written Program Report is compiled using text, spreadsheets, graphs, and diagrams. The report becomes an official document distributed to the client, developer, broker, attorney, and others who are involved with the project.

Program Reports serve a dual purpose. The designer or space planner and other members of the immediate design team need to know all of the finite details of a project, such as the quantity of files or the size of each room, to plan the space for the client's requirements onto a floor plan. On the other hand, many recipients of the Program Report are normally more interested in macro-information. They are looking at this report from an economic or feasibility standpoint and simply want

a summary of the information: What is the total square footage? What is the total number of people? What is the average square feet per person?

PROGRAM REPORT BOOKLET

Generally, the graphic and written portions of the Program Report explain much of the same information, but in different ways. Reports or booklets are typically divided into eight or nine sections depending on the number of topics included under Additional materials:

- Preliminary matter
- Executive summary
- Organization charts
- Adjacency diagrams
- Quantitative and detailed information
- Typical work area and support room layouts
- Additional materials

Preliminary Matter

Preliminary matter helps to both formalize a Program Report and to provide a level of comfort to the reader. Preliminary matter may include but not be limited to a cover sheet, title page, cover letter, and table of contents.

Cover Sheet and Title Page

The cover sheet and title page may be one and the same, or they may be separate pages, depending on the size and formality of the project or style of the booklet. Elements on this page typically include the name of the client, branch or division name if applicable, name of the design firm, the date of the report, the address of the project if it has already been selected, and the title, *Program Report*, or something similar.

Cover Letter

A cover letter is often included after the title page. It should be addressed to the primary client contact or senior person in charge of the project. The letter should be brief, formally thanking the organization for its contributions and cooperation in providing the necessary information; it should conclude by expressing the design firm's appreciation for the opportunity to compile the information into a report. Finally, the cover letter should be signed by a senior member of the design team or firm.

Table of Contents

A table of contents will help the client easily access various parts of the report. It also serves as a quick reference for a list of sections included within the report.

Executive Summary

A written summary of two to six pages consolidates information and quantities from all sections of the report in traditional paragraph form. Some people find it easier to comprehend information presented in this manner as opposed to looking at diagrams, tables, drawings, and graphs.

The summary may cover all sections equally, or it may focus on selected sections and information. For example, some companies may be interested in personnel growth, whereas another company may be more interested in the types of work areas requested by its staff. In these situations, the summary can present a thorough discussion of these subjects rather than just a list of the raw data.

Other parts of the written summary include an opening statement, objectives of the report, methods used for gathering the information, and conclusions reached based on the data. Finally, the summary should address incomplete or inconclusive data and future actions that should be taken to complete these deficient areas.

Organization Charts

Organization charts are a critical component of the planning process (Figs. 12.1 and 12.2).

FIGURE 12.1 Organization chart: Top level overall company

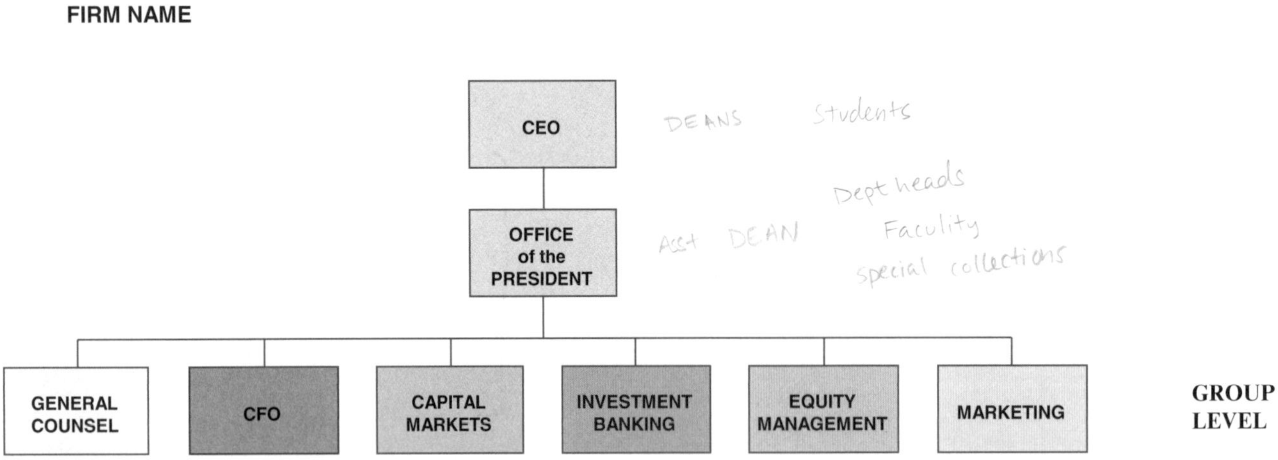

Figures 12.1, 12.2, 12.3b, and 12.4 through 12.9, based on original Programming Effort and Report for "Kemper Securities, Inc.," ML Design, Chicago, IL, 1991, have been edited and updated to reflect current industry trends.

The charts may show corporate departments as they relate to each other overall, or they may show specific staff positions within each department. The charts typically display the hierarchy relationships within the company or show how the departments relate to each other. Charts are helpful for understanding the makeup of the company and aid in organizing the data and criteria in the main quantitative section of the Program Report. Typically, companies have three or four levels of hierarchy, but there is no standardization of level names from one company to the next. One company may use the term *department* as the highest level within its organization, and another company may use the same term *department* to represent the second level of hierarchy within its organization. Other level names include but are not limited to division, section, group, branch, team, and unit. The designer should follow the terminology used by each client for all documentation on their respective projects, knowing that the terminology will change from one client to the next client.

Many companies already have charts that can be attached to questionnaires, or each group can draw its chart on a piece of paper and attach it to the questionnaires. Charts typically consist of several parts:

- A primary or top-level chart showing the major divisions or departments of the overall company (Fig. 12.1)
- Second-level charts for each division or department (Fig. 12.2)
- Additional charts for the lower levels of sections or groups within a division or department

Although the client-supplied charts can be used in Program Reports, designers frequently redraw charts for a consist look in the final report. Often, it is beneficial to color code each group on the charts. Those colors can then be used consistently to represent each group throughout the report in other graphic drawings, such as adjacency and stacking diagrams.

Adjacency Diagrams

Adjacency relationships refer to both internal and external departmental interactions and associations. Internal relationships include individuals, units or groups, and support functions within the immediate group of reference. External relationships include interaction with another department, division, or firm-wide special use areas. Relationships include physical and paper interactions but generally not telephone interactions. Adjacency or non-adjacency

FIGURE 12.2 Organization chart: Second level

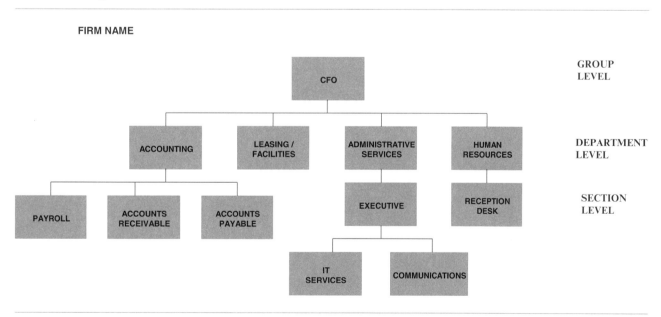

requirements may also include the need for off-site spaces and on-site separation between certain groups. Physical separation may be an internal desire, such as when a president requests that the executive area be separated from the personnel office, or it may be a Securities and Exchange Commission (SEC) regulation stating that retail and certain financial divisions within a corporation may not occupy joint floor space. Requesting an off-site location is generally based on economics, such as housing old records in less expensive facilities.

Based on client input on the questionnaires, desired or requested relationships and interactions can be expressed through graphic or adjacency diagrams (Fig. 12.3a and b). Generally, most clients are fascinated by adjacency diagrams and find them fairly easy to read in order to understand desired associations between various groups within a firm. Adjacency diagrams present a visual tool with a lot of information, yet they do not require a great deal of analytical thinking.

Adjacency diagrams are used for three purposes. First, when a client's organization will occupy more than one floor, the designation of less stringent interactions and associations help determine which groups can be separated when stacking them on different floors within a building. Second, the designation of more critical associations determine placement of groups on the same floor. Third, the designation of workflow helps with space planning each specific group layout.

Relationship Requirements

Relationship requirements can range from being very critical, to a close spatial alliance, to a desirable closeness, to no requirements at all, or even to physical separation from another group or particular support function. Requests for desired relationships may flow from both directions, meaning that two groups both ask for a close, or non-close, association with each other, or just one of the groups asks for a particular alliance, but not the other group. Differences in adjacency requests should be addressed with each group during programming interviews or in follow-up conversations before floor plans are finalized.

FIGURE 12.3a Adjacency diagram: Circle form

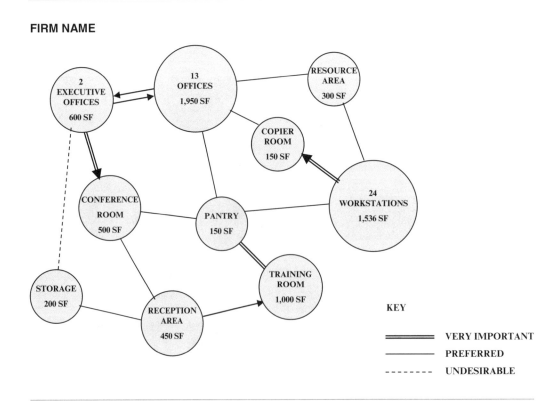

FIGURE 12.3b Adjacency diagram: Oval form

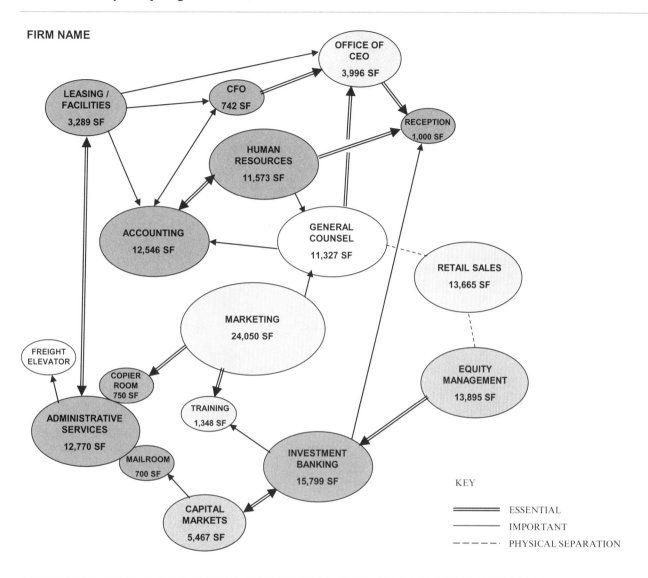

FIRM NAME

KEY

═══════ ESSENTIAL

──────── IMPORTANT

– – – – – PHYSICAL SEPARATION

Diagram Styles

Adjacency diagrams can be created in several distinct forms, including a grid form (Fig. 12.4) or the more popular circle form used by many interior design firms. Other shapes, such as rectangles or ovals, can be used in place of circles (Fig. 12.3b).

Nomenclature used in the diagrams should correspond to the vocabulary used on the questionnaire. For example, if the words *essential, desired,* and *physical separation* were used on the questionnaire, then these same words should be used on the diagram. If words such as *critical, important,* and *undesirable* were used instead, then those words should be used on the diagram.

Graphic lines of various styles, weights, or number of lines are assigned to each relationship word and then used to depict the relationships on the diagram. Arrows help communicate the direction of each request. A key or legend listing the relationship terms and the assigned line graphics should be included as a part of each diagram.

Adjacency vs. Bubble Diagram

Although adjacency diagrams may appear to be similar to the bubble diagram used in planning many homes and other new buildings, there are some primary differences between the two

FIGURE 12.4 Adjacency diagram: Grid form

FIRM NAME

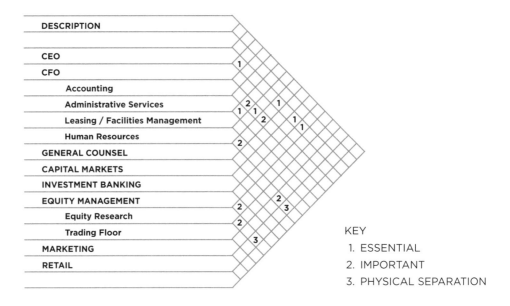

KEY
1. ESSENTIAL
2. IMPORTANT
3. PHYSICAL SEPARATION

diagrams. Bubble diagrams are developed during the conceptual or schematic phase in which an attempt is made to place bubbles in exact spatial relationships, emanating in a final floor plan layout. Adjacency diagrams are created during the programming phase to represent workflow relationships. Preliminary bubble diagrams may truly be bubbles, or they may take on desired room shapes. Whether a bubble or room shape, bubble diagrams usually allocate one room per bubble, whereas adjacency diagrams may incorporate a whole department within a single circle. On a bubble diagram, arrows or double sets of lines indicate door and entry locations, whereas arrows and lines represent spatial relationships on adjacency diagrams.

The designer can make an attempt to arrange the adjacency circles in some type of spatial relationship for a final plan, however, because the actual floor space may not yet have been selected, any attempt to do so may be ambiguous. For instance, positioning the point of entry or reception circle will depend on whether the floor space is at street level, on an upper floor, directly off the elevator lobby, at the end of the corridor, or split between several floors. Depending on the final building or floor plate size, the client may lease one floor or multiple floors,

which means department circles may all need to go to the left, or right, or be split around the reception circle. Because there are so many unknowns, it is not easy to place the adjacency circles in a truly spatial relationship on the diagram.

Number of Circles and Terminology

The number of circles depends on the client and the size of the project, but it is often best to simplify the diagram with fewer circles for visual clarity. Obviously, a smaller project will have fewer requirements, resulting in fewer circles, whereas a larger project will have many circles. A circle can symbolize individual rooms, a group of rooms, or a whole department. Oftentimes, there are a number of different ways to use circle representations. For example, if there are four workstations and two offices, the diagram can show one circle for each work area, resulting in six circles, or the diagram can combine all workstations together in one circle and the two offices in another circle for a total of two circles. When circles encompass whole departments and groups, it may be prudent to show the reception area, copy room, and other selected support rooms as separate circles, as these areas have important relationships to more than one group.

Circle names or terms should follow vocabulary used by clients on their questionnaires. Circle names rarely, if ever, use employees' actual names.

Size of Circles

To some extent, different sizes of circles can be used to represent larger or smaller amounts of square footage. Different sizes of circles can quickly indicate visually that the reception area and copier rooms require less space than the finance department or that the cafeteria requires more space than the conference room.

Only three or four diverse circles, each representing a range of square footage, should be used to depict all groups or rooms displayed on a diagram. When too many sizes are used, the diagram will appear disorderly. If the circles are too small, it is difficult to place the necessary information within the circle. If one circle is too large (even though the space requirement may truly be large), it will dominate the diagram. Good sizes to use for circles are $1/2$ inch (in.), $3/4$ in., $7/8$ in., and 1 in.

Quantitative and Detailed Information

The backbone of space planning, the crux of the Program Report, and the nuts and bolts of the design are based on the detailed information quantified under the square footage and numbers segment for each level of hierarchy; information that is compiled from the questionnaires, interviews, walk-throughs, typical layouts (Chapters 6–11), and other means. It is beneficial for the designer to input data into the computer fairly quickly after each interview; follow-up questions can be answered while the information is fresh in everyone's mind.

Where the information is straightforward, such as the headcount and work area types for each staff position (questions 3 and 4 in questionnaire in Appendix C), data are easily entered. When room sizes need to be calculated based on items to be housed within (questions 8 and 9 in questionnaire in Appendix C), it is a good idea for the designer to draw a sketch and attach it to the questionnaire to show how the square footage was calculated (see Table 11.2 and Figs. 11.9a and b). This attachment provides backup data and is a good reference when square footages need to be validated in the future.

Formatted Page Layouts

Information should be entered starting with the lowest levels of hierarchy and then summarized upward. Each level should receive its own stand-alone spreadsheet or page. Although it is best to use a true database program that can sort the information, many firms use a standard spreadsheet program, such as Excel. Page layouts can be formatted as the designer chooses.

There are two types of information that should appear on each level's page: project identification and group detailed information. Project identifying elements to remain consistent on standard page layouts may include (Fig. 12.5):

- Client name
- Level name
- Level code (if applicable)
- Hierarchy information
- Report name
- Design firm name
- Page number

Detailed Information

Once a page layout for the Program Report is established, formulas are set up in all cells that require a calculated number; numbers should not be calculated outside the spreadsheet and then entered as a whole number. Obviously, with formulas, the cells will recalculate as the data changes, and there will be changes to some of the data. Quantitative entries follow a fairly typical columnar layout of information (Fig. 12.6).

- Staff positions (per the organization charts)
- Rank or grade (if applicable)
- Typical work area type
- Support rooms and areas
- Support room type (if applicable)
- Net square footage (NSF) assignments
- Existing or current staff headcount
- Existing or current support quantities
- Existing or current net square feet (calculated in cell by formula of headcount or support quantities times NSF assignments)
- Projected staff headcount
- Projected support quantities
- Projected net square feet (calculated in cell by formula of projected headcount or support quantities times NSF assignments)

FIGURE 12.5 Program Report: Lowest-level quantitative summary

Firm Name ← CLIENT NAME

PERSONNEL AND SUPPORT AREAS ← REPORT NAME

GROUP: CFO ←
DEPARTMENT: Accounting ← LEVEL NAME
SECTION: Payroll ←

ITEM	GRADE	DESCRIPTION	FUNCTION TYPE	NSF	2015 CURRENT STAFF	SUPPORT	NSF	2017 MOVE-IN STAFF	SUPPORT	NSF
1		Manager	PO-3	150	1		150	1		150
2		Payroll - Research	P100	100	4		400	0		0
3		Payroll - Processing	P100	100	5		500	0		0
4										
5		Payroll - Research	WS-1	60	0		0	3		180
6		Payroll - Research	WS-2	48	0		0	2		96
7		Payroll - Processing	WS-1	60	0		0	2		120
8		Payroll - Processing	WS-2	48	0		0	4		192
9		Vertical Letter Files		8		7	56		7	56
10		Vertical Letter Files		10		3	30		3	30
11		36" Lateral Files		14		4	56		6	84
12		24 x 60 Work Table		25		0	0		1	25
13		Storage Cabinets		14		1	14		1	14
14										
15		Professional - Payroll Control	WS-2	48	1		48	2		96
16										
17		Visitor Workstation	WS-2	48		0	0		2	96
18		Shredder		6		1	6		1	6
19										
20										
21		**Notes:**								
22		1 All sections of Accounting will share a copier / Fax Room.								
23		2 Research and processing personnel currently occupy 100 sf offices - they will move into								
24		workstations in the new location.								
25										

NET SQ. FT. (NSF)   1,260   1,145

     50% CIRCULATION   630   573

TOTAL USABLE SQ. FT. (USF)   **1,890**   **1,718**

TOTAL PERSONNEL   **11**   **14**

     TOTAL SQ. FT. / PERSON   172   123

DESIGN FIRM NAME

ML DESIGN _____ ←

PROGRAM REPORT
Page 11

PAGE NUMBER →

FIGURE 12.6 Program Report: Mid-level quantitative summary

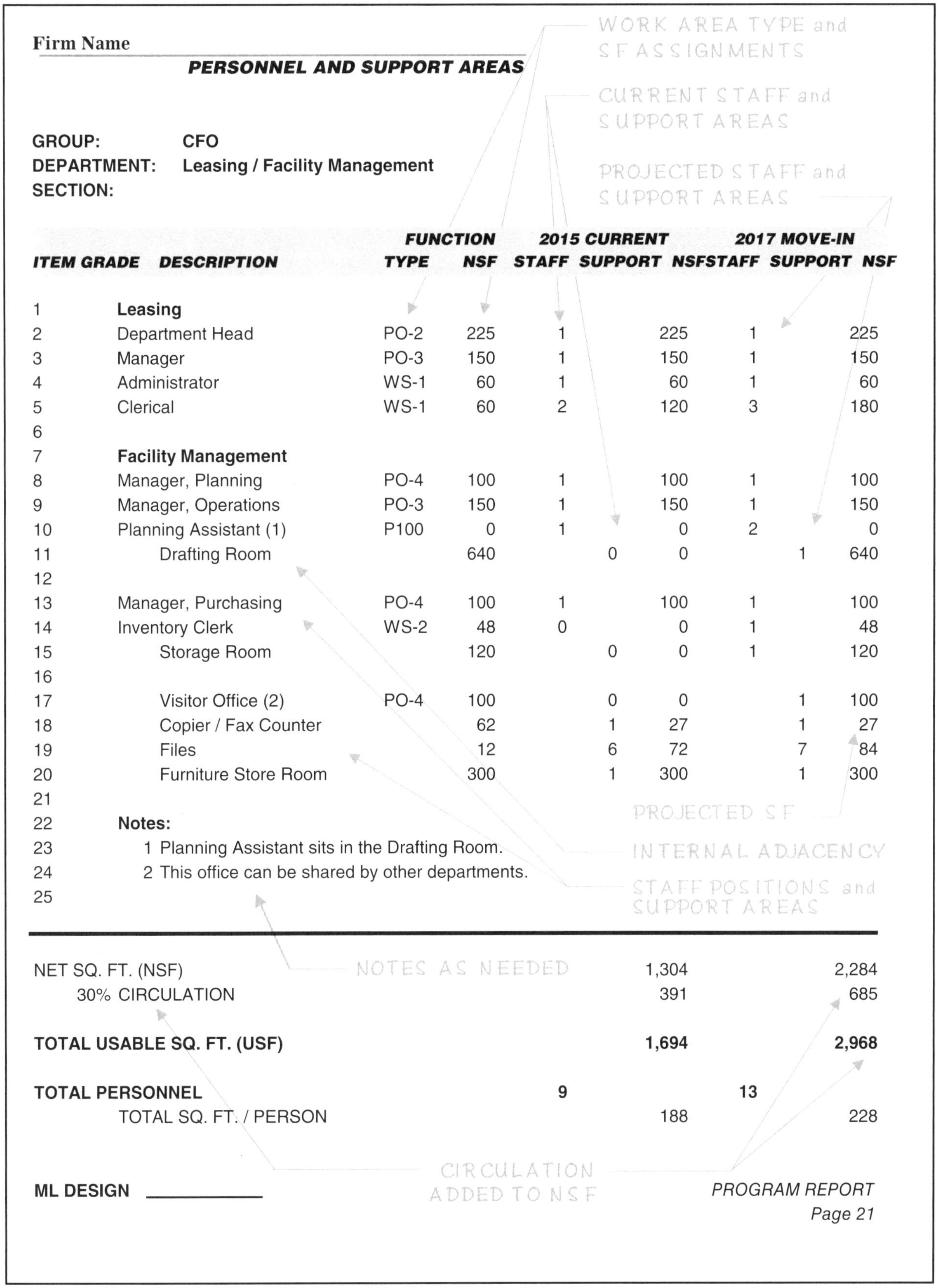

Firm Name

PERSONNEL AND SUPPORT AREAS

GROUP: CFO
DEPARTMENT: Leasing / Facility Management
SECTION:

ITEM	GRADE	DESCRIPTION	FUNCTION TYPE	FUNCTION NSF	2015 CURRENT STAFF	2015 CURRENT SUPPORT	2015 CURRENT NSF	2017 MOVE-IN STAFF	2017 MOVE-IN SUPPORT	2017 MOVE-IN NSF
1		**Leasing**								
2		Department Head	PO-2	225	1		225	1		225
3		Manager	PO-3	150	1		150	1		150
4		Administrator	WS-1	60	1		60	1		60
5		Clerical	WS-1	60	2		120	3		180
6										
7		**Facility Management**								
8		Manager, Planning	PO-4	100	1		100	1		100
9		Manager, Operations	PO-3	150	1		150	1		150
10		Planning Assistant (1)	P100	0	1		0	2		0
11		Drafting Room		640		0	0		1	640
12										
13		Manager, Purchasing	PO-4	100	1		100	1		100
14		Inventory Clerk	WS-2	48	0		0	1		48
15		Storage Room		120		0	0	1		120
16										
17		Visitor Office (2)	PO-4	100		0	0		1	100
18		Copier / Fax Counter		62		1	27		1	27
19		Files		12		6	72		7	84
20		Furniture Store Room		300		1	300		1	300
21										
22		**Notes:**								
23		1 Planning Assistant sits in the Drafting Room.								
24		2 This office can be shared by other departments.								
25										

	2015	2017
NET SQ. FT. (NSF)	1,304	2,284
30% CIRCULATION	391	685
TOTAL USABLE SQ. FT. (USF)	**1,694**	**2,968**
TOTAL PERSONNEL	**9**	**13**
TOTAL SQ. FT. / PERSON	188	228

ML DESIGN __________

PROGRAM REPORT
Page 21

WORK AREA TYPE and SF ASSIGNMENTS
CURRENT STAFF and SUPPORT AREAS
PROJECTED STAFF and SUPPORT AREAS
PROJECTED SF
INTERNAL ADJACENCY
STAFF POSITIONS and SUPPORT AREAS
NOTES AS NEEDED
CIRCULATION ADDED TO NSF

Rank or grade used by the government and some other companies and institutions, when applicable, is often used as an association for assigning typical work areas and square footage for staff positions. For instance, all grades above 13 may be assigned 300 square feet (SF), whereas all grades below an 8 may be assigned 48 SF, along with the appropriate work area types.

Both existing and projected quantities of personnel and support areas should be listed in the report. Clients know what they have today, but the designer needs to plan for the future. Some clients find it hard to project growth patterns, but it is essential for them to understand the importance of looking at their future needs. Mature companies will probably have limited growth patterns and therefore will want to keep their growth numbers very low or possibly flat. On the other hand, young, fast-growing companies probably have much higher growth numbers, which will require more space to accommodate all of their new members on the move-in date. It is critical, however, to be realistic about growth and not project growth that is not sustainable by the company's business goals.

Some designers prefer to list all personnel positions first and then all support areas. At other times, it is possible to indicate some internal adjacency requirements by listing a support area immediately after the position that requires the adjacency, such as a private bathroom or conference room directly below the director's position on the report or a drafting room listed directly below the planning assistant position (see Fig. 12.6). When all support areas are listed together after staff positions, it usually indicates that these rooms are shared by all of the staff.

Notes or comments can be added as necessary. However, these should be kept to a minimum, as this portion of the report is a quantitative rather than a qualitative analysis.

Data Entry

Using the second-level organization chart (see Fig. 12.2), there are four levels of hierarchy shown for the CFO: level 1—group; level 2—department; level 3—section; level 4—unnamed. Two of the departments have section levels as the lowest levels, thus the program information is first entered under each section level, such as for the

Payroll section (Fig. 12.5). Once data are entered for all sections of a given level, in this case, Payroll, Accounts Receivable, and Accounts Payable, with each level receiving its own sheet, then all sections are summarized under their respective department level, in this case, Accounting (see Fig. 12.7).

Continuing with the same organization chart, the department of Leasing/Facilities Management has no section levels. In this case, it is the lowest level in their department, and as such, its information is entered without summary from any lower levels (Fig. 12.6).

Just as all sections are summarized under their respective departments, in a similar manner all departments are summarized under the next level up, in this case a group level. In this example, Leasing/Facilities and Accounting are combined with the other two departments and their executive group to be summarized under their group level (Fig. 12.8). Group levels are summarized, in turn, under the firm summary showing the total number of personnel, the total required square footage, and the average square feet per person (Fig. 12.9). It is this top-level firm summary, and perhaps the next level down or group level summaries, that are of most interest to the majority of people viewing the Program Report. The balance of the pages and levels serve as backup information to be validated by the lower-level groups involved and then used by designers for space planning.

Quantitative and Square Footage Data

Once the information has been entered and summarized, a draft copy of the data should be given to the client for review. In turn, clients may distribute portions or all of the data to each group or level that provided input information for their concurrence and agreement, or corrections and revisions as necessary. It is very important that clients approve the stated detailed information, as this information is used for lease negotiations, space planning, special construction requirements, security implementation, and many other aspects during the design phases. Although the designer looks for data approval at this point, there is yet another opportunity for clients to update or revise the data when they receive a copy of the completed Program Report.

FIGURE 12.7 Program Report: Departmental quantitative summary

Firm Name

DEPARTMENT SUMMARY

INDIVIDUAL STAFF and SF SUMMARIES for EACH GROUP or SECTION ARE SHOWN UNDER THEIR DEPARTMENT HEAD

GROUP: CFO
DEPARTMENT: Accounting
SECTION:

ITEM GRADE	DESCRIPTION	2015 CURRENT STAFF	NSF	2017 MOVE-IN STAFF	NSF
1	Department Manager	5	1,075	6	1,075
2					
3	Payroll	11	1,896	14	1,703
4					
5	Accounts Receivable	17	3,396	20	3,400
6					
7	Accounts Payable	18	3,575	22	3,790
8					
9	Support Areas		1,075		1,136
10					
11					
12					
13					
14					
15					
16					
17					
18					
19					
20					
21	**Notes:**				
22	1 All sections of Accounting will share a copier / Fax Room.				
23	2 Research and processing personnel currently occupy 100 sf offices - they will move into				
24	workstations in the new location.				
25					

LATERAL LEVELS or SECTIONS ARE SUMMARIZED UNDER THEIR DEPARTMENT HEAD

NET SQ. FT. (NSF)		11,017	11,104
5% CIRCULATION		551	555
TOTAL USABLE SQ. FT. (USF)		**11,568**	**11,659**
TOTAL PERSONNEL	**51**	**62**	
TOTAL SQ. FT. / PERSON		227	188

ML DESIGN _____

PROGRAM REPORT
Page 9

FIGURE 12.8 Program Report: Second-level quantitative summary

Firm Name

GROUP SUMMARY

GROUP: **CFO**

ITEM GRADE	DESCRIPTION	2015 CURRENT		2017 MOVE-IN	
		STAFF	NSF	STAFF	NSF
1	Executive	2	742	2	690
2					
3	Accounting	51	11,562	62	11,674
4					
5	Leasing / Facilities Management	9	1,694	13	2,968
6					
7	Administrative Services	59	9,719	72	13,220
8					
9	Human Resources	33	7,267	40	7,873
10					
11					
12					
13					
14					
15					
16					
17					
18					
19					
20					
21	**Notes:**				
22	1				
23	2				
24					
25					

LIKE LOWER LEVELS, LATERAL DEPARTMENTS ARE SUMMARIZED UNDER THEIR GROUP LEVEL

	2015 CURRENT	2017 MOVE-IN
NET SQ. FT. (NSF)	30,983	36,425
4% CIRCULATION	1,239	1,457
TOTAL USABLE SQ. FT. (USF)	**32,223**	**37,882**
TOTAL PERSONNEL	**154**	**189**
TOTAL SQ. FT. / PERSON	209	200

AVERAGE SF PER PERSON

ML DESIGN _____

PROGRAM REPORT
Page 6

Firm Name

PROGRAM SUMMARY

GROUP: **FIRM**

ITEM GRADE	DESCRIPTION	2015 CURRENT STAFF	NSF	2017 MOVE-IN STAFF	NSF
1	CEO and Office of President	4	3,273	5	3,387
2					
3	General Counsel	38	6,313	54	11,327
4					
5	CFO	154	32,223	189	37,882
6					
7	Capital Markets	13	3,436	21	4,167
8					
9	Investment Banking	33	10,092	52	11,960
10					
11	Equity Management	35	8540	51	10,895
12					
13	Marketing	73	15,980	114	21,898
14					
15	Common Facilities	0	9,295	0	15,839
16					
17					
18					
19					
20					
21	**Notes:**				
22	1				
23	2				
24					
25					

STAFF and SF ARE SUMMARIZED FOR ALL GROUPS TO PROVIDE A TOTAL FIRM REQUIREMENT

NET SQ. FT. (NSF) — 89,152 — 117,355
2% CIRCULATION — 1,783 — 2,347

TOTAL USABLE SQ. FT. (USF) — 90,935 — 119,702

TOTAL PERSONNEL — 350 — **486**
TOTAL SQ. FT. / PERSON — 260 — 246

ML DESIGN _____

AVERAGE SF PER PERSON

PROGRAM REPORT
Page 1

Information Summaries

The designer must total existing and projected personnel and the square footage for each group. This allows for a quick comparison between existing situations and requested new spaces. It is not necessary to total support areas, as that total would have little meaning because it includes a variety of areas such as file rooms, pantries, or copy rooms. Occasionally, a company may want to know how many conference or LAN (local area network) rooms have been requested. In these cases, separate queries can be made for specific information.

Square Footage

Up to this point, square footage listings and discussions have generally referred to net square feet (NSF) or the exact amount of space required for a function, for instance, 225 NSF (15×15) offices, 48 NSF (6×8) workstations, or 150 NSF (10×15) coffee rooms. In addition to the NSF, circulation space is required for people to walk and operate throughout the office space. When added to the NSF, this new total square footage is known as usable square feet (USF; see Box 12.1).

BOX 12.1 Square Feet

Net Square Feet

Net square feet (NSF) is the specific amount of space required for a private office, workstation, support or special use area, or any other required spaces. Also known as assigned space, it does not include any circulation or core items.

Usable Square Feet

Usable square feet (USF) includes the total net square feet plus the internal circulation and any unassigned space within an office suite. It does not include any building core elements, primary circulation, or external walls.

Rentable Square Feet

Rentable square feet (RSF) includes the usable square feet plus the common building areas on each floor, including the corridors or primary circulation, restrooms and telephone closets, building lobby, loading dock, and other common use areas within the building. It does not include any vertical building penetrations, such as elevator shafts or any spaces such as window shelves that are contiguous to an outer building wall with a dominant portion of glass and a clear finished height of less than 5 feet (ft).

Gross Square Feet

Gross square feet (GSF) is the total area of the building, including all circulation (stairs, escalators, elevators), mechanical spaces, core areas, and building support spaces. The area extends to the outer surface of the exterior walls and windows. It does not include parking or the roof.

Building Core

The building core includes portions of both the gross and rentable square foot items, such as the restrooms, telephone and mechanical closets, stairs, and elevators. It also includes vestibules into these areas and the elevator lobby. These items are generally bundled together and positioned near the center of the building, or occasionally offset to a selected perimeter edge in smaller footprint buildings (see Chapter 13).

Rentable Factor

Because tenants use many common building areas such as corridors and restrooms, they pay lease rates based on rentable square footage, which includes both those building common areas and their own usable square footage. Rentable square footage is calculated for both single and multi-tenant floors. Standard practice typically calls for the rentable factor to be added to the total usable square footage. If the building is very efficient and provides little beyond the basic code requirements for the primary corridors and restrooms, the factor may be as low as 8–9 percent of the usable square footage. When a building offers many amenities and is very generous with space, such as large lobbies or atriums, the core factor may be as high as 18–22 percent of the usable square footage.

A typical industry standard for the core factor is 12–14 percent of the usable square footage during the initial design phases.

Circulation

During the micro-planning or space planning phase, it is easy to calculate the exact amount of circulation dedicated to each area (see Chapter 5). However, during the programming or macro-planning phase, when all of the specifics are not known, circulation is calculated as a percentage factor of the NSF (Box 12.2). Historical experience has demonstrated that although the circulation factor will vary from one type of function to another, it remains fairly consistent for like functions. For instance, offices, regardless of size, habitually require that a factor of approximately 25–30 percent be added to their NSF, whereas workstations of any size require a higher factor of 45–60 percent (Box 12.3).

Generally, the circulation factor is added to the total NSF at the bottom of each data sheet. The specific factor can vary from group to group based on the mixture of offices, rooms, and workstations required for each individual group. Departments or sections with more offices can receive a smaller factor, whereas departments or sections with more workstations should receive a higher factor (Figs. 12.5 and 12.6).

Occasionally, clients request that circulation factors be calculated on an individual function basis rather than a total basis. This is achieved by adding another column next to the NSF column on the report. Separate factors are then added to each office, workstation, and so on (Table 12.1). When this occurs, a separate circulation factor is generally not included at the bottom of the report sheet.

Clarifying Circulation Factors

There is often much conversation about the circulation factor. After all, it will regularly add at least 30–50 percent more square footage to the minimum required net square footage needed for offices, workstations, and other support rooms. Due to building architecture, configuration, and size, some buildings allow for more efficient use of internal space and thus require lower circulation factors. Other buildings, or the nature of the program requirements, may not allow for efficient use of internal space and thus require higher circulation factors. Regardless of the reason for higher factors, the client pays rent based on the total usable square footage, not the

TABLE 12.1 Circulation Added to Individual Rooms and Areas

DESCRIPTION	SIZE	NSF	%	USF
Office*	15' × 20'	300	1.25	375
Office*	15' × 15'	225	1.25	281
Office*	10' × 15'	150	1.25	188
Workstation**	7'-6" × 8'	60	1.55	93
Workstation**	6' × 8'	48	1.55	74
Auditorium	30' × 50'	1,500	1.1	1,650

*See Fig. 6.11 for office size layouts
**See Fig. 7.2 and Illustrated Table 7.2d for workstation size layouts

net square footage. In addition, a rentable factor as defined by the landlord is added to the total usable square footage.

Building management and landlords recognize the circulation factor to be critical in lease negotiations. They often promote their buildings as having efficient circulation factors. But it is important to clarify the terminology when speaking about circulation or efficiency factors because designers and building landlords generally use different language and calculations for defining circulation factors (Box 12.4).

Average SF per Person

Finally, the average square feet per person is calculated by dividing the total usable square footage by the total number of personnel (Figs. 12.8 and 12.9). Company management periodically uses an average USF per person as a benchmark to compare their firm with another firm or to start lease negotiations for new space (see Chapter 2). Average SF also serves to inform the client about a definable amount of space, 207 USF per person as opposed to, for example, envisioning fifty-one staff in 10,569 SF.

Some groups or areas such as a library will have very high usable square footage per person, which is understandable because only one or two people have a permanent work area in this room; other groups may have low usable

BOX 12.2 Circulation[1]

Circulation provides for the movement of people (and materials) through a building as part of their daily activities. Typical circulation paths include corridors and aisles. There are two types of circulation:

- Primary building circulation
- Internal departmental circulation

Primary Building Circulation

Primary circulation is that portion of a building that is a public corridor or lobby, or part of a required route for access on all floors to the stairwells, elevators, restrooms, and building exits and entrances to be used by all occupants and visitors of the building. This circulation is determined by identifying a reasonable minimum corridor or route connecting these building areas and the tenant (departmental) suite entry points. In addition to providing entry, the primary corridor must also meet life-safety access and egress requirements.

Occasionally, bridges, tunnels, and atria, which do not meet the strict definition of a primary corridor but which are not readily used for another purpose, are also included as part of the circulation.

Standard practice typically calls for a primary circulation allowance to be based on a factor of 5 percent of the total usable square footage.

Internal Departmental or Secondary Circulation

Internal or secondary circulation occurs within each suite of offices for all departments, divisions, and groups. Internal circulation is made up of several components, including corridors; main walkways; aisles between workstations; access space to shelving, storage, and equipment; and space for opening furniture or equipment doors, drawers, and other parts.

Internal circulation is an allowance based on a factor of the total net square footage. It is a bit more complex and subjective when assigning an internal circulation factor, as there are four scenarios that should be considered.

1. When the plan is predominately private offices and other rooms, a 25–30 percent factor is applied to the net square footage.
2. When there is a fairly even mix of offices and workstations, a 35 percent allowance is typically applied to the total net square footage.
3. When the number of workstations greatly exceeds the number of offices, a 45–60 percent factor should be applied to the net square footage.
4. Special use areas are usually self-contained rooms with some circulation already built into the assigned square footage. For these areas, the circulation factor can be reduced to 10–15 percent applied to the net square footage.

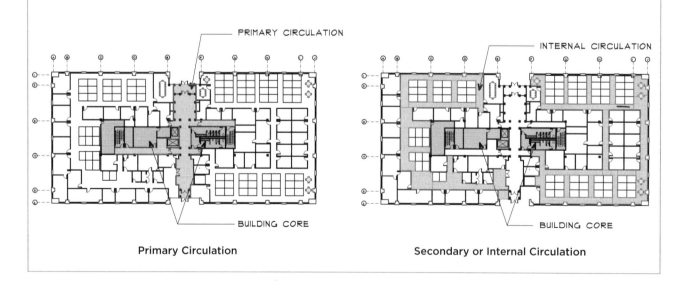

Primary Circulation

Secondary or Internal Circulation

BOX 12.3 Calculating Internal Circulation[2]

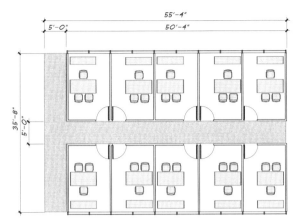

Offices—150 NSF

10 PRIVATE OFFICES
 2 GROUPS OF OFFICES
 1 AISLE OF CIRCULATION

WORK AREA: 1,546 NSF
CIRCULATION: 430 NSF
TOTAL USABLE: 1,976 USF

CIRCULATION
28 PERCENT OF WORK AREA NSF
OR
22 PERCENT OF TOTAL USF

Circulation around offices

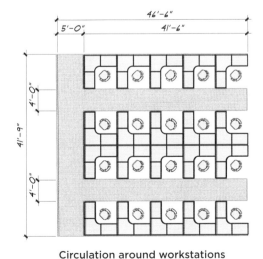

WORKSTATIONS—64 NSF

20 WORKSTATIONS
 2 GROUPS OF WORKSTATIONS
 3 AISLES OF CIRCULATION

WORK AREA: 1,390 NSF
CIRCULATION: 723 NSF
TOTAL USABLE: 2,113 USF

CIRCULATION
52 PERCENT OF WORK AREA NSF
OR
34 PERCENT OF TOTAL USF

Circulation around workstations

WORKSTATIONS—64 NSF

20 WORKSTATIONS
 3 GROUPS OF WORKSTATIONS
 2 AISLES OF CIRCULATION

WORK AREA: 1,400 NSF
CIRCULATION: 546 NSF
TOTAL USABLE: 1,946 USF

CIRCULATION
39 PERCENT OF WORK AREA NSF
OR
28 PERCENT OF TOTAL USF

Circulation around workstations

Note: SF and percentages have been rounded up or down slightly.
Formulas: Circulation ÷ Work area = Percentage NSF
          Circulation ÷ Total usable = Percentage USF

BOX 12.4 Circulation Factors

It is wise to be cautious when discussing circulation factors with the client and landlord, broker, or developer.

Calculating circulation square footages can be based on either the projected NSF or the existing USF space. The first mode is an ADDITIVE measure, while the second mode is a SUBTRACTIVE measure, resulting in a different percentage factor for each calculation.

Design and architectural firms ADD the circulation factor to the NSF of a Program Report. This requires a higher factor than the Subtractive Method.

75 NSF x 34%   = 25 SF Circulation
75 NSF + 25 SF = 100 USF

Building managers and brokers SUBTRACT the circulation factor from the USF of existing space. This results in a lower factor than the Additive Method.

100 USF x 25%   = 25 SF Circulation
100 USF – 25 SF = 75 NSF

Under either method, additive or subtractive, the resulting amount of circulation is 25 SF. However, the percentage factor used to achieve that 25 SF is higher or lower, depending on the method used to calculate it.

It is critical to establish whether one is talking about circulation based on the NSF or the USF.

---

square footage per person when there are only a few support rooms or support rooms are small. Firms with a lot of offices, such as three group levels in the Program Report example ranging between 210–230 USF per person (Table 12.2),

will have higher averages of usable square footage per person than does a department that is workstation intensive, such as accounting in this example with 188 USF per person (Fig. 12.7). Excessive support areas and amenities, such as a cafeteria, conferencing center, or wider circulation corridors, found under the common facilities in the report example with 33 USF per person (Table 12.2), will also increase the average USF per person, in this case to an overall 246 USF per person. Individual group usable square footage is important, but it is the firm's overall USF per person that should be used for the initial basis of planning.

Even though firms are frequently looking to lower their SF averages, as seen in these examples, it is often tough to achieve truly low averages. A single 15' × 15' office is already at 225 NSF, increasing to 281 USF once circulation is added (Table 12.1), well above the desired averages of 190 to 215 USF discussed below under "Historical Average Square Footage." To attain low square foot averages, firms will need to embrace smaller office sizes, more workstations over any office sizes, and consider mobility and teleworking scenarios where staff share work areas in some type of arrangement through reservations or a buddy system.

TABLE 12.2 Average USF per Group in Example (Fig. 12.9)

GROUP	CURRENT USF	MOVE-IN USF
CEO	818	677
General Counsel	166	210
CFO	209	200
Capital Markets	264	198
Investment Banking	306	230
Equity Management	244	214
Marketing	219	192
Common Facilities	27	33

*Note: Normally, these USF averages are found at the bottom of each group summary page, similar to the CFO example (Fig. 12.8).

Corporate Philosophy

When comparing average square footage, it is important to identify the type and philosophy of the firms a client uses as benchmarks. Although two companies may have the same business background, corporate philosophy can greatly alter the USF per person. For example, many insurance companies house the majority of underwriters and analysts in workstations. One insurance company may believe that better production is received from employees seated in large 100 NSF cubicles (almost the size of an office). Another company may feel that the same amount of work can be achieved from employees occupying 64 NSF (see Illustrated Table 7.2e) or 80 NSF cubicles.

Thirty-six or 20 NSF per person can make a huge difference in the total SF required for lease and thus the amount of rent to be paid. It is important to discuss the work area standards with clients at the beginning of each project. Clients should be made aware of how each work area standard could affect the final outcome of their space and financial obligations.

When average square footages appear higher than current trends, this may be the time to revisit the work area mix of offices vs. workstations (see Chapter 2) discussion with the client, which presumably took place near the start of gathering the programming information in order to establish work area typicals to include as part of the questionnaire package. Or, the client may be interested to learn more about worker mobility and telecommuting work area options (see Chapter 2 and Chapter 7), which can also reduce average square footages. Designers should always respect clients' wishes and desires for the number of offices allowed or the change from offices to workstations. After all, it is their space. Yet, at the same time, designers should not be timid about pointing out how choices may increase or decrease the average square footages per person and the overall firm square footage.

Building Footprint Efficiencies

Building footprints can also affect the average SF per person. Odd-shaped or angled buildings often produce less than desirable or unusable spaces (see Chapter 5, "Leftover, Unusual, or Angled Spaces"). Although these otherwise unusable spaces frequently create greater interest and employee satisfaction than buildings with more efficient space, these additional spaces and square footage also increase the average USF per person.

Ultimately, the USF per person is transformed into rentable square footage (RSF) per person, which is the basis for lease negotiations. Buildings with high core or amenity factors, while beautiful and impressive, also generate higher lease rates. It is important that clients understand the design factors that might impact their lease rates.

Historical Average Square Footage

During the late 1980s and early 1990s, 235 USF per person represented a good planning average for a typical corporation to use. Since then, averages have been reduced for three reasons. First, as costs for construction, rent, and new furniture escalate, many companies look for ways to reduce their total square footage. Second, with a computer now sitting in most work areas, certain positions, such as typists and proofreaders, as well as their workstations, have been eliminated from the workforce, thus saving square footage. Third, as the workforce moves to alternate work styles, employees often share work areas through hoteling and touchdown arrangements. Current averages are somewhere between 190 and 215 USF per person, but as businesses continue to evolve, the average USF will once again adjust based on prevailing trends.

Typical Work Area and Support Room Layouts

The average person has little concept as to what constitutes 150 SF or 500 SF. A few people may be able to visualize a room that is 10 × 15 or 20 × 25, but dimension sizes can be a bit confusing to many people. Therefore, it is beneficial to include with the Program Report copies of the typical private office and workstation layouts, and support room layouts as appropriate that were attached to the questionaires (see Chapter 3 and Chapters 6–11).

Although not everyone can read and fully comprehend all aspects of a floor plan or typical layout, most people can understand at least some of it. It is especially helpful when the furniture is listed alongside the layouts (see Figs. 6.5, 7.2, and 8.8).

Additional Materials

Occasionally Program Reports will include additional materials and information that aid clients in making better decisions for their projects. Such aspects of the report may consist of, but not be limited to, parking requirements, interview summaries, initial floor-blocking plans and stacking diagram calculations, existing or future floor plans, budgets, glossaries, and any other information that may be deemed pertinent by the designer, depending on the scope of the project and the client's needs.

When additional items are added to the report, it is important for the design firm to understand the scope of these desired services so that proper fees and resources can be requested and allocated appropriately.

STACKING DIAGRAMS

For tenants with multi-floor requirements, it can be helpful to include a stacking diagram (opening diagram this Chapter 12) as part of the Program Report. This diagram takes the adjacency requirements and quantitative SF totals from the Program Report to the next, or first, level towards developing a space plan by assigning departments, groups, sections and firm support rooms and areas onto various floors of a multi-floor building. Assigned areas can be color-coded to match the org chart and adjacency diagram color assignments for each department, group, etc., so that the client can quickly identify where each group is to be located.

With a stacking diagram, it is also helpful to include a table or spreadsheet, probably on a separate page, that shows each floor listing the groups and their respective square footages to be housed on that floor, and a total square footage for each floor. For the initial presentation, total square footages for each of the floors will not equal or be the same square foot totals as on other floors. Floors will have higher and lower square footages, because at this point, everything is conceptual, even when the specific building is known. The reason to present this

flexibility is two-fold. First, square footages in the program are based on best guesses of quantity of items, items required and percentages of circulation. Any of these items could change between the time of filling out questionnaires, preparing the report, and space planning, thus increasing or decreasing the final quantities and square foot numbers. Second, the client may have a different point of view where they really, really want two groups to be on the same floor, even if it means splitting one of the groups between two floors or they may not want certain groups on the same floor even though the presented solutions work best based on the raw SF numbers. By presenting the unadulterated SF totals for each floor, the client can see that there is plenty of room for discussion and decision making.

When the client has already selected a particular building, then those floor plate square footages should be used for calculating the groups and support areas that can be assigned to each floor. If the building has not been chosen, then the designer can use average building floor plate sizes for the area where the client intends to locate. For instance, if the client is looking at a campus setting in a suburb where buildings tend to be low-rise buildings with large, horizontal footprints, the designer will want to display a stacking diagram based on approximately 50,000 SF per floor, whereas if the client wishes to locate in a downtown, metropolitan city that has many high-rise buildings, it is probably better to use between 25,000–30,000 SF per floor.

Technically, stacking diagrams fall under the Conceptual Design Phase II (see Box 1.1). So, though it may be a benefit to include this diagram, or optional diagrams displaying different stacking scenarios, in the Program Report, Phase I, designers will want to verify that there are sufficient fees under the programming contract to cover their efforts to calculate and draw the diagrams.

BLOCK PLANS

It is less likely that block plans will be included as part of the Program Report as a building truly has to already have been selected in order to develop a block plan. Particularly for larger projects, prior to drawing in, or space planning, all typical rooms, workstations, and individual pieces of furniture and equipment onto the floor plan, designers frequently block out chunks or areas of floor space on the selected building floor plate based on adjacency requirements, stacking diagrams, and sub-total square footages for groups, departments, support rooms, or other listings found in the Program Report. This big picture, non-detailed concept plan is a versatile tool to show and discuss with clients. It greatly aids the client to understand not only which groups go on each floor but also where each group will be located on their respective floors. As the client digests this information, suggests swapping two groups, either on the same floor or between different floors, even though the adjacency diagram may say something else, or decides to squeeze more support areas onto a given floor, it is much easier to relocate, reshape, or realign blocks of colored shapes than it is to move rows of offices and workstations around. Once this conceptual flow "feels" right, the designer will then plan individual program items or rooms within each chunk of blocked space that meet the client's needs and desires.

As with stacking diagrams, this task officially falls under the Conceptual Design Phase II. Block plans also move quickly into the actual space planning task, so designers should be careful about how much and what is included in the Program Report. After all, the primary essence of the report is to provide square foot requirements along with an idealized concept of the client's desires, wishes, and needs. It is only after the Program Report has been approved that block plans and space planning should proceed.

REPORT BOOKLETS

Because the data in a Program Report usually consist of several sections, files, and media types, it is generally printed and compiled into booklet form rather than distributed electronically. Design firms may have a standard format to be used for each section, or they may develop a new layout for each new project. Data can be printed from live files or turned into PDF files and then printed, depending on the type of file created for each section of the report. Once

printed, pages and sections are usually collated and assembled by hand.

Reports can be spiral-bound or inserted into three-ring notebooks. They can be tabbed or not and be printed in black and white, color, or a combination of both. Whichever method is selected for presentation, the designer should always keep in mind that the report is a representation of the design firm and the firm's quality of work and services. It is also important to note that the report becomes a legal document.

Report Format

In this book, examples displayed in Figs. 12.1–12.9, organization charts, adjacency diagrams and quantitative report sheets, and typical layouts (Figs. 6.5, 7.2, and 8.8) are shown in both portrait and landscape format to demonstrate that either format is acceptable. However, one format should be selected, and it should be used consistently throughout the final report. Continuity is broken when a reader is turning the report back and forth to first read a portrait layout, then a landscape layout, and then back to a portrait layout.

PRESENTATION OF THE REPORT

Program Reports are usually presented and reviewed at a meeting scheduled specifically for such action. In addition to the primary client contact, some or all of the questionnaire interviewees may be included at this meeting, along with other project team members, such as the broker, developer, or building manager. Each person should receive his or her own copy of the report. It is a good idea to bring along several extra copies of the report as well.

As the meeting begins, it is important to allow time for the participants to leaf through the report in an attempt to acquaint themselves with the report makeup. This may be the first time that many people have seen such a report, and it is probably the first time they are seeing this kind of detailed information about their own company.

Presentation of the report can be made either formally, with the designer standing at the front of the room, or informally, with the designer sitting at the table with everyone else. It may be prudent for the designer to start by reading aloud the written summary and then moving on to other sections. The designer will want to point out major aspects of the report, explain the process of generating the report, and touch upon open issues that are not addressed in the report. Time should be allowed for the participants to ask questions both during and after the presentation.

Review and Approval

Very few decisions will be made at this meeting. Clients should not be expected to give final approval of the report at this time. Rather, clients will want time to digest all of the information after the meeting has concluded, confer among themselves, make some changes or additions, and then ask for an updated report. Approximately one to two weeks should be allowed for the client review.

Report Sign-Off

Once the client has reviewed the Program Report and all changes have been made, it is very important to have the client actually sign and date the report as a legal document. Brokers may solicit building options based on typical office configurations and corporate philosophy. Lease negotiations may be based on the total square footage shown on the summary page. Designers will use the adjacency diagrams to lay out the groups within a building floor plate. This report is used as the basis for space planning. Therefore, forward movement of the project is based on official approval of the Program Report.

Generally, there is no specific, designated line for signing off on the report. Nevertheless, a signature and date made by the president, a board member, or other senior officer of the company should appear near the front of the booklet, perhaps on the title or cover letter page.

START OF SPACE PLANNING

After sign-off on the report, depending on the size of the project and the type of client, there may be a time lapse of between two weeks and six months before space planning begins. Clients may still be looking for a building. They may be negotiating the specific amount of square footage to be leased or the floor location, or they may be conducting internal studies. If this is a government project, time is required to secure funding. Some projects, commercial or government, never go beyond programming.

When space planning does begin, the Program Report becomes the source for every aspect of the planning process.

PROJECT

Write and assemble a Program Report

Students should plan to write and assemble a Program Report for their client using the tools discussed in this chapter. Not only is it important to develop an accurate concept of each client's wants, needs, and wishes at the start of each new project, but this information must be presented in a coherent manner for other vested parties to see and understand. Reports turn the raw data into synthesized graphs and charts for quick reference and information.

There are two options for choosing the client on which to base the report:

1. Use the client profile that was selected from Appendix A for other projects thus far.
2. Use the client who filled out the questionnaire in Chapter 3.

In either case, students should follow the same procedures to develop a final report:

1. Assign typical work area types to each staff member.
2. Calculate the support room sizes.
3. Compute total usable square footages.
4. Add circulation factors.
5. Draft an adjacency diagram.
6. Write an executive summary.

Keep in mind that typical layouts are often inserted into Program Reports. Therefore, the Program Report format should probably follow either the portrait or landscape format already established for the typical layouts.

13

BUILDING FOOTPRINT AND PROJECT INFORMATION

Location! Location! Location!
Like first impressions in the reception room, building location says a lot about a company and the image they wish to convey to their employees, visitors, and clients. A location on the 72nd floor of a landmark building in downtown Chicago, facing Lake Michigan, can provide a commanding view of the "world" for well-established firms or up-and-coming entrepreneurs. On the other hand, being situated in low-rise buildings on a rolling 200-acre campus in the suburbs, along an interstate highway, or in moderate buildings located across the country can provide a relaxed, secure position for any industry or small business.

Each location has its amenities.
Each location has its own character.
Each location has a slightly different set of program requirements.
Each location provides a philosophical outlook for space planning.
Each location may have similar or diverse code requirements.
Each location could serve the same firm should the client so choose.

Each location could serve many different types of client.

Whether companies remodel their existing space or relocate within the same building, down the street, across town, to the suburbs or into the city, over state lines, or out of the country, companies generally perform careful due diligence to ascertain the effect such a move will have on many aspects of their businesses. They consider their client base, employee base, morale and personnel turnover, rent and other financial costs, corporate image, business mission, availability of local amenities, and transportation accessibility. Any move, even a minor one, can affect any one or all of these issues.

Space planners should also perform due diligence on the building and site location prior to the start of space planning. Space planners may need to do some code research, particularly when the project will be in a location or building with which they are not familiar. It is beneficial to tour the building and surrounding sites. The more information the designer can acquire about the specific space to be planned, the better the final space plan.

SITE LOCATION

Companies choose their locations based on a number of factors, such as the locale being a source of raw materials, a hub of national or international centers, a cluster of similar types of businesses or a hometown of the owners. The locale may also be significant for consumer and employee bases and may provide a certain desired image. There is no golden rule as to where companies might choose to relocate. As a firm applies new strategies and updates its vision or mission statement, any number of factors may influence the site of its new office space.

Site Tour

To start a relocation process, clients and their brokers often use square footage information as stated in the client's existing lease to select and tour various buildings to be considered for new office space. When the design firm has already been selected, designers are normally invited to join in a tour of those buildings. At other times, clients will first request a design firm to provide programming services, establish the amount of actual required square footage, and then tour selected buildings to consider for new office space.

Sometimes the client has already chosen the new location prior to receiving feedback from or retaining a design firm. For some smaller projects, there may be limited interaction between the client and the design firm because the design firm has been retained by either a building manager or a developer who will include design fees as part of the new lease rate. In this case, the building manager or developer becomes the client and the company for whom the space is being planned is referred to as the tenant.

If the designer has not participated in a building tour with the client or tenant, the designer should still visit the building and surrounding site, when possible, to gain both an accurate picture of what currently exists and a mental picture or concept of what could exist in the space to be planned and designed.

- How will the type of building or its location affect the space plan?
- How will the building footprint affect the plan?
- How will the specific floor level affect the layout?

Site Analysis

In some cases, a floor plan will reflect the building location. Many older urban buildings were developed with narrow front or curb dimensions and deep interiors. Regardless of the type of business being planned for one of these buildings, the floor plan regularly results in a front-to-back procession of offices and rooms with a corridor down the middle or along one side of the building. Newer and suburban buildings tend to have wider or more lateral building frontage, which customarily opens up the space plan to any variety of floor layouts. Location can make a difference in how the designer approaches the space planning.

On the other hand, some branded companies, such as fast-food chains, drop their same typical footprint into various building footprints in cities all over the world. To these companies, location and building type makes no difference.

BUILDING SELECTION

When looking at specific buildings, companies consider many factors during the selection process (see Appendix B). Answers to the following questions eventually translate into or suggest the design approach and development:

1. Is it important to have a highly visible address such as Broadway or Pennsylvania Avenue? Or will a parallel, perhaps lesser-known street be acceptable? From a design standpoint, well-known addresses or buildings genuinely evoke a more spacious ambience or an added punch with higher circulation factors whereas lesser-known addresses often result in more standard layouts and circulation factors.

2. Will the building be a new, expensive building with high lease rates; an older building; or just any building with available floor space? New buildings often implicitly convey a higher design budget and fees whereas an older building may indicate a conservative budget.

3. Can the building be either a high-rise or low-rise building? In high-rise buildings where there are usually smaller floor plates, employees may be spread over several floors, resulting in a desired or implied hierarchy. In low-rise buildings, which regularly have larger floor plates, everyone may be located on the same floor.

4. Can the building be contemporary with lots of glass and steel? Or will a more traditional stone and colonnade building be a better selection? A contemporary building may suggest an avant-garde layout whereas a symmetrical layout may be a better tactic in a traditional building.

5. Is it desirable for the building tenant roster to have similar businesses? Or can the building contain any variety of business types? Similar businesses could either suggest a similar design approach or, alternatively, a design to set the client apart from the others.

Building selection frequently expresses a qualitative space planning and design approach. By validating reasons for the building selection, designers can incorporate the client's vision into the space plan.

PROJECT INFORMATION

Once the building has been selected and the project starts, it is important for the designer to compile the building and project information (Box 13.1). This information is used to determine applicable building codes, and it is required to be listed on the cover sheet of all construction drawing sets submitted for permits. The design firm may already have a standard form, or the designer may simply list the information on a sheet of paper placed in the project file.

This basic information will not change during the course of the project, yet it will determine many aspects of the space plan and project. For instance, under International Building Codes (IBC), Occupancy Group A-Assembly, subgroup A-1, in training rooms with fixed seats, only one wheelchair space is required for every 25 seats, whereas under subgroup A-2, cafeterias

---

BOX 13.1 Building and Project Information

Building address: _____

Local governing jurisdiction: _____

Building code and code year: _____

Building construction type: _____

No. of floors in building: _____

Sprinkled or non-sprinkled: _____

Floor Plate SF: _____

Use group: _____

Project SF: _____

---

with movable tables and chairs, the total allotted area for those tables and chairs is required to be wheelchair accessible.[1]

Although some code requirements and specifics of each project become second nature to the experienced designer, it is still a good idea to compile the information for each new project. That way, as new members join the design team, the information is readily available for review.

Building Address

All correspondence, drawings, and construction documents should display part or all of the new project address. Everyone wants and needs to know where the building is located.

Local Jurisdiction

Not only does each jurisdiction have a specific set of building codes (see Chapter 5), but it may also have additional amendments and requirements unique to that particular jurisdiction. For example, The City of Chicago still maintains use of the *Municipal Code of Chicago*, while many of the Chicago suburb jurisdictions have adopted use of the IBC codes. A jurisdiction is where an application for the building permit is filed; therefore, it is important to ascertain the governing jurisdiction of the project.

Building Code and Code Year

Codes are generally updated every three years. Many of the updates are subtle, but as new technology and means and methods of construction and installation enter the market, there may be major code changes that will affect a space plan. Jurisdictions often lag behind by several years for adopting the updated versions of codes, so it is best to verify which code year is in use at the time of the project. It is possible that several code years are in effect at the same time within a jurisdiction depending on when a project was started, how far along the design has been developed, when the updated codes were adopted, or when the project is submitted for permit review.

Building Construction Type

Although the interior designer generally has no say in the building construction type, it is important to know the type in order to develop the best space plans and final design of the space. Codes divide construction types into noncombustible, combustible, and a combination of noncombustible/combustible building types, with several subdivisions, for a total of five categories. Noncombustible types use concrete and masonry materials, which do not burn and therefore can be left exposed as part of the finished design—think "nice brick wall in older buildings." Although wood will burn, large wooden beams will char long before they burn. Therefore, it too can be left as an exposed material when used in heavy timber construction.

On the other hand, steel framing, the primary material used for skyscrapers, loses strength at high temperatures and then melts. As such, it is considered a combustible material, which must be protected with approved insulation such as spray-applied, fire-resistant materials. This is not an attractive material and is almost never used as an exposed material in the final design. Generally, most of the walls and ceilings in this type of construction are covered with Sheetrock, paneling, acoustic tiles, or other applied finishes.

Concrete Construction

While exposed concrete ceilings and brick walls in noncombustible building construction can add charm, natural beauty, or a high-tech feel to the designed space, these types of buildings often come with low slab-to-slab or ceiling heights due to the very nature of their construction and materials. Low slab heights, approximately 10 feet (ft) high, are one of the reasons

to expose the ceilings in the first place. Approximately 2 ft of clearance is required to accommodate infrastructure such as HVAC (heating, ventilation, and air conditioning) ducts, electrical wiring, and light fixture housings. When a dropped ceiling is installed, this leaves 8 ft for ceiling heights, which tends to feel a bit low in large, open office spaces.

By exposing the ceilings, or technically, the underside of the slab above, the designer can give the allusion that the vertical space is much higher than it really is, even though the infrastructure is still taking up space at the ceiling line (Fig. 13.1). Initially, this may seem like a cost savings since no actual ceiling is installed. However, this design technique paradoxically requires better quality materials and better installation of the infrastructure for a good appearance, thus resulting in higher installation costs.

Steel Frame Construction

Steel frame construction is typically constructed with 13–14 ft slab-to-slab floor heights. This provides ample space for adequate plenum heights of 2–4 ft, leaving 9–10 ft ceilings throughout the space, and the ability to raise ceilings in certain areas where needed or desired in order to create a grand ambience. Steel framing generally offers the greatest expanse of perimeter wall glazing, which can add to the impact of the design.

Wood Frame Construction

Wood frame construction includes both heavy timber as found in many older warehouse buildings and 2 × 4 or 2 × 6 wood studs as used in residential and small commercial construction. When converting old warehouses to offices or residences, for example, timbers can be exposed to provide a warm, cozy ambience. Wood studs on the other hand, like steel structures, are seldom left exposed.

When the designer knows the building construction at the time of space planning, this information can be used to enhance the layout. While the client is counting offices and workstations, design concepts can be suggested for a raised ceiling here or an exposed brick wall there.

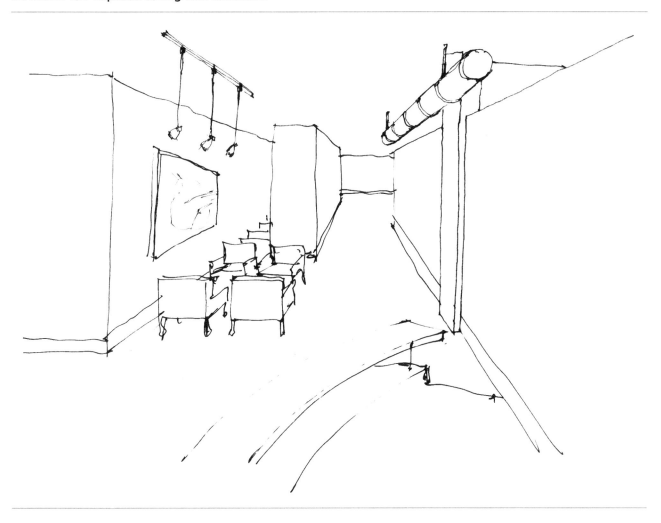

Number of Floors in the Building

There are several code requirements based on the height of a building (Box 13.2). For instance, buildings over four floors high are required to have an elevator. Buildings over 75 ft tall (five to seven floors, depending on construction type) are required, among other provisions, to have an automatic sprinkler system. By knowing this information, designers can incorporate items such as sprinkler heads, based on the sprinkler consultant's design and layout, into the reflected ceiling plan (RCP).

Sprinkled or Non-Sprinkled Building

In today's market, most commercial buildings have sprinkler systems installed throughout the building, even buildings less than 75 ft tall.

When a project is going into an older, non-sprinkled building, the designer will need to research several sections of the code because there are some major differences in code requirements for sprinkled vs. non-sprinkled buildings.

Building Floor Plate

The building floor plate generally refers to a blank floor plan of the entire building (Fig. 13.2). Obviously, the shape of the building or floor plate can help determine the final space plan and design development. More importantly, though, it is the size or amount of square footage on each floor plate and the type of occupancy that determines many specific code requirements such as occupant load, number of egress doors, egress (corridor) width, and travel distance.

BOX 13.2 IBC Number of Floors in a Building[2-4]

DEFINITIONS

HIGH-RISE BUILDING. A building with an occupied floor located more than 75 feet (22,860 mm) above the lowest level of fire department vehicle access.

SECTION 403
HIGH-RISE BUILDINGS

403.1 Applicability. *High-rise buildings* shall comply with Sections 403.2 through 403.6.

[F] 403.3 Automatic sprinkler system. Buildings and structures shall be equipped throughout with an *automatic sprinkler system* in accordance with Section 903.3.1.1 and a secondary water supply where required by Section 403.3.3.

SECTION 1009
ACCESSIBLE MEANS OF EGRESS

1009.2.1 Elevators required. In buildings where a required *accessible* floor is four or more *stories* above or below a *level of exit discharge*, not less than one required accessible *means of egress* shall be an elevator complying with Section 1009.4.

Occupant Load

Occupant load refers to: "the number of persons for which the *means of egress* [see Box 5.4] of a building or portion thereof is designed"[5]; in other words, the maximum number of people permitted to occupy a space at any given time, based on an allowable square feet per person. For office space, there are six functions of space to consider: standard office or business areas, assembly areas with fixed seating, assembly areas with movable table and chairs, library areas, platforms (in assembly areas), and storage rooms (Table 13.1). Each of these areas allocates a separate (mostly different) amount of gross or net square footage per person that must be considered when planning space (see Box 2.1).

Occupant load is not the same as the average square feet per person (as discussed in Chapters 2 and 12). Firms may provide as much (or little) square footage per employee or patron as they desire, provided it is not less square footage than listed in the applicable code for the jurisdiction

■ FIGURE 13.2 Plan view: Typical building floor plate

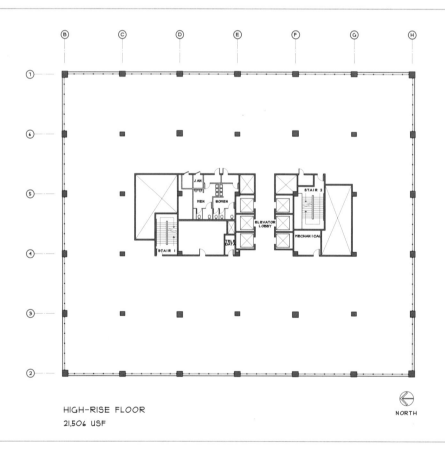

HIGH-RISE FLOOR
21,506 USF

NORTH

TABLE 13.1 IBC Occupant Load[6]

TABLE 1004.1.2
MAXIMUM FLOOR AREA ALLOWANCES PER OCCUPANT

FUNCTION OF SPACE	OCCUPANT LOAD FACTOR[a]
Accessory storage areas, mechanical equipment room	300 gross
Agricultural building	300 gross
Aircraft hangars	500 gross

Airport terminal
  Baggage claim
  Baggage handling
  Concourse
  Waiting areas
	
	20 gross
	300 gross
	100 gross
	15 gross

Assembly
  Gaming floors (keno, slots, etc.)
  Exhibit gallery and museum
	
	11 gross
	30 net

Assembly with fixed seats	See Section 1004.4

Assembly without fixed seats
  Concentrated (chairs only—not fixed)
  Standing space
  Unconcentrated (tables and chairs)
	
	7 net
	5 net
	15 net

Bowling centers, allow 5 persons for each lane including 15 feet of runway, and for additional areas	7 net
Business areas	100 gross
Courtrooms—other than fixed seating areas	40 net
Day care	35 net
Dormitories	50 gross

Educational
  Classroom area
  Shops and other vocational room areas
	
	20 net
	50 net

Exercise rooms	50 gross
Group H-5 Fabrication and manufacturing areas	200 gross
Industrial areas	100 gross

Institutional areas
  Inpatient treatment areas
  Outpatient areas
  Sleeping areas
	
	240 gross
	100 gross
	120 gross

Kitchens, commercial	200 gross

Library
  Reading rooms
  Stack area
	
	50 net
	100 gross

Locker rooms	50 gross
Mall buildings—covered and open	See Section 402.8.2
Mercantile Storage, stock, shipping areas	60 gross 300 gross
Parking garages	200 gross
Residential	200 gross

Skating rinks, swimming pools
  Rink and pool
  Decks
	
	50 gross
	15 gross

Stages and platforms	15 net
Warehouses	500 gross

For SI: 1 square foot = 0.0929m², 1 foot = 304.9 mm.
a. Floor area in square feet per occupant.

Functions of space most applicable for commercial office space planning

in which the space is located. Many commercial businesses provide much more square footage than the occupant requirement for egress.

Either inductive or deductive methods may be used to calculate occupant load (Table 13.2). When the actual number of occupants is known for the space being planned, the number of actual persons is multiplied by the allowable square footage to determine the total minimum amount of required square footage needed for that client's plan. Conversely, when a definable amount of space is being considered by the client for a new location, the actual allowable number of persons who can occupy the space is determined by dividing the given amount of square footage by the allowable occupant square footage as per code.

Egress Doors

In general, most use groups require at least two exit doors from its space, although office areas under 3,000–5,000 square feet may provide only one exit door, depending on the code in use (Box 13.3). As the amount of square footage on the building floor plate and occupant load increases, the number of required exit doors and corridor widths may also need to increase. Other code requirements to consider include the maximum distance for a common path of travel and the total travel distance from any point within the space to an exit door. As the size of the floor area increases, additional exit doors may be required to meet the travel distance, although the doors may not have been required because of occupant load.

Egress Corridors

Egress corridors are planned based on a minimum width of 44 in. (see Box 5.2), use group (see Box 2.1), occupant load (Box 13.4), and whether the space is sprinkled or non-sprinkled. For sprinkled commercial office buildings, a 44-in.-wide corridor can serve floor plates up to 22,000 square feet (SF) (Table 13.3). As floor plate sizes increase, wider corridor widths will be required based on actual square footage and occupant load.

Travel Distance

Travel distance is defined as the distance that an occupant could travel from any given point within a building space before reaching a point of exit access. Depending on the use group, the maximum distance varies from 75 ft to 400 ft under the IBC. For Use Group B, the maximum travel distance is 200 ft in buildings without sprinkler systems and 300 ft in buildings with sprinkler systems (Box 13.5 and Fig. 13.3). When the design distance exceeds the distance as defined by the applicable code, additional stairwells may need to be added in buildings with more than one story or additional exit doors added to single-story buildings to provide a shorter travel distance.

Common Path of Egress Travel

What distance should people have to traverse together before they have an option to take another path to safety or exit door (Boxes 13.3 and 13.6)? Although the path to two separate exits may occur within tenant space, it often occurs at the point of entering the public corridor (Fig. 13.4a).

TABLE 13.2 Occupant Load Calculations

Actual Persons—Training Rooms (Assembly)
50 occupants (people) × 15 NSF = 750 NSF minimum floor area

Actual Space—Office Space (Business)
5,000 GSF (floor area) ÷ 100 GSF occupant load = 50 occupants (people) maximum

*See Table 13.1 for SF per occupant.

TABLE 13.3 Corridor Width Calculations

To maintain a minimum 44" corridor width (see Boxes 5.2 and 13.4)

44" ÷ .2" per occupant = 220 maximum occupants on a floor

220 × 100 SF per occupant = 22,000 SF maximum total floor plate size

Larger floor plates require wider corridors

30,000 SF floor plate ÷ 100 SF per occupant = 300 occupants

300 occupants × .2" per occupant = 60" minimum corridor width

BOX 13.3 IBC Number of Egress Doors[7]

SECTION 1006
NUMBER OF EXIT AND EXIT ACCESS DOORWAYS
1006.2 Egress from spaces.

1006.2.1 Egress based on occupant load and common path of egress travel distance. Two *exits* or *exit access doorways* from any space shall be provided where the design *occupant load* or the *common path of egress travel* distance exceeds the values listed in Table 1006.2.1.

TABLE 1006.2.1.1 IBC Spaces with One Exit or Exit Access Doorway

Occupancy	Maximum Occupant Load of Space	MAXIMUM COMMON PATH OF EGRESS TRAVEL DISTANCE (feet)		
		Without Sprinkler System (feet)		With Sprinkler System (feet)
		Occupant Load (OL)		
		OL ≤ 30	OL . 30	
A[c], E, M	49	75	75	75[a]
B	49	100	75	100[a]
F	49	75	75	100[a]
H-1, H-2, H-3	3	NP	NP	25[b]
H-4, H-5	10	NP	NP	75[b]
I-1, I-2[d], I-4	10	NP	NP	75[a]
I-3	10	NP	NP	100[a]
R-1	10	NP	NP	75[a]
R-2	10	NP	NP	125[a]
R-3[c]	10	NP	NP	125[a]
R-4[c]	10	75	75	125[a]
S[f]	29	100	75	100[a]
U	49	100	75	75[a]

For SI: 1 foot = 304.8 mm.
NP = Not Permitted.

a. Buildings equipped throughout with an *automatic sprinkler system* in accordance with Section 903.3.1.1 or 903.3.1.2. See Section 903 for occupancies where *automatic sprinkler systems* are permitted in accordance with Section 903.3.1.2.

b. Group H occupancies equipped throughout with an *automatic sprinkler system* in accordance with Section 903.2.5.

c. For a room or space used for assembly purposes having *fixed seating*, see Section 1029.8.

d. For the travel distance limitations in Group I-2, see Section 407.4.

e. The length of *common path of egress travel* distance in a Group R-3 occupancy located in a mixed occupancy building or within a Group R-3 or R-4 *congregate living facility*.

f. The length of *common path of egress travel* distance in a Group S-2 *open parking garage* shall be not more than 100 feet.

(continued)

BOX 13.3 IBC Number of Egress Doors[7] *(continued)*

1006.2.1.1 Three or more exits or exit access doorways. Three *exits* or *exit access doorways* shall be provided from any space with an occupant load of 501 to 1,000. Four *exits* or *exit access doorways* shall be provided from any space with an occupant load greater than 1,000.

1006.3.1 Egress based on occupant load. Each *story* and *occupied roof* shall have the minimum number of *exits*, or access to *exits*, as specified in Table 1006.3.1. A single *exit* or access to a single *exit* shall be permitted in accordance with Section 1006.3.2. The required number of *exits*, or *exit access stairways* or *ramps* providing access to *exits*, from any *story* or occupied roof shall be maintained until arrival at the *exit discharge* or a *public way*.

TABLE 1006.3.1 IBC Minimum Number of Exits or Access to Exits per Story

OCCUPANT LOAD PER STORY	MINIMUM NUMBER OF EXITS OR ACCESS TO EXITS FROM STORY
1–500	2
501–1,000	3
More than 1,000	4

1006.3.2 Single exits. A single *exit* or access to a single *exit* shall be permitted from any *story* or occupied roof where one of the following conditions exists:

  2. Rooms, areas and space complying with Section 1006.2.1 with *exits* that discharge directly to the exterior at the *level of exit discharge*, are permitted to have one *exit* or access to a single *exit*.

BOX 13.4 IBC Corridor Widths[8]

SECTION 1005
MEANS OF EGRESS SIZING
1005.2 Minimum width based on component. The minimum width, in inches (mm), of any *means of egress* components shall be not less than that specified for such component, elsewhere in this code.

1005.3 Required capacity based on occupant load. The required capacity, in inches (mm), of the *means of egress* for any room, area, space or story shall be not less than that determined in accordance with Sections 1005.3.1 [stairways] and 1005.3.2 [other]:

1005.3.2 Other egress components. The capacity, in inches, of *means of egress* components other than *stairways* shall be calculated by multiplying the *occupant load* served by such component by a means of egress capacity factor of 0.2 inch (5.1 mm) per occupant.

1005.4 Continuity. The minimum width or required capacity of the *means of egress* required from any story of a building shall not be reduced along the path of egress travel until arrival at the public way.

1005.7 Encroachment. Encroachments into the required *means of egress* width shall be in accordance with the provisions of this section.

   1005.7.1 Doors. Doors, when fully opened, shall not reduce the required width by more than 7 inches (178 mm). Doors in any position shall not reduce the required width by more than one-half.

   1005.7.2 Other projections. *Handrail* projections shall be in accordance with the provisions of Section 1014.8. Other nonstructural projections such as trim and similar decorative features shall be permitted to project into the required width not more than 1½ inches (58 mm) on each side.

For Use Group B, the maximum common path of travel in a sprinkler building is 100 ft. If the common path of travel in the desired layout exceeds the allowable distance, the designer must revise the space plan to meet code requirements. In some layouts, it may be necessary to extend the public corridor or to create additional corridors within the tenant space (Fig. 13.4b).

When clients wish to incorporate a large training room or other assembly rooms into their designed space, the common path of travel cannot exceed 30 ft, at which point two exits are required (Box 13.6).

Use Group Classification

Although Use Group B does not have any sub-group classifications, as do some other occupancy groups, there may be other occupancy areas within an office space (see section "Occupant Load" in this chapter and single or multiple classifications in Chapter 2).

Identifying and listing the use group classification and occupancies at the beginning of each project can help everyone move the project along in an expeditious manner. For the designer, it is much easier to look up specific code requirements as the plan and design progress. Code reviewers often look for some of these very elements when reviewing the drawings for permit. It is assumed that if these basic elements are met, then there is a likely chance that more obscure code requirements will be met as well.

Project Square Footage

Like the type of building, the project square footage will also dictate which code requirements may be used or required. As already stated in Chapter 9, when the project is small enough, the entry door may swing in, whereas egress doors for the building will need to swing out. When the building floor plate is greater than 22,000 SF, public corridors need to be wider than 44 in., whereas the tenant space corridors may remain at 44 in. wide provided their space is no more than 22,000 SF (Table 13.3). By calculating the project square footage at the start of the process, time is saved by providing code compliance space plans up front.

BOX 13.5 IBC Travel Distance[9]

SECTION 1017
EXIT ACCESS TRAVEL DISTANCE
1017.2 Limitations. *Exit access* travel distance shall not exceed the values given in Table 1017.2.

1017.3 Measurement. *Exit access* travel distance shall be measured from the most remote point within a story along the natural and unobstructed path of horizontal and vertical egress travel to the entrance to an *exit*.

TABLE 1017.2 IBC Exit Access Travel Distance[a]

OCCUPANCY	WITHOUT SPRINKLER SYSTEM (FEET)	WITH SPRINKLER SYSTEM (FEET)
A, E, F-1, M, R, S-1	200	250[b]
I-1	Not Permitted	250[b]
B	200	300[c]
F-2, S-2, U	300	400[c]
H-1	Not Permitted	75[d]
H-2	Not Permitted	100[d]
H-3	Not Permitted	150[d]
H-4	Not Permitted	175[d]
H-5	Not Permitted	200[c]
1-2, 1-3, 1-4	Not Permitted	200[c]

For SI: 1 foot = 304.8 mm.

a. See the following sections for modifications to exit access travel distance requirements:

....

Section 1006.3.2: For buildings with one exit.
Section 1029.7: For increased limitation in assembly seating.
Section 3104.9: For pedestrian walkways.

c. Buildings equipped throughout with an *automatic sprinkler system* in accordance with Section 903.3.1.1.

FLOOR SELECTION

Once the location and site have been narrowed to a particular building or several buildings, the client must consider which floor they wish to occupy. In low-rise buildings, the first or ground floor is generally the most desirable location.

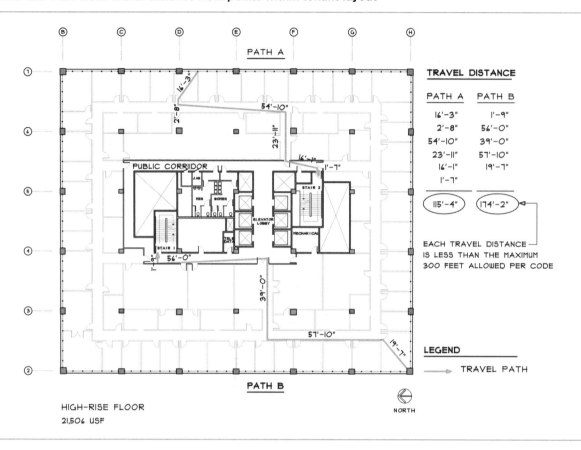

HIGH-RISE FLOOR
21,506 USF

TRAVEL DISTANCE

PATH A	PATH B
16'-3"	1'-9"
2'-8"	56'-0"
54'-10"	39'-0"
23'-11"	57'-10"
16'-1"	19'-7"
1'-7"	
115'-4"	174'-2"

EACH TRAVEL DISTANCE IS LESS THAN THE MAXIMUM 300 FEET ALLOWED PER CODE

LEGEND

→ TRAVEL PATH

BOX 13.6 IBC Common Path of Travel[11, 12]

CHAPTER 2
DEFINITIONS

COMMON PATH OF EGRESS TRAVEL. That portion of *exit access* travel distance measured from the most remote point within a *story* to that point where occupants have separate access to two *exits* or *exit access* doorways.

SECTION 1029
ASSEMBLY

1029.8 Common path of egress travel. The *common path of egress travel* shall not exceed 30 feet (9144 mm) from any seat to a point where an occupant has a choice of two paths of egress travel to two *exits*.

Exceptions:

1. For areas serving less than 50 occupants, the *common path of egress travel* shall not exceed 75 feet (22,860 mm).

Employees and visitors can walk right in off the street or from the parking lot rather than walk up or take an elevator up two to four floors. In high-rise buildings, the higher floors are thought to be more desirable because of the views.

Many high-rise buildings bundle floors in several groups—premium, midlevel, or low level—and then set lease rates accordingly. Rent for the same amount of space in the same building can vary by several dollars per square foot depending on the floor selection. Building managers even go so far as to vary the lease rate from one side of the floor or building to the other side on multi-tenant floors based on views.

It behooves the designer to discuss the specific floor selection with the client prior to the start of space planning. Floor level and associated views (see Figs. 1.3 and 1.4) often affect the design philosophical approach for placing offices or workstations along window walls; the general location of particular groups, departments, or support rooms; and the entry door position.

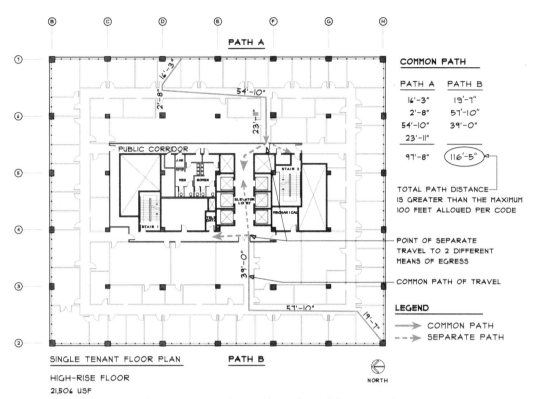

a. Common path of travel based on initial space plan

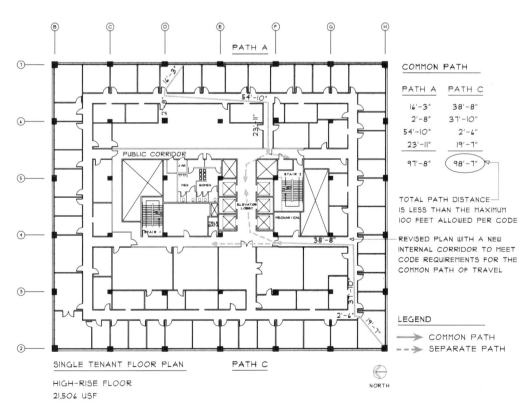

b. Revised layout to meet code requirements for common path of travel

Floor Plate Information

Buildings, and thus floor plates, may be rectilinear, curved, angled, stepped, or a combination of shapes (Fig. 13.5a and b). The building may be a single floor, have multiple stacked floors either above or below ground, or have different sizes of floor plates that are either larger, because they overhang lower floors, or smaller, because they are set back from the outer perimeter edges of the floors below. Floor plates may be column-free or contain any number of columns, which may or may not all be the same size. There may be continuous floor-to-ceiling windows or individual inset windows. Buildings may use a

■ FIGURE 13.5 Plan views: Building architecture

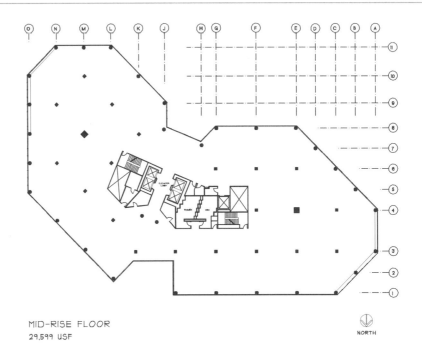

MID-RISE FLOOR
29,599 USF

NORTH

a. Angled building floor plate

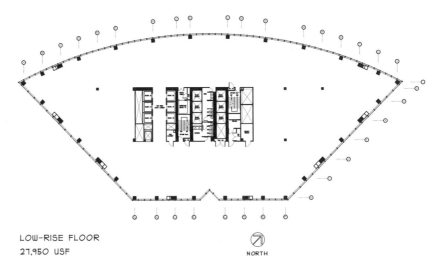

LOW-RISE FLOOR
27,950 USF

NORTH

b. Curved building floor plate

convection HVAC system along the perimeter walls or VAV (variable air volume) boxes above the ceilings. Building standards may dictate that there shall be no floor cores or that all elevator lobby finishes must be consistent with all other floors, even for single-tenant floors. Each building is unique and should be analyzed prior to the start of space planning.

When a site tour is conducted, it is a good idea to document specific architectural elements (see Appendix D). Designers should also request a copy of all building standards from the building management; ask if there is leeway in using or not using any or all standards.

Building Core

The functional center of each floor plate, known as the building core (Fig 13.6), consists of the following rooms or areas:

- Elevator cabs
- Elevator lobby
- Restrooms
- Exit stairs
- Air shafts
- Mechanical rooms
- Telephone and electrical (utility) closets
- Storage or miscellaneous rooms

All elements may be grouped together as one chunk or mass of space or be split into two or three masses of space. A majority of high-rise buildings group half of the elevator cabs and one exit stairwell together as a smaller chunk of space and the remaining elevator cabs, the second exit stairwell, and balance of the rooms together as a larger chunk of space, with a 10-ft-wide elevator lobby separating the two masses of space (Fig. 13.6a). Even though there are two masses of space, the core is considered a whole entity, located somewhat centrally within the floor plate.

Low-rise and some small floor plate, high-rise buildings may have only two or three elevator cabs, in which case all of the elements are combined into a single mass with the elevator lobby being an imaginary 10-ft space in front of the elevator cabs. In this case, the core is often offset in the floor plate along one of the perimeter walls (Fig. 13.6b).

Really large floor plates of 40,000–50,000 SF and larger may require a third or even fourth exit stairwell. In these situations, the primary core is very similar to the split core arrangement in typical high-rise buildings. Then a third stairwell is offset to one side of the floor plate, often within a tenant space, based on a distance as outlined in the appropriate code.

Core Size and Massing

Core shape and sizes vary from one building to the next based on the total square footage of each floor, the intended use group, the type of mechanical systems used, and the building classification. For instance, the restroom size is based on the number of fixtures, which is based on the floor occupancy load, which in turn is based on the use group and size of floor. As each of these elements increases or decreases in number or size, the restrooms and core will become larger or smaller.

Regardless of size, massing, or location, cores are basically duplicated and stacked on top of each other from floor to floor within a specific building. This provides for vertical penetrations of all core elements such as air shafts, plumbing stacks, and electrical closets.

Building cores are usually planned and set by the building architect during the initial building design phase. Very seldom does the interior designer have any say in the core size, configuration, or location unless the building is being designed specifically for the client and the interior design firm has been selected early in the process. In this case, the interior designer may be able to work with the architect to locate the core elements. But generally, the core will be set and the designer must plan the interior space around the core.

Exit Stairwells

During times of fire and emergencies, elevators are turned off, leaving public corridors and stairwells as the only means of exit. Per building code, there must be a minimum of two means of egress to the exterior of the building from any point on the floor. On ground floors, public corridors lead directly to an outside exit, whereas on upper floors, public corridors typically lead to exit stairwells, which in turn lead to outside exits.

Although the two exit stairwells are customarily connect by public corridors, it is feasible

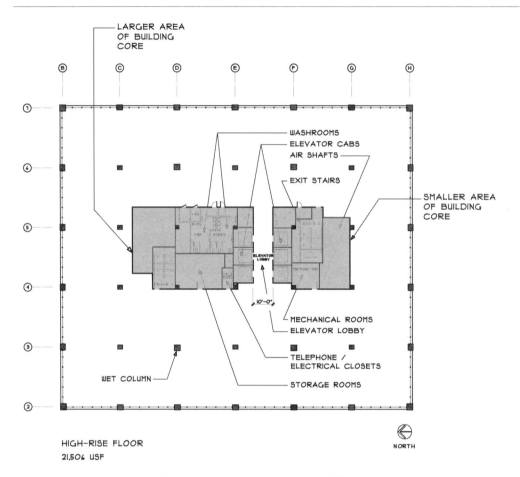

a. High-rise typical centralized building core

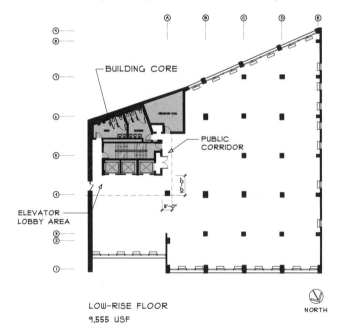

b. Offset building core plan

for one or more exit stairwells to be located within the tenant space rather than in the core or connected to a public corridor. However, since everyone must have access to at least two stairwells, this generally means that the tenant must leave their entry doors unlocked in order to provide direct access to those stairwells within their spaces. Because most tenants wish to secure their space, the exit stairwells are habitually a part of the core, connected to a public corridor.

Internal Staircases

Internal office suite staircases connecting several floors of a multi-floor tenant do not qualify as a legal means of egress. These staircases are generally designed as open, showcase elements within the space for both ambience and convenience. People may use these staircases to exit the building or floors where possible. However, they must be in addition to exit stairwells, which, as required by code, are enclosed structures that lead directly to the exterior of the building and have a minimum two-hour fire rating.

Public Corridors

Public corridors, also known as primary circulation paths or *means of egress*, shall be provided on each floor as required. In addition to a means of exiting from the building, public corridors, particularly on multi-tenant floors, provide right of entry into tenant spaces, restrooms, exit stairwells, and other elements within the core without going through tenant spaces (Box 13.7).

Existing Corridors

In most situations, for existing buildings with an existing tenant roster, the public corridors will already be established. The designer can start laying out the new tenant space without much consideration given to the public corridor (Fig. 13.7).

New Corridors

For new construction, or when an existing floor has been fully demolished down to raw space, the designer will want to start a space plan by first blocking out the public corridors. Although 44 in. is the minimum requirement for corridor widths, many commercial buildings typically provide 5-ft-wide public corridors for several reasons:

BOX 13.7 IBC Public Corridors[13, 14]

SECTION 1004
OCCUPANT LOAD

1004.6 Multiple occupancies. Where a building contains two or more occupancies, the *means of egress* requirements shall apply to each portion of the building based on the occupancy to that space. Where two or more occupancies utilize portions of the same *means of egress* system, those egress components shall meet the more stringent requirements of all occupancies that are served.

SECTION 1016
EXIT ACCESS
1016.2.1 Multiple tenants. Where more than one tenant occupies any one floor of a building or structure, each tenant space, *dwelling unit* and *sleeping unit* shall be provided with access to the required *exits* without passing through adjacent tenant spaces, *dwelling units* and *sleeping units*.

---

1. Five-foot corridors eliminate the necessity for calculating appropriate widths for many buildings, unless the floor plate is really large (see previous section on egress).
2. Five-foot corridors have become an industry standard.
3. Five-foot modules are easier to work with than 3'-8".
4. Doors that open into the corridors have their own set of code requirements, which cannot always be met under 44-in.-wide corridors.
5. Five-foot-wide corridors allow two people to walk abreast, whereas 44-in. corridors do not (see Fig. 5.2).
6. Finally, more spacious 5-ft-wide corridors help give the impression of a high-quality building rather than an average building.

Z-Corridors

Z-corridors normally provide the shortest route for connecting all core elements and the exit stairwells by passing through the elevator lobby. Some codes allow a Z-corridor, but some codes do not. Smoke and heat rise up through the elevator shafts and can seep out into the elevator lobby, which can potentially impede the means of egress (Fig. 13.8a).

Looped, Wrapped, or Donut Corridors

Looped corridors wrap around one or both ends of the core. This allows a means of egress to both

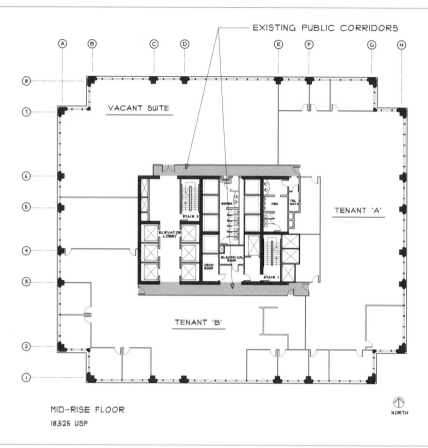

MID-RISE FLOOR
18,525 USF

NORTH

stairwells without passing through the elevator lobby (Fig. 13.8b).

Looped corridors often provide short-cuts for the tenant when traveling from one point within the office or core to another point without having to go through the entire office space or around through the elevator lobby. While this is beneficial to tenants, public corridors are non-usable space but still considered rentable space. This means that the tenant is paying for this convenience without being able to use the space in any manner other than traversing through the hallways. Therefore, the landlord tends to discourage donut corridors in favor of Z-corridors where allowed by code.

Dead-End Corridors

Dead-end corridors do not lead to a means of egress. They may lead to a tenant entry door or core element such as a restroom, but they do not lead to a stairwell for exiting the building (Fig. 13.8c and Box 13.8).

In a non-sprinkled building, dead-end corridors may not exceed 20 ft. In sprinkled buildings, these corridors can be up to 50 ft per the IBC or another length as specified, depending on the code in use.

Occasionally, when a core element such as a mechanical room is located at the far end of the core, the doorway of that room may need to open into tenant space in order to avoid creating a dead-end corridor by extending a public corridor for access. In this situation, building maintenance people will need to access this room through the tenant space. This is something that needs to be discussed with the client and agreed to during lease negotiations (Fig. 13.9).

Corridor Doors

After the number of required egress doors has been determined, three primary factors must be considered when planning for doors that open into a public corridor: the degree of separation, the direction of door swing, and the clearance.

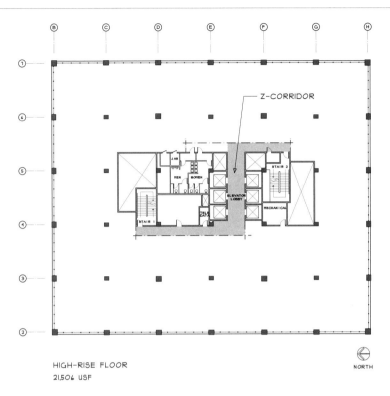

a. Z-corridors

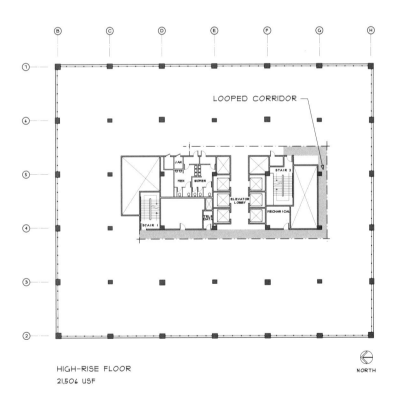

b. Looped, wrapped, or donut corridors

(Figure continues)

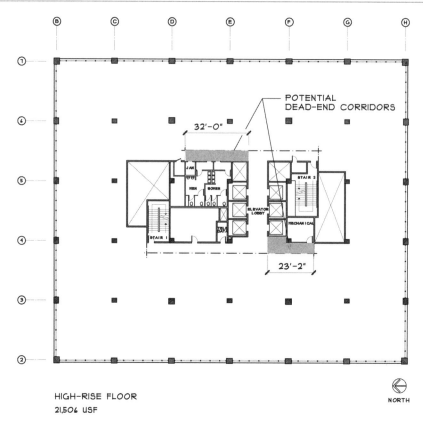

HIGH-RISE FLOOR
21,506 USF

NORTH

c. Dead-end corridors

Degree of Separation

Exit doors are required to be separated by an appropriate distance based on the assumption that approximately one-half of the occupants will travel through one exit and the other half of the occupants will travel through another exit. Without this separation, when doors are located in close proximity, people will bunch up as they are exiting (Fig. 13.10a).

As noted under the code exception, the actual distance between door placements depends on whether the building is sprinkled or non-sprinkled (Box 13.9). In a sprinkled building, the doors need to be separated by only one-third of the overall distance. In a non-sprinkled building, the required separation is much greater: one-half of the distance.

Direction of Door Swing

All exit or egress doors, including doors that open into a public corridor, into stairwells, or from assembly areas, must swing out in the direction of travel (Box 13.10). This allows people to push the door open outward and away rather than pull the door open toward themselves and people behind them (Fig. 13.10b).

This code requirement is applicable to doors in the path of egress only. Doors into typical

---

BOX 13.8 IBC Dead End Corridors[15]

SECTION 1020
CORRIDORS

1020.4 Dead ends. Where more than one exit or *exit* access doorway is required, the *exit access* shall be arranged such that there are no dead ends in *corridors* more than 20 feet (6,096 mm) in length.

Exceptions:

1. In occupancies in Groups B, E, F, I-1, M, R-1, R-2, R-4, S and U, where the building is equipped throughout with an automatic sprinkler system in accordance with Section 903.3.1.1, the length of dead-end *corridors* shall not exceed 50 feet (15,240 mm).

■ FIGURE 13.9 Plan view: Core elements located within tenant space

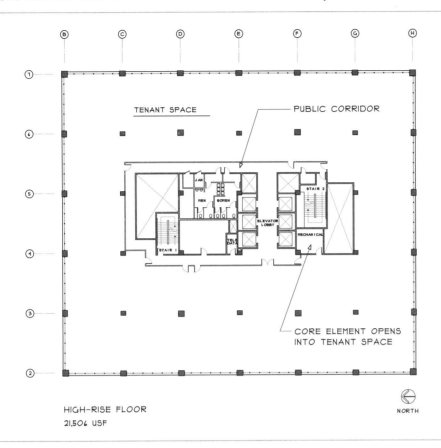

HIGH-RISE FLOOR
21,506 USF

NORTH

offices and other non-assembly rooms can swing into the room or be of the sliding type.

Clearance

In an open position, exit doors shall not impede the path of cross-travel or encroach into the required minimum corridor width (see Box 13.4).

If the client or landlord wishes to maintain the minimum corridor width of 44 in., then the exit doors will need to be inset into the tenant space so that when in an open position the doors do not project more than 7 in. into the minimum corridor width requirements (Fig. 13.10c).

The second part of this restriction means that when the door is fully open, there must be one-half of the minimum corridor width between the end of the door and the opposite corridor wall. One-half of a minimum 44-in.-wide corridor is 22 in. When added to a 36-in.-wide door, the resulting width is 58 in. A 5-ft-wide (60 in.) corridor will satisfy this code requirement (Fig. 13.10d).

When wider doors are used, such as a 42- or 48-in. door rather than a standard 36-in.-wide door, which may be the case for assembly rooms or mailrooms, the designer will need to plan corridors and door insets accordingly.

Tenant Occupancy

Some tenants are large firms that require entire floors or even several floors. Other tenants are small companies that need only a portion of a floor, in which case they will share the floor with other tenants who also need only a portion of the floor. The two scenarios are referred to as *single tenant* and *multi-tenant* floors, respectively.

Single Tenant Floors

Single tenants generally have greater options for planning floor layouts. Public corridors can be planned outside of the secured tenant space (Fig. 13.4b) with entry doors separating the tenant suite from the public corridors, or the corridors

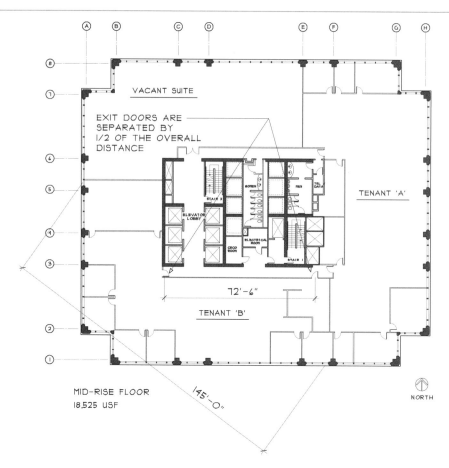

a. Exit doors are separated by a distance equal to at least one-half of the overall longest diagonal distance of the space

---

BOX 13.9 IBC Separation of Exit Doors[16]

SECTION 1007
EXIT AND EXIT ACCESS DOORWAY CONFIGURATION
1007.1.1 Two exits or exit access doorways. Where two *exits*, *exit access doorways, exit access stairways* or *ramps*, or any combination thereof, are required from any portion of the *exit access*, they shall be placed a distance apart equal to not less than one-half of the length of the maximum overall diagonal dimension of the building or area to be served measured in a straight line between them. . . .

Exceptions:
1. Where a building is equipped throughout with an *automatic sprinkler system* in accordance with Section 903.3.1.1 or 903.3.1.2, the separation distance shall not be less than one-third of the length of the maximum overall diagonal dimension of the area served.

1007.1.2 Three or more exits or exit access doorways. Where access to three or more *exits* is required, not less than two *exit* or *exit access doorways* shall be arranged in accordance with the provisions of Section 1007.1.1. Additional required *exit* or *exit access doorways* shall be arranged a reasonable distance apart so that if one becomes blocked, the others will be available.

BOX 13.10 IBC Exit Doors to Swing Out[17]

SECTION 1010
DOORS, GATES AND TURNSTILES
1010.1.2 Door swing. Egress doors shall be of the pivoted or side-hinged swinging type.

1010.1.2.1 Direction of swing. Pivot or side-hinged swinging doors shall swing in the direction of egress travel where serving a room or area containing an occupancy load of 50 or more persons or a Group H occupancy.

Exceptions:
1. Private garages, office areas, factory and storage areas with an *occupant load* of 10 or less. . . .
2. In other than Group H occupancies, manually operated horizontal sliding doors are permitted in a *means of egress* from spaces with an *occupant load* of 10 or less.

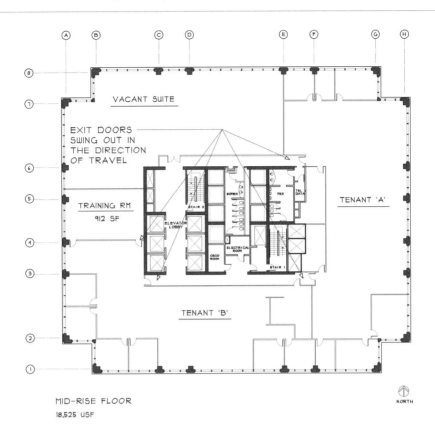

b. Exit doors shall swing in the direction of egress

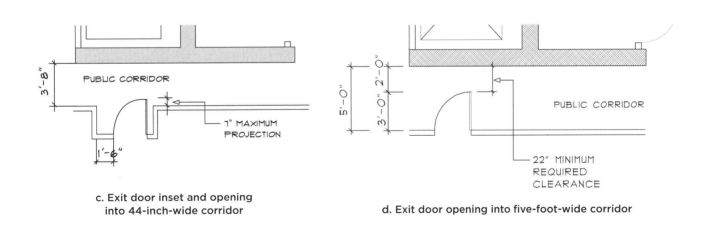

c. Exit door inset and opening into 44-inch-wide corridor

d. Exit door opening into five-foot-wide corridor

can be incorporated into the overall layout as an open walkway or an internal corridor with no entry doors (Fig. 13.11). Obviously, there needs to be entrée to the restrooms and other core elements, but access into these rooms can be through the tenant space since the core elements serve primarily only one tenant.

The primary advantage for incorporating public corridors into a single tenant space is the ability to gain usable floor space by eliminating part or all of some circulation spaces and the ability to back support rooms and offices up against the core walls.

A second advantage for single tenant floors is that the reception area can be located directly off or incorporated as part of the elevator lobby. Although such a layout may cause the reception area to be outside the secured office space, it provides a visual impact for visitors when the elevator doors open (Fig. 13.12).

There are two potential disadvantages to incorporating the public corridor within the tenant space or locating the reception in the lobby area. First, there is some lack of security for the receptionist. Second, because the exit stairwells are within the tenant space, the tenant space must be open at all times to allow any persons on the floor, those in the restrooms, cleaning people at night, visitors, or even anyone who accidentally steps off the elevators on the wrong floor, to have a means of egress to two exit stairwells. People cannot be left trapped in the elevator lobby or anywhere on the floor.

To provide a level of security for the reception area and prevent non-employees from wandering around on the floor during off-hours, many high-rise buildings install keycard systems in each elevator cab, which can be programmed to stop or not stop at selected floors based on security requirements for each tenant. With this system,

■ **FIGURE 13.11 Plan view: Public corridors incorporated into tenant space on single tenant floor**

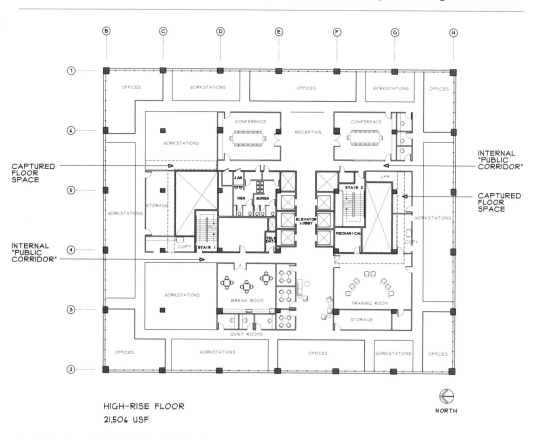

HIGH-RISE FLOOR
21,506 USF

NORTH

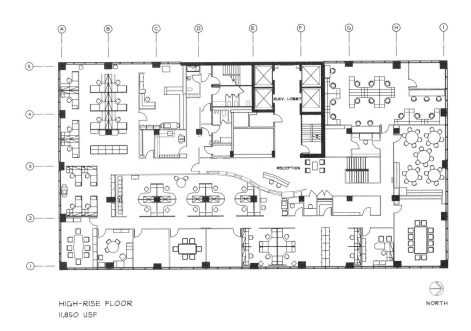

HIGH-RISE FLOOR
11,850 USF

NORTH

only those people with security clearance to access a particular floor or visitors accompanied by a person with such clearance can gain entry to the floor and reception area via the elevator.

Finally, one other advantage that many single floor tenants regularly enjoy is the waiver received for being required to use building standard finishes. More often than not, building management will allow single floor tenants to select and install any finishes and interior doors as desired, provided those finishes and materials do not conflict with building viewpoint or other ramifications. In some cases, single floor tenants may still need to conform to some building standards such as installing all light fixtures in the same direction or not install outlets on window walls, but in general, single floor tenants usually have more latitude when it comes to selecting architectural and design ambience.

Multi-Tenant Floors

The specific number of tenants on a multi-tenant floor depends on the size and configuration of the floor plate, square footage requirements of each tenant, building class, and building management philosophy. While most buildings have at least one multi-tenant floor with tenants occupying office suites of 3,000–15,000 SF, some buildings are known for having a greater number of multi-tenant floors with many small office suites, ranging between 500–2,000 SF, that may cater to a particular trade or industry, such as medical offices or talent agencies.

All multi-tenant floors must have a public corridor. After means of egress (Box 13.7), the most logical reason for a public corridor on these floors is the ability for tenants to lock and secure their spaces while still having access to all of the core elements without going through another tenant's space.

The most desirable suite location on a multi-tenant floor is an area that allows the tenant's entry door or doors to be directly opposite the elevator lobby for immediate visibility once someone steps off the elevators. When this location is not available, the next desirable location is to have an entry door at the end of the public corridor so that it is easily visible once a visitor turns into the corridor. Good directional signage is a must on multi-tenant floors (Fig. 13.13).

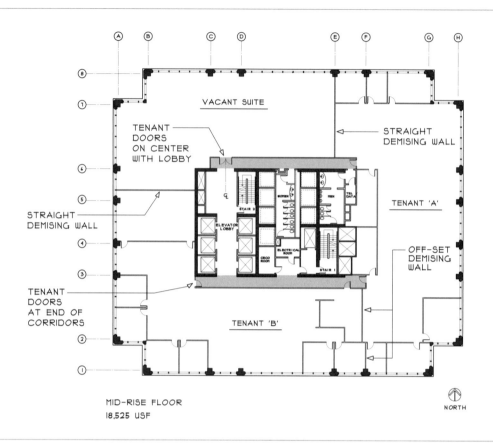

STRAIGHT DEMISING WALL

STRAIGHT DEMISING WALL

TENANT DOORS ON CENTER WITH LOBBY

VACANT SUITE

TENANT 'A'

OFF-SET DEMISING WALL

TENANT DOORS AT END OF CORRIDORS

TENANT 'B'

MID-RISE FLOOR
18,525 USF

NORTH

Demising Partitions or Party Walls

Commonly known as *demising partitions* or *party walls* in the design industry (although this term is not specifically used in the IBC Code Book), these walls or partitions separate one tenant from another tenant or one use group from another use group on a multi-tenant floor or within a multi-tenant building. In fully sprinkled buildings, when tenants are of the same use group, demising partitions are constructed in the same manner as are other typical walls. However, when tenants are in different use groups, whether on the same floor or on different floors, demising partitions and floor and ceiling assemblies must be constructed as fire-resistant assemblies. In non-sprinkled buildings, demising partitions between any two tenants, even tenants in the same use group, are also required to be fire-resistant partitions.

Demising Wall Placement

For the first tenant to be planned on a multi-tenant floor, along with public corridors (see previous section), demising partitions are located on the floor plan at the start of space planning. Sometimes the space planner has the occasion to randomly select any area on the floor plate for the new client space plan, but customarily the location is based on direction from the landlord, who, with the client, has agreed to a general area on the open floor plate. Once the space planning begins, the landlord and client then rely on the designer to specifically locate the demising walls based on the required amount of square footage and eventual space plan. When construction starts, these partitions are also the first partitions constructed on a floor to separate and contain new tenant spaces from other areas, even big, wide, open areas, on the floor.

When other tenants already exist on a multi-tenant floor, the corridor and demising walls will already be in place. However, the designer should still verify these wall locations at the start of space planning as the existing walls shown on old floor plans may have been altered over time.

Demising Wall Jogs

From an ideal point of view, straight demising walls are more practical, especially for potential tenants considering the other side of the demising wall for their new space. However, from a space planning perspective, this does not always happen. Many demising walls have at least one offset or jog. Logistically though, it is best to keep the turns and jogs to a minimum in a demising wall when planning the layout (Fig. 13.13).

Fire-Rated Assembly Partitions

In addition to tenant separation in non-sprinkled buildings, some rooms within a tenant space, such as laboratories and storage rooms, require fire-resistant partitions around all sides. Fire-resistance partitions are generally rated as 1-hour, 2-hour, 3-hour, or 4-hour resistant, with a 1-hour rating being the most common in typical office spaces when a rating is required. To achieve a basic 1-hour fire rating for drywall partitions, wall assemblies are constructed using metal studs and type-X or type-C gypsum board on either side of the studs. The constructed wall assembly is sealed with caulk at the top and bottom to the floor decks above and below (see Appendix D).

When constructed with gypsum board, fire-resistant partitions visually appear the same as demising partitions and typical wall construction. Even so, when referring to the various wall constructions, designers should always use appropriate terminology.

TEST FITS

Once clients have selected a particular building for their new location, they simply need to decide which floor to lease based on availability and lease options. When several buildings are being considered, both the broker and the various building managers will probably suggest

that a *test fit* be done for each building based on either the client's actual or anticipated program requirements.

Test Fit Plans

Test fits are just that—a quick study or test as to how the client's program requirements might fit into a space or onto a floor. A test fit is a first-step floor plan; it is not the final layout. The final layout may look similar to the test fit plan or look completely different. A test fit simply gives the client an idea of what and how many rooms, workstations, or areas might be accommodated in a particular space or building (see Fig. 14.3b).

Even though two or more buildings may offer approximately the same amount of square footage and lease options, the actual floor plates may look and function differently. One building may be long and rectangular, and another building may be squarer. The rectangular building will probably offer more lineal feet of window space, whereas the square building will provide greater amounts of interior spaces. Core-to-perimeter wall depth, another factor to consider, is important when laying out great quantities of workstations.

Of all plan types (see Chapter 15), test fits show the least amount of furniture, perhaps only in the lunchroom, conference room, and reception area. Rooms are normally labeled based on staff positions such as partner, administrative assistant, or receptionist. Room sizes, for example, 10 × 15, 12 × 18, or square footages, for example, 150 SF, 216 SF, are also shown below room names. Room numbers are rarely shown.

Test fits are generally printed at ⅛-in. scale for distribution to the prospective client, broker, building manager, and any other involved parties. Clients can quickly see their various program requirements as shown in each building plan and can compare them for efficiency before selecting the final building.

Test Fit Planner

If the design firm has already been selected by the client, it is probably wise for them to have that design firm do test fits for all buildings under consideration. This should provide better control and consistency of planning the program requirements into each building. The firm can prepare a matrix comparison table for the spaces under consideration based on the various building test fits (Table 13.4).

When a design firm has not already been selected, most buildings have a design firm of record to provide test fits or design services. Whether it is a firm of record or the client's designated designer, each firm providing a test fit receives a token fee, approximately 12–18 cents per SF based on the actual square footage planned, from each building management for whom the test fit was done.

Test Fit Services

Test fit services generally include an initial meeting and one or two follow-up meetings with the client and an initial test fit plan that may receive one or two minor revisions based on the follow-up meeting conversations. At this point, space planners should always keep in mind that this is a test fit, not a design project. Therefore, while designers may wish to satisfy as many client requests as possible, in many cases, the client is not yet a client. This is only a test fit with a limited amount of fees. Because the actual SF will vary slightly from one building to the next, so too will the fees vary slightly for each of the various buildings and plans, but the services will remain the same. These fees and services are outside of any fees and services later contracted between the client and design firm for providing services required for a complete design project.

FINAL BUILDING SELECTION

There are many factors for clients to consider when selecting a new building site and location. Initially, they must look at the relocation

TABLE 13.4 Building Comparison Summary				
MID-RISE FLOOR	**BUILDING A**	**BUILDING B**	**BUILDING C**	**BUILDING D**
15 × 15 offices	11	11	12	12
10 × 15 offices	25	22	22	22
Conference rooms	2	4	2	2
Board rooms	1	1	1	1
Mobile file stacks	No	Yes	Yes	Yes
Standard file room	Yes	No	Yes	Yes
Library	Yes	Yes	Yes	Yes
Single tenant USF	20,714	19,347	18,621	23,419
Core/lobby SF	4,654	3,774	3,865	4,533
TOTAL RSF	**25,368**	**23,121**	**22,486**	**27,952**
Rent ratio	18.35%	16.32%	19.19%	16.2%
Window module	2'-8"	5'-0"	5'-0"	5'-0"
Ceiling height	8'-9"	9'-0"	9'-0"	9'-0"

on a macro-level. Where is the general area in which they wish to be located? Who is the employee base, and where will these people live? Is there a specific street they would like for an address?

After these questions, and more, are addressed, then the company can consider the move on a micro-level. How much space will they need? Which floor do they wish to lease? How will the floor lay out?

PROJECTS

Project #1: Interview a local building manager and site-measure parts of the building interior

To better understand the parameters of planning in various buildings, it is beneficial to talk directly with a building manager and to do a walk-through of the building spaces.

1. Students should find a local building where their chosen client could relocate, or the instructor can pre-select a building.
2. Schedule a time to meet with the building manager to discuss several topics.
3. Topics can include:
   a. Negotiate a lease for approximately 4.500 square feet of new office space.
   b. What is the desired length (number of years) for a new lease?
   c. Inquire about floor options, areas on the floor, and building standards.
   d. Is there an existing public corridor? If not, what is the desired width for planning?
4. Share information about the prospective client with the manager to achieve the best lease deal for the client.
5. Ideally, there are some raw, unconstructed spaces within the building that can be seen during the building tour.
6. Do an assessment of the raw space; take and record dimensions, photographs, etc. (see Appendix D).

Project #2: Write a two-page summary of the interview

1. What impression did the building manager provide for a favorable lease deal?
2. How will the site location, specific building, and floor add value in the space plan?
3. How could the building standards affect the space plan?

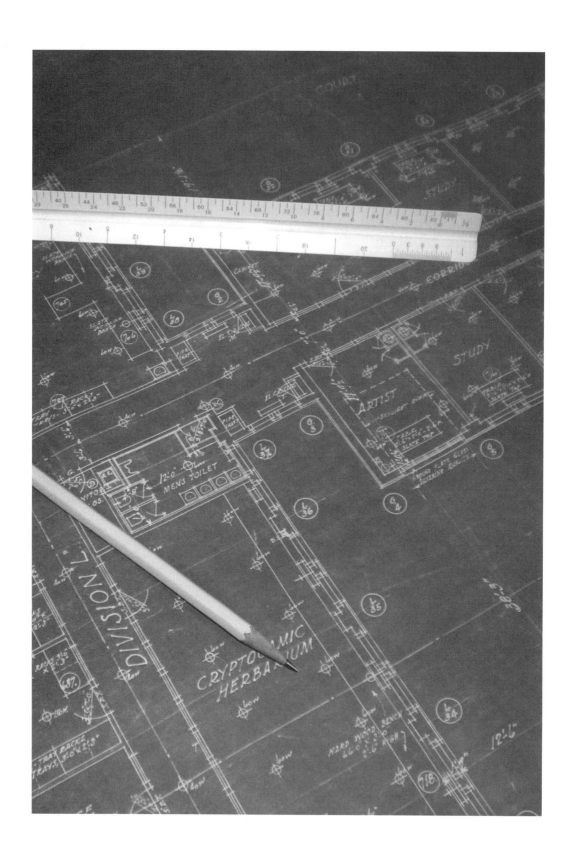

14

SPACE PLANNING

Some people may compare space planning with piecing a puzzle together. In a way, they are right. In space planning, all of the program requirements need to fit within a defined amount of space on a given floor plate. Just like puzzle pieces, sometimes the program components need to be moved around and looked at several times before they fall into place. There are adjacency requirements and outer edge pieces, or rooms. There are centers. There are focal points. And there are pieces that just do not seem to fit anywhere!

Keep in mind though, puzzle pieces fit together in only one way. Space planning, on the other hand, offers many options for a final outcome or plan. When one part does not fit where it is first placed, it may work better in another location. Some parts can be swapped, rotated, or changed in shape to work better in the overall flow. It is up to the designer to massage the plan and all its various parts and components to create a good space plan.

The hardest part may be just to get started. A blank floor plate can be quite intimidating. As intimidating as it may seem, however, a blank floor plate also presents an opportunity and creative challenge for designers to display their ability to bring all components together in a pleasing and exciting space plan that will meet with the client's approval.

STARTING A SPACE PLAN

Blank space. . .

Empty space. . .

Space for:
Offices
                    Workstations
        Furniture
                    Reception areas
Support rooms
            Spontaneous areas
    Creative ideas
                    Conference rooms
                Internal circulation
    Entry doors
Means of egress
                Adjacencies
More conference rooms

Pantry and coffee rooms
Client vision
Code requirements
Coat closets
Green building requirements
Public corridors
Egress doors
Paths of travel

The space plan also allows for:

Philosophical outlook
Traditional, contemporary, modern,
and high-tech styles
Exposed building materials
The building itself

Once there is a plan on paper, whether the plan is good or just so-so, it is much easier to move rooms and areas around to meet the final objectives (both tangible and intangible), code requirements, and desired design aesthetics. First, however, the space planner must start the planning process, then make adjustments as *desired or needed*. As a simple example, consider a single office (Fig. 14.1a). When codesigners or clients see the plan, it is easy for them to quickly suggest:

"Oh, why don't you move the door to the other side of the wall?" (Fig. 14.1b), or

"What about moving the furniture to the other side of the wall?" (Fig. 14.1c), or

"Why not rotate the furniture?" (Fig. 14.1d), and

"What happens if the door is moved to the middle of the wall?" (Fig. 14.1e).

There are any number of ways to conceptualize a space plan. Later, modifications can and should be made to the plan. However, these changes should not be made needlessly nor continue unabated. Some clients may really like the plan with the door opposite the desk. Although, at first glance, it may seem that the door is impeding on the guest chairs, the occupant of this office may reason:

- Guest chairs are seldom used, and when not in use, the chairs can be pushed under the recessed desk front (Fig. 14.1f).
- A small table can be added in the opposite corner of the room, perhaps eliminating

the need for guest chairs in front of the desk.
- Best of all, the occupant can now look directly out of the door to see his or her executive assistant across the aisle.

A space planner should always keep in mind that there are no absolutes when it comes to laying out a space plan. There are:

Possibilities
Recommendations
Better recommendations
Requirements
Alternatives
Options
Client's desires
Practicality
Creativity
Logical order
Status quo
Responsibility
Client vision
Building location
Building configuration
Client philosophy

Any number of nouns and adjectives can be used to describe the process of space planning. The important thing is to keep an open mind and consider a variety of options before finalizing a space plan.

Set-Up for Starting a Space Plan

Many designers carry three to seven projects at any given time. As long as projects are in different phases of the design process, or at least not all starting at the same time, most designers are fairly comfortable with this multi-tasking between projects and phases of each project.

And yet, for all of the multi-tasking that designers can do, for space planning it is best to clear both one's mind and the work area. Space planning is multi-tasking in and of itself. There are many diverse parts and pieces to consider for each new space plan (Box 14.1). Some parts are tangible, such as the various building blocks accumulated along the way; other parts are less tangible, such as client vision and green credits. Space planning requires concentration and focus to bring all of the components together as a cohesive whole.

■ FIGURE 14.1 Plan views: 15 x 15 private office—optional layouts

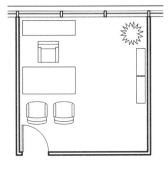

OPTION A

a. Initial office layout

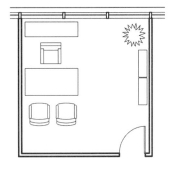

OPTION B

b. Office layout with
mirrored door

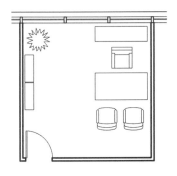

OPTION C

c. Office layout with
mirrored furniture

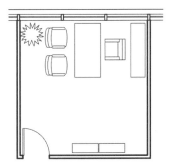

OPTION D

d. Office layout with rotated
furniture

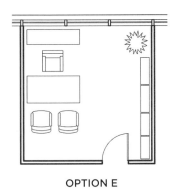

OPTION E

e. Office layout with
relocated door

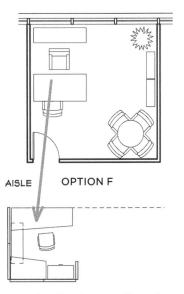

AISLE   OPTION F

f. Office layout adjusted
per client wishes

BOX 14.1 Space Planning

Desired vs. *Building Standards*

Desired vs. *Code Requirements*

Program Requirements vs. *SF Available*

Hand sketching vs. *CAD*

Stated vs. *Gleaned*

Stated vs. *Vision*

Building Blocks and Tools

In addition to clearing one's mind and primary work area, designers may want to gather together all tangible tools and building blocks for easy reference (see Fig. 1.1) because they will need to consider or use each of these items to create a successful final space plan:

1. Building footprint—hard copy
2. Or—CAD file—or both
3. Floor area being planned
4. Program Report
5. Adjacency diagrams
6. List of existing furniture to reuse
7. Copies of typical work areas
8. Code books as applicable
9. Green or LEED credits to implement

Other tools and aspects of the project to be considered and kept in mind are less tangible, but no less important:

1. Client vision
2. Client's business type
3. Building location
4. Building history
5. Function of spaces
6. Designer's creativity

■ **FIGURE 14.2 Hand sketching: Law Firm Layout 1**

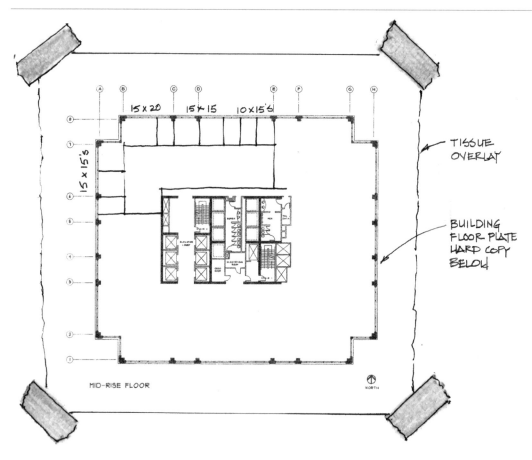

a. Start space planning by hand sketching on tissue

Space Planning

To actually start a space plan, depending on the size of the project, number of floors to be planned, building configuration, scope of services, deliverables to the client, visual presentations for the client, design fees and experience of the designer, designers may want to start with a block plan, or plans when there are multiple floors (see Chapter 12), or even a single floor, and then move into planning individual rooms and items. Or the designer may be able to go directly into micro-planning without first developing block plans.

Once the micro-planning begins, another form of blocking takes place; it is often easiest to begin by clustering offices or other large rooms together. Regardless of whether clients request that some or all of their offices be placed along window walls or in interior locations, consecutive rooms provide a concrete start for planning. There are two means for sketching and laying out a new plan: old-school hand drafting and new-school computer drafting programs. Both means offer advantages and disadvantages.

Hand Sketching

Although there are few drafting boards around anymore, designers can still *draft* or sketch initial space plans by hand. The designer lays or tapes a hard-copy computer-generated building floor plate (see Chapter 13), printed at 1/8 in. (inch) scale, on a primary worksurface and then lays tissue (bum wad, sketch, or tracing paper) over the floor plate (Fig. 14.2a). Designers rarely sketch directly on hard-copy plans for initial planning and sketching. By using tissue, the designer can draw ideas, throw them away, and then draw more ideas on new layers of tissue. By layering new

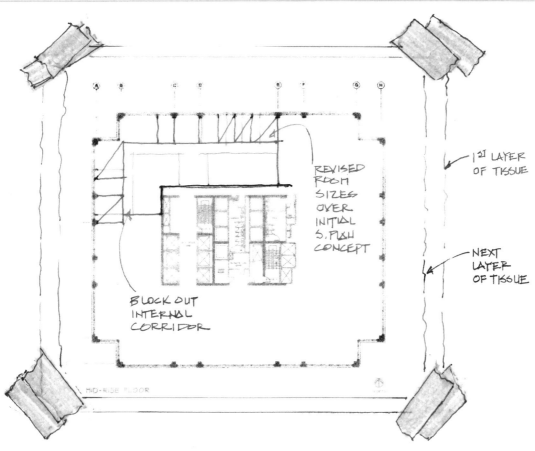

b. Revise space plan by overlaying new tissues

tissues over successive tissues, designers can see through several layers of ideas or concepts before continuing on with the next creative concepts.

Using the selected building base plan in Appendix B, Fig. B.4 and the program requirements from the law firm client, Smith, Jones & Associates (Appendix A.1), we need to plan for one 15 × 20, two 15 × 15, and four 10 × 15 offices along the window wall and four 10 × 12 offices located anywhere (Fig. 14.2a).

On the first go-round the count does not seem quite right: there appear to be four 15 × 15 and five 10 × 15 offices, and no 10 × 12 offices!

For initial hand sketching there are no doors, no furniture (to speak of), and no details. Single lines rather than double lines are drawn for walls. The idea is to block out and plan the overall concept. Details will come later once all of the components are arranged in a reasonably good layout. As changes are made, such as enlarging rooms, making them smaller or relocating them, the designer will continue to draw on top of the same tissue, habitually drawing a diagonal line from one of the lower corners to the opposite upper corner to indicate the extent of the newly planned room or rooms (Fig. 14.2b). When the tissue has reached a point of too many lines and diagonals to understand clearly, or the designer is somewhat satisfied with the evolving plan, or a wholly new concept comes to mind, then the designer will tear a new tissue to place over the top of the existing tissue. Favorable parts of the plan can be retraced; unfavorable and overworked traces can be discarded. Lower tissues may be removed or stay as is while the designer continues with space planning concepts. Designers often end up with five, six, or a dozen layers of tissue before reaching a final space

■ **FIGURE 14.3 Finalizing a space plan: Law Firm Layout 1**

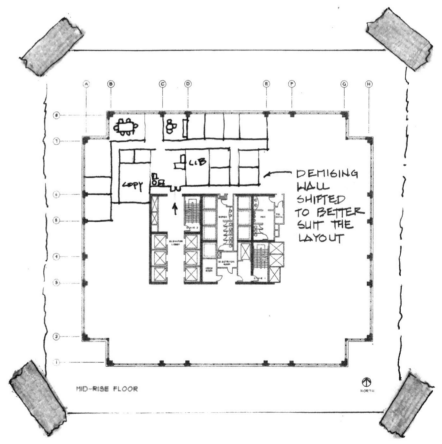

a. Continue space planning to include all program requirements

plan; drawing, tracing, switching tissues around to draw from an earlier version, tracing again and then starting with other fresh ideas.

Depending on each designer's preference, either fat or thin markers can be used to draw freehand lines at approximately the correct dimensions required for each office, room, or area. New designers will initially want to scale out the correct dimensions. With practice, however, experienced designers are able to draw or sketch fairly accurately to any dimensions required, $^1/_8$ in., $^1/_4$ in., half size, and other scales as appropriate.

Once the offices are blocked out and moved around as necessary, internal circulation is incorporated; a reception area is sketched in and then the balance of the program requirements are added per adjacency requests (Fig. 14.3a). When the client is the first tenant on an open floor, demising walls may be shifted slightly to better

accommodate the desired layout. Furniture is often sketched in for reception areas, conference rooms, and other support rooms to ensure the fit of desired pieces and to give the designer (and eventually the client) a sense of perspective for room sizes. Once a space plan has been finalized and the designer is pleased with the overall concept, it can be drafted on the computer for further use (Fig. 14.3b).

Computer-Aided Design and Drafting (CADD)

Space planning directly on the computer follows a format similar to hand drafting. The selected building floor plate is X-reffed (see Glossary) into a new file, and the designer starts to block out office walls on a new layer. As changes and thoughts occur, the designer can switch to another layer in order to preserve initial planning and then proceed with new ideas and

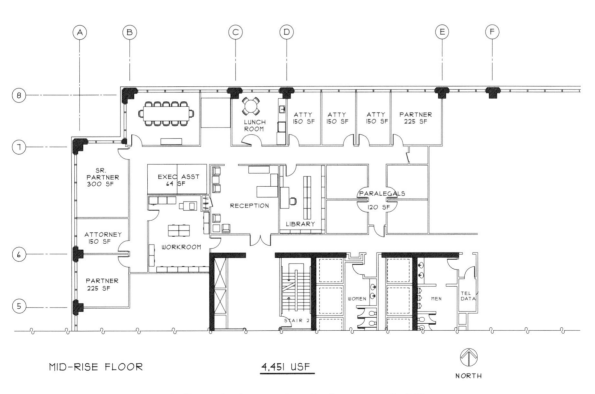

MID-RISE FLOOR   4,451 USF   NORTH

b. Conceptual space plan, also known as a test fit

concepts. Rooms or wall lines can be shifted or relocated to conjure up a better plan, adjacencies, or circulation flow.

Using program requirements from the accounting firm client, Bailey and Marks Accounting, Appendix A.2, and the base plan, Appendix B, Fig. B.4, the designer can block out the desired number of offices, in this case, interior offices since the client seemed open-minded about this concept (Fig. 14.4a). Initially, there will be no doors, no furniture, and no details. The plan needs to remain fluid until all requirements are in place.

Two differences between computer and hand drafting are *exact* dimensions and drawing two-line walls. Because the computer screen can be zoomed in and out, it is much harder to establish a visual concept of dimensions. When desired dimensions are known, it is best to type in the desired dimensions such as 5'-0" widths for

corridor walls or a 15'-0" depth for office walls. Walls may eventually be moved or stretched to be of either a greater or lesser dimension on the final plan, but the designer is at least starting with known requirements.

Because it is just as easy for the computer to draw two-line walls as a single line, it makes sense to draw two-line walls right from the start. However, during the initial planning concepts, because walls are often moved, stretched, angled, or changed, it is not necessary to clean up the wall intersections. This can be done once the plan is finalized.

Workstation Dominant

Although many designers start by laying out offices and other hard-walled rooms, occasionally it is prudent to start the planning process with the workstations, particularly when there are many more workstations than offices. For

■ FIGURE 14.4 CAD drafting: Accouting Firm Layout 1

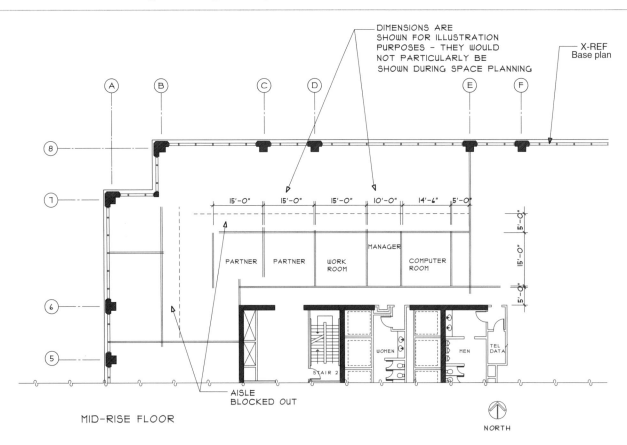

a. Start computer-generated space plan by importing an X-ref base plan and then draft on a new layer

initial planning, either with hand drafting or on the computer, the designer will want to use an open box based on the typical workstation sizes or footprints as shown to the client. It is important to add panel thicknesses around all four sides of the box to calculate overall dimensions of workstation clusters (see Chapter 7). There are several concepts to keep in mind when laying out workstations:

1. Offices and rooms can be adjusted by 2 in., $1^3/_4$ in., $3^1/_4$ in., or any fraction thereof as needed to fit within the allotted space to make a plan work.
2. Workstations can be adjusted in 6 in. increments only. There must be a sufficient amount of space to accommodate the overall workstation dimensions.
3. Office sizes are typically based on window mullion dimensions and furniture layouts within, thus establishing a general footprint in addition to a square footage amount.
4. Workstations sizes are usually based on an allocated amount of square footage and thus are subject to change in layout shape or footprint to meet the needs of the occupant or the given space.

With these concepts in mind, the designer will need to measure the given floor space more carefully to plan workstations. Continuing with the accounting firm client, first determine the overall width and length of a desired cluster of workstations (WS). A cluster of four 8 × 8 WS, including panel thicknesses, measures 16'-9" × 16'-9". When two WS are replaced with two 8 × 10 supervisor WS, the new size is 16'-9" × 18'-9". For access, place an aisle along the length of each run of WS (Fig. 14.3b). Per code, these aisles

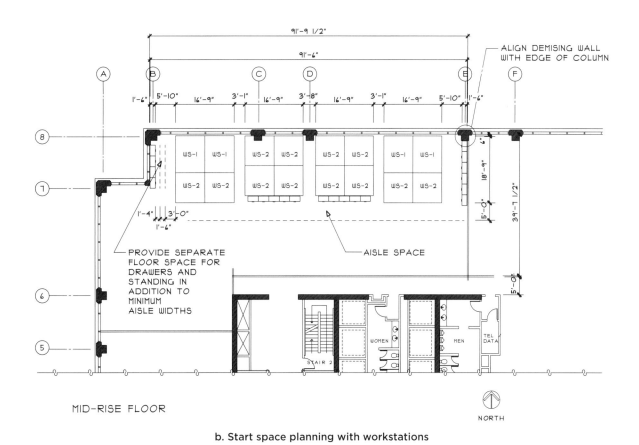

b. Start space planning with workstations

(Figure continues on p. 286)

should be a minimum width of 44". However, when an aisle serves fewer than fifty occupants, it can be reduced to a minimum width of 36", which can help conserve space where necessary (see Box 5.2).

Aisle Widths Plus Door/Drawer Floor Space

When there is a bank of files, shelving, or work-tables opposite the last cluster of stations or between two clusters of stations, sufficient clearance or additional floor space must be added to the minimum aisle widths to accommodate any drawers, doors, or chairs that might open or move into the aisle space (see Chapter 5). For instance, approximately 34"–36" of floor space is required for someone to open a lateral file drawer (see Appendix E.11–13). When added to the minimum aisle width, the overall aisle width is 70" or 5'-10". In high-traffic areas, it may be wise to provide even more floor space for a person to stand at an open file drawer, for an overall aisle width of 72"–84".

Overall Dimensions

In the example shown, the overall length or width of floor space required to lay out four clusters of workstations and a bank of files at each end is 91'-6" × 18'-9". In addition, some amount of space is required between the furniture and a wall. It is not possible to place the furniture absolutely tight up against the wall. There is a rubber, wood, or stone base along the wall to consider. The walls may not be plumb. Depending on the furniture system selected, the panel base may extend beyond the panel by 1/4 to 1/2 in. Therefore, it is good planning to increase the required overall dimensions by some amount; approximately 1/2 to 1 in. should be added at each end of the furniture layout.

To achieve this layout, it is necessary to shift the demising wall at column line E slightly from on center to the right edge of the column to accommodate the furniture as shown. If the demising wall had been at a window mullion where it could not be shifted or was already set by another tenant

■ **FIGURE 14.4 CAD drafting: Accounting Firm Layout 1** (continued)

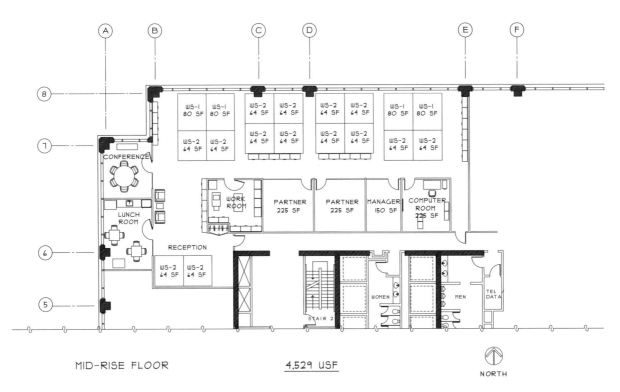

MID-RISE FLOOR   4,529 USF   NORTH

c. Final space plan with all rooms and work areas

occupying space on the other side of the demising wall, an alternate layout would need to be planned that could work within the prescribed space.

Internal Circulation

Once the workstations are laid out, internal circulation is blocked out along the front of the stations in the same manner as with offices and other rooms. Hard-walled rooms and offices can then be planned around and within the remaining areas on the floor plan. In this building and in this layout, coincidently, the remaining space in front of the workstations and aisle is 15'-0", the exact depth requested for offices listed in the Program Report (Fig. 14.4c). When the remaining space is less or greater than the desired dimensions, room and office sizes can generally be slightly shortened or elongated and still house the furniture and a layout as needed.

Space Plan Adjustments

Whether hand or computer drafted, plans should remain in flux until the designer feels that all program requirements have been met in the best possible manner. Even then, the designer should still consider various options: functions can be moved from interior positions to window wall locations or vice versa, and they can be enclosed within a room or arranged as open areas where feasible.

Every attempt should be made to provide adjacency and square footage requests per the Program Report. Many of those requests, however, can seem a bit ambiguous. For instance, our law firm wants the lunchroom located near the reception area. Does this mean that the lunchroom should be immediately next to the reception area, sharing a common wall, possibly with a door for direct access (Fig. 14.5)? Can it be located across the corridor opposite the reception area (Fig. 14.3b)? Can it be one door down the corridor from the reception area opening (Fig. 14.6)?

Two groups in the accounting firm have 22 files between them, requiring 370 to 400 square feet (SF), a large amount of floor space. Since these files can either go into an enclosed room or out in the open area, it may be possible to conserve space in one location over the other.

Sketching, revising, redoing, moving, and adjusting will continue until all program requirements, circulation, and codes have been met and placed within the allotted floor plan space *and*

the designer is not only satisfied with, but also excited about, the ambience of the space plan.

Peer Review

During the process of creating a final (initial) space plan, whether it is hand sketched or created on the computer, designers should always consult with codesigners. Such collaboration brings out a suggestion here, points out a code violation there, or offers another thought on how to arrange rooms and areas. Obviously, with hand drafting, the designer and peers will be viewing a hard copy of the space plan. New tissue can be overlaid on the plan under review and marked up as the designers conceive of new ideas. With computer drafting, peer review can be done by viewing the drawing on the computer screen with changes made directly in the file, or a hard copy can be printed and then marked up as the designers are "jamming."

The designer may choose to accept and apply the suggestions and thoughts offered by a codesigner or may not. However, before rejecting comments made by peers, designers should carefully consider their comments. After all, the designer has been concentrating and focusing so much on making sure that everything fits into the plan, sometimes it is easy to miss the big picture.

Before sharing the plan with codesigners, and definitely before showing the plan to the client, the designer should always print out the computer plan to review in hard copy form. It is much easier to see missing lines, double lines, or other goofy computer errors on a hard copy than it is on the computer screen. Finally, always, always run a spell-check over the entire plan before printing a copy to give to the client.

Creative Layouts

Many, maybe even the majority, of space plans will be straight, 90-degree rectangular layouts. Clients are used to such layouts. Straight lines fit into our everyday lives; streets and roads are regularly built on a 90-degree grid, and homes and other buildings are customarily rectangular or square. It is often easier to plan with parallel and perpendicular lines.

Nevertheless, not everything has to be, and indeed, is not, laid out with 90-degree angles. There are diagonal streets and round traffic circles, octagonal buildings, even a famous oval office. These variants add creative aspects and interest to our lives.

We need to be careful, though, with avant-garde layouts and ideas. Some creative, unexpected designs and layouts work better than others. Selected designs and layouts may be controversial, whereas others may be considered innovative. Recall the Vietnam Memorial Wall. When first presented in the early 1980s, the concept was something totally unheard of for national monuments and memorials; two triangular walls joined at an obtuse angle below grade. Initially, there was much controversy over the design; some people embraced it, and some people belittled it. Once built, the vast numbers of people who visit the wall understand the simplicity and healing powers of an interactive memorial.

Other creative designs are not always so well received, either initially or after they are built. John Silber, former president of Boston University, has written a book entitled *Architecture of the Absurd*, expounding "against the excesses of 'designer' architects and urban-planning utopians."[1] He discusses both buildings that are conceived in absurd ways and buildings that become absurd due to construction mishaps. He maintains that designers should not be creative just to be creative, if that creativity is not practical.

Localized Creativity

Creativity can be achieved in numerous ways. Not all space plans will lend themselves to angled, curved, rotated, or skewed walls. Plans with these creative wall concepts tend to require additional floor space to adequately incorporate minimum circulations, notably in the corridor areas (see Fig. 3.1). Plans with lots of offices and rectangular furniture do not conform easily to angled or curved walls.

Sometimes, however, angled or curved walls can be localized for use around selected rooms. Reception and conference rooms, for instance, tend to be less rigid in their layouts and often more generous in space to begin with, which can allow for easy rotating of furniture and angling or canting of walls. By considering an alternate

■ **FIGURE 14.5** *Localized creativity* **using angled walls for reception area and rooms on either side of reception area: Law Firm Layout II**

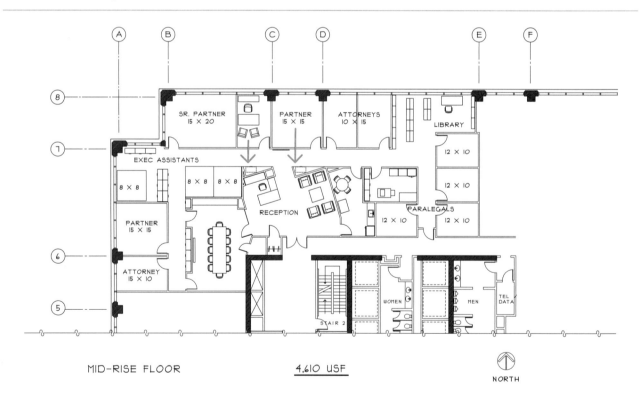

MID-RISE FLOOR   4,610 USF

NORTH

layout for our law firm, walls in the reception room are angled, as a floor-to-ceiling glass wall leading into the conference room and as a solid wall for a seating group (Fig. 14.5). This sets a great backdrop for dynamic first impressions and impact while leaving the balance of the plan fairly conventional. It also creates some niches on the corridor side that can later be developed as functional or playful spaces.

Visual Creativity

Sometimes plans can achieve visual excitement by creating focal points of interest rather than by using angled walls. In a third space plan option for the law firm, the positioning of the conference room, with an interior glass wall opposite the reception area, offers the northern skyline of the city below as the first sight for visitors (Fig. 14.6).

Impact Creativity

What a feeling it is when the designer sees, recognizes, creates, or is offered the opportunity to plan something truly different: curved walls, round walls, canted walls, angled walls, oddly shaped rooms and spaces, even curved and canted furniture. Perhaps it is the nature of the business, or the building, or the clients themselves that inspire the concept of a truly unconventional space plan.

There are various ways to start a plan with curved or angled walls. Using program requirements from the advertising firm client, Mundelein Advertising (Appendix A.3), the designer may select a form, such as a circle, and *roll* it around (Fig. 14.7a). Forms can be enlarged to extend beyond the confines of the building or the designated space (Fig. 14.7b); they may be broken, imaginary, pulled apart, mirrored, or rotated (Fig. 14.7c). Parts of the form may become ceiling lines or changes in flooring material. Selected pieces of furniture may be drawn to ensure that it will adequately fit within the creatively designed rooms. With time, patience, trial and error, and more sketching, these creative, non-linear plans will come together in much the same manner as linear plans (Fig. 14.7d).

■ **FIGURE 14.6** *Visual creativity* **using focal point, such as view outward from upper floor windows: Law Firm Layout III**

MID-RISE FLOOR   4,476 USF   NORTH

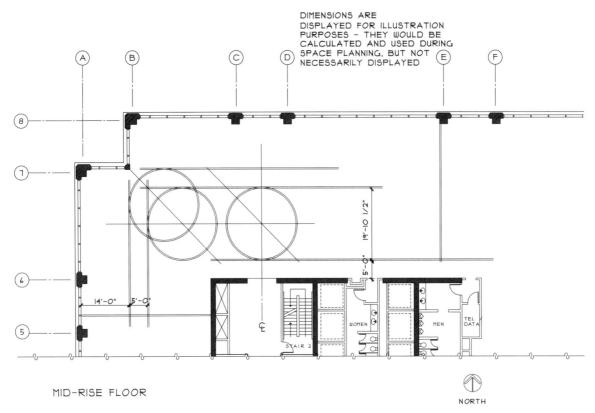

a. Start space planning by selecting a form and playing with it

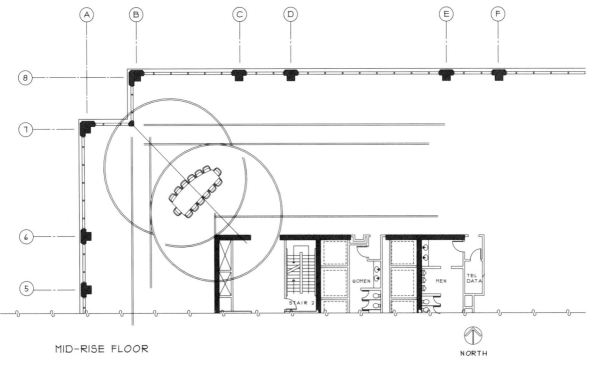

b. Extend forms beyond space or building, split forms, pull forms apart

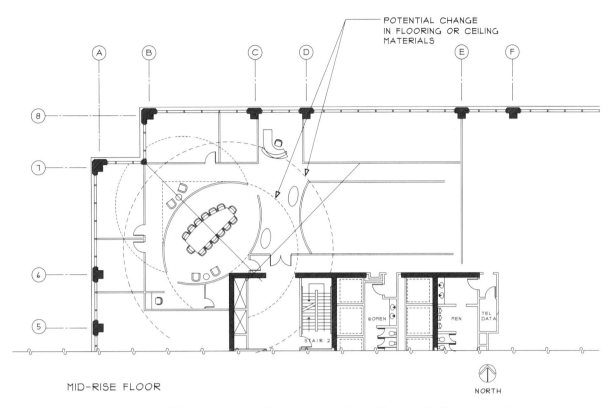

MID-RISE FLOOR

NORTH

c. Break forms up, move them around, enlarge them, make them suggestive
by continuing the form as floor or ceiling material changes

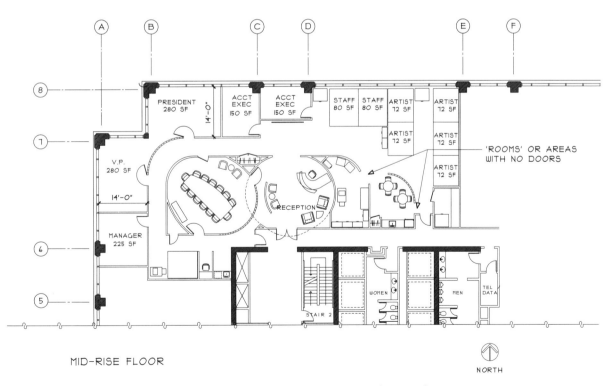

MID-RISE FLOOR

NORTH

d. Final space plan labeled with room names and square footages

Doors and Curved Walls

It is very unlikely that we will see many curved doors in today's market because they are expensive to manufacturer. To install straight doors in curved walls, it is important to consider the selected door type. For a typical framed, hinged door, at least 5'-0" of the wall will need to be straight: 3'-0" for the door, 1'-6" for the American with Disabilities Act (ADA) code clearance on the strike side (see Box 6.2), and 6" on the hinge side to support the frame (Fig. 14.8). For a frameless, full-height pivot door, it is conceivable that the walls on either side of the door may be curved, but the door itself will be straight, thus breaking a continuous curve or circle. Depending on the severity of the curved wall and approach to the door, approximately 12–18 in. of the wall on the strike side of the pivot door may also need to be straight to meet ADA codes.

Angled Layouts

Placing workstations on an angle can add another very interesting facet to floor plans (Fig. 14.9). Informal meeting areas can be incorporated at the end of a run of workstations. Greater privacy is often achieved between cubicle occupants due to the offset of cubicle entrances when stations are on an angle. At the same time, visual variation can be accomplished due to the visual "break up" of panels and worksurfaces along the aisles of a cluster of cubicles as opposed to straight panels along the front run of straight clusters of workstations.

Void Spaces

When planning angled or curved layouts, an important feature to address is the non-square wall angles that naturally evolve on these plans. Obtuse angles create areas that are more desirable because they can be used for tables and chairs, plants, and other items, whereas acute-angle wall areas generally become unusable space. In many instances, it is best to box out acute angles, thus forming void spaces (Fig. 14.9 and see also Fig. 9.1b). Sometimes void spaces will be just that, void spaces. At other times, these spaces can be used for vertical plumbing lines, ductwork, or heavy bundles of wiring and cabling.

■ **FIGURE 14.8 Enlarged plan: Straight doors in curved wall**

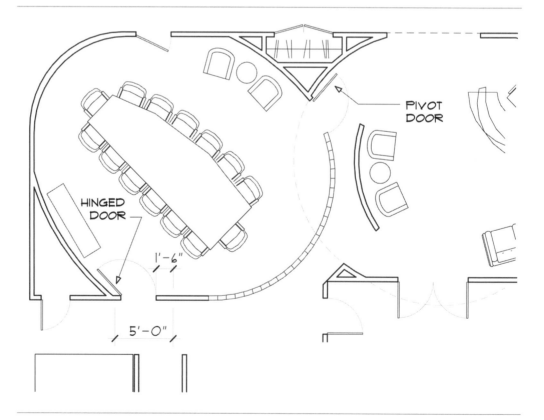

Even though void spaces can be disguised, it is best to keep them to a minimum. After all, the client is paying rent for all of the floor space and would like to be able to use as much space as possible.

Draw in 2-D While Thinking in 3-D

Space planning is flat, it is 2-dimensional, just lines on paper; yet, eventually, all lines will elevate themselves into 3-dimentional entities. Everything looks "good," and the "same," on plan view! Haven't we already seen that with conventional and contemporary work areas (see Illustrated Table 7.1a-c, Illustrated Table 7.2c and Fig. 7.19)? The same can be true for wood doors and framed glass doors, they are both 1³/₈" to 1³/₄" thick, two 3 ft capped lines on a floor plan.

So, while design development (DD) has not yet actually started, DD is part of phase III and space planning is part of phase II, the designer/space planner, can, and should, be thinking in 3-D. Develop conceptual ideas (also part of phase II and the next task after a space plan has been approved), doodle on sketch paper, tear out magazine photos, start a file of ideas, and then incorporate some of those ideas into the space plan. Will the entry doors be wood or will they be glass pivot (Illustrated Table 14.1a and b)? Although glass pivot doors should be drawn as 1 in. thick doors, when printed at ¹/₈ in. scale, they may appear the "same" as wood doors. However, 3-D thinking may then "call for" an adjacent glass wall, which will appear different from typical wall construction (Fig. 14.14b) or a dropped soffit above the door header, which can lead to a dropped soffit in the reception area.

The angled wall corridor niches in Fig. 14.5 are too large to just box out as void spaces, yet too small to accommodate soft seating or a table and chairs. By thinking and sketching in 3-D, perhaps these spaces can be functional by installing a 2- or 3-drawer file cabinet below a counter top, or maybe these are great areas to display the owners' 3-D sculpture pieces. Quick sketches instill many ideas in the designer's creative mind (Illustrated Table 14.1c and d), which can then be further developed during the design phase. *Draw 2-D—Think 3-D!*

FIGURE 14.9 Workstations and some partitions on angled layout: Accounting Firm Layout II

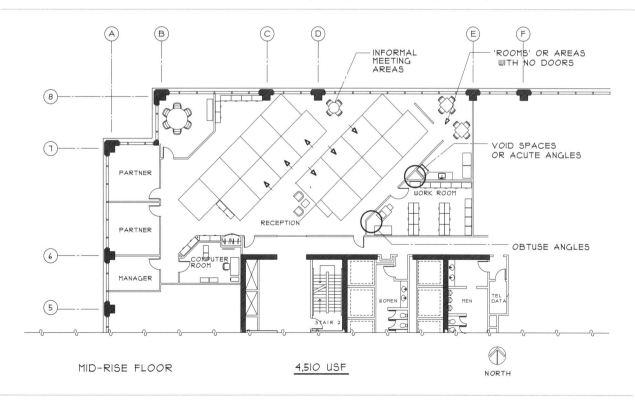

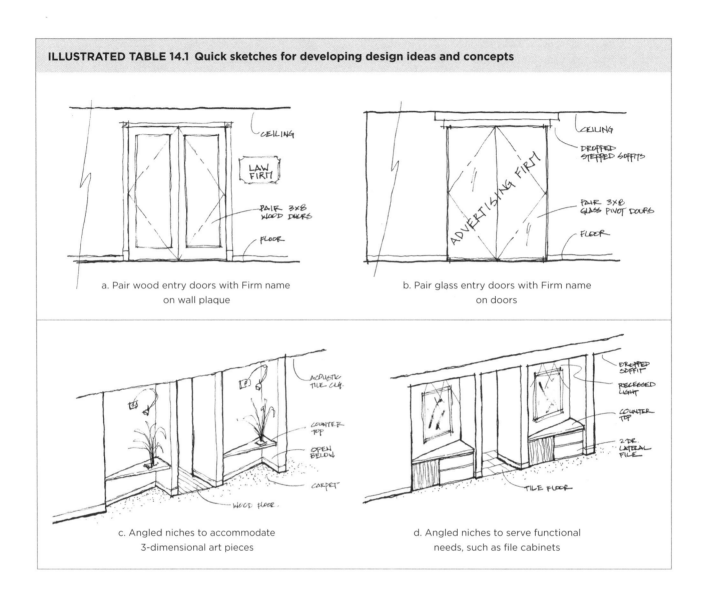

a. Pair wood entry doors with Firm name
on wall plaque

b. Pair glass entry doors with Firm name
on doors

c. Angled niches to accommodate
3-dimensional art pieces

d. Angled niches to serve functional
needs, such as file cabinets

Program Variances

Whenever rooms, particularly offices and workstations, are adjusted in size or dimension to better fit within the space plan, it is a good idea to point out these differences to the client. Many people are not adept at reading floor plans and therefore do not automatically see that the plan is not providing exactly what is stated in the Program Report.

Oftentimes, these small discrepancies make little or no difference, and it may not be necessary to make an issue of slight variances, but the designer should not automatically assume that the client does not care. For the advertising firm, the Program Report calls for two 15 × 20 offices. To create the ellipsis conference room to seat 14 people, the main offices were reduced from the program requested depth of 15'-0" to a space plan depth of 14'-0" (see Fig. 14.7d). Fourteen feet is more than adequate for an impressive desk, credenza, and guest chair layout, especially considering the width of each room (see Fig. 14.12). Winter sunsets as seen from these offices offer such gorgeous sights that a mere foot may soon be forgiven.

In other situations, changing the requirements as listed in the Program Report may not be acceptable, particularly when quantities are changed. An office or workstation must be provided in the space plan for every person listed within the report. Granted, at times it may be necessary to reduce the size of the work area, but the area must be on the plan. Of course, if the plan allows, there can always be extra offices, workstations, files, or other items over and above the requested quantities as listed in the Program Report; however, there cannot be fewer items than requested.

Finalizing a Space Plan

Eventually, everything comes together. All program requirements and circulation seem to be laid out in a logical order. There are some creative walls and other design concepts incorporated within the space plan. Now is the time to add details: doors, plants, and furniture, as might be suitable, and to clean up wall intersections on computer drawings. Glass can be added to offices and other rooms to allow penetration of daylight into interior spaces (Fig. 14.10). Floor or ceiling design concepts are indicated with dashed lines for presentation plans (Fig. 14.7c). Rooms should be labeled with names and sizes or square footage as appropriate. In addition, the designer will want to mentally "walk" through the entire planning procedure and then carefully analyze the plan from several viewpoints to ensure that there are no glaring mistakes or omissions.

PLANNING PROCEDURE

Each designer will develop his or her own method for space planning, use their own creativity, or follow a proven path. There are, however, some basic procedures that all designers should follow or take into account.

1. **Building footprint:** Carefully consider and measure the overall building footprint. How will these dimensions relate to the program requirements? Is the building an historical building, a new building, or a renovated building under a new use group? What are the building standards to consider? How is the building positioned in relationship to the path of travel for the sun at different times of day or year? Answers to these questions may or may not dictate where or how space planning begins on a floor plan.

2. **Public corridors:** Start each plan by blocking out the public corridor on new floors that have not previously housed tenants or verify existing corridors on floors that currently house tenants.

■ **FIGURE 14.10 Finalize floor plans: Add details, sidelights, doors, room names, clean up wall intersections, etc.**

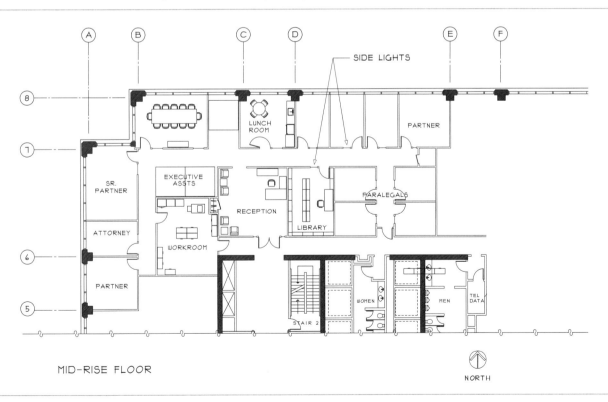

3. **Offices**: Since most private offices are fairly typical in size and layout, it is often easiest to initiate actual space planning by beginning with the offices. It is good practice to discuss placement of the offices as window or interior rooms with the client prior to start of planning.

4. **Reception**: High visibility of the entry doors, and thus the reception area, is normally desired by most clients. Depending on whether the space is located on an upper or ground-floor level, this typically means that the reception entry door is positioned on center with the elevator lobby, at the end of a corridor, or immediately to the right or left of the building entry doors. The final size of the reception room will probably fluctuate in size, shape, and exact location, depending on how the balance of the plan lays out.

5. **Support rooms**: One might assume that support rooms are never placed along a window wall, but rather they are in interior positions only. After all, why would a file room receive natural daylight while employees sit in interior rooms with no natural daylight? However, there may be some employees who have a permanent work area in the file room. Lunchrooms along a window wall may be occupied only 20 percent of the day, but while occupied, the natural daylight can be very uplifting for those employees who otherwise sit in interior locations. Each support room should be individually considered for the best location on the floor plan.

6. **Workstations**: Workstations generally start out as square footage (48 SF), evolve into a stated size (6 × 8) as a typical layout, and then often are adjusted once the space planning starts: perhaps 7 × 7 at 49 SF or 6'-6" × 7'-6" at 48.75 SF. Since buildings can vary greatly in their depths from window wall to core and in widths, workstations often are adjusted to these variances in footprint layouts to allow for maximum planning of workstations. Workstations can be planned around offices and other hard-walled rooms; they can be single and stand-alone, backed up to walls, share common panels, be straight or rotated.

There are many options when planning workstations. Designers should remember two main factors: add panel thicknesses to overall nominal workstation sizes and provide aisle space along one side of each and every workstation.

7. **Adjacencies**: Designers should verify that rooms and areas are either as close or as far away as possible per the adjacency diagrams and requests.

8. **Circulation**: Minimum aisle and corridor widths are 44 in. There are exceptions, but it is better to plan for the minimum rather than the exception. All rooms, offices, cubicles, and items of furniture and equipment need to be accessed via an aisle or corridor.

9. **Leftover space**: No plan fits perfectly within a given amount of space. There will always be some amount of space left over on a floor plan. This space can be incorporated into wider aisles and corridors, used for casual meeting areas or seating groups, or encapsulated into various rooms such as the conference room or lunchrooms. Sometimes leftover space can be used as relief space in an otherwise fully laid-out floor plan.

10. **Layouts**: Rectangular or straight 90-degree lines and rooms are the most common and will make up the vast majority of space plans. When layouts are angled, the most familiar angle is 45 degrees. Curved walls look great on a plan, but they are harder and more costly to construct. Nevertheless, when it is feasible or desirable to create unusual space plans, designers should by all means bring out the best space planning techniques possible.

ANALYZING A SPACE PLAN

Once a designer has *finalized* a plan, the plan should be printed for review. Most commercial projects are printed at $1/8$-in. scale, unless the area of the project is quite small, in which case it can be printed at $1/4$-in. scale.

It is a good idea to let the plan sit overnight, or from morning until the afternoon, so the designer may clear his or her mind and become detached from the planning process. With a little time lapse, the designer can truly analyze the space plan from an objective point of view, from the client's point of view, from the employees' point of view , from a green point of view, and finally, from a code reviewer's point of view.

Objective Point of View

Envision the client seeing the plan for the first time. Envision visitors entering into the reception area. It is helpful for designers to close their eyes, turn off the lights when feasible, and sit in a restful position to contemplate "walking" through the to-be-built environment, not necessarily the finished, designed space (that will come later), but rather a 3-dimensional space of the floor plan. Designers should consider physically standing inside the entry doors or by the reception desk, looking around, and then proceeding down the corridors, asking, *What are the sights?*

Exciting or Ungainly Sights

Consider the Law Firm Layout II; there are three points of view immediately inside the entry doors and two more points of view as one approaches the reception desk (Fig. 14.11a). Two of these views are anticipated, expected even: the receptionist and seating. The other three views may not have been considered during space planning, but these points of view will most definitely be seen: the associate attorney sitting behind his office desk (Fig. 14.11b), the coffee counter through the lunchroom door (Fig. 14.11c), and the large wall behind the conference table.

Most likely, the designer has already pondered the type of artwork that will look best on the conference wall. More than likely, however, those thoughts were in conjunction with being inside the conference room, not from outside of the room looking through what appears to be a glass wall. If the wall is glass, artwork will then first be seen from the reception area. The designer may or may not want to reconsider the artwork on this wall.

For the attorney office, the door was positioned opposite the column to provide the best furniture layout. If left as shown, then not only will visitors be able to peer into the office from the reception area, but more than likely, the attorney's concentration will be interrupted each

time visitors speak with the receptionist due to direct travel paths of noise. In this situation, it may be better to mirror the door and furniture. Granted, the credenza will be offset from the desk, but now visitors will see either a blank wall or artwork, and the attorney will not be distracted by direct noise (Fig. 14.11d).

Coffee counters may not make the best first impression, as they are habitually messy with dirty cups, old coffee packets, and other sundry items. A closer can be installed on the lunchroom door, which closes the door automatically each time it is opened. Doors with closers are typically drawn as only partially open, at approximately 25–30 degrees vs. 90 degrees open. Or, the designer could also consider switching the layout around so that the table is opposite the door and the counter is out of sight. True, the table might also get messy, but a table is more likely to hold newspapers or other items that are not as "gross" as dirty cups. A framed poster can then be hung on the wall behind the table to detract from any items on the table (Fig. 14.11d).

It is important for the designer to *see* the built environment long before it is actually constructed. Once constructed, it is much more costly to make changes. And, even though this is still the space planning phase, design development can and should be floating around in the designer's mind as creative imagery in order to achieve the best layouts.

Best Use of Space

Upon entering the Advertising Firm Layout l (Fig. 14.12a), there are two initial points of view and then two more points of view as one approaches the reception desk. Directly inside the entry doors, the visitor gets an interesting glimpse of what appears to be a glass block wall; two more steps, and the glass block is gone, leaving the curved desk and curved wall as the main focal point. Moving into the reception area brings a view of artwork (in the distance) and, as one turns around, perhaps hoping to see the glass block again, but instead, sees a partial curved wall, conceptually continuing from the curved wall behind the reception desk, that serves as a backdrop for lounge chairs. Initially, this looks like a really exciting plan with nothing amiss. But, is this the best possible layout?

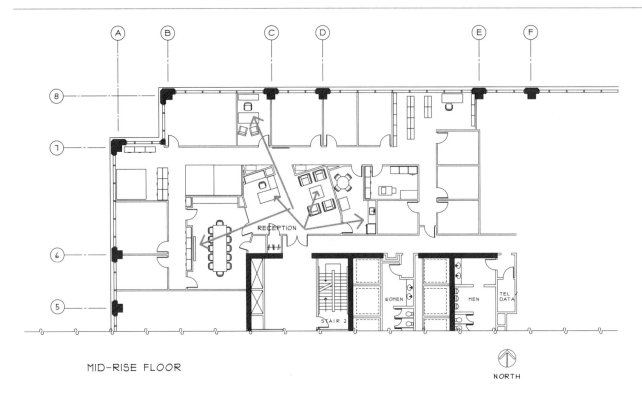

a. Plan view: Points of view from reception area

b. Direct view of office occupant
from reception area

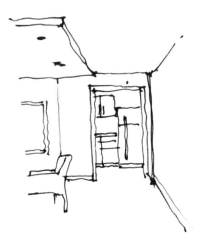

c. View of coffee counter through
door from reception area

(Figure continues)

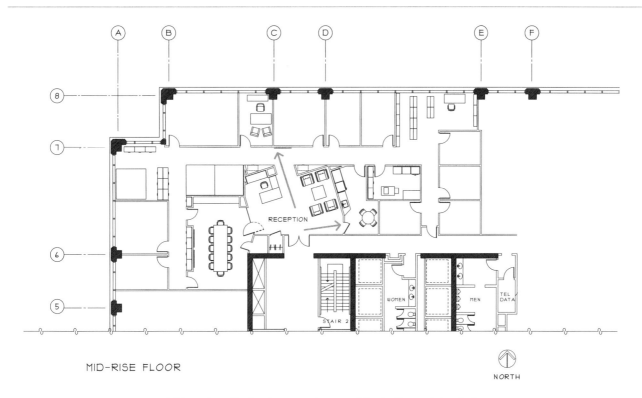

d. Plan view: Revised space plan provides better points of view

Further consideration of this plan suggests three flaws. The account executive at column line C will need to walk past the reception area each time he or she goes to meet with the artist housed on the right side of the plan. Both owners will see files at the end of the corridor each time they walk from their offices to the reception area. Finally, the workroom is a bit tight.

By slightly revising the reception area, removing the backdrop and relocating the coat closet from the left to the right side of the opening between the reception area and internal corridor, a more functional plan can be realized (Fig. 14.12b). Technically, the reception area is the same size in both layouts. However, with the backdrop gone, the area feels larger, and the full effect of the curved, glass-block wall can be felt without having to peak around the backdrop. The continuous concept of the curved wall behind the desk can be captured by using two different materials on the floor. With a straight wall on the back of the coat closet, artwork or the company logo can now be installed directly in the reception area and not just across the corridor.

The conference room becomes its own entity without the attached closet. Additionally, the passage from the reception area now leads primarily to the two owners' offices, the main people who will receive visitors and use the conference room. With this slight movement of the closet, it makes sense to reposition the files, which then leads to enlarging the workroom. Much has been gained by objectively analyzing the finished space plan.

Corridor Widths

Although designers regularly plan corridors to be 5 ft wide, it may be desirable, prudent, or sometimes necessary to reduce that width in order to accommodate all program requirements or to gain additional floor space in certain rooms. However, when reducing corridor widths, it is important to consider all aspects of the plan. Looking at Law Firm Layout II, note that the corridor across the top of the plan can be reduced

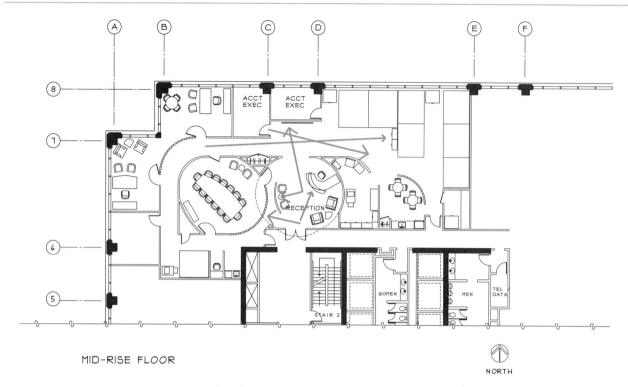

a. Plan view: Points of view from reception area

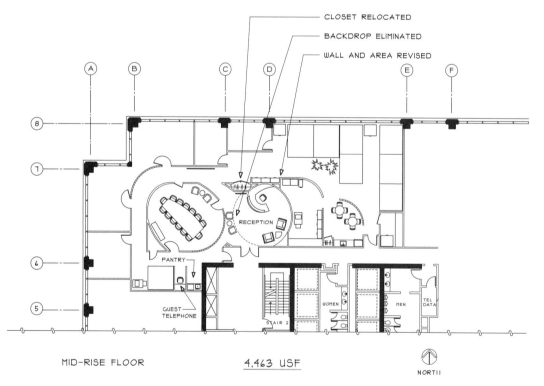

b. Plan view: Revised space plan for better use of space

to a minimum of 44 in. because there are no doors or drawers that open into this corridor, but the corridor along the left side cannot not be reduced to 44 in. because the file drawers, when opened, would encroach upon the minimum required corridor width (Fig. 14.13).

Do these narrower corridors really gain much for the space plan? Where the corridors are long or enclosed on either side with floor-to-ceiling walls, occupants may experience a tunnel effect. Two people cannot walk abreast. No doors or drawers can open into these corridors. Visually, the space plan appears confining compared with 5 ft corridors (Fig. 14.11d). Therefore, it is important for designers to carefully consider each aspect of the plan before making decisions for a final space plan.

Client's Point of View

Even though the designer is excited about the completed space plan and has even taken the time to be objective by making some minor changes, the real question is: Is the client excited and happy with the space plan?

Less Than Exciting Space Plans

Not all firms will agree to accept interior offices for the owners and other upper-level positions, even though the space plan provides a nice, clean layout as in Accounting Firm Layout I (Fig. 14.4c). An alternate plan whereby the workstations are rotated 45 degrees, thus producing several angled walls and rooms with acute and obtuse corners, also provides a clean layout (Fig. 14.9). The first space plan has no corner offices, and the second plan provides only one of the partners with a corner office. Status is very important for most people. It is unlikely the partners will want to flip a coin to determine who will occupy which office. It is possible that one partner office can be switched with the conference room, but the offices will not be equal in size or layout.

A third space plan provides both partners with a corner office (Fig. 14.14a). However, the balance of space becomes a maze of aisles and workstations with limited zing in the overall plan, plus this plan requires 4,671 SF as compared to 4,529 SF for layout I and 4,510 SF for layout II. Is the client willing to lease an

FIGURE 14.13 Corridors based on minimum widths: Law Firm Layout II

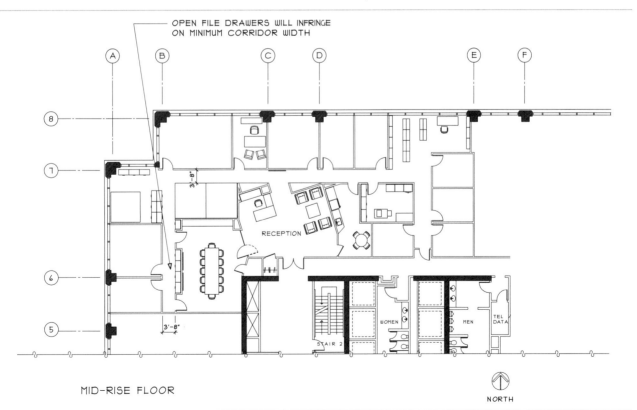

MID-RISE FLOOR

NORTH

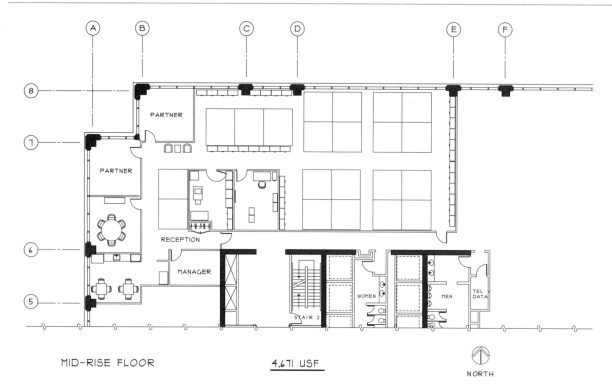

MID-RISE FLOOR   4,671 USF

NORTH

a. Alternate space plan with two corner offices, but perhaps displaying a more mundane or less exciting layout: Accounting Firm Layout III

additional 150 SF of floor space to acquire two corner offices when other plans offer a more exciting layout in less square footage?

Alternate Exciting Plans

Exciting can mean many things and be achieved in many ways. Glass block and other atypical construction materials can provide a lot of pizzazz, often as much pizzazz or more than angled or curved walls. Perhaps the client prefers clear glass or etched or laminated glass as opposed to glass block. Glass panels, like doors, will be straight, not curved. But when panels of glass are installed at slight angles, one after another, the wall can appear to be curved (Fig. 14.14b).

To use glass panels, a new plan is needed because the 20 ft curved wall in Advertising Firm Layout I is probably too tight to simply replace the glass block with straight panels of glass and still achieve the same curvature. Glass block comes in widths of 4, 6, 8, and 12 in., with 6 in. being the most common width for interior work. These small dimensions allow for tighter curves.

For full-height glass, panels need to be a minimum of 15–18 in. wide to prevent torque. Depending on both the panel widths and installation angles selected, the curvature may appear to be smooth or to be a faceted wall. Neither option is bad, wrong, best, or right; they are just alternate exciting ways to produce a wonderful space plan!

The curved wall as shown in Advertising Firm Layout II uses 28 in. wide on center, frameless, full-height glass panels installed at 4–9 degrees with the panel before and after, resulting in a 40 ft diameter arch. Advertising Firm Layout II appears to be just as exciting as layout I. In some ways, layout II is more exciting. The entry is definitely unique. Visitors are drawn wholly into the space via the reception seating on the window wall. The executive or owner area is completely divided from the rest of the staff. Plus, the receptionist has better access to the pantry.

But layout II requires almost 150 more square feet than layout I. Layout II requires 4,609 SF and layout I requires 4,463 SF (Fig. 14.12b). Is the client willing to pay rent for the additional square footage?

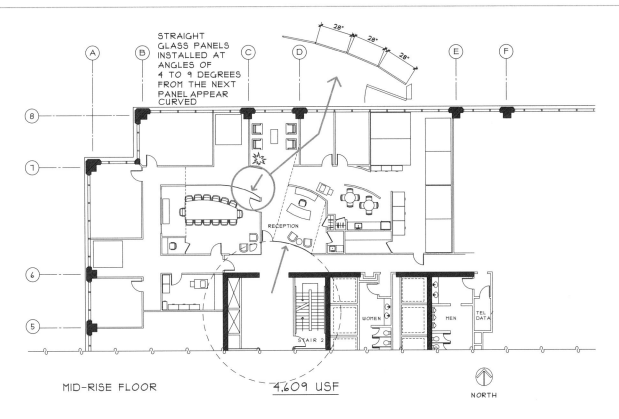

STRAIGHT GLASS PANELS INSTALLED AT ANGLES OF 4 TO 9 DEGREES FROM THE NEXT PANEL APPEAR CURVED

MID-RISE FLOOR

4,609 USF

NORTH

b. Alternate space plan displaying level of excitement: Advertising Firm Layout II

Budgetary Objective

Has the plan been considered from a budgetary point of view? No matter the client's reference point—a low, medium, or high budget objective—there is always a budget, and there are always more items to add to that budget. When money is saved in one area, it can often be reallocated and spent in another area.

One way to reduce costs during space planning is to eliminate doors on certain rooms, such as a copy room or lunchroom (Figs. 14.7 and 14.9). Doors into these rooms are seldom closed; they tend to remain open unless the door is equipped with a closer. So, why install these doors? Another method for reducing costs, when feasible, is to lower the wall heights surrounding these rooms to three-quarter height, thus saving more money during construction and life-cycle costs for HVAC.

It is important to discuss these and other options with the client. Depending on the location of each room in relation to other rooms in the space plan, the client may wish to actually close doors to those rooms to contain smells or noise. In any case, the designer should always think about the space plan from the client's point of view.

Green Point of View

Recycling, reducing waste, reducing energy consumption and operating costs, improving air quality, specifying products from renewable resources, and maintaining and improving our health are all parts of going green. Designers regularly address many of these issues during design development and documentation by selecting products that offer green amenities. Actually, greening and consideration for employee health and well-being and energy conservation can be incorporated right from the start during space planning. Employees spend 6, 8, 10, 12 hours a day inside the workplace. That is a lot of time to be inside a building. According to one article:

There is some evidence of reduced absenteeism and increased productivity in green buildings....

For instance, contact with nature and sunlight penetration has been found to enhance emotional functioning. Positive emotions, in turn, are associated with creativity and cognitive "flow," a state of high task engagement. Other green building features, such as indoor and outdoor relaxation areas with vegetation and views, are likely to enhance social interactions and sense of belonging—both of which are associated with organizational attachment, a topic of enormous interest among organizations today.[2]

Natural Daylight and Views

Under the Leadership in Energy and Environmental Design (LEED) rating system, up to three credits can be achieved by providing natural daylight and exterior views for 75 to 90 percent of the built space (Box 14.2). Additionally, the designer may want to consider open relief areas within the overall plan that provide spontaneous gathering areas where people can gather to talk with coworkers.

BOX 14.2 LEED CI Natural Daylight for Everyone[3, 4]

Indoor Environmental Quality Credit
DAYLIGHT
EQ Credit (1–3 points) Commercial Interiors
Intent
To connect building occupants with the outdoors, reinforce circadian rhythms, and reduce the use of electrical lighting by introducing daylight into the space.

Requirements
Provide manual or automatic (with manual override) glare-control devices for all regularly occupied spaces. Select one of the following three options.

OPTION 1. Simulation: Spatial Daylight Autonomy and Annual Sunlight Exposure (2–3 points)

Demonstrate through annual computer simulations that spatial daylight autonomy . . . of at least 55%, 75%, or 90% is achieved. Use regularly occupied floor area. . . .

OPTION 2. Simulation: Illuminance Calculations (1–2 points)

Demonstrate through computer modeling that illuminance levels will be between 300 lux and 3,000 lux for 9 a.m. and 3 p.m., both on a clear-sky day at the equinox . . . Use regularly occupied floor area. . . .

OPTION 3. Measurement (2–3 points)
Achieve illuminance levels between 300 lux and 3,000 lux for the floor area . . .

Indoor Environmental Quality Credit
Quality Views
EQ Credit (1 point) Commercial Interiors
Intent
To give building occupants a connection to the natural outdoor environment by providing quality views.

Requirements
Achieve a direct line of sight to the outdoors via vision glazing for 75% of all regularly occupied floor areas.

View glazing in the contributing area must provide a clear image of the exterior, not obstructed by frits, fibers, patterned glazing, or added tints that distort color balance. Additionally, 75% of all regularly occupied floor area must have at least two of the following four kinds of views:

- multiple lines of sight to vision glazing in different directions at least 90 degrees apart;
- views that include at least two of the flowing: (1) flora, fauna, or sky; (2) movement; and (3) objects at least 25 feet (7.5 meters) from the exterior of the glazing;
- unobstructed views located within the distance of three times the head height of the vision glazing; and
- views with a view factor of 3 or greater, as defined in "Windows and Offices; A Study of Office Worker Performance and the Indoor Environment."

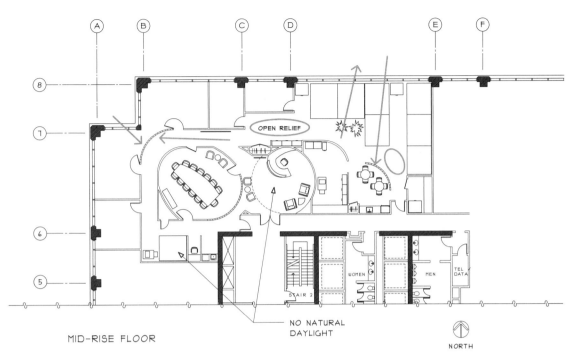

a. Open relief areas and natural daylight for some areas of revised space plan: Advertising Firm Layout I

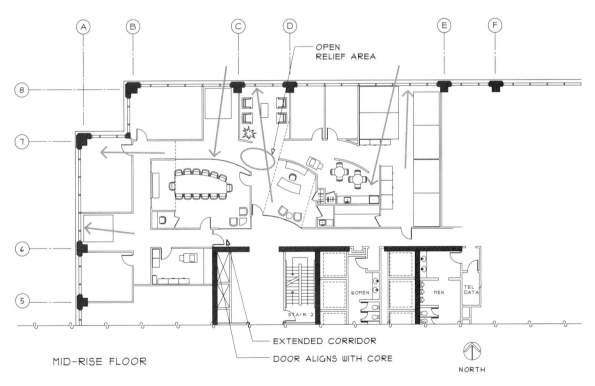

b. Natural daylight for all areas of space plan: Advertising Firm Layout II

Advertising Firm Layout I (Fig. 14.15a) provides several open relief areas, but no natural daylight for the receptionist and one assistant. Layout II (Fig. 14.15b) provides views and natural daylight for all employees, plus the conference room. All plans should be checked to ensure they provide daylight to employees and then be adjusted or revised accordingly.

Energy Conservation

Although some cities began embracing green construction techniques years ago, more and more cities and states are now adopting the newly published IgCC (see Chapter 1) to augment building, mechanical, electrical, fire and safety, and other codes already in use. The biggest impact of the green code for office interiors is the requirement to reduce artificial lighting via motion and daylight sensors (Box 14.3).

Even though motion sensors are required only in selected areas, many firms request that sensors also be installed in rooms used sporadically during the week, such as LAN, storage, and coat rooms. Other rooms, often used or occupied intermittently throughout the work day, such as conference, collaborative, and break rooms, may also be included on this list. The code indicates that fixtures need merely to be dimmed, but in many situations, particularly in the rooms just listed, sensors are designed to be off until such time when an occupant enters the room, at which time the light level immediately turns on 100 percent. When light fixtures are off, no energy is used; monthly utility costs go down and energy is conserved.

Although motion sensors are really more a part of DD than space planning, daylight harvesting truly falls under space planning. All light fixtures within approximately 15 ft of all perimeter walls will need to be installed with a daylight sensor. As side information, generally speaking, sensors are able to serve 8-10 fixtures; fluorescent fixtures require an upgraded ballast, both of which will be designed and specified by the electrical engineer during the DD and CD phases.

With daylight sensors, light levels dim rather than turn off as with motion sensors. The amount of dimming is dictated by the amount of natural daylight entering each area of the floor plan. Thus, southern exposures (in the northern

hemisphere), which naturally receive more direct sunlight and daylight than the opposite northern side of the floor plan, will probably experience a wider range of dimming in the fixtures than those fixtures on the north side. With this knowledge, space planners may arrange program requirements; offices, workstations, based on the anticipated perimeter light levels. Perhaps workstations with individual light controls (see Box 7.1) should go along the window walls while conference rooms, sometimes requiring higher light levels for presentations, could be interior rooms, because unless a permit reviewer grants a variance, there will be no control over turning certain light fixtures on from off.

Code Reviewer's Point of View

All floor plans and accompanying documentation must be presented to code reviewers for approval and permitting. Code violations raise red flags; the permitting process is slowed down because the reviewer will send the drawings back to the designer for correction. If the corrections are extensive, not only will the designer need to spend time and fees to correct the problems but also, it may be necessary to reprint copious drawings, an added expense. It is a very good idea to analyze the space plan from a code requirement perspective at each step of the design process.

Eight code requirements (discussed in Chapter 13) are briefly summarized below:

- Corridors—public, dead-end, and widths
- Exit doors—quantity, direction of swing, and separation
- Travel distance and common path of travel

Two additional code requirements to be considered during space planning are:

- Intervening rooms
- Ceiling heights

Corridors

Assuming that the public corridors are laid out per landlord directions, there should be few code issues to address at this juncture. The landlord may push to encapsulate some of the corridor space into tenant space as shown with the coat closet in Law Firm Layout II (Fig. 14.16), or the corridor may be a bit longer as shown in other

BOX 14.3 IgCC Daylight Harvesting[5]

SECTION 608
BUILDING ELECTRICAL POWER AND LIGHTING SYSTEMS
608.3 INTERIOR LIGHT REDUCTION CONTROLS.
Occupant sensor controls shall be provided to automatically reduce connected lighting power by not less than 45 percent during periods when occupants are not present in the following locations:

1. Corridors and enclosed stairwells;
2. Storage and stack areas not open to the public; and
3. Parking garages.

Exception: Automatic power reduction is not required for the following:

1. Where occupant sensor controls are overridden by time switch controls that keep lights on continuously during peak occupancy periods.
2. Means of egress lighting required by the *International Building Code* or the *International Fire Code*.

608.5 AUTOMATIC DAYLIGHT CONTROLS.
Automatic *daylight controls* shall be provided in daylit areas complying with Section 808.3.1 or Section 803.2 to control the lights serving those areas. . .

Exception: Automatic *daylight controls* are not required for the following spaces and equipment:

1. Toplighting . . . skylight . . .
2. Sidelighting . . .
3. Daylit areas served by less than 90 watts of lighting.
4. Spaces where medical care is directly provided.
5. Spaces within dwelling units or sleeping units.
6. Lighting required to comply with Section C405.2.3 of the *International Energy Conservation Code*.

608.6 PLUG LOAD CONTROLS.
Receptacles and electrical outlets in the following spaces shall be controlled by an occupant sensor or time switch as follows:

1. In Group B office spaces without furniture systems incorporating wired receptacles, not less than one controlled receptacle shall be provided for each 50 square feet (4.65 m²).
2. In Group B office spaces with furniture systems incorporating wired receptacles, not less than one controlled circuit shall be provided at each electrical outlet used for powering furniture systems.
3. In classrooms in Group B and Group E occupancies, not less than four controlled receptacles shall be provided in each classroom.
4. In copy rooms, print shops, and computer labs, not less than one controlled receptacle shall be provided for each data jack.
5. In spaces with an overhead cabinet above a counter or work surface, not less than one controlled receptacle shall be provided for each work surface.

SECTION 808
INDOOR ENVIRONMENTAL QUALITY AND COMFORT
808.3 DAYLIT AREA OF BUILDING SPACES.
In buildings not greater than two stories above grade, not less than 50 percent of the net floor area shall be located within a daylit area. In buildings three or more stories above grade, not less than 25 percent* of the net floor area shall be within a daylit area.

NOTE:
*Twenty-five percent transcribes into an area of roughly 15 ft. around all perimeter walls.

plans by aligning a tenant door with the edge of the core elements (Fig. 14.15b). A code reviewer should easily approve either option.

In Law Firm Layout II, there is an interior 37 ft long dead-end corridor on the left side of the plan (Fig. 14.16). Granted, the corridor leads to an office and a conference room, but it does not lead to a means of egress. This would not be acceptable in a non-sprinkled building, which allows a maximum 20-ft dead-end corridor. With sprinkled buildings, the International Building Code (IBC) allows dead-end corridors up to 50 ft in length, so this plan should be approved by a code reviewer since it is a sprinkled building (see Box 13.8).

When looking at an enlarged section of the Advertising Firm I Layout (Fig. 14.17a), at first glance this short corridor or passageway along the glass block wall appears to fall within an allowable ADA code constraints: it meets the 32 in. minimum width requirement (see Box 5.3). However, not only are there generally more than

one set of codes to consider but there are often separate conditions within a given code that need to be met.

In addition to the minimum width, that width can continue for only 24 in. in length (see Box 5.3). As initially drawn, the passageway was 28 in. long. For a final plan, the passageway was revised and reduced to 24 in. long in order to pass code reviews (Fig. 14.17b).

Exit Doors

Most floor plans require two exit doors unless the square footage is really large or the building is non-sprinkled, in which case additional doors will be required, or if the square footage is quite small, in which case only one exit door may be required. Even though the layouts are less than 5,000 SF, a size that could allow for only one exit door under some codes, they have been planned for two or three doors in each space plan. Even when only one exit door is allowable, it is still good planning to provide at least two exit doors

■ FIGURE 14.16 Plan view: Dead-end corridor and separated exit doors: Law Firm Layout II

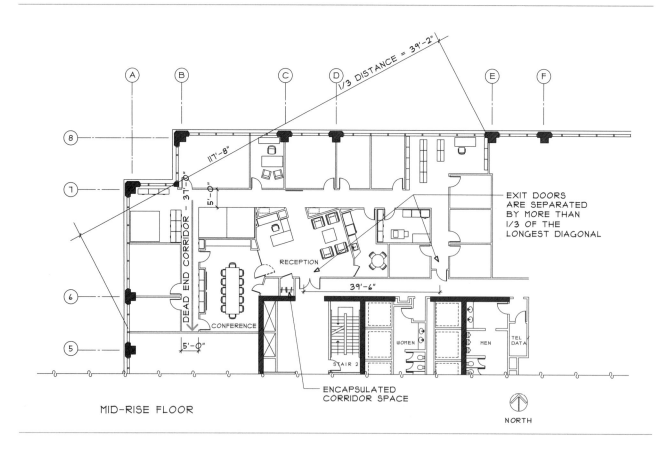

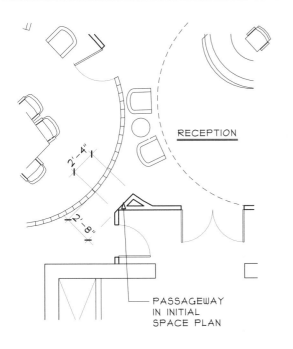

RECEPTION

2'-4"

2'-8"

PASSAGEWAY
IN INITIAL
SPACE PLAN

**a. Initial layout of passageway, which does
not meet code due to length that exceeds
maximum length for reduced passage width**

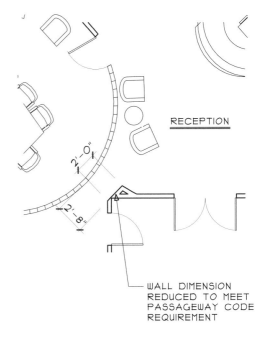

RECEPTION

2'-0"

2'-8"

WALL DIMENSION
REDUCED TO MEET
PASSAGEWAY CODE
REQUIREMENT

**b. Revised passageway layout to
meet code requirements**

when possible. It is better to over-design in some situations; no one wants to be caught at the wrong end of the floor space with limited egress during a fire. Additionally, all doors in the plans swing out in the direction of egress travel (see Box 13.10.)

Finally, when two exit doors are required, based on minimum exit door separation requirements of one-third distance of the longest diagonal dimension in sprinkled buildings (see Box 13.9), both the Law Firm Layout II (Fig. 14.16) and Advertising Firm Layout I (Fig. 14.18a) are able to exceed the separation requirement. Doors are separated by 39'-6" (vs. MIN 39'-2") and 49'-3" (vs. MIN 38'-6") of the respective diagonal lengths of 117'-9" and 115'-6".

The exit doors for Law Firm Layout I (Fig. 14.18b) are separated by only 36'-0", a dimension less than the required one-third distance of 39'-9" of the 119'-4" diagonal distance. Under the IBC code, this plan would not be allowed (if the space were larger than 5,000 SF) based on the minimum one-third distance separation code requirement. On the other hand, the plan

would have been allowed under the old Building Officials Code Administrators (BOCA) code requirements, as that separation is only one-fourth the diagonal distance, or 29'-0". Some state codes were modeled after the BOCA code, which means that some states may still allow the shorter distance. As always, it is important to know under which set of codes and jurisdiction the space is being planned.

Travel Distance and Common Path of Travel

In general, most interior spaces will meet or fall below the total allowable travel distance because this distance had to be calculated at the time that the architect designed the building (see Chapter 13). Still, it is always a good idea to actually measure travel distances on each floor plan.

A common path of travel, a maximum of 100 ft in sprinkled buildings, can be calculated only after a space plan has been laid out (see Chapter 13). Common paths may be part of the maximum travel distance, but they are also any paths traveled in common with other people. The longest distance of common path travel

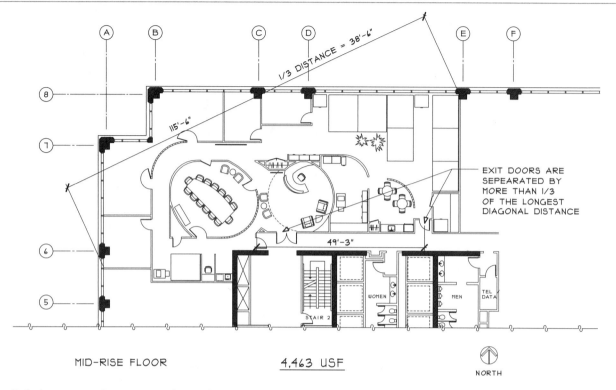

a. Exit door separation meets code requirements of one-third the longest diagonal distance: Advertising Firm Layout I

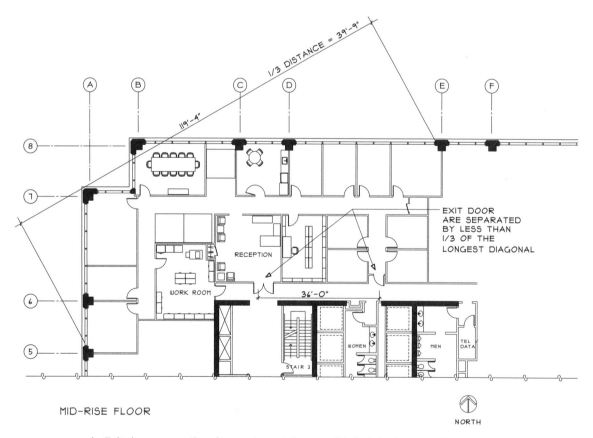

b. Exit door separation does not meet the one-third of the longest diagonal length separation requirement: Law Firm Layout I

for the Accounting Firm Layout II, 70'-9", falls within the code requirements (Fig. 14.19).

Intervening Rooms

As one means of exiting, reception areas are one of the most common intervening rooms through which the path of travel will traverse. Other allowable intervening rooms depend on the code requirements in use (Box 14.4).

In Law Firm Layout I, which did not meet door separation requirements under the IBC codes (Fig. 14.18b), when a path of travel is routed through the workroom to an exit door leading to a public corridor, the door separation is increased to 48'-9", easily meeting the separation requirement (Fig. 14.20). The question, however, in this case is how will the code reviewer interpret the room label "workroom"? Might the reviewer wonder if this room is really a storage room or similar type of room?

If reviewers deem the term *workroom* to be the same as or similar to the term *storage room*, they may find this means of egress to be unacceptable under IBC code. The term *file room*

■ **FIGURE 14.19 Plan view: Common path of travel: Accounting Firm Layout II**

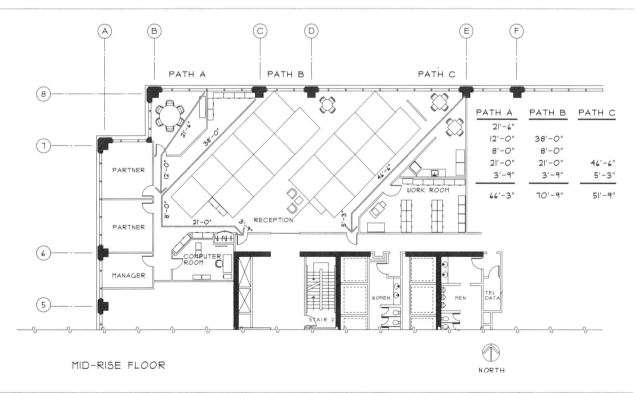

	PATH A	PATH B	PATH C
	21'-6"		
	12'-0"	38'-0"	
	8'-0"	8'-0"	
	21'-0"	21'-0"	46'-6"
	3'-9"	3'-9"	5'-3"
	66'-3"	70'-9"	51'-9"

MID-RISE FLOOR

NORTH

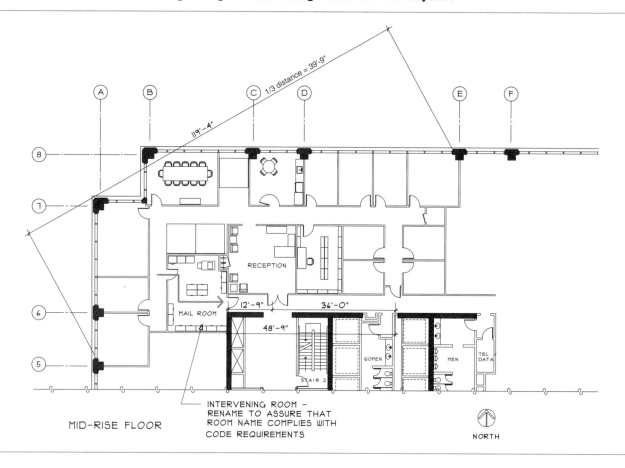

MID-RISE FLOOR

INTERVENING ROOM –
RENAME TO ASSURE THAT
ROOM NAME COMPLIES WITH
CODE REQUIREMENTS

NORTH

could also be interpreted as another term for *storage room*. It may be wise to label the room as *copy room* or another term that will be acceptable to reviewers.

Ceiling Heights

Although it may seem a bit early to consider ceiling heights at the time of space planning, this is an important area to keep in mind, particularly in concrete-constructed buildings, which tend to have low ceiling heights (see Chapter 13). Occasionally, portions of these floor slabs may be thicker, which means those portions on the underside slab are dropping even lower than the already low ceiling heights. Per code, two areas that require minimum ceiling heights are general office areas and the means of egress (Box 14.5).

In built-out or existing spaces, there are many electrical and mechanical elements suspended from the slab above, or the exposed ceiling. When a space is to be remodeled or if some existing items will be reused in a new space, it may be prudent to field verify the exact locations of existing elements prior to planning a new floor layout. In some space plans, it may be necessary to locate storerooms or closets where those existing elements hang below allowable code heights.

Code Compliance

In addition to these code requirements, there are other equally important requirements that need to be addressed, especially as the floor plates and space plans increase in size or square footage and the project moves into the next phases. With experience, many code requirements become second nature during space planning and design development, but designers should not become complacent because codes and requirements change and are updated every three years. Generally speaking, when there are major changes to a particular code requirement, various organizations, such as American Institute of Architects (AIA) or the International Interior Design Association (IIDA), produce advertisements and hold seminars to help keep designers abreast of the changes. Changes or no changes, it is the designer's responsibility to apply all appropriate code requirements to each and every space plan.

Occasionally, it is prudent to request a meeting with a code reviewer in the permit office to discuss certain areas of a space plan. Depending on the design of the building floor plate, the location of the space plan on the floor plate, the amount of square footage involved, the use group classification, the nature of the client business, or any number of parameters, it is sometimes difficult to fully comply with one or more particular code requirements (see Chapter 2). By scheduling a meeting with a code reviewer, these areas can be discussed. Perhaps the reviewer interprets the code a little differently than does the designer so that, in fact, the layout will be acceptable. Maybe the reviewer will offer an option not known to the designer, an option that will also be acceptable. Sometimes the reviewer will grant a variance or exception to a code requirement to allow the designer to proceed with the plan as shown.

Depending on the design firm and the permitting office, these reviews are handled in several different ways. Some firms have one designated employee who handles only code review meetings. Other firms allow any of their designers to schedule and attend review meetings. Some permit offices allow walk-in meetings at any time, whereas other offices require the designers to schedule such meetings.

When review meetings are held, it is important to fully document all information obtained during the meeting, including the date and attendees. After all, space planning is step one in a *long* process between starting a design project, completing construction documents, and then permitting. No one wants to go down a path where the designer thinks and assumes certain

decisions were made but no one can remember or prove them ten months or two years later when everything has been designed and is ready for permitting and construction.

FINALIZING A SPACE PLAN

The space plan is laid out and drawn. It has been analyzed from various points of view. All program requirements have been checked and verified. All requirements are included on the plan. Adjacency requests have been juggled to place critical rooms together or separated as deemed appropriate. Code requirements have been addressed. Some design suggestions and client visions have been incorporated into the layout. All areas are labeled, furniture has been added, and workstation blocks are replaced with components. The plan has been printed at least once and has been reviewed for glaring mistakes such as missing doors, overlapping lines, misspelled words, etc. It is now time to present the plan to clients for their review and approval (Fig. 14.21).

BOX 14.5 IBC Ceiling Heights[7, 8]

SECTION 1003
GENERAL MEANS OF EGRESS
1003.2 Ceiling height. The *means of egress* shall have a ceiling height of not less than 7 feet 6 inches (2,286 mm).

Exceptions:
1. Allowable projections in accordance with Section 1003.3.

1003.3 Protruding objects. Protruding objects on *circulation paths* shall comply with the requirements of Sections 1003.3.1 through 1003.3.4.

1003.3.1 Headroom. Protruding objects are permitted to extend below the minimum ceiling height required by Section 1003.2 where a minimum headroom of 80 inches (2,032 mm) is provided over any walking surface, including walks, *corridors, aisles* and passageways. Not more than 50 percent of the ceiling area of a *means of egress* shall be reduced in height by protruding objects.

Exception: Door closers and stops shall not reduce headroom to less than 78 inches (1981 mm).

SECTION 1208
INTERIOR SPACE DIMENSIONS
1208.2 Minimum ceiling heights. Occupiable space, *habitable spaces* and *corridors* shall have a ceiling height of not less than 7 feet 6 inches (2,286 mm). Bathrooms, toilet rooms, kitchens, storage rooms and laundry rooms shall be have a ceiling height of not less than 7 feet (2,134 mm).

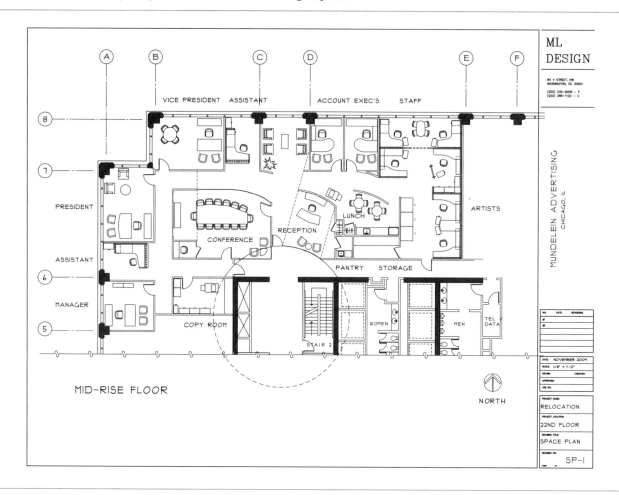

PROJECTS

Project #1: Create and draft a space plan:

Using building blocks and typical layouts created during earlier projects, Chapters 6–12, and circulation and code requirements, Chapters 5 and 13, respectfully, students should space plan a floor layout that will meet the needs of their selected client from Appendix A or client selected for questionnaire in Chapter 3.

1. The instructor should provide a CAD file for a designated base building floor plate that students can use for this space planning project.

2. There are two options for creating the space plan:
   a. All planning can be performed directly and only on the computer.

   b. A ⅛" scale base plan can be printed to use for initial hand sketching on trace paper laid over the hard-copy plan.

   c. Once a hand-sketched plan is deemed appropriate, the ideas and concept should be transferred to a computer drawing.

3. Visual presentation of the floor plan is half the battle when gaining the client's interest and approval. Be sure to use appropriate line weights, a title block, and insert a north arrow onto the final plan.

4. The final space plan should be printed from the computer at ⅛" scale on 18" × 24" bond paper, or a paper size as designated by the instructor.

5. Graded copies can be revised and then resubmitted for additional credit.

Project #2: Create and draft a test fit plan:

The client has decided that another building should also be considered for their new space before they make a final decision where to locate their new office space.

1. The instructor should provide a CAD file for a second base building floor plate that students can use for this test fit planning project.

2. The same two options listed above for creating a space plan, either computer or hand sketching, can also be used for this project.

3. Use appropriate line weights, a title block, and insert a north arrow onto the final plan.

4. The client likes this plan and building more than the initial space plan. Therefore, this plan will be used in the client presentation (see Chapter 15 projects).

5. Develop the test fit plan further as needed to meet and address all program requirements for a full space plan presentation.

6. The final space plan should be printed from the computer at ⅛" scale on 18" × 24" bond paper, or an alternate size as designated by the instructor, or printed on heavy bond paper or glossy paper for the final project.

Project #3: Develop and draft elevations and cross-sections:

It is important for students to understand in 3-D and built space what they are drawing and proposing on their 2-D space plans.

1. Elevations and design development may be based on either Project #1, the first building, or Project #2, the second building.

2. Elevate and draft three or four millwork items, special feature walls, or custom items.

 a. Elevations may include reception desk, built-in credenza or ledge, reception or conference wall, coffee counter, entry doors, workroom counter, etc.

 b. Provide all dimensions, notes, cross-section markers, and other information as required for a millworker or contractor to construct and install the items.

 c. Elevations are customarily drawn and printed at ⅜" or ½" scales.

3. Provide two cross-sections or details of one or two of the elevations.

 a. Provide all dimensions, notes, enlargement detail markers, and other information as required for a millworker or contractor to construct and install the items.

 b. Cross-sections are generally drawn and printed at ¾" or 1" scales.

 c. Details are generally drawn and printed at 1½", 3" or half-size scales.

4. Elevations, cross-sections, and details will eventually become part of the client presentation (see Chapter 15 projects).

Project #4: Select and develop a basic design concept:

While space planning, most designers are thinking about, analyzing, envisioning, and developing design concepts in their minds. This is the opportunity to show the audience what influenced the space planning concepts and layouts.

1. Start to develop a file of ideas to include as part of the final presentation (see Chapter 15 projects).

 a. Select and provide copies of key furniture items to be used.

 b. Create some doodles, 3-D sketches, or isometrics.

 c. Select materials and finishes for the furniture and other key elements of the space plan.

15

PRESENTATION OF PLANS

The space plan is completed. It looks *fantastic*! Program requirements have been checked off. Code requirements have been analyzed and met. Rooms, offices, and people are adjacent as requested, or nearly as adjacent as possible. Natural daylight has been provided to at least 70 percent of the space. The plan meets the needs and desires of the client. It is functional, and yet it has excitement and pizzazz.

Now it is time to present the space plan to the client.

It is vital for the client to understand the space plan: the flow of one space or area into other spaces, rooms, and areas; the size or scale of areas; and how their program requirements fit into the plan. Then the client must formally approve the plan. Upon client approval of the plan, many people in many disciplines join the design team: CAD operators; a whole production team; junior, intermediate, and other designers; engineers; furniture dealers; outside consultants specializing in acoustics, lighting, and other areas; and perhaps even the general contractor. Each new person or discipline uses the space plan as a background on which to build their respective designs, products, takeoffs, cost

estimates, and more. Thus, an approved plan is critical to ensure continuity of design among the various disciplines.

ASSOCIATED PLAN TYPES

Designers can present plans to the client in various ways using various media, both formally and informally, depending on the scope of the project. A space plan represents one type of plan in a line of project plans. It is a key plan and the driving force for releasing a project. It is also the plan to be approved by the client. To get to that point of understanding and approval, in addition to a space plan, there are at least another half-dozen plans that may be presented to the client at or near the start of a project.

Test Fit Plans

Test fits are the first floor plans that a client might see, but not every project requires them (see Chapter 13). Test fit plans, though they may seem to be a type of space plan, are rarely referred to as such. In fact, they are not even called plans; rather, they are just called *test fits*. Furthermore, terminology used for generating these plans is *providing* or *doing* test fits, rather than *space planning* a test fit.

Marketing or Spec Plans

Whereas test fits and space plans are based on real clients and real client needs, marketing or spec plans are conceptual plans created by designers to show what a floor plan could look like for a potential client, any client (Fig. 15.1). As a separate project, developers or building managers often request these plans so they can use them as marketing tools to show prospective tenants how their requirements might lay out on a given floor.

Rooms, except perhaps the reception and workrooms, are rarely labeled because there is no actual client and thus no actual positions or titles to accommodate. Most rooms include a full furniture layout, which provides a visual concept in lieu of labels. This allows potential tenants to think about their own staff titles as they count work areas and contemplate moving into such a space.

Marketing plans are customarily brought into an imaging program where color, various fonts, and other text can be added to the plans or page layouts. Pages can be turned into slides, sent via electronic transfer, or kept as print materials. Although drawn to scale, most plans cannot, and are not intended to, actually be scaled for dimensions because many of these layouts are printed on 8½ × 11 sheets of paper, which are too small for scaling. The sole purpose of marketing or spec plans is just as the name implies—marketing.

Presentation Plans

Presentation plans are decorous and embellished space plans (Fig. 15.2a and b). For formal presentations, these plans are frequently printed on slick photographic paper rather than traditional bond paper: they are often dry mounted by a print company to foam-core board, which allows display of the boards on easels or chalk rails. When the presentation is informal, presentation plans are occasionally printed on a heavyweight bond paper. Unless there is a reason to print these plans at either a larger or smaller scale, most presentation plans are printed at ⅛-in. scale.

To add punch and charisma to these plans, designers normally poché all walls, add a few plants in offices or the reception area, and include furniture layouts in essential rooms such as partner offices, the reception area, conference rooms, and some file rooms and specialty areas. In addition to room labels, room numbers are often added to the plan at this point to facilitate identification of rooms. Floor covering or ceiling designs are periodically suggested by dashed or

■ **FIGURE 15.1 Marketing plan that illustrates how a multi-tenant floor could lay out**[1]

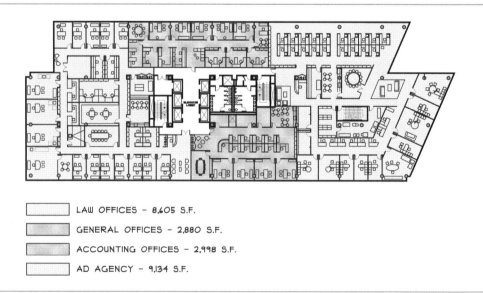

LAW OFFICES – 8,605 S.F.

GENERAL OFFICES – 2,880 S.F.

ACCOUNTING OFFICES – 2,998 S.F.

AD AGENCY – 9,134 S.F.

FIGURE 15.2 Presentation boards

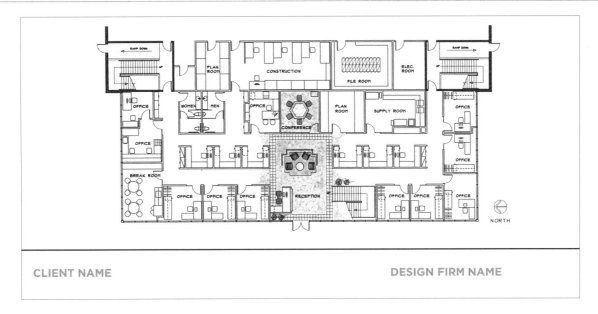

CLIENT NAME

DESIGN FIRM NAME

a. Presentation plan with colored pencils applied[2]

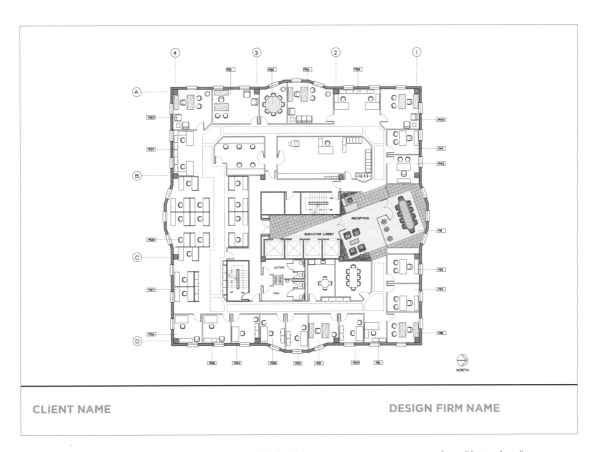

CLIENT NAME

DESIGN FIRM NAME

b. Presentation plan with color applied using a computer program such as Photoshop[3]

lighter-weight lines. Occasionally, color is added to further enhance the appearance of the plan.

Although presentation plans may be kept for a time by the design firm, these plans are regularly left with clients to be displayed in their lobby or conference room. Staff and visitors can then view the plans, which helps generate excitement and feelings of inclusion regarding the new space. In a sense, presentation plans are a type of marketing tool for both the design firm and designer to sell clients on the space plan and design concept.

Not all projects include presentation plans. Besides the added design or production time required to embellish the plans, there is a cost to print and mount the plans. Not all clients are willing to pay for these extra fees and expenses; therefore, it is important to assess the need for creating presentation plans.

Final Floor Plan

Even though the client, in concept, may approve and sign off on a space plan as shown, there are bound to be a few changes, revisions, or additions to the plan. A door may need to move a little this way or that way. Two rooms might combine into one large room, or a large room will divide into two or three rooms. Walls may extend to create a file niche or be replaced with

frameless glass. There could be any number of both small and major changes.

It is important to make all changes as needed or desired prior to starting construction documents. This is probably the last time the plan will be a single plan. From this point forward, more plans evolve—ceiling plans, power and data plans, dimension plans, and more. Beyond this point, each change to the plan means changes to many plans. Not only must designers remember to distribute changes to all disciplines involved and hope they will make the needed changes, but designers must also remember how or why certain decisions were made along the way and how those decisions might be affected by new changes to the plan. As a courtesy, and for due caution, it is wise to send a copy of the adjusted plan to the client for the final nod of approval.

Base or Background Plan

Once a space plan is deemed final, a base or background plan (Fig. 15.3) can be set up. Base plans appear as blank floor plans and are used solely as background for other plans, for instance, the furniture plan, the finish plan, etc. In CAD, a base plan is usually X-reffed into a new file, which ensures that it is not inadvertently changed, erased, stretched, or adjusted

■ **FIGURE 15.3 Base or background plan with only walls, doors, and room numbers**

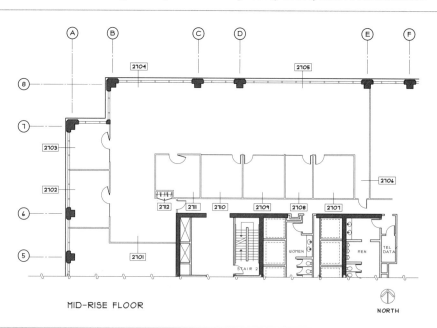

as the designer works *live* on other layers of the construction documents.

Base plans consist of numerous layers, with each layer containing separate construction items, partitions, doors, glazing, etc. This way a layer can be turned on and off as needed; for instance, the door layer is turned off on the ceiling plan. There are no room labels or sizes, furniture, plants, or other embellishments on the plan, but it should include room numbers, along with all basic plan and project information.

Construction Documents

Construction documents, or CDs, comprise all of the working drawings and specifications required to obtain a building permit and construct the finished space. Drawings include, but are not limited to, the dimension plan; reflected ceiling plan (RCP); power and data (P&D) plan; finish plans; elevations and sections by the designer or architect; mechanical, electrical, and plumbing (MEP) plans by the engineers; other consultant plans as appropriate; and structural plans as needed. Although it may be tempting to start work on the CDs prior to approval of a space plan, it is wise to wait. It is best to finalize the base plan and then use it as a background for other plans, knowing there will be a restricted number of changes. By strict definition, CDs do not include the furniture plan. Nevertheless, many firms habitually insert this plan as a reference to use to explain details on other plans.

Furniture Plan

Although clients may approve their space plan based on room labels, sizes, and typical layouts, many clients still want to see a plan with all of the furniture laid out in every room: every desk, chair, file, and table. As construction documents develop, the designer will also want to see a plan with complete furniture and equipment detail. This ensures accurate placement of the electrical outlets, light fixtures, and circulation clearances, and a basis for eventual furniture specification check list.

It is relatively easy to create CAD templates for each client project based on the typical layouts created during the programming phase; templates that show appropriate furniture—panels, worksurfaces, desk, credenza, chairs—for each typical layout. Many manufacturers have already created templates for their standard product lines, which can be used by the design team when they select and specify that given manufacturer's product line. Templates can be inserted into the furniture layer or plan, copied, rotated, or mirrored as a single entity. Other templates can be created for various layouts, which may not be actual typical layouts developed during the programming phase, but are a repetitive layout on the space plan, such as a table and four chairs for lunchrooms, a bank of two or three files, shelving stacks, etc., or furniture can be drawn as individual items and then inserted where needed.

When a client already has a working relationship with a furniture dealer, designers may ask the dealer to input the furniture on the plan, particularly when the plan is heavy with workstations. This initiates a team approach for a successful project. If there is no established relationship, it may be an opportune time to discuss with the client how and by whom the furniture will be supplied.

Drawing and Plan Information

All plans should include basic information that identifies the project and plan, thus allowing each plan to stand alone. In addition, viewers should be able to orient themselves within the plan. Information can be divided into two parts, project information and plan information.

Title Blocks and Project Information

Most firms set up title blocks, generally along the right edge of the sheet, which includes the design firm name and address and a standard form or block for inserting the project and plan information. Typical information includes the client name, project address, floor number, scale, original date, and any revision dates. Plans printed for distribution to the client or to other disciplines should *always* be printed on these title block sheets with all pertinent information included (Fig. 15.4).

Presentation Plans

An exception to using right-edge title blocks may occur when printing presentation plans.

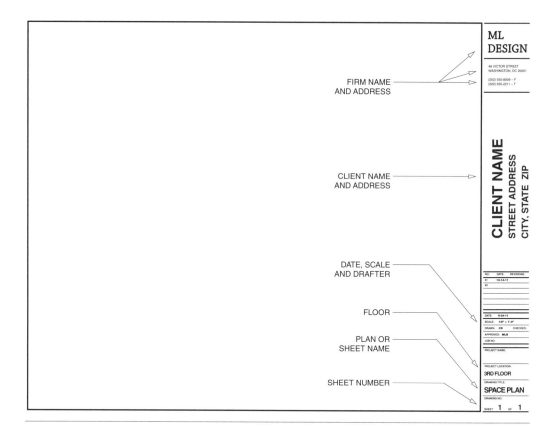

For a visually balanced presentation board, the title block information is often printed along the bottom edge of the plan rather than on the side edge (Fig. 15.2a and b). Nevertheless, the title block still includes pertinent project and plan information.

Plan and Sheet Information

While project information remains consistent from one sheet to the next, some plan or sheet information will vary. Except for the base or background plan, all other plans should always be labeled with a plan name, such as, space plan, furniture plan, etc. Other information may include room names, light fixture schedules, etc., as applicable.

Regardless of the type of plan, all plans should clearly display a north arrow, column lines and numbers, and room numbers. These entities provide easy orientation and reference points on the plan (Fig. 15.3).

COLOR IN PRESENTATION PLANS

When possible, color is often added to presentation plans. According to one article, "when [color is] applied to presentation materials, people—clients—read it very easily."[4]

Color Media

Both the computer and traditional media (film, colored pencils, and markers) can be used to add color to a plan. Sometimes designers combine various media to achieve effects that are more dramatic.

Computer Application

In today's market, computer applications are probably used the most often for adding color to plans. This enables plans to be printed as often as desired, either in-house as letter- or legal-size handouts or by print shops as large presentation boards. Colors can be solid, ranging in tonal value from very light to intense or textured with added effects (Fig. 15.2b).

Colored Film

Another solid-color treatment is a sticky-back film that can be applied over selected areas of a plan that has been printed on photographic paper. Film comes in several dozen colors and tonal values. Although the final appearance is similar to a computer-rendered color plan, this media is used when designers wish to set a plan apart from computer-rendered plans. Colored photocopies can be made of smaller plans, but it is often difficult to make copies of large presentation boards.

Colored Pencils

Use of colored pencils on plans adds a certain artistic flair (Fig. 15.2a). It is easy to manipulate shading, design patterns, and depth of color by using colored pencils. They can be used on either bond or photographic print plans. Working with colored pencils takes both time and skill to create a professional presentation plan, so it is important to allow enough time before the presentation for this option. Although photocopies can be made, color pencils sometimes print at slightly lighter shades than the original artwork.

Markers

Art markers add vibrancy, intensity, and depth of color to a plan. However, they take training and skill to create good visual presentations. When this is the preferred medium, print an extra plan, either standard or heavy bond, on which to practice.

Area of Plans to Receive Color

With any space plan, there are two basic ways to address color: the entire plan can receive color or selected areas of the plan can receive color. The option chosen may depend on the particular media selected, the time available, or the purpose for adding color to the plan.

Full Floor Plan Color

Occasionally, designers use a light color for the entire floor plan simply to set the plan apart from the white background of the overall print or board. More often, when color is added to the overall plan, it is done to easily distinguish one area from another (Fig. 15.1). Corridors may be one color,

offices another color, and workstations or chairs additional colors. Or, there may be only two colors, one color for circulation and another color for all other areas. Other options include color-coding various groups on the same floor or color-coding the same function on multi-floor plans.

Partial Floor Plan Color

In lieu of using color for the entire floor plan, it is often effective to color a selected area of the plan, such as the reception area leading into the conference room (Fig. 15.2b). This will draw the eye to what is often the focus of the space plan and design. When a floor finish pattern has already been conceptualized, it may be beneficial to use colors to emphasize that pattern rather than an entire room. Sometimes a diagonal or curved line is lightly drawn through a section of the plan whereby rooms and areas to the right or left are colored and areas on the other side of the line are left as a black-and-white plan.

ALTERNATIVES TO A PLAN

Although the designer can envision the built space, clients are ordinarily not as able to visualize as designers are. Sometimes the plan by itself may not sell a unique concept, particularly when the layout is rotated or there are rooms in unusual shapes. Clients may be a little hesitant to take a chance on something out of the ordinary. Occasionally, to assist the client with understanding, appreciating, and signing-off on such a wonderful space plan, it may be necessary to provide other means of presentation.

Alternate Layouts

It may help to draw an alternate, conventional layout so that the client can compare a less exciting plan with a more creative idea (see Figs 14.9 and 14.14a). The risk in this approach is that the client may not care about the exciting plan and simply want the ordinary plan as shown in the alternate solution.

Axonometrics, Isometrics, and Perspectives

While doodling and space planning, many designers draw quick axonometrics, isometrics, or perspectives. Once concepts are solidified within the designer's mind, these sketches can be refined, redrawn, detailed, or left loose. They can be easily adjusted for changes in the design concept and then presented to the client as part of the design development (Fig. 15.5; see Fig. 9.8 for plan view.) Designers can add color to photocopies to quickly show the client alternate schemes. Although this is an easy tool to use in many situations, hand sketches are not generally used for formal presentations unless the designer is very skilled at sketching.

For formal presentations, designers customarily rely on computer 3-D modeling programs to generate isometrics, derivatives of the floor plan. This method of producing isometrics tends to be quicker than formal hand sketching, also quicker to change, rotate, or rethink. Color can be added to the drawings, or drawings can be printed in black-and-white. When color is added in the computer, the color is often a solid mass of color, or, in some cases, degrees of shading and texture can also be added.

For those designers who love the appearance of hand sketches, they will print copies of computer isometrics and then with hand-flair, sketch directly on the copies or on trace paper to recreate the desired isometrics for presentations. The new sketches can be scanned into the computer to then have color added. These presentations offer panache not available with strictly computer-produced drawings. But, keep in mind, hand drawings take skill and practice, something that is unfortunately not being acquired by many designers these days as more and more work is done on the computer.

Renderings

A professional outside consultant, retained on a project-by-project basis, usually executes renderings for an agreed-upon fee. Because renderings can be expensive, they are typically used on a limited basis. Even so, when the project is high-end or presented to a large group of people, this may be the best route to take. Renderings are often left with clients to put on display at their existing office along with the presentation plan.

■ **FIGURE 15.5 Axonometric of building entry used as part of a design presentation[5]**

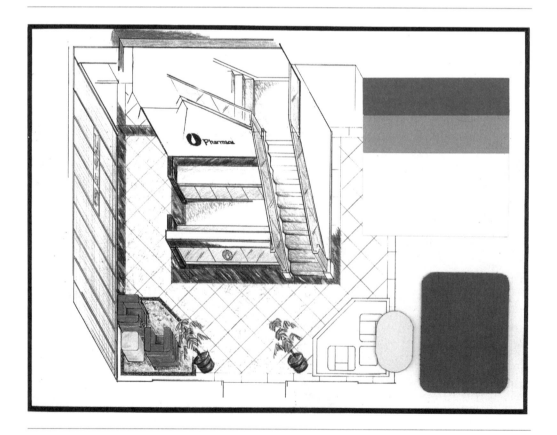

3-Dimensional Modeling and Virtual Tours

With the computer, many designers use 3-dimensional modeling to capture design concepts and then use other programs to add color to the drawings. Presentations can be given via a virtual tour of a single space or the entire space. Clients tend to be quite impressed with these "tours." As with renderings, these presentations often come with an associated fee, with hours and fees built into the design contract or as a separate fee.

Models

Sometimes a client needs to see a model. Many architectural firms regularly commission professional model builders when designing new buildings. This 3-dimensional tool makes the plan much easier to explain and understand as a tangible item than when compared to drawings or renderings.

Professional models are expensive to build and are seldom used to display interior spaces. Nevertheless, when the entry, reception area, and conference or other areas are planned as unique shapes, there is no reason why a model cannot be built to display the design concept. If the space is a very high-end design, clients may enjoy having this visual aid to show off their new and upcoming office space and therefore may be willing to pay for such a service.

When the budget is limited, if a designer has model-building skills, the designer may want to construct a model to demonstrate an envisioned built space. One such case was a client who, when first viewing a 20/70-angled reception layout for their new space (see Fig. 9.1d), which corresponded to the angles found in the building bay windows, indicated a less than enthusiastic response. Even when color was added to the space plan (Fig. 15.2b), the client was still hesitant to approve the angled layout.

I knew that if this plan were going to succeed, some kind of additional presentation would be required to convince the client of the design strategy. It was difficult to capture the true essence of this plan with an axonometric, and there were no fees in the budget to commission a rendering. On my own time, I built a reasonably good model that sold the plan (Fig. 15.6).

■ **FIGURE 15.6 Model for a reception area and conference room[6]**

After move-in, the client was very happy to have approved such an unusual plan. But, a word of caution should be given here: for a designer to build a model, even though this is a skill learned by many designers in school, it is a bit unconventional in standard design practice.

PRESENTATION OF PLANS

There are several methods for presenting the various plans, both in person and not in person. The method selected is often based on the plan to be presented, the size of the audience, or the ability of the audience to read plans.

Electronic Transfer

With electronic transfer of plans, the designer is not present to explain or discuss portions of the plan. Either the plans should be very clear and easy to understand, or the audience should be adept at reading plans.

CAD Drawing Files

Computer-aided design (CAD) files are easily transferred back and forth between the designers, engineers, furniture dealers, and other design disciplines via email or the internet for interdisciplinary design use. On the other hand, most clients are not set up to receive electronic drawing files unless they are a large organization with a facilities group set up with CAD capabilities. Even when clients do have CAD groups, they generally wait until after construction documents are completed and then receive drawing files as a set of record.

PDF of a Marketing Plan

Marketing plans are normally sent electronically as PDF files. Building management or other persons seeking marketing plans are usually skilled at reading floor plans, and thus they ordinarily do not need much direct explanation from the designer. When they do have questions, or wish to make some minor changes, these things can be discussed easily via emails or the telephone. Changes can be made, and then new PDFs can be sent again by electronic transfer.

PDF of a Space Plan

PDFs of a space plan should be sent to clients only after an in-person presentation has been given. Because many clients are not skilled at reading or understanding plans, it simply would not be a wise decision to send a plan to clients without the benefit of their hearing the rationale, design concept, the excitement, the actions for meeting the vision, and the many thought processes that went into creating this wonderful space plan.

After an in-person presentation of the space plan, by all means send a PDF version of the plan to clients, especially once the plan has been approved. That way, clients can print as many copies as desired to display in their office, pass out to staff, or give away to interested parties. At that point, clients can enthusiastically articulate the philosophy and approach inherent in the plan.

Delivery via Mail or Messenger

For many plans, the standard method of delivery is via the US postal system or a messenger service. However, like electronic transfer, the designer is not present to explain the plan layout or answer questions. Therefore, the designer should make sure the recipients are familiar with how to read and understand the plans or these delivered plans occur after a presentation has been given in person to the client.

Test Fits

Three to five printed $\frac{1}{8}$-in. full-scale test fits are normally delivered to building managers, developers, and brokers without an in-person presentation. Generally, these career people are familiar with all types of plans; therefore, they need little assistance from designers to comprehend the essence of the plan. In turn, they are the ones who then walk their prospective tenants through the plan.

Space Plans

Once the client has participated in a design presentation for the selected building and the client understands how to read plans, $\frac{1}{8}$-in. full-scale space or furniture plans are often sent via mail or messenger to the client upon request. After changes and revisions have been made to space plans as needed, final plans are also sent via mail or messenger service.

Construction Documents

Completed construction document sets are usually delivered via mail or messenger to the client, contractor, and anyone else needing these drawings. Though, prior to sending the finished documents, the designer should strongly consider an in-person presentation to the client for selected sheets within the set that show design aspects of the finished space. Such sheets may include the reflected ceiling plan, floor and wall finish plans, elevations, and details.

Rolled Drawings

Obviously, $\frac{1}{8}$-in. plans, printed on either 24" × 36" or 30" × 42" sheets, cannot be sent lying flat either by mail or messenger service. Except for presentation boards, even when the plans are personally handed to the client or other parties, people are not going to carry these huge prints as is. The drawings must be rolled or folded.

When rolling up plans, the natural tendency is to lay the plans face up and then start rolling from one end or the other with the floor plan facing inward. The correct way, however, is to turn the plan or plans over with the blank backside facing up, then starting with the left side, the side opposite the title block, roll the plans up so that the plan itself is facing out. Plans are rolled this way for two reasons.

First, by rolling plans to face outward, when completely rolled up, the title block and project information are fully visible. With a stack of numerous rolled plans, it is easy to grab the desired plans by quickly observing the project information. Otherwise, when plans are rolled facing inward, it is necessary to unroll drawings to find the desired plans.

Second, after rolled drawings have been stored for some time, when unrolled for viewing, they tend to curl in the same direction in which they were rolled. This means that if the plans were rolled facing inward, when placed flat for viewing they will keep rolling back up, making it necessary to hold the corners of the plan down to keep it flat for viewing.

For drawings rolled with the plans facing outward, the curl is now against the horizontal surface on which the plans are laid. There may be a slight curvature to the overall plans or along the

edges, but by and large the plans will lie flat for easy viewing.

Folded Drawings

It is possible to send rolled drawings through both the postal system and messenger service. But, when only a few drawings are to be sent, it is sometimes practical to fold the drawings, especially if it is felt that the client will fold the drawings anyway to place in a file. As with rolled drawings, folded drawings should be folded with the title block facing out. To achieve this, lay the drawing flat, this time facing up. Fold the drawing in half, with the right edge to the left edge, making a firm crease along the folded edge. Next, fold the top half back toward the creased edge so that the right one-quarter of the sheet with the title block is now facing upward. Make another crease along the left side of this fold. Turn the entire sheet over, leaving the right half folded, and then fold back the remaining left side of the sheet for an accordion fold and crease. Finally, fold the folded sheets in half, or thirds, depending on the sheet sizes, with the title block on top, resulting in folded sizes of roughly 9" × 12" or 10½" × 10", a much easier carrying sizes.

Informal Presentations

Depending on the size of the project, the number of people attending the presentation, and the ability of the attendees to read space plans, nearly 50 to 60 percent of all presentations may be informal, with everyone, including the designer, sitting around a conference table at either the design firm or client's existing location. This provides an intimate setting: clients feel less intimidated or embarrassed to ask "silly" questions. Everyone is close enough to read room labels and other information on the plan; point to areas in question; look at each other without needing to turn to the left, right, or around; and speak in conversational tones.

Informal presentations are best done when there are no more than six to ten people present, otherwise some people may need to stand or sit at the far ends of a long table where they cannot clearly see the plan. The designer should sit in the middle of the table rather than at the head of the table, with the client's primary decision maker seated directly across the table. Drawings should be turned around or rotated to face the client, not the designer. This allows clients to view the drawing from a readable position while the designer views the drawing from an upside down position.

Upside Down and Backwards

Viewing a drawing from an upside down position can be a strange sensation, particularly after having worked for many hours on the plan in a normal, readable position. If it seems funny to designers, imagine clients trying to read upside down when they have not previously seen the plan. Therefore, to help clients in every way possible to enjoy seeing and learning about their proposed new space, place the plan in front of them in a normal position. To acclimate themselves to this new point of view, designers should take time to review the plan in this upside down position before going to the presentation.

Design and Drafting Tools

As a matter of course, designers should come to all presentations and meetings fully prepared and equipped. For a presentation or any meeting involving plans, it is always wise to bring along typical design tools. Typical tools include a scale, tissue or bumwad, markers, red pen, drafting tape or dots, straight edge, tape measure, and calculator. Even the Program Report should be brought along to a space plan presentation.

As the presentation proceeds, comments, notes, additions, changes, corrections, and more can and should be notated directly on the space plan, which then serves as the basis for documentation and meeting minutes. Tissue paper can be torn and taped to the space plan for sketching out new ideas. Sizes or square footage for selected rooms on the plan can be scaled, measured, calculated, and then validated by referring to the Program Report.

Back to Upside Down

Writing notes, at least simple notes, and sketching are done upside down and backwards by skilled designers as changes are discussed over the plans. This is not a gimmick. It is a useful talent acquired and used by experienced designers for several reasons. From the beginning to the end of the presentation, clients will continually be able to read the information on the plan without needing to crank their heads around or ask designers to repeat to them what was written upside down to their view. When the plan is brought back to the design office for corrections, the CAD operator is able to easily read the plan and comments without having to turn it this way and that to read upside down writing.

Writing upside down and from right to left does take practice. But, like any talent, once learned it becomes a very useful tool.

Presentation Content

Informal presentations are generally conducted with the immediate decision makers and daily client contacts. This is the group of people responsible for ensuring a successful relocation, for ensuring that all staff members are happy with their new accommodations, and for ensuring that all aspects are met as appropriate. Now is the time to address every aspect of the plan: the designer can reiterate that every file cabinet and room has been accounted for, particulars of the workroom or lunchroom are confirmed, and existing furniture to be reused is identified as to its location. Together, the designer and client can count the number of offices and workstations. Code issues and compliance can be pointed out on the plan. Daily client contacts need to be as intimate with the space plan as is the designer.

Formal Presentations

As the scope of a project increases in size, complexity, and dollar value, it is customarily prudent to make a formal presentation to clients and their audience. In addition to the daily client contacts and design team, participants may include a board of directors, CEO, CFO, client broker or attorney, selected client staff members, outside vendors, public citizens, and building management.

This audience is looking for an overview of the project and space plan. Because they are not daily participants making requests and decisions, they may not necessarily need or want to know how many file cabinets are located on the plan or that a public corridor was shortened for whatever reason. These items can and should be pointed out to the daily client contact at separate meetings, but for a formal presentation, the designer should focus on the big-picture information.

For these participants, it is relevant for them to know how the overall square footage of the final space plan relates to the square footage approved in the Program Report. They want to understand how the mission statement and vision are projected into the space plan and how the reception area, the first point of entry, reflects their desired public image. Granted, the CEO wants to know where his or her office and administrative assistant are located, but he or she also wants to learn how the new corporate philosophy of more open work areas and fewer enclosed private offices was incorporated into the plan. Beyond these global concerns and interests, this audience is not overly eager to learn the particulars about copy rooms or lunchrooms. It is sufficient simply to hear that these rooms exist.

Location and Set-Up

Depending on the size of the audience and type of project, this presentation may be held at the client's existing location, at the design firm office, or at a local conferencing facility. When held at either the client's or design firm's location, many of the participants will probably sit around a conference table, facing forward, with chairs brought into the room and set along the walls for additional participants. In a conferencing facility, there will most likely be rows of chairs for seating, all facing forward.

The presenting designer will want to stand at the front of the room and use presentation boards, PowerPoint slides projected onto either flat-screen monitors or a large projection screen, or a combination of the two to give the presentation. To aid in pointing out aspects of the plan, some designers use their hands and others like to use a wand or infrared pointer.

Presentation Boards

All presentation boards for any given project should be consistent in size and orientation and coherent in terms of color, title strips, font or lettering, and arrangement. Typically, 24" × 36" or 30" × 42", the boards can be displayed either horizontally or vertically. For a formal presentation, the design may have developed through the conceptual phase so that some colors and finishes can also be shown on presentation boards.

People sitting more than 10–15 feet from where the presentation boards are displayed at the front of the room will not be able to read room labels and other fine features on the plan. Therefore, the designer must clearly identify each area of the plan as he or she explains the design concept. It is also practical, before starting the presentation, to ask the participants to walk around the room to view the boards to familiarize themselves with the plans prior to start of the discussion.

Overhead or PowerPoint Presentation

For some audiences, it might be advantageous to give the presentation as a PowerPoint presentation. The plans can also be printed on 8½ × 11 sheets for distribution and reference during the presentation. At the same time, it is wise to have scalable plans on hand either as regularly printed drawings or as presentation plans. There is always an audience member who wants to know how large is *that* room!

Audience Participation

While it seems natural for clients to interject comments and questions during informal presentations, they are less inclined to do so during formal presentations. Audiences tend to listen as long as the designer is speaking. Therefore, it is imperative for the designer to strategically pause while presenting and explicitly ask, "Are there any questions?"

Once the designer finishes with the verbal portion of the presentation, he or she should again ask if there is any commentary or questions. Discussions can often be initiated by specifically calling on the highest-level client in attendance. After this person has offered some remarks or questions, other attendees then feel comfortable to make statements or ask additional questions.

ORAL PRESENTATION

"Hello." "Good afternoon." "Good evening" [or other salutation].

> *"My name is . . .."*

Without a doubt, always, always state your name at the beginning of a presentation. Even when someone else provides an introduction as to who will be presenting, you, the presenter, should still state your name to start the presentation. In addition, it is wise to state the name of the design firm and the name of the client, such as, "Our firm, Design Layouts, is pleased to have this occasion to present this space plan for our client, XYZ Company."

Oral presentation is the opportunity to amplify the space plan concept: to explain how the oval conference room suggests an artist's pallet for an advertising firm, how an angled reception room dispels fears of unapproachable attorneys. This is the time to explain that some green building practices have been implemented: by placing offices in interior locations rather than along windows, this allows all staff to have the ability to enjoy natural daylight throughout the day. An alternate approach included placing the administrative assistant workstations, lunchroom, and other non-enclosed support areas intermittently between continuous window offices to allow staff to enjoy glimpses of natural daylight throughout the day; or a final method of bringing daylight into the interior spaces was to construct sidelights or other glazing in the front wall of perimeter offices.

As the designer, you should explain why and how the space plan evolved; the approach taken to incorporate the needs, desires, and expectations of the client; and how the plan will implement the client's vision and improve their financial balance sheet. Before delving into these full explanations, however, first orient the audience to the space plan, as this may be the first time many participants are seeing it.

Plan Orientation

Briefly walk the audience through the overall plan. Start by indicating the north arrow on the plan and the direction the building is facing. State whether they are looking at a full building floor plate or a partial floor. Point out the main entry to the building for a ground level floor or the elevators on an upper floor. From that point, proceed to the client's reception area and then groupings of areas within the space plan. Once you are assured that the audience is comfortable with the overall concept of the plan, you can delve into the particulars.

Body Language

Body language is important. Stand straight and confident to one side or the other of the presentation boards or screen to prevent blocking a view of the plans. Look toward the audience when speaking rather than at the plans with your back to the audience.

Eye Contact

Not only look toward the audience but also look the audience in their eyes to capture their attention and interest. When the speaker is looking at the ceiling or floor, his or her enunciation may sound muffled and the audience will follow the direction of the speaker's eyes, wondering what is so important *over there*?

It can be very nerve-wracking to look people in their eyes, especially when the speaker is not familiar with the audience. To overcome this sensation, it is often helpful to look at the audiences' foreheads or mouths, as this gives the appearance and feeling that the speaker is looking at and talking with the audience. Be sure to look around the room, to the left, to the right, and to the center, so everyone feels included. No one wants to watch the presenter speaking only to the group *on that side of the room*. With practice, you will eventually feel comfortable enough to look each individual in his or her eyes.

Hands and Nails

Designers talk with their hands. Designers point out individual rooms and areas on a plan with this hand or that hand. They use their hands to sketch in front of the client and to hand out plans. Look at your hands the day before a presentation. What do you see? What will the client see?

It is a personal choice whether or not a woman wears colored nail polish. Care must be taken, though, to make sure the hands are well-groomed with no chipped nail polish or broken, uneven nails.

Men, too, may manicure their nails with a clear polish, or not, but in either case, the nails need to be clean and evenly cut. Everyone should take the time to attend to personal appearance before presenting the plan to the client.

Dress Attire

A level of professionalism should be reflected in the clothes worn for a presentation. Consider the audience. How will they be dressed? In commercial office settings, many men wear suits as a matter of course. Women wear either skirts or slacks, although women in decision-making positions tend to wear suits of some kind. For best impressions, it is wise to consider dressing in traditional business attire and dress shoes.

Voice Modulation and Word Terminology

By employing a few subtle techniques, you can deliver a much stronger presentation and capture the audience's full attention.

First, since design projects are normally a team effort, be inclusive and systematically use the pronouns *we* and *our* rather than *I* and *my*.

Second, learn and use appropriate design terminology: halls should be called *corridors* and walls are customarily called *partitions*. Although the audience may not know the exact design process, they are generally quite knowledgeable regarding construction and furniture terminology.

Third, consider your voice pitch. If your voice is naturally soft, force yourself to speak louder during informal presentations or arrange to have a microphone at formal presentations. When your voice is naturally loud, this may be great for formal presentations because everyone can hear in the back of the room. However, for informal or smaller presentations around a table, it may be hard, but learn to tone down the volume. It can be uncomfortable and off-putting for many people when they are forced to listen to someone speaking very loudly.

Fourth, use inflections in your voice: get excited, show some caution, speak louder or softer to emphasize a point. Monotone presentations can become boring.

Finally, prepare your oral presentation in advance to allow time to practice speaking. Look in a mirror as you practice: give the presentation to peer designers to help develop a fluid, easy manner where you feel comfortable. Definitely ask these listeners to point out each time you say, "Um," "ya know," or "and." Too many of these nervous pauses and awkward expressions, such as, "I *stuck* this color. . .," detract from an otherwise great space plan.

Speech Preparation

Know what you are going to say before you arrive at the presentation; do not try to "wing it"! Without preparation, it is very easy to forget some key points, mix up some facts, or present items out of order.

Writing the entire presentation speech and memorizing it is one option. Unfortunately, this choice often leads to monotones. When speakers forget a line, they habitually stumble over their words, making an awkward interruption. It also invites fewer spontaneous questions should the audience feel so inclined.

By writing an outline listing all pertinent points, you have more latitude to deviate from a strictly ordered presentation. You can pause to look at notes, check off the points already discussed, jump forward if the client interjects a question about something farther down on the list, and then go back to where you left off. An outline allows you to cover all necessary points, yet present in a more relaxed manner than when delivering a memorized speech.

Closing

The audience has been introduced to the space plan. You have discussed how the offices and workstations conform to the two or three typical layouts agreed upon prior to programming; corporate philosophy regarding the importance of staff has been covered; and questions have been answered. The oral presentation is coming to an end.

Like the opening statements, closing statements need to be strong. Do not end a presentation by saying, "That's all I can think of," or something similar. Not only do you want the audience to be impressed, but you want them to agree with the overall space plan and the direction of design as presented. A strong closing statement could be, *"I believe all of the relevant points listed in the Program Report have been covered in the space plan. We, our team, at Design Layouts, are happy to have this opportunity to work with you, the client, on this plan for your new office location. With your approval, we will move forward into design development. Thank you for your attention. Are there any additional questions?"*

SIGN-OFF FOR THE APPROVED SPACE PLAN

Approval of the space plan is the final step under the programming and space planning phase. No matter how creative the designer, how the building inspired the layout, how unique, how original, how great the space plan, we as designers are planning for other people. We are interpreting the design, needs, and desires of those other people, our clients, who are paying our fees. When all of this comes together, the space plan is ready to receive a formal approval by the client.

Approval Signature

Like the Program Report, an approved space plan becomes a legal document. When the daily client contact has the authority, he or she may sign the space plan. It is usually prudent, however, for the president or CEO of the client firm to sign the space plan. The CEO's signature, along with the date, may be affixed over the space plan, below the space plan, or in the title block (Fig. 15.7).

Space planning is a matter of interpretation!

■ **FIGURE 15.7 Sign off on space plan by client**

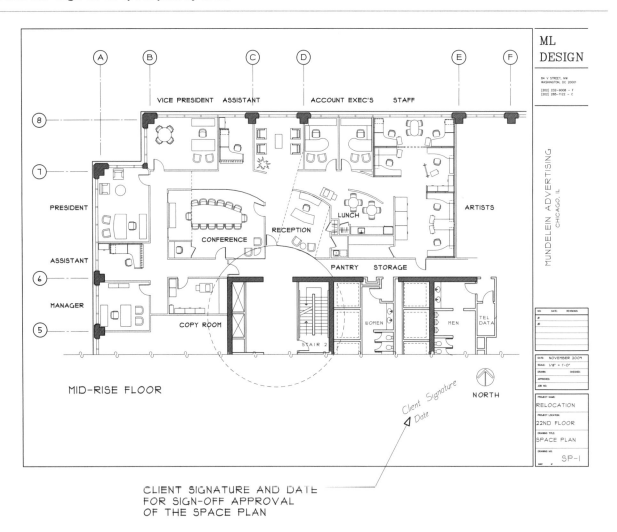

CLIENT SIGNATURE AND DATE FOR SIGN-OFF APPROVAL OF THE SPACE PLAN

PROJECTS

Project #1: Prepare visuals for a presentation to the client:

Use selected floor plan from Chapter 14 project, along with elevations, cross-sections, and details and furniture and finish selections to prepare a presentation for the client.

1. Depending on direction from the instructor, visuals may be mounted on presentation boards, left loose for a more informal presentation, or a combination of loose and booklet form.
    a. Presentation Boards
        i. Board sizes should be 18" × 24", or a size as designated by the instructor.
        ii. All boards should be the same size, color and oriented in the same direction.
        iii. Provide a title strip on all boards.
        iv. Projects will probably require three or four boards, depending on the quality and size of items to display, and the organization of the items.
        v. Instructor should provide a handout or further instructions on PRESENTATION BOARDS protocols.
    b. Loose Presentation
        i. Loose presentations are normally shown in less formal, more informal settings.
        ii. Plans may be loose or mounted on boards.
        iii. Materials, finishes, and furniture brochures are left loose.
        iv. The presenter will show, briefly explain, and then lay down each item, plans, materials, and finishes.
        v. Items are often layered one on top of each other. This allows the audience to pick up and examine individual items of interest.
    c. Booklet Form
        i. Periodically it is a good idea to leave a presentation booklet with the client. This allows the client to later review and consider the various options under more relaxed conditions.
        ii. Booklets can be 8½ × 11, 11 × 14 or 11 × 17.
        iii. Media can include spiral, three-ring or other types of binders.
        iv. Individual sheets within the booklet may be the same size as the overall booklet, or other sizes as appropriate, and then folded within the booklet.
        v. In addition to a reduced size floor plan within the booklet, it is normally wise to also bring along a full size floor plan.
        vi. Items could be scanned for printing from the computer or mounted on heavier card stock directly within the booklet.
2. For the final presentation plan, it may be a good idea to embellish the plan with some suggestions for design concepts, such as change of flooring materials, wood designation on desks, plants, etc.
3. Another option for the final presentation plan is to add color.

Project #2: Give an oral presentation to the client:

In this case, the client is the other students in the class. Other students, instructors, or school administrative personnel can be invited to participate as part of the audience.

1. Each student should give an oral presentation of their selected project.
2. Each presentation should last about 10 minutes.
3. Topics of the presentation should include information about:
    a. The client
    b. Why the client selected the particular building
    c. How the client's program requirements were met in the space plan.
4. Props should include the space plan, elevations and cross-sections, and materials and finishes in the media selected for the first project above (see Chapter 14 projects).
5. Students should dress in appropriate business attire.

6. After each presentation, there should be about 10 minutes for other students to ask questions of the presenter.

7. Students should be prepared to answer questions and respond to comments about their space plan and project.

8. Students should also be prepared to ask questions following other student presentations.

9. Instructor may want to provide further handouts or instructions on ORAL PRESENTATIONS.

APPENDIX A

CLIENT PROFILES

The following profiles, which describe program requirements for four separate, diverse firms having different office-to-workstation ratios, can be used for all chapter exercises. The first three firms are used in Chapter 14 to explain space planning.

- Client A.1: law firm—a majority of offices with a few workstations
- Client A.2: accounting firm—a majority of workstations with a few offices
- Client A.3: advertising firm—approximately half and half offices and workstations
- Client A.4: nonprofit organization—mobility and collaborative work areas

CLIENT A.1

Smith, Jones & Associates—Program Requirements

SMITH, JONES & ASSOCIATES is a small law firm practicing civil cases in The Loop area of downtown Chicago. They have been at their current address for ten years. Now that their 3,900 SF lease is about to expire, they want to move to a new location at 77 West Wacker Drive, Chicago, Illinois (see Appendix B), a fully sprinkled building near the courtrooms located in the County building on La Salle Street. They are not sure, but they think they will need additional square footage to accommodate new employees, and therefore they wish to retain a design firm to first program their needs and then space plan the new layout.

Mr. Smith died last year, so Mr. Jones is the remaining senior partner and the only person who will need a large office. He would like the new overall office space to be impressive. The ambience should create a sense of awe and inspire confidence in both existing and new clients.

Both existing and new personnel, along with work areas, are listed below:

EXTG QTY	NEW QTY	TITLES	TYPE	APPROX. SIZE
2	1	Senior partner	PO-1	15 × 20
2	2	Partners	PO-2	15 × 15
2	4	Associate attorneys	PO-3	10 × 15
3	4	Paralegals	PO-4	10 × 12
2	3	Executive assistants	WS-2	8 × 8
1	1	Receptionist	Desk	
TOTAL	**TOTAL**			
12	15			

Mr. Jones has his own executive assistant. The other attorneys share one assistant for every three attorneys. Assistants each have four 36-in.-wide four-drawer lateral files that can be located either in a file room or near their stations.

There is a workroom for the copier and office supplies. The new room should be about 150 SF. The firm would like to reuse some of their existing 30 × 24 metal shelving in this room. Assistants want to include a shared scanner and color printer in the room, but they want the two B&W printers near their workstations.

One large conference room should seat 12 people and be near the reception room. The room should have a credenza or horizontal ledge for serving coffee and assortments of food for early morning meetings. There should also be space for a videoconferencing setup, which will need a 24" wide × 26" deep storage area to house the equipment.

The reception room should have seating for four people and a guest coat closet. The receptionist sits in the reception area at a traditional desk with a return. He or she has a laptop with two monitors on the return and a credenza.

A lunchroom should be adjacent to the reception area, as the receptionist will serve coffee to guests, if they so desire. This room has a refrigerator, counter for a microwave and coffeemaker, a table with four chairs, and one vending machine. The firm will reuse existing furniture and appliances in the lunchroom.

The library has twenty 36-in.-wide wood shelves, and a Lexus and a shared computer terminal that both sit on a table. The firm will reuse an existing table or tables for this equipment. The library can be in a separate room or an open area. It should be located near the paralegals.

Mr. Jones does not want the paralegals near his office. They make too much noise while they are talking and researching over the telephone or collaborating on cases.

Smith, Jones & Associates will reuse the pieces of furniture previously mentioned along with any other items it makes sense to reuse. They will buy new panel systems and private office furniture. The budget is medium to medium-high. The style does not have to be overly traditional, but it should not be too contemporary.

They plan to sign a lease for approximately 4,500 SF of space (to be adjusted based on the programmed amount of square footage) on the northwest side of the 31st floor (see Appendix B, Fig. B.4). The building manager states that the demising wall on the west side starts at 10 feet (ft) below column line 6. The floor space continues along the north side of the building to column line E. He says the demising walls may be adjusted by 5–10 ft in either direction, but the total amount of space should remain at approximately 4,500 SF.

Finally, it is very important for the entry door(s) to be on center with the elevator lobby so that clients will be able to see the firm name as soon as they step off the elevators.

CLIENT A.2

Bailey and Marks Accounting—Program Requirements

BAILEY and MARKS is a small accounting firm. Many of their clients are furniture manufacturers with showrooms in the Merchandise Mart. Since hiring several new employees to meet increasing client demands, their existing 3,900 SF office space located on Wabash Avenue is very confining. To improve work areas, B&M has decided to relocate to a new, fully sprinkled building, located at 77 West Wacker Drive, Chicago, Illinois, within easy walking distance of The Mart (see Appendix B).

Mr. Bailey and Mr. Marks feel that they should take a conservative approach to their new office design to reflect the difficult times some of their clients are experiencing during a recent slump in furniture sales. This philosophy should be considered for all areas of the design: office size, aesthetic finishes, and the amount of new furniture.

All personnel and space requirements are listed below:

EXTG QTY	NEW QTY	TITLES	TYPE	APPROX. SIZE
2	2	Partners	PO-2	15 × 15
1	1	Manager	PO-3	10 × 15
2	3	Supervisors	WS-1	10 × 8
3	5	Inventory control	WS-2	8 × 8
3	4	Accounts payable	WS-2	8 × 8
2	3	Accounts receivable	WS-2	8 × 8
0	1	Administrative assistant	WS-2	8 × 8
1	1	Receptionist	WS-2	8 × 8
TOTAL	**TOTAL**			
14	20			

The inventory control staff have nine file cabinets, the accounts receivable staff have 11 file cabinets, and the accounts payable staff have five file cabinets that they need adjacent to their work areas. The first two groups can share a file room or have their files out in the open office space. The files are 36-in.-wide four-drawer laterals. There is one supervisor for each group. Each group would like one new file cabinet.

There should be one workroom similar to the 225 SF workroom in their existing office space. They would like to reuse all of the existing items within the room, which includes a copier, a 30 × 60 table for sorting copies, four 30 × 24 metal shelving units for storing forms and office

supplies, and the mail machine. In addition, the firm will acquire one new color scanner/printer, to be shared by all staff members, so this equipment can be located in this room. The room should be close to the reception area, as the receptionist acts as a second administrative assistant. This room could also be enlarged to combine it with a file room.

The reception area does not need to be a separate room; rather, it can be part of the open office area. Seating for only two people is required because Mr. Bailey and Mr. Marks usually go to their clients' offices for appointments. They receive very few visitors.

A conference room to seat six people should be located near the partners' offices. They would like to purchase new furniture for this room, including a small credenza on which to set the telephone and a coffee urn. They want a flat-screen monitor on a mobile cart, to primarily remain in the conference room, but it can also be wheeled into the main office area for large staff presentations. At first, the partners wanted their offices along the perimeter window walls. Upon hearing about the benefits of green construction and daylit views, they agreed that their offices could be located anywhere within the new space.

The computer room should be 216 SF, though it could be a bit smaller if floor space is appropriately allocated elsewhere. The room should be large enough to house an old metal desk with a terminal, two 18 × 24 racks, a 42 × 36 backboard, one vertical file, and two 30 × 15 shelving units. The manager is responsible for this room.

A lunchroom should include space for two tables with four chairs each. There are two vending machines. Mr. Marks says they will reuse the existing furniture and appliances in this room. A coatroom should be close to the lunchroom.

Bailey and Marks will reuse only the items mentioned above. They will buy new systems furniture and other furniture as required. Keep in mind, though, the budget is low or moderate.

Last week they agreed to sign a lease for space on the northwest side of the 27th floor (see Appendix B, Fig. B.4). The building manager states that the demising wall on the west side starts at 10 ft below column line 6. The floor space continues along the north side of the building to column line E. He says the demising walls may be adjusted by 5–10 ft in either direction, but the total amount of space should remain at approximately 4,500 SF.

It is not essential for the entry door(s) to be seen from the elevator lobby.

CLIENT A.3

Mundelein Advertising—Program Requirements

MUNDELEIN ADVERTISING is a small advertising firm currently located on the second floor above a hardware store on Grand Avenue. The president and her cousin started the firm five years ago with only two other people when the hardware store chain asked her to create some advertisements for a national magazine.

Now Ms. Mundelein has decided to move to a fancy new high-rise building overlooking the Chicago River where they want an impressive, high-profile office design for eliciting confidence from both existing and new clientele. The fully sprinkled building is located at 77 West Wacker Drive, Chicago, Illinois (see Appendix B). Both Ms. Mundelein and her cousin play an equal role in entertaining and attracting new clients, so both should have large offices.

All personnel and space requirements are listed below:

EXTG QTY	NEW QTY	TITLES	TYPE	APPROX. SIZE
1	1	President	PO-1	15 × 20
1	1	Vice president	PO-1	15 × 20
0	1	Manager	PO-2	15 × 15
2	2	Account executives	PO-3	10 × 15
1	2	Staff	WS-1	10 × 8
3	4	Artists	WS-2	7 × 9
1	2	Assistants	WS-3	7 × 8
0	1	Receptionist	Custom	
TOTAL	**TOTAL**			
9	14			

The reception area was small and cramped. Now they would like an area or room with a large, spacious feeling. There should be seating for three to six people, a coat closet, and a custom-built receptionist desk. First impressions are very important. Immediately next to the reception area there should be a conference room with a table to seat 14 people. In addition, there should be one or two side groupings of more casual seating within the conference room. This room needs a media center for a large flat-screen TV, AV equipment, storage, a projection screen, and a credenza on which to set the AV gizmos. For making more private or lengthy telephone calls, a telephone could be located in this room or in a small adjacent room, with a counter and chair.

A small coffee pantry should be accessible from both the conference room and reception area. A small storage room is required for the projector cart and mobile marker board. This room should be accessible from the conference room or immediately adjacent to it.

Both the president and vice president want corner offices for the best views. They would like to be close to the conference room. The manager should be close by, as all three of these people share the assistants.

The assistants need a copy room of about 150 SF. They will reuse one or two 30 × 24 metal shelves and a vertical file in this room. The counter must be large enough to hold the binding machines, postage machine, scale, staplers, and other accessories and provide plenty of room for collating the many proposals that are put together each week to attract new clients.

Account executives each have two artists and one staff member working under them. The staff people share six 30-in.-wide three-drawer laterals. All of these groups share a second copier and color scanner/printer that sit in the general staff area.

The artists want a storage room of 100 SF with 30-inch-deep lower millwork cabinets for storing display and poster boards and upper shelving for art supplies, etc. They share three drafting files that are 48"w × 42"d × 38"h. These files can be out in the open or in an enlarged storage room. This group should not be close to the reception area because they tend to be messy.

Ms. Mundelein would like a separate lunchroom with seating for eight people. This should not be close to the reception or conference room. There is not room enough for any vending machines, but the firm will reuse existing furniture and appliances. There is a small coat closet in this back area.

This week they are signing a lease for space on the northwest side of the 22nd floor (see Appendix B, Fig. B.4). The building manager states that the demising wall on the west side starts at 10 ft below column line 6. The floor space continues along the north side of the building to column line E. He says the demising walls may be adjusted by 5–10 ft in either direction, but the total amount of space should remain at approximately 4,500 SF.

Finally, it is very important for the entry door(s) to be on center with the elevator lobby so that clients will be able to see the firm name as soon as they step off the elevators.

CLIENT A.4

Verdant Environments Nonprofit—Program Requirements

VERDANT ENVIRONMENTS is a nonprofit organization currently located in a western suburb of Chicago. They write grants and raise funds to restore and stabilize land and water environments, specializing in four areas; loss of wetlands, soil erosion, over usage of fertilizers, and runoffs into natural waterways.

Although many original grant writers lived in suburbs when the organization first started 15 years ago, the directors and officers realize that the newer, younger staff now live along the west side of the Chicago River in old, renovated printing press buildings; they do not overly enjoy the reverse commute. Even several older staff have sold their big houses and moved to newly renovated high-rises in The Loop. Everyone wants to walk to work; they enjoy the outdoor atmospheres. Therefore, VE has decided to relocate their offices downtown to the second floor of a fully sprinkled building, 77 West Wacker Drive, Chicago, Illinois (see Appendix B).

All personnel and space requirements are listed below:

EXTG QTY	NEW QTY	TITLES	TYPE	APPROX. SIZE
1	1	Director of Development	PO-3	10 × 15
1	1	Executive Director	PO-3	10 × 15
1	2	Fund Raising Officers	WS-1	10 × 12
1	1	Major Gifts Officer	WS-1	10 × 12
1	2	Accountants	WS-2	6 × 8
1	1	Copy Writer / Editor	WS-2	6 × 8
15	20	Grant Writers	WS-3	6 × 6
1	1	Receptionist	Custom	
TOTAL	**TOTAL**			
22	29			

VE hosts large fund raisers about six times a year, sending out 75–100 invitations for most events and up to 170 invitations for the holiday party at year's end. They would like to be able to fully open at least one end of the conference room adjacent to the reception area for a large entertainment space. It is important to calculate the SF of standing occupants to ensure there is sufficient open floor space to accommodate this assembly of people.

When in use, the conference room needs to seat all 18 board members. To facilitate set-up for events, VE would like tables that can be ganged for meetings, then un-ganged, tilted, and moved into a nearby storage room during events. Two or three tables can be repositioned and used as needed by the caterers. They would like two 70" monitors in this room and storage for the AV equipment, plus one entire wall to be coated as a marker board writing surface.

The reception area should have a large, spacious feeling with seating for four to six people, a walk-in coat closet to house up to 80 winter coats, two smaller flat-screen monitors and a custom-built receptionist desk. First impressions are very important.

A café should be easily accessible from the conference room, reception area, and open plan workstations. Generous counter space will hold serving trays, a cappuccino coffee maker, and two microwaves. There is a wide, double-door refrigerator, one or two vending machines, and recycle bins. They would like seating for eight, preferably at bar height tables or counter. No doors are required as this area is also part of event congregating areas.

In the spirit of conservation, the directors and officers decided to occupy small private offices or panel systems offices. When they need more space for meetings, there are two collaboration rooms and two 36"-diameter meeting tables in the open spaces that can easily be reserved or used spontaneously. There are also groupings of soft seating near the window. Mobile working and less concern for privacy in nonprofit organizations lead to much openness.

The accountants and copy writer/editor will sit in permanent workstations, while the grant writers will reserve work areas when they come into the office. There is roughly one work area for every 1.67 writers and one locker for every two writers. Everyone shares six 30-in. –wide three drawer lateral file cabinets and a 6 ft wide coat closet.

A copy room, approximately 240 SF, will have two copiers, one B&W and one color; a white-paper recycle bin; and a secured paper bin for shredding. They would like a millwork counter large enough to hold two printers, binding machines, postage machine, scale, staplers, and other accessories and provide plenty of room for collating the many proposals that are put together each week to attract new donors. Nearby, there is a 120 SF LAN room.

Because VE opted for the 2nd floor, where rent is considerably less than the upper floors, they believe the off-set in lower rent is enough to lease an additional 100 SF of space than originally planned. These savings also allow them to afford a moderate to moderate-high construction and furniture budget. The ambiance, materials, and finishes should reflect the environments served—after all, they are requesting funds for ecosytems of the greater community. Keep in mind, though, this is a nonprofit organization; they do not want to appear ostentatious.

This week they are signing a lease for space on the northwest side of the building (see Appendix B, Fig. B.4). The building manager states that the demising wall on the west side starts at 10 ft below column line 6. The floor space continues along the north side of the building to column line E. He says the demising walls may be adjusted by 5-10 ft in either direction, and the total amount of space can be increased to approximately 4,600 SF.

Finally, it is very important for the entry door(s) to be on center with the elevator lobby so that donors and visitors are able to see the firm name as they step off the elevators.

APPENDIX B

BUILDING LOCATIONS

Companies choose office site locations for a
variety of reasons. These examples show amenities and tools that a firm might consider when
selecting their final site; an amenities map, a
transportation map, and office building sites
offering city views to enhance the work environment. The building floor plate, Fig. B.4, is used in
Chapter 14 for space planning the clients listed
in Appendix A.

BOX B.1 LEED Certification or Higher

For projects being designed with LEED (certi-
fied, silver, gold, or platinum) in mind, or even
for just sustainable-minded clients, up to two
credits can be achieved when the site is located
within a Ð mile of public transportation access
and/or places of basic services such as banks,
post offices, and restaurants (see Figures B.2
and B.3). Most central city buildings will meet
these requirements. For suburban or rural sites,
designers may need to look for other LEED
credits or work with local planning boards to
develop new or additional sustainable performance attributes (see Box B.2).

BOX B.2 LEED CI Amenities Within Walking Distance[1, 2]

Location and Transportation Credit
SURROUNDING DENSITY and DIVERSE USES[1]
LT Credit (1–8 points) Commercial Interiors

Intent
To conserve land and protect farmland and wildlife habitat by encouraging development in areas with existing infrastructure. To promote walkability, and transportation efficiency and reduce vehicle distance traveled. To improve public health by encouraging daily physical activity.

Requirements
OPTION 2. Diverse Uses (1–2 points)
Construct or renovate a building or a space within a building such that the building's main entrance is within a Đ-mile (800 meter) walking distance of the main entrance of four to seven (1 point) or eight or more (2 points) existing and publicly available diverse uses (listed in Table 1).
The following restrictions apply.
- A use counts as only one type (e.g., a retail store may be counted only once even if it sells products in several categories).
- No more than two uses in each use type may be counted (e.g., if five restaurants are within walking distance, only two may be counted).
- The counted uses must represent at least three of the five categories, exclusive of the building's primary use.

TABLE 1: Use Types and Categories

Food retail
- Supermarket
- Grocery with produce section

Community-serving retail
- Convenience store
- Farmer market
- Hardware store
- Pharmacy
- Other retail

Services
- Bank
- Family entertainment venue (e.g., theater, sports)
- Gym, health club, exercise studio

- Hair care
- Laundry, dry cleaner
- Restaurant, café, diner (excluding those with only drive-thru service)

Civic and community facilities
- Adult or senior care (licensed)
- Child care (licensed)
- Community or recreation center
- Cultural arts facility (museum, performing arts)
- Education facility (e.g., K–12 school, university, adult education center, vocational school, community college)

- Government office that serves public on-site
- Medical clinic or office that threat patients
- Place of worship
- Police or fire station
- Post office
- Public library
- Public park
- Social services center

Community anchor uses (BD+C and ID+C only)
- Commercial office (100 or more full-time equivalent jobs)

Location and Transportation Credit
ACCESS TO QUALITY TRANSIT[2]
LT Credit (1–7 points) Commercial Interiors

Intent
To encourage development in locations shown to have multimodal transportation choices or otherwise reduced motor vehicle use, thereby reducing greenhouse gas emissions, air pollution, and other environmental and public health harms associated with motor vehicle use.

Requirements
Locate any functional entry of the project within a Đ-mile (400 meter) walking distance of existing or planned bus, streetcar, or rideshare stops, or within a Đ-mile (800 meter) walking distance of existing or planned bus rapid transit stops, light or heavy rail stations, commuter rail stations, or commuter ferry terminals. . . .

■ FIGURE B.1 High-rise office buildings, 1991. Right building—solid facade with punched windows; center building—curtain wall construction[3]

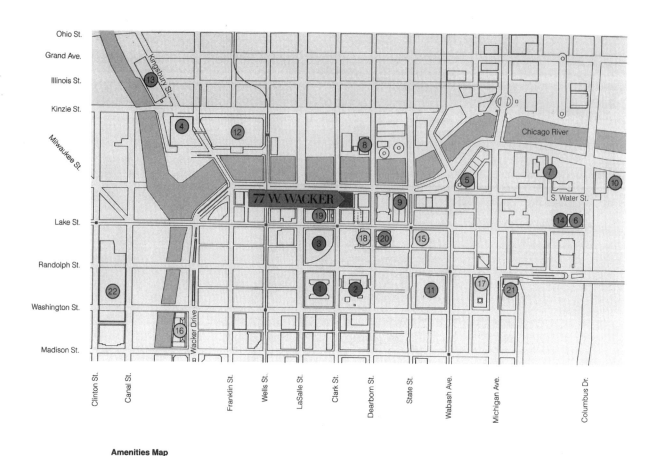

Amenities Map

Key

River North Art, Restaurant and Entertainment District

Central Business District

Government Buildings
1. City Hall/County Building
2. Richard J. Daley Center
3. State of Illinois Center

Hotels
4. Apparel Center/Holiday Inn
5. Executive House
6. Fairmont Hotel
7. Hyatt Regency Hotel
8. Nikko Hotel
9. Stouffer Hotel
10. SwissAir Hotel

Shopping
11. Marshall Field's
12. Merchandise Mart

Health Clubs
13. East Bank Club
14. Sporting Club

Cultural
15. Chicago Theater
16. Civic Center for Performing Arts
17. Cultural Center
18. Harris-Selwyn Theatres

Parking Facilities
19. 203 N. LaSalle
20. Theater District Self-Park

Railroad Terminals
21. Illinois Central Gulf Station
22. North Western Station

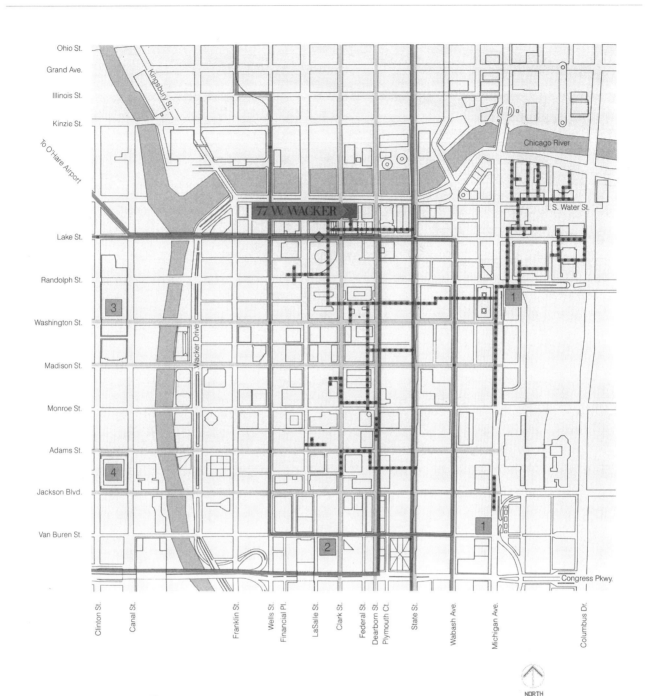

Transportation Map

Key

CTA Rapid Transit Routes
Bus Routes
Subway Routes
Elevated Routes
Major Subway Stop

Underground Pedestrian Walkway
Elevated Pedestrian Walkway

Railroad Terminals
1. Illinois Central Gulf Stations
2. LaSalle Street Station
3. North Western Station
4. Union Station

■ FIGURE B.4 Typical building floor plate for a high rise curtain wall building[6]

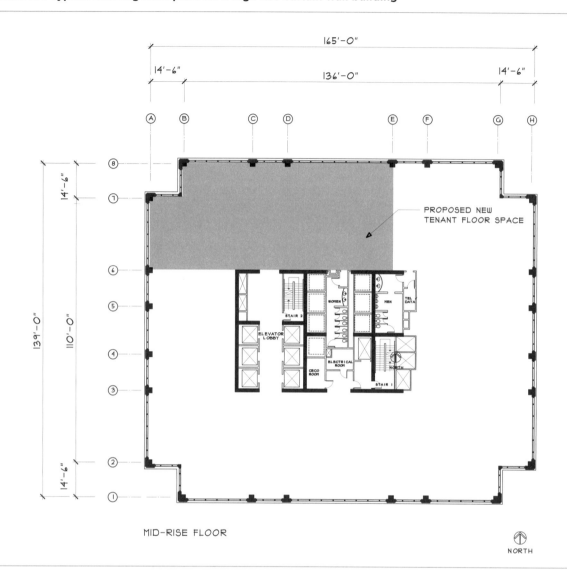

MID-RISE FLOOR

NORTH

PROGRAM QUESTIONNAIRE

This questionnaire is used in Chapter 3 to gather information from a client. Although most of the questions are typical or standard questions asked on all projects, the actual form is usually customized, as required, for each new project. Shown in portrait format here, it could also be formatted in landscape, often overlaid on the design firm's letterhead as part of their marketing or branding package.

Generally, typical layouts for private offices (see Fig. 6.5) and workstations (see Fig. 7.2) are attached to the questionnaires to aid clients with

answering questions 3 and 4 regarding personnel and assigned work areas. Occasionally, suggestive layouts for conference rooms (see Fig. 8.8), food rooms, or selected support rooms may also be attached to the questionnaire to provide clients with a better understanding of what to anticipate in the final plan.

In Chapter 12, the answers and information gathered from the questionnaires, interviews, and walk-throughs are compiled into a Program Report used for space planning in Chapter 14.

PRELUDE

The first step for planning new office space is for the design firm to gather information about each of the departments and groups within the client's firm. This information will help the designer to space plan each area in the best possible way to meet operational needs. Answers on this questionnaire provide an opportunity for each department or group to define how it functions on a daily basis, list basic needs and requirements, and to explore future wants and wishes. Please take the time to look beyond the traditional way of doing things and impart your vision for an optimum work environment of the future. All answers and comments are voluntary and as such, will be kept in strict confidences.

COMPANY NAME: _____

CONTACT NAME: _____

TELEPHONE NO.: _____

EMAIL: _____

GROUP NAME: _____

DEPARTMENT: _____

DATE: _____

1. Briefly describe the function of your department or group and its relationship to the remainder of the company or firm.

2. Please attach a copy of your department organizational chart to this questionnaire, draw your organizational chart below, or you may draw one on a blank sheet of paper if one does not already exist.

EXISTING AND PROJECTED PERSONNEL

3. Please list all personnel within your department by job position or title. Personal names should not be listed, as personnel may change over time. If there is more than one group in your department, please list each group separately, i.e., accounts receivable, accounts payable. Then indicate the type* of office, workstation, or other workspace that each job position should occupy. Finally, list the number of existing personnel for each position. Then list a desired number of personnel projected for the new space.

	Job Position/Title	Type*	Current Personnel	Projected Personnel

* Select a Private Office (PO), Workstation (WS), or an Alternate Work Area type for each job position or title from the typical layouts attached at the end of this questionnaire. In situations where none of the typical layouts is applicable, leave the space under "type" blank. It can be discussed during a face-to-face interview.

PART-TIME/CONTRACT WORKERS AND VISITOR WORK AREAS

4. Part-time, temporary, and contract workers make up a portion of the workforce for many organizations. These positions can be listed and tracked separately from the permanent personnel, yet incorporated as part of the general population. In addition to these workers, many organizations like to provide a few open private offices and workstations for occasional visitors. Please list all such requirements for your department.

	Job Position/Title	Type*	Current Personnel	Projected Personnel

* Select a Private Office (PO), Workstation (WS), or an Alternate Work Area type for each job position or title from the typical layouts attached at the end of this questionnaire. In situations where none of the typical layouts is applicable, leave the space under "type" blank. It can be discussed during a face-to-face interview.

ALTERNATE WORK STYLES

5. Alternate work style arrangements, if applicable, can provide enhanced productive use of your facilities. Please list and describe any personnel or other workers who may share work areas (shift work), use teaming areas (lounge set-ups), require hoteling areas, work from home, or require two or more work areas, or no work area at all.

RECEPTION AREAS

6. Most firms have one main reception area to receive all visitors. Occasionally, however, separate reception areas are required for a particular department due to the number of visitors received by a given group (employee training) or due to the nature of the departmental services (human resources). Please indicate your department's visitor and reception area requirements for any given week.

Visitor Requirements	Internal Staff	Sales Reps. and Vendors	General Public	Planned Meetings
Average number of groups				
Average number of people per group				
Average wait (minutes, hours)				
Scheduled, impromptu, or walk-in				
Room setup: • Straight chairs • Lounge seating • Receptionist in room • Receptionist enclosed behind wall • Interactive touch screen • Pantry • Coffee bar • Coat closet • Guest telephone • Other				

CONFERENCE AND TRAINING ROOMS

7. Conferencing and training requirements are a combination of many elements. With careful planning, these rooms can be designed to be stand-alone rooms or to satisfy diverse functions. Please indicate your department's on-site requirements for any given week.

	Conferencing Requirements	Small 3–6 People	Medium 7–12 People	Large 13–20 People	Other > 20 People
	Average number of meetings per day or week				
	Average duration (minutes, hours)				
	Meeting type (staff, vendor, other)				
	Scheduled or impromptu				
	Ownership (shared, exclusive use)				
	Room setup: • Videoconferencing/phone conferencing • Marker/tackable boards • Fixed/movable tables • Projector/screen • TV/DVD player • Food service • Podium/other				

	Training Room Requirements	Small 3–6 People	Medium 7–12 People	Large 13–20 People	Other > 20 People
	Average number of meetings per day or week				
	Average duration (minutes, hours)				
	Scheduled or impromptu				
	Ownership (shared, exclusive use)				
	Room setup: • Videoconferencing/phone conferencing • Marker/tackable boards • Movable tables/fixed seating • Projector/screen • TV/DVD player • Food service • Podium/other				

SPECIAL USE AND COMMON USE AREAS

8. Special and common use areas are generally under the jurisdiction of a given department or group but intended to be used by all company personnel, consultants, part-time workers, and, in some instances, visitors. These areas are usually more centrally located, accessible to the main entrance or other main corridors, and not necessarily located within or adjacent to the department or group responsible for that area.

Although the core team for the project and the group responsible for each of the areas listed below will determine final requirements and concepts for each area, in order to make better-informed decisions, comments and input from each department are welcomed.

Room/Area	Comments
Main Reception	
Main Conference	
Central Records	
Duplication Center	
Computer/LAN room	
Mailroom	
Health club	
Auditorium	
Cafeteria	
Other	

Please make additional comments about each room as desired.

INTERNAL DEPARTMENTAL SUPPORT AREAS

9. In addition to special and common use rooms, internal departmental support rooms, areas, or functions are essential for completing the make-up of office space. First, identify required support areas for your department. In the next section, list specific information for each room or area.

	Room/Area	Comments
	Copier room/ workroom	
	Mail/delivery area	
	Supply storage	
	Filing/storage room	
	Project/team rooms	
	Telephone booths	
	Library	
	Coffee room	
	Other	

	Freestanding Files	Number of Drawers	Front-to-Back	Side-to-Side	Existing Qty	Desired Qty	Locks Required
	30" Lateral file						
	30" Lateral file						
	36" Lateral file						
	36" Lateral file						
	42" Lateral file						
	42" Lateral file						
	15" Vertical file						
	18" Vertical file						

INTERNAL DEPARTMENTAL SUPPORT AREAS (continued)

10. Please make a separate copy of this page for each Internal Departmental support room, area, or function listed on the previous page. Then list the requirements for each room.

SUPPORT ROOM/AREA _____

	Equipment/ Furniture	Existing Qty	Required Qty	Manufacturer (if known)	Model No. (if known)	Size W × D × H

Please make additional comments about each room as desired.

ADJACENCY REQUIREMENTS

11. Adjacency requirements refer to both internal and external departmental relationships between groups, individuals, support areas, or special use areas. Relationships generally include both physical (face-to-face) and paper interactions, but not telephone interactions. In order of priority, please list close or required associations, interactive or desired relationships, and any important physical separations.

	External Departments/Groups/ Special Use/Other	Essential Adjacency	Desired Adjacency	Physical Separation

	Internal Personnel/Areas/ Support Rooms/Other	Essential Adjacency	Desired Adjacency	Physical Separation

Please make additional comments about each room as desired.

SECURITY REQUIREMENTS

12. Please describe general security requirements for your department. List specific requirements such as holding areas, vaults, eye recognition devices, and any other suggestions or needs.

HOURS OF OPERATION

13. Most mechanical systems are designed to operate during normal hours of business from approximately 7 AM to 6 PM. If your department operates outside of these hours, please list your hours of business so that the HVAC system can be designed accordingly.

OVERALL COMMENTS

14. Please describe any overall thoughts regarding facility related matters that currently exist or that you wish to address for the new office location.

RAW SPACE

Many aspects of a project building and site location may and can affect space planning and design efforts. The following Box D.1 and checklist of questions on the next two pages contain just some of the many details that a designer should notate and be aware of at a job site.

BOX D.1 Isometrics: Wall Partitions

Walls, or partitions as they are known in the commercial industry, may look like a single unit in the built environment, but they are actually an assembly of parts and pieces. First, sole plates or channels, depending on the material of studs used, are anchored to the floor. Studs are erected in a vertical position, generally at 16" OC with intermittent bracing for support; gypsum boards are attached to both sides of the studs with drywall screws. Next a layer of compound is troweled over the gyp board joints and screws and then drywall tape is pressed into the compound. Then another layer of compound is added. When everything is dry, the compound is sanded to a smooth finish to receive paint or another type of finish, such as wallcovering, ceramic tile, or granite slabs.

The partition thickness is generally based on the size of stud and type of gypsum board used to construct the wall (Figures D.1 and D.2) When drawing typical rooms or floor plans it is important to accurately depict the appropriate thickness of each wall.

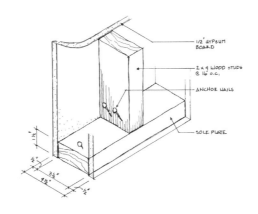

FIGURE D.1 Wood stud partition

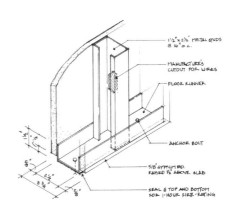

FIGURE D.2 Metal stud partition

RAW FLOOR PLATE SPACE

BUILDING ADDRESS: _____

FLOOR NUMBER: _____

1. Is there an existing public corridor, and if so, what is the width?

2. Draw an elevation of the perimeter window wall or walls; then dimension all parts.

   A. Typical perimeter wall   B. Perimeter wall no. 2   C. Perimeter wall no. 3

3. Draw a cross-section of each elevation. Provide dimensions.

   A. Typical perimeter wall   B. Perimeter wall no. 2   C. Perimeter wall no. 3

4. Provide the following dimensions:

   _____ Mullion width   _____ OC width of mullions and glass
   _____ Clear glass width   _____ Mullion depth to window
   _____ Clear glass height   _____ Other

5. Provide the following column dimensions:

_____ Round column diameter
_____ Large (wet) column width   _____ Large (wet) column depth
_____ Small (typical) column width   _____ Small (typical) column depth

6. What is the center-line to center-line column dimension?

_____ N-S dimension of typical columns
_____ E-W dimension of typical columns
_____ E-W dimension of a typical column to the perimeter wall
_____ N-S dimension of a typical column to the perimeter wall

7. Are there convection units and if yes, what is the depth, width, and height of the units?

8. What is the standard ceiling height?

9. Draw a cross-section of how the ceiling tile and grid attach at the following locations:

A. Perimeter wall   B. Demising wall   C. Interior wall

10. What is the slab-to-slab height?

11. What items can be seen in the plenum?

12. Are there any other items to be noticed and noted?

CIRCULATION PLAN VIEWS*

Plan views and item sizes can be used to calculate square footage for various furniture items, and appropriate or required circulation paths. While Tables E.1 through E.37 show very specific items, this section can be used as a reference to calculate the square footage for a wide variety of items in any office space plan.

SHELVING / BOOKCASES

TABLE E.1 Library Shelving

36" w x 10" d

42" h ± — 3 shelves
84" h ± — 7 shelves

4'-8" x 11'0" = 51.37 SF + 6 = **8.56 SF**/unit
= **9 SF** / unit nominal

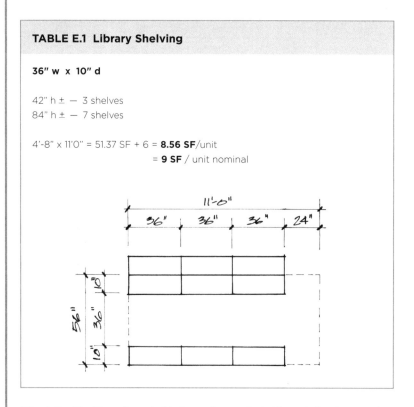

Circulation Plan Views shown in this Appendix are adapted from similar views used at Reel/Grobman & Associates, Los Angeles, CA, 1988.

TABLE E.2 Bookcases

36" w x 12" d

30" h ± — 2 shelves
42" h ± — 3 shelves
54" h ± — 4 shelves
60" h ± — 5 shelves

3'-0" x 3'-0" = **9 SF**

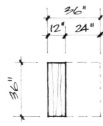

TABLE E.3 Bookcases

36" w x 15" d

30" h ± — 2 shelves
42" h ± — 3 shelves
54" h ± — 4 shelves
60" h ± — 5 shelves

3'-0" x 3'-3' = **9.75** SF
        = **10 SF** nominal

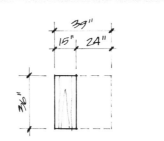

KEY:

Open floor space for a person
to stand while accessing
furniture or equipment

CABINETS / WARDROBES

TABLE E.4 Storage Cabinets

36″ w x 18″ d

42″ h ±
66″ h ±
78″ h ±

3'-0″ x 5-0″ = **15 SF**

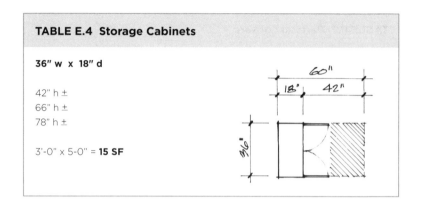

TABLE E.5 Storage Cabinets

36″ w x 24″ d

42″ h ±
66″ h ±
78″ h ±

3'-0" x 5'-6' = **16.5 SF**
= **17 SF** nominal

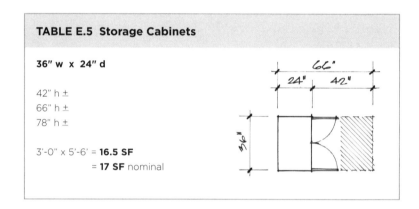

TABLE E.6 Wardrobe Cabinets

36″ w x 24″ d

60″ h ±
78″ h ±

3'-0" x 5'-6" = **16.5 SF**
= **17 SF** nominal

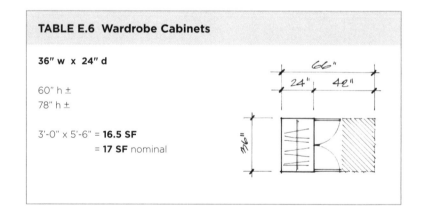

LOCKERS / FILE CABINETS

TABLE E.7 Vertical Lockers

12" w x 18" d

51" h ±
66" h ±

1'-0" x 4'-6' = **4.5 SF**
       = **5 SF** nominal

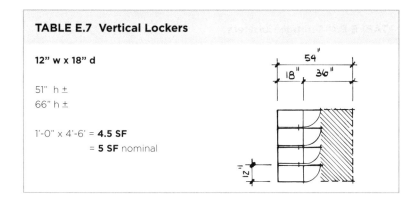

TABLE E.8 Vertical Lockers

15" w x 24" d

51" h ±
66" h ±

1'-3" x 5'-3' = **6.5 SF**
       = **7 SF** nominal

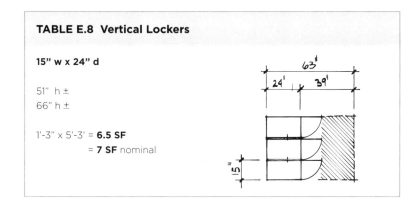

TABLE E.9 Vertical Files

Letter Size

30" h ± — 2 drawers
42" h ± — 3 drawers
54" h ± — 4 drawers
60" h ± — 5 drawers

1'-3" x 6'-4" = **7.9 SF**
       = **8 SF** nominal

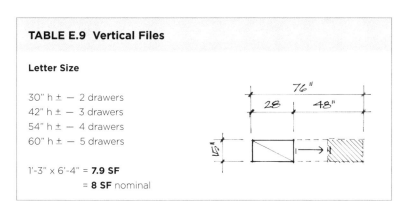

TABLE E.10 Vertical Files

Legal Size

30" h ± — 2 drawers
42" h ± — 3 drawers
54" h ± — 4 drawers
60" h ± — 5 drawers

1'-6" x 6'-4" = **9.5 SF**
       = **10 SF** nominal

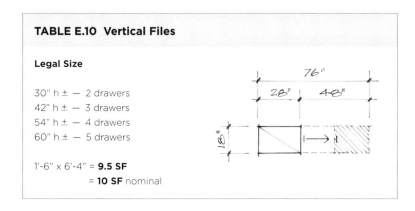

FILE CABINETS

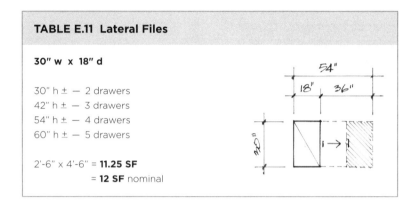

TABLE E.11 Lateral Files

30" w x 18" d

30" h ± — 2 drawers
42" h ± — 3 drawers
54" h ± — 4 drawers
60" h ± — 5 drawers

2'-6" x 4'-6" = **11.25 SF**
             = **12 SF** nominal

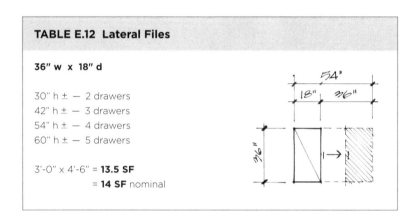

TABLE E.12 Lateral Files

36" w x 18" d

30" h ± — 2 drawers
42" h ± — 3 drawers
54" h ± — 4 drawers
60" h ± — 5 drawers

3'-0" x 4'-6" = **13.5 SF**
             = **14 SF** nominal

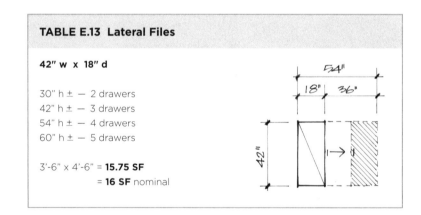

TABLE E.13 Lateral Files

42" w x 18" d

30" h ± — 2 drawers
42" h ± — 3 drawers
54" h ± — 4 drawers
60" h ± — 5 drawers

3'-6" x 4'-6" = **15.75 SF**
             = **16 SF** nominal

FLAT FILES

TABLE E.14 Flat Files

42" w x 30"d

16 h ± — 1 stack (5-drs)
35" h ± — 2 stacks (10-drs)
51" h ± — 3 stacks (15-drs)

3'-6" x 7'-0" = **24.5 SF**
              = **25 SF** nominal

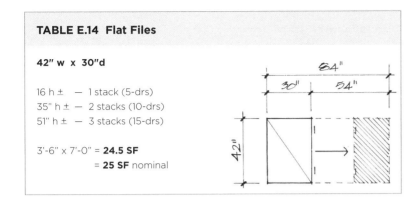

TABLE E.15 Flat Files

48" w x 36" d

16 h ± — 1 stack (5-drs)
35" h ± — 2 stacks (10-drs)
51" h ± — 3 stacks (15-drs)

4'-0" x 8'-0" = **32 SF**

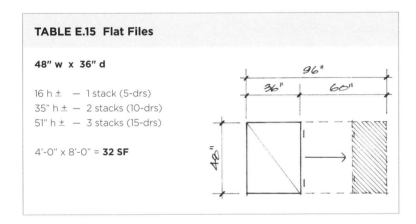

TABLE E.16 Flat Files

42" w x 54" d

16 h ± — 1 stack (5-drs)
35" h ± — 2 stacks (10-drs)
51" h ± — 3 stacks (15-drs)

4'-6" x 9'-0" = **40.5 SF**
              = **41 SF** nominal

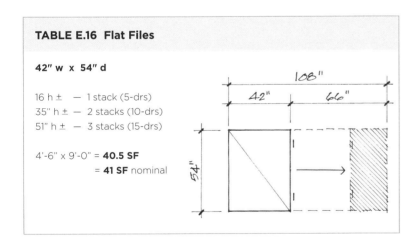

METAL SHELVING, ANY HEIGHT

TABLE E.17 Metal Shelves

36" w x 12" d
Any Height

3'-0" x 3'-0" = **9 SF**

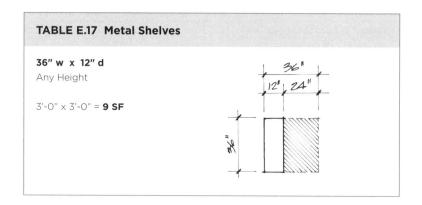

TABLE E.18 Metal Shelves

36" w x 18" d
Any Height

3'-0" x 3'-6" = **10.5 SF**
          = **11 SF** nominal

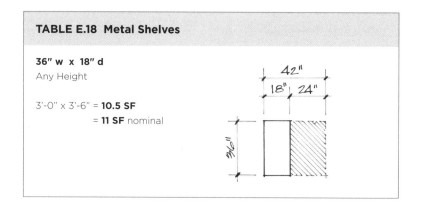

TABLE E.19 Metal Shelves

36" w x 24" d
Any Height

3'-0" x 4'-0" = **12 SF**

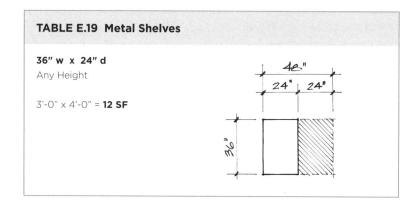

METAL SHELVING, ANY HEIGHT

TABLE E.20 Metal Shelves

42" w x 12" d
Any Height

3'-6" x 3'-0" = **10.5 SF**
　　　　　　 = **11 SF** nominal

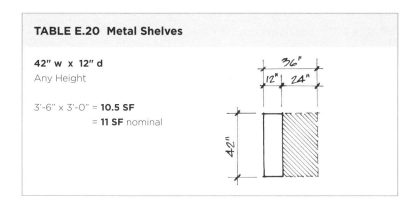

TABLE E.21 Metal Shelves

42" w x 18"d
Any Height

3'-6" x 3'-6" = **12.25 SF**
　　　　　　 = **13 SF** nominal

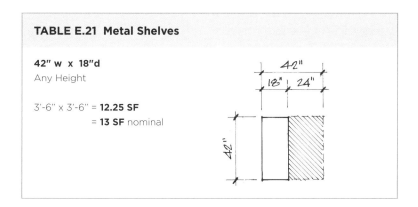

TABLE E.22 Metal Shelves

42" w x 24"d
Any Height

3'-6" x 4'0" = **14 SF**

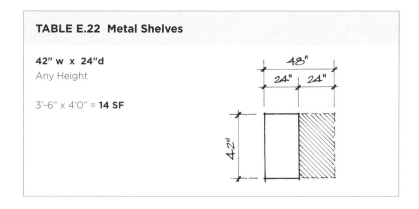

TABLES

TABLE E.23 Table: Access One Side

30" x 48"

4'-0" x 5'-6" = **22 SF**

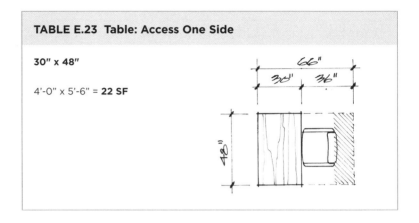

TABLE E.24 Table: One Side Access

30" x 60"

5'-0" x 5'-6" = **27.5 SF**
            = **28 SF** nominal

TABLE E.25 Table: Access Two Sides

30" x 60"

5'-0" x 8'-6" = **42.5 SF**
            = **43 SF** nominal

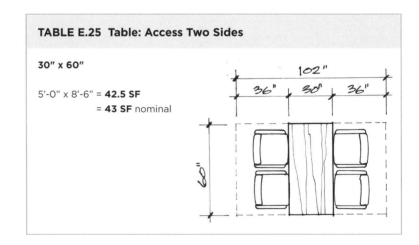

TABLES

TABLE E.26 Table: Access Two Sides

30" x 72"

6'-0" x 8'-6" = **51 SF**

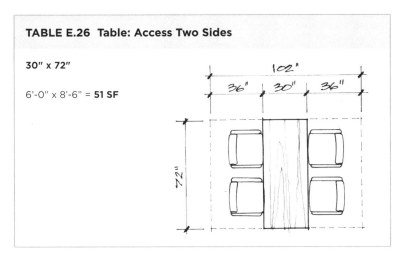

TABLE E.27 Table: Access Four Sides

30" x 60"

8'-6" x 11'-0" = **93.5 SF**
           = **94 SF** nominal

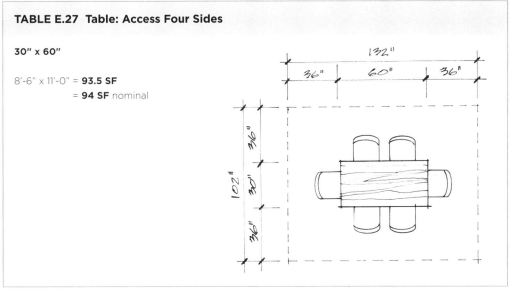

TABLE E.28 Table: Access Four Sides

30" x 72"

8'-6" x 12'-0" = **102 SF**

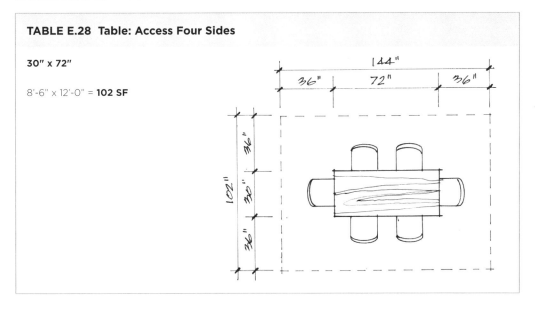

TABLES

TABLE E.29 Table: Access One Side

42" x 96"

6'-6" x 8'-0" = **52 SF**

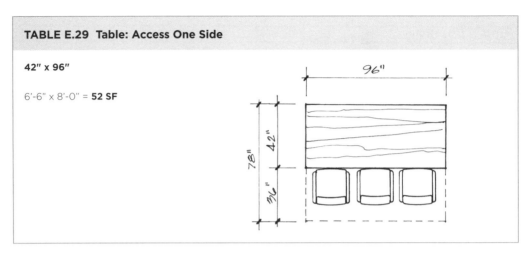

TABLE E.30 Table: Access Two Sides

42" x 96"

9'-6" x 8'-0" = **76 SF**

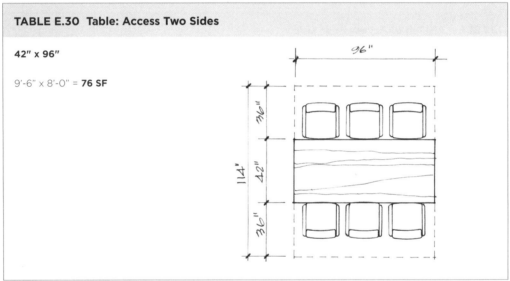

TABLE E.31 Table: Access Four Sides

42" x 96"

9'-6" x 14'-0" = **133 SF**

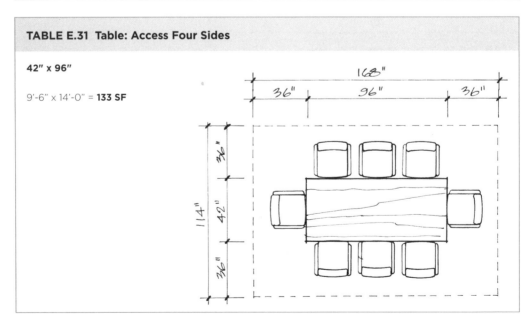

ROUND TABLES

TABLE E.32 Round Tables

36" Diam.

79 SF

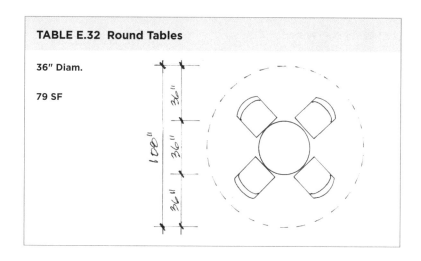

TABLE E.33 Round Tables

42" Diam.

87 SF

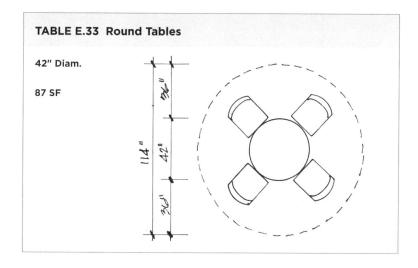

TABLE E.34 Round Tables

48" Diam.

95 SF

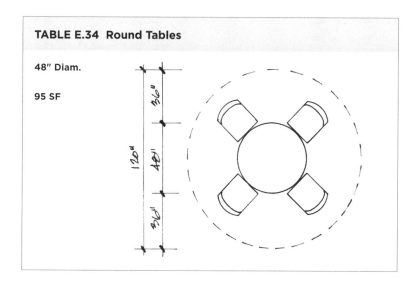

EQUIPMENT

TABLE E.35 Water Cooler

15″ w x 12″ d

2'-3" x 4'-0" = **9 SF**

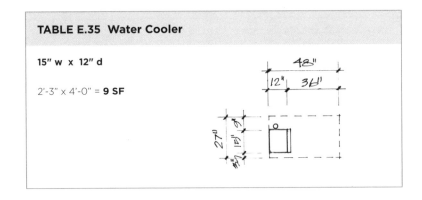

TABLE E.36 Plotter

74″ w x 38″ d ±

9'-2" x 7'-2" = **65.7 SF**

= **66 SF** nominal

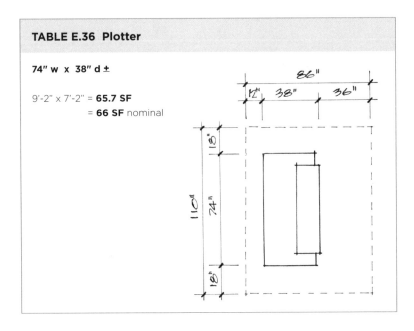

TABLE E.37 Medium Size Copier

60″ w x 30″ d

9'-6" x 6'-6" = **61.75 SF**

= **62 SF** nominal

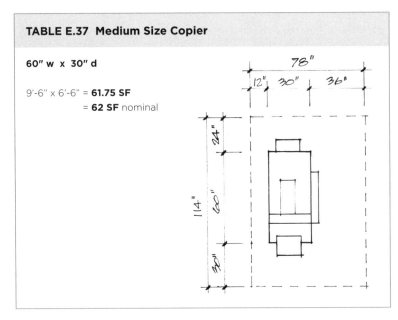

INVENTORY FORMS

To keep track of furniture, equipment, and appliances that will be reused on a project, it is helpful to use standard forms that capture the same information for all items. There are two ways to record items—by room or by item.

INVENTORY BY ROOM

When all items within one room will be relocated as a group into a single room within the new location, such as a private office, it may be best to inventory by room (see "Inventory by Room" form on p. 377) even if the items in the next room to be reused are identical to the first room. The next room will then also be inventoried as a separate room. Often people feel an attached ownership to "their" furniture, meaning that when they relocate, they want their specific furniture and not someone else's furniture that looks the same or similar to their items in the previous location.

INVENTORY BY ITEM

When one-of-a-kind items or a quantity of identical items, such as file cabinets, are to be reused, it may be best to inventory by an item list. Items that are identical in color, size, design, and finish material can be listed one time; then item quantities from various rooms, along with the room numbers, can be listed and totaled on the same form (form not included). When items vary in any manner, such as color, even though all other attributes are the same, the second item is listed as a separate inventoried item. Depending on the number of different items, and the number of rooms or locations for each of the items, when inventorying by item, individual items may be listed on separate forms, or all items can be listed on a continuous, single form.

INVENTORY OF EQUIPMENT AND APPLIANCES

Because furniture seldom displays the manufacturer's name or model number, this information is generally not recorded on those forms. On the other hand, most equipment and appliances clearly display manufacturers' names and model numbers on the front or top of the items. Electrical information such as voltage or amperage can usually be found on stickers on the back, side, or underside of the items. It is important to record this information as it will have to be provided to the engineers during the design development phase (see Chapter 11). Equipment and appliances can be recorded by room or item, just as furniture, but because there are ordinarily far fewer of these items, an item form is typically used (see second form "E&A Inventory").

It is wise to photograph some or all of the items to be reused. Photographs should be labeled and organized according to the recorded forms. Finally, under a move coordination task, actual items are usually tagged with identifying information, such as coded numbers relating to the recording form, the existing location, and the new location.

FURNITURE INVENTORY BY ROOM

WORKSHEET

Client:

Address:

Department:

Group:

Contact:

Telephone:

E-Mail:

Room No:

Date:

Inventory Completed By:

QTY	ITEM	DESCRIPTION	SIZE			FINISH #1 or COLOR #1	FINISH #2 or COLOR #2	COMMENTS
			W	D	H			

ML Design

EQUIPMENT and APPLIANCE INVENTORY

WORKSHEET

Client:

Address:

Department:

Group:

Contact:

Telephone:

Email:

Date:

Inventory Completed By:

QTY	ITEM	DESCRIPTION	SIZE			ROOM LOCATION	HVAC, POWER, OTHER	MANUFACTURER	MODEL NUMBER
			W	D	H				

ML Design

Page:

METRIC CONVERSION TABLE

LENGTHS	
ENGLISH	**METRIC**
1 inch	2.54 centimeters/25.4 millimeters
1 foot	0.3048 meter/30.38 centimeters
1 yard	0.9144 meter
METRIC	**ENGLISH**
1 millimeter	0.0394 inch
1 centimeter	0.3937 inch
1 meter	3.280 feet
AREAS	
ENGLISH	**METRIC**
1 square inch (in^2)	6.4516 cm^2
1 square foot (ft^2)	0.093 m^2
1 square yard (yd^2)	0.8361 m^2
METRIC	**ENGLISH**
1 square centimeter (cm^2)	0.155 in^2
1 square meter (m^2)	1.196 yd^2

General formula for converting:
Number of Units × Conversion Number = New Number of Units

To convert inches to centimeters:
(number of inches) × 2.54 = (number of centimeters)
To convert centimeters to inches:
(number of centimeters) × 0.3937 = (number of inches)
To convert feet to meters:
(number of feet) × 0.3048 = (number of meters)
To convert meters to feet:
(number of meters) × 3.280 = (number of feet)

To convert square inches to square centimeters:
(number of square inches) × 6.4516 = (number of square centimeters)
To convert square centimeters to square inches:
(number of square centimeters) × 0.155 = (number of square inches)
To convert square feet to square meters:
(number of square feet) × 0.093 = (number of square meters)
To convert square yards to square meters:
(number of square yards) × 0.8361 = (number of square meters)
To convert square meters to square yards:
(number of square meters) × 1.196 = (number of square yards)

GLOSSARY

Accessories

1. Items generally purchased from an office supply store, including wastebaskets, letter trays, tape dispensers, etc.; **2**. supplemental items to office furniture and equipment, such as rolling carts, plants, and artwork; **3**. work tools such as letter trays, pencil cups, etc. made specifically by panel system manufacturers to coordinate with their workstation lines.

Actual workstation sizes

Overall size of a workstation including panel thicknesses as opposed to nominal sizes. See *nominal workstation sizes*.

ADA codes

A Department of Justice set of federal rules and regulations that bars architectural barriers so as to make each and every building and structure accessible and usable by all persons, including those persons with any type of disability.

Adjacency diagrams

A graphic depiction—circles, ovals, or rectangles including connecting lines, or grids—that displays the desired geographic relationship between two or more groups, departments, divisions, rooms, or areas to be planned on any given floor.

Agenda

An outline of topics to be discussed at a meeting, distributed either before or at the start of a meeting.

Aisles

Open passageways between workstations, groups of other furniture, fixed auditorium seating, or other sections of seating.

Alternative work styles

An arrangement that allows employees to work in a manner other than at a traditional desk or cubicle. Such arrangements include working from home, a touch-down location, sharing a seat with second shift personnel, or sharing a work area on a first-come, first-served basis.

Average SF per person

The total square footage (SF) of floor space occupied by a company or firm divided by the total number of employees.

Background plan

See *base plan*.

Base plan	An approved interior architectural floor plan that shows all partitions, doors, room numbers, and north arrow, and is used as the base or background plan for all other plans in a set of construction drawings. Same as a background plan.
Benching	A row of worksurfaces, tables, or counters, typically without high dividing panels or screens, and mirrored with a similar row of worksurfaces, tables, or counters that can be used by employees, visitors, and other personnel on a first-come, first-served basis.
Benchmark	A point of reference at a given point of time.
Block plans	Building floor plate with chunks or areas of space blocked out, color coded, and arranged based on adjacency requirements and sub-total square footages for groups, departments, support rooms, or other listings found in the Program Report.
Blueprint	**1**. A reproduction of a drawing on light-sensitive paper producing a negative image consisting of white lines on a blue background (archaic); **2**. a method that replaced the original blueprint reproduction of a drawing by using chemically sensitive paper to produce an imagine consisting of blue lines on a white background (no longer in use); **3**. a generic term used to refer to copies of construction drawings. **4**. now, generally replaced with newer terms of plots or prints.
Boardroom	A large, spacious room, similar to a conference room, used for meetings of the board of directors of a corporation or organization.
Branch office or location	**1**. A commercial organization operating with more than one location of business; **2**. generally a smaller office location set up by a corporate headquarters to service outlying customers and their needs.
Break room	A central gathering place where employees within the firm can relax or interact with other employees who they may not otherwise see during the day.
Building analysis	Analytical report of a prospective building, site, and location based on the client's needs and program requirements.
Building architecture	The style and manner in which a building is constructed.
Building codes	A set of rules and regulations adopted by a jurisdiction for the purpose of constructing and maintaining all property, buildings, and structures to ensure that the structures are safe and fit for their intended usages.
Building construction type	The materials and methods used to construct a building per the building codebook.
Building core	A group or massing of rooms typically found on each floor within a building structure. Rooms include, but are not limited to, mechanical rooms, shafts, public restrooms, elevators, and utility closets.
Building floor plate	A blank floor plan or drawing of the entire building.
[Building] Shell and Core	Normally referred to simply as *Shell and Core* or *Core and Shell*. Generally a commercial building, or possibly an industrial building, with unfinished, or raw, interior floors and spaces that the prospect client will contract to finish construction and make improvements to suit their needs. See also *warm lit shell* and *cold lit shell*.

Building standards	A list of interior finishes or other items, including paint, carpet, ceiling tile, light fixtures, door style and size, window treatment or any other finishes that building management may include as part of the lease rate or require tenants to use in newly leased spaces. Consistency of products between tenants usually provides for reduced maintenance costs in the future. Standards may also include installation methods such as installing all light fixtures in the same direction or no outlets on window walls.
Business category	Terminology used to describe the type of business conducted by a company or firm, such as law firm, accounting firm, hospitality, residential, etc.
Casegoods	Office furniture, such as desks, credenzas, and bookcases, constructed primarily of wood or metal, that provides storage and horizontal writing surfaces for the office user.
Center line (₵)	A line representing an axis of symmetry, usually shown on drawings as a long-short-long broken line and with the symbol intersecting through or overlaid on the line.
Circulation	**1**. A means of exit egress from a building as required by building code; **2**. a means of travel through a building or company space in addition to the primary means of egress; **3**. unoccupied floor space, in addition to and often adjacent to required circulation paths, that is necessary to perform certain functions such as opening doors or drawers is included as part of the overall circulation square footage amount; **4**. free and unoccupied floor space not allocated to any other process that is included as part of the overall circulation square footage amount. (see Boxes 12.2 and 12.3)
Circulation factors	A percentage that is subtracted from existing space or added to anticipated program space requirements to calculate an approximate amount of square footage dedicated to circulation. (see Box 12.4)
Client	A business, organization, company, firm, or individual that receives professional services. As opposed to a customer.
Client needs, desires, and expectations	Expectations of the client for their prospective project that designers implement into a space plan and built space.
Closer	Hardware that, when installed on a door, automatically closes the door each time it is opened. Also called a door closer, this hardware is generally installed at the top of the door and then is attached by means of a scissor closing arm either from the door to the jamb above the door or from the door to the wall above the door.
Coat closet	A small room containing a horizontal rod and hat shelf above, often adjacent to the reception area, used for hanging coats.
Codes	See *building codes* and *ADA codes*.
Code years	Most building codes are updated or revised every three years, so it is important to know which codes are in use for the jurisdiction in which the project is located.
Coffee room	A room with basic provisions such as kitchen cabinets and counters, single- or double-bowl sink, refrigerator, and coffeemaker.

Cold lit shell	A building, generally commercial, with totally unfinished interior spaces, lacking HVAC and usually without lighting, plumbing, ceilings, or interior walls. The prospective tenant must contract for all new construction. See also *warm lit shell*.
Common path of travel	That portion of exit access that occupants are required to traverse together before two separate and distinct paths of egress travel to two exits are available.
Company logo	A symbol or font style that is used consistently by a company as a representation of the firm.
Computer room	A small room to house servers and other network computers for a firm.
Construction documents	Scaled drawings, produced by an architect and other design industry professionals such as engineers, acoustic consultants, and fire and life safety firms; intended for use by a contractor, subcontractor, or fabricator, which form part of the contract documents for obtaining a building permit and constructing the building project; also known as construction drawings or working drawings.
Contemporary workstation layouts	Cubicles or work areas often using low panels or no panels, glass inserts, and mobile worksurfaces and storage units.
Contract documents	A group of documents including construction drawings; plans; contracts or agreements between the owner and contractor; conditions for doing the work; specifications; all addenda, modifications or revisions; changes; and other items as stipulated.
Conventional workstation layouts	Cubicles with fixed panels, worksurfaces, and storage units, often enclosed with high panels surrounding the work area.
Copy or copier area/room	A designated area or room containing a photocopier and related provisions such as various papers, sorting counters, staplers, hole punchers, and other paraphernalia.
Core and shell	A building structure consisting of the exterior envelope, all core elements, and basic HVAC, plumbing, and electrical systems, but left unfinished, raw, and devoid of any interior partitions and finishes. See also *[building] shell and core*.
Corporate philosophy	The beliefs and outlook possessed by a company regarding its style and structure, such as autocratic or democratic, traditional or casual dress code, ratio of offices to workstations, etc.
Corridor	**1**. An interior passageway, either open or enclosed, that provides access to several rooms or areas; **2**. a public means of access from several rooms or spaces to an exit.
Credenza	A horizontal storage unit, generally positioned approximately 45 in. behind a desk in a private office.
Cross-section	A drawing that represents an object as it would appear if cut by an imaginary plane, showing the internal structure.

Cubicle, cubical	**1**. The spelling of this word is often associated with the practice in use in various areas of the country; **2.** a group of furniture components, including horizontal worksurfaces, storage units, and vertical dividers, assembled to form individual, enclosed work areas, often with high panels. Although there is no official designation as such, *cubicle* is probably a slightly less formal term than some other terms with which it is used interchangeably. See also *workstations, panel systems, furniture systems, open-office furniture, systems furniture, modular furniture, landscape furniture*, and *stations*.
Curtain wall facade	A nonload-bearing exterior building wall between or in front of pilasters or columns. It does not support the beams or girders of the building skeleton frame.
Custom furniture	Generally one-of-a-kind pieces of furniture that are designed for a specific project or client and fabricated by a millworker or factory.
Customer	Typically used to describe a person shopping in a retail store or shop.
Cut sheet	A single-sheet brochure from a manufacturer showing a particular product and associated information, also known as a tear sheet.
Daylight harvesting or daylight control	A device or system that provides automatic control of electric light levels based on the amount of daylight in a space.[1]
Dead-end corridor	A corridor, longer in length than acceptable by building code that does not lead to a means of egress.
Dead space	On a floor plan, and then in the built space, a portion of floor space that is walled over and inaccessible for use. Also known as *void spaces*.
Delivery room	A room designated as the central point to receive and distribute deliveries of all kinds, including mail, packages, supplies, and other items; often combined with other functions. See also *mailroom*.
Demising wall	A wall separating one tenant from another tenant, also known as a party wall.
Direction of door swing	The direction in which a door opens into or out of a room.
Discipline	**1**. A field of study; **2**. other professions, such as engineers, contractors, consultants, etc. involved on a project.
Donut corridor	A corridor that forms a continuous loop around the building core. See also *looped corridor* and *wrapped corridor*.
Door separation	A minimum distance, per building code, by which two or more egress doors must be separated.
Drywall	An interior partition constructed with gypsum board or Sheetrock.
Egress corridors	An enclosed exit access component that defines and provides a path of egress travel to an exit.
Egress doors	Doors along the path of travel and means of egress. Doors must swing out or in the direction of travel.
Electrical closet	A small room located on each floor in a building, generally as part of the building core that houses the electrical panels to provide a direct wire connection from the local electrical supply source to the tenant space.
Elevation	A drawing showing the vertical elements of a building, either exterior or interior.

Employee lounge	A room often found in manufacturing plants, warehouses, or other industrial buildings that generally includes some lounge seating in addition to vending machines or other types of coffee and lunch-break eating provisions.
End user	**1**. The company or business that ends up with and uses a manufacturer's product; **2**. The ultimate consumer of a finished product.
Envelope	See *office envelope* and *room envelope*.
Equipment	Items found within an office setting that generally require an electrical power source and either dedicated floor or counter space.
Exposed ceiling	**1**. Technically the underside of the slab above; **2**. a room where there is no specific material installed as a finished ceiling.
File, file cabinet	A storage unit with drawers designated to store and file papers, manila file folders, and hanging folders. Files are designated as either lateral or vertical files.
File room	A room, often lockable or secured in some manner, designated for storing file cabinets.
Final floor plan	A revised and approved space plan that will be used to set up the base or background plan.
Fire-resistance wall assembly	An assemblage of specific materials or products that are designed, tested, and UL approved to withstand a burning fire for a designated period of time, usually one hour, two hours, three hours, or four hours.
Floor plan	A drawing of a horizontal section taken above a floor, at approximately 30–68 in., to show diagrammatically the enclosing walls of a building, its doors and windows, and the arrangement of its interior spaces.
Focus Rooms	See *telephone booths*.
Footprint	A drawing representative of an area or room to be drawn on a floor plan.
Framed construction	Base or upper cabinets constructed with a frame set behind the doors and drawers. The frame provides structure for attaching door hinges or other hardware.
Frameless construction	Base or upper cabinets constructed without a frame where the hinges are attached directly to the inside of the cabinet.
Free-address	A work style in which employees or visitors may sit anywhere in an open work area on a first-come, first-served basis. See also *hoteling* and *JIT*.
Furniture plan	A floor plan displaying all intended furniture, equipment, accessories, and other items to be used in the built space.
Furniture systems	Generally, a broader term that includes both panel system components, and freestanding or partially freestanding furniture that works or attaches in conjunction with a compatible panel system to form individual or shared work areas. See also *workstations, cubicle, cubical, landscape furniture, modular furniture, open-office furniture, panel systems, stations*, and *systems furniture*.
Game room	A room with selected recreational accommodations, such as pool or ping-pong tables, pinball machines, or putting greens, to be used by employees while taking a break from their daily workloads.

Glazing	A transparent material or glass used in a window.
Green design	Reusing and recycling existing materials, reducing energy consumption while producing new materials, using rapidly renewable materials, and reducing landfill.
Grommet	**1**. A hole, approximately 1½ to 2 in., cut into a surface to allow passage of electrical and data cords and cables from the equipment to the source of power, which then typically conceals the cords and cables as opposed to those cords and cables dangling in sight. **2**. To protect and conceal the raw surface material of the newly cut hole, a plastic or metal ring is installed in the hole. A cover plate is also typically added over the grommet hole.
Gross square feet (GSF)	**1**. The total square footage of a building footprint. **2**. For interior projects, designers often refer to GSF as the total square footage on a building floor plate that can be used for rooms, areas, functions, or circulation and primary corridors. It does not include the building core areas. (see Box 12.1)
Gypsum board (GYP BD)	A wallboard, having a gypsum core and paper surfaces, used over studs as the outer member of a partition. See also *sheetrock* and *drywall*.
Hallway	A corridor or passageway; a term generally used in residential construction.
Hardwired Connection	Equipment that is permanently connected by a licensed electrician to electrical wires vs. having a cord and plug that can be disconnected by the user.
Headquarters	The main business location for a company often having other, smaller branch locations.
Health, safety, and welfare	Building codes, green design, National Council for Interior Design Qualification (NCIDQ), and other organizations are all concerned about providing for the health, safety, and welfare of all peoples.
Hoteling	The arrangement in which employees who work less than 50 percent of the time within an office setting, or visitors, may call ahead to reserve a workspace in a manner similar to renting a room at a hotel. See also *free-address* and *JIT*.
Infill	Material used to fill the spaces within a frame or between structural members in a building, windows, or other units.
Infrastructure	The underlying framework and basic facilities of a building or space, such as plumbing, electrical, HVAC, and IT systems.
In-house	Services that are performed within the business sector, which could otherwise be contracted out to another company.
In stock	Furniture, equipment, or other product items that are manufactured and then warehoused either at the factory or dealership, ready to be shipped when ordered.
Intervening room	A room between a means of egress and an exit door.
Interviews	See also *programming interviews*.
JIT (just in time)	Based on the just-in-time philosophy, this arrangement provides a work area when it is needed for a person who spends limited time in the office setting. See also *free-address* and *hoteling*.

Job title description	The title, rank, or category that describes an employee's job function or duties.
Jurisdictions	The local governing body or authority, city, county, state, or federal, responsible for enforcing laws and building codes.
LAN room	An acronym for local area network, otherwise known as computers connected to each other via a server terminal.
Landscape furniture	**1**. Also known as office landscape furniture, this term is the forerunner of open-office planning, (as opposed to enclosed offices), which then evolved into panel systems. Originally, landscape furniture referred to freestanding desks and other conventional furniture arranged in irregular layouts, with plants often serving as the primary dividers between work areas; **2**. currently refers to a group or layout of workstations and other furniture in the floor plan. See also *workstations, cubicle, cubical, furniture systems, modular furniture, open-office furniture, panel systems, systems furniture*, and *stations*.
Lateral file	A horizontal storage unit 30 in., 36 in., or 42 in. wide, with two to five stacked drawers used for filing papers, manila folders, or hanging folders.
Lead time	**1**. The amount of time it takes to place an order and then receive the product; **2**. the time between the beginning of a process and the appearance of its results.
Lease costs	Rent costs for commercial space.
Leftover or unusual space	Floor space that is not specifically assigned to a room, area, or function, or floor space that is awkward to assign to a specific function, such as a corner of an angled building. See also *unassigned space*.
Legal classification	The manner in which a company or firm files for a business permit; classifications include, but are not limited to, non-profit, for profit, public entity, private sector, corporation, sole proprietor, etc.
Library	Any room or area containing shelving to store books and other reference materials.
Life-cycle costs	The cost of a building, equipment, or furniture based not only on the initial expenditure but also on its maintenance and operating costs over its entire lifetime.
Lockers	Storage units that can be permanently assigned to staff or utilized on a daily basis by mobile staff workers.
Looped corridor	See *donut corridor* or *wrapped corridor*.
Lunchroom	A small room, generally containing a counter, sink, refrigerator, coffee machine, and table and chairs to seat between three and ten people.
Mailroom	A room, often combined with other functions such as a copy room, designated as the central point to receive and distribute deliveries of all kinds, including mail, packages, supplies and other items. See also *delivery room*.
Manager	A subjective job title applied to several different levels of management, including management of people, offices, products, and processes.
Marketing or spec plan	Hypothetical floor plans used for marketing a floor or building to potential tenants.

Means of egress	A continuous and unobstructed path of vertical and horizontal egress travel from any occupied portion of a building or structure to a public way and the exit.
Millwork	**1.** Ready-made products that are manufactured at a wood-planing mill or woodworking plant, such as moldings, trims, frames, etc.; **2.** cabinetry built at a woodworking shop for a specific client and project, based on drawings from a designer or architect.
Mobile filing system	See also *movable shelving system.*
Mobile pedestals	A pedestal on casters, sometimes with a cushioned seat on top.
Modesty panel	A panel attached to the front of a desk or table.
Modular furniture	Similar to or the same as furniture systems. See also *workstations, cubicle, cubical, furniture systems, landscape furniture, open-office furniture, panel systems, systems furniture,* and *stations.*
Modular panel systems	Conventional panel systems that require worksurfaces and components to be equal in width to one or more panels in order for them to be installed or hung from those panels.
Movable shelving system	Also known as high-density filing, this system consists of metal shelving that can be rolled together via a track on the floor in order to conserve floor space by sharing and reusing the same aisle space for each row of shelving. See also *mobile filing system.*
Move in	The act of moving into the new space.
Mullions	A vertical member separating (and often supporting) windows, doors, or panels set in a series.
Multi-tenant floor	A building floor that is divided into two or more spaces and occupied by more than one company or business.
Multiple location company	An organization with more than one location of business.
Net square feet (NSF)	The exact amount of floor space required for a function, room, or area. It does not include any circulation SF (see Box 12.1).
New school	The method and manner of designing, sketching, and producing drawings by using computers.
Nominal workstation sizes	The stated size of a workstation, such as 6 × 8, which does not include the panel thicknesses, as opposed to actual workstation sizes.
Non-modular panel systems	Contemporary panel systems that allow worksurfaces and components of any width to be installed or hung from panels of any width and at any location along a panel run. Also known as *offset panel systems.*
Non-typical workstation layouts	Although the majority of employees within a given firm occupy typical or duplicate workstations and cubicles, occasionally it is imperative to provide a workstation that is different from the rest of the stations.
Non-wet areas	Areas, such as a workroom counter, where there is limited potential for the area to get wet due to the lack of localized water supply. See also *wet areas.*
Number of attendees per meeting	To determine the best size to make a conference table and room, it is customary to determine the average number of people to sit around the table for an average meeting.

Occupancy group	Building codes classify all building structures into one of ten categories based on the type of group to occupy the structure (see Box 2.1).
Occupant	A term used by codebooks to mean a person.
Occupant load	The number of persons for which the means of egress of a building or portion thereof is designed.
Office	Although the term can refer to a place of business, in the design industry *office* generally refers to private, individual offices.
Office envelope	See *room envelope*.
Office-style workstations	Workstations designed to feel and look like hard-walled offices by using panels that are at least 80 in. high or to the ceiling in order to accommodate a hinged or sliding door.
Off-set panel systems	See *non-modular panel systems*.
Old school	The method and manner of designing, sketching, and producing drawings by hand drafting before the advent of computers.
On board	As a project progresses, various disciplines join the team or come *on board*.
On center (OC)	The distance between the center line of one element, member, part, or component, such as a stud, and the center line of the next element, member, part, or component.
Open-office furniture	Panel systems, workstations, systems office furniture, or any other furniture used in an open-office layout. See also *workstations, cubicle, cubicals, furniture systems, landscape furniture, modular furniture, panel systems, systems furniture*, and *stations*.
Operating costs	Utility, maintenance, and other costs required to operate a business each month.
Oral presentation	Presenting a space plan, final floor plan, design concepts, or any other materials and information to the client at a formal meeting.
Organization charts	A graphic depiction using circles, ovals, or rectangles and lines that displays the divisions, departments, or sections within an organization in a hierarchical manner.
Outlets	A receptacle to receive a plug or jack for either an electrical, telephone, or data device.
Overheads	Open shelving or enclosed storage units that are hung off panels over worksurfaces.
Panel creep	That which occurs when clusters of workstations are space planned using their nominal sizes rather than actual sizes, which should include panel thicknesses. During installation of the workstations on-site, nominal workstation sizes will *creep* along the floor, thus taking up more floor space than on the plan.
Panel systems	**1**. Typically, the overall term used to describe a group of furniture components, including worksurfaces, storage units, panels, and other vertical dividers, that can be assembled together to form individual or shared work areas; **2**. often refers to a whole cluster or overall layout of workstations rather than individual workstations. See also *workstations, cubicle, cubicals, furniture systems, landscape furniture, modular furniture, open-office furniture, systems furniture*, and *stations*.

Pantry	A very small room, often with a short counter, small bar-style sink, an undercounter refrigerator, and small coffeemaker to be used on a limited basis.
Partition	A dividing wall within a building, either loadbearing or nonload-bearing.
Pedestal	A two-drawer file that can be freestanding, suspended below a worksurface, or on casters.
Peer review	The act of reviewing drawings, sketches, and design ideas with co-designers or team members to garner new ideas, validate existing concepts, catch mistakes, and generally improve and refine a space plan or other design presentations.
Pivot doors	A door having small pins at the top and bottom that are installed into overhead framework and the floor, around which the door can pivot or swing in and out, as opposed to a door hung on hinges.
Plan, plan view	See *floor plan*.
Plan analysis	Reviewing a plan from several perspectives, including creativity, efficiency, meeting the client's needs and desires; building code and ADA requirements; and technical requirements.
Plenum	**1**. In suspended ceiling construction, the space between the suspended ceiling and the main structure above; **2**. a space that receives air from a blower for distribution.
Plot	**1**. A reproduction of a CAD drawing on bond paper using ink-filled pen points of various widths to plot out a drawing from a computer file (obsolete); **2**. a generic term used to refer to blueprints or copies of construction drawings.
Potable water	**1**. Water of sufficiently high quality that can be used and consumed for drinking; **2**. water without risk of immediate or long-term hazard.
Preliminary budget	An initial discussion at the start of a project as to how much money the project may cost or how much money the client plans to spend. Dollar amounts may be based on historical data of similar projects, a figure the client has allocated to capital investments, or a number simply pulled from the air. This budget should be, and needs to be, updated as the project progresses through each design phase.
Presentation plan	An embellished space plan displayed to the client during a formal presentation.
Primary circulation	Public corridors, lobby, and any portions of a required exit access route through a building (see Box 12.2).
Print	**1**. The current method to reproduce CAD drawings using laser or inkjet technology; **2**. a generic term used to refer to copies of blueprints or construction drawings.
Private office	An enclosed room, often on a perimeter window wall, to house one occupant.
Program Report	A bound report, based on information gleaned through a programming effort, which details and summarizes the client's needs, wishes, and desires for new space, often depicted through both graphic and written methods.

Programming	A method whereby a designer gathers and documents information about a client via questionnaires, interviews, walk-through of existing spaces, and research.
Programming Interviews	Separate meetings between the programmer or designer and a client's department heads to determine the needs, desires, and wishes of the client for the new or modeled space. See also *programming*.
Project directories	A list with pertinent contact information of all persons, disciplines, and other consultants involved on a project.
Project room	An open area or enclosed room temporarily taken over by a group working on a particular project.
Public corridors	Corridors outside of a tenant space that serve as a means of egress through a building; also known as primary circulation.
Punched openings	Doors or windows set in a solid wall facade.
Questionnaires	A formal list of questions regarding the client's needs, desires, wishes, expectations, philosophy, vision, security concerns, etc., that can be submitted via hard copy or electronically.
Quiet Rooms	See *telephone booths*.
Raw space	Interior space, either new or demolished space, within a building in which there are no walls, ceilings, finishes, mechanical systems, etc.
Reception desk	A desk, workstation, or custom-built unit that is often larger than a standard desk. It generally is an upgraded piece of furniture with special finishes.
Rentable square feet (RSF)	All usable floor square footage plus common public areas such as washrooms, the loading dock, etc. toward which the tenant pays rent. It does not include building shafts, elevators or window shelves (see Box 12.1).
Room envelope	The real or imaginary shape of a building or room, including the floor, walls, and ceiling, indicating its maximum volume. See also *envelope* and *office envelope*.
Room location	**1**. The floor on which the room is located; **2**. the location of a room on a floor with respect to the elevator lobby, the window wall, an interior position not on the window wall, or any other defining point on the floor plan.
Room size	**1**. The physical width, depth, and height of a room; **2**. the room size and shape based on the desired use and ambience of the room.
Sales rep	**1.** Abbreviated term for sales representative; **2.** A person responsible for representing a manufacturer and manufacturer's products with the intent to persuade a designer or architect to specify those products to the end user for their projects.
Seating	Any piece of furniture on which a person may sit, including stack chairs, lounge chairs, office chairs, sofas, benches, etc.
Secondary circulation	Internal corridors and other means of passage through a tenant space (see Box 12.2).
Shared equipment	Equipment, such as scanners and fax machines, used only occasionally and thus shared by all employees.
Sheetrock	Trade name for wallboard with gypsum core and paper surfaces. See also *gypsum board* and *drywall*.

Shell and Core	See *[building] shell and core* and *core and shell*.
Shipping/receiving room	A term sometimes used in place of mailroom or delivery room.
Shop drawings	Drawings, diagrams, illustrations, and other data prepared by the contractor, subcontractor, or millworker that illustrate how specific portions of the work or items will be fabricated and/or installed. This information is sent to the designer or architect for review and approval prior to construction and installation of said items.
Sick room	A room, generally containing a sofa or cot, to be used by employees during the workday when experiencing a short bout of illness.
Sign-off	A legal designation of approval and acceptance of a task, phase, or drawing by a client who formally signs the drawing or other documentation at hand, at which time the project can proceed to the next task or phase.
Single-location company or firm	An organization operating out of a single location of business.
Single tenant floor	A floor within a building that is occupied entirely by a single company or business.
Site analysis	The evaluation of a particular site for an appropriate usage based on natural terrain, local codes and zoning laws, and location.
Sitting space	Open floor space in which a person seated in a chair can freely move.
Sizing a conference room	A method for calculating the width and depth of a room based on the number of people to be seated around the conference table.
Slab above	A reinforced concrete floor above the floor in question.
Solid wall facade	A building constructed of masonry units, such as brick, with punched windows.
Space plan	An initial floor plan that shows rooms, areas, and corridors based on the client's program requirements. This plan is typically revised, adjusted, and changed based on client reviews, as it eventually evolves into a final floor plan to be used for construction documents.
Space planner	A designer who provides space planning services.
Space planning	The process, both methodically and creatively, of laying out or planning an initial two-dimensional floor plan, known as a space plan, based on the client's program requirements.
Space to move items	Open floor space throughout the building, often part of typical corridors or hallways that can be used to freely move, rest, or transport mobile equipment, chairs, and other movable items.
Space to open doors and drawers	Open floor space in front of furniture units, equipment, or other areas used to freely open doors and drawers.
Spandrel glass	An opaque glass in windows and curtain walls used to conceal beams, columns, or other internal construction elements.
Specifications	A written technical description of materials, equipment, standards, and workmanship, which is included as part of the contract documents.
Stacking diagrams	Conceptual diagrams that display how groups or departments will be assigned to a particular floor in a multi-floor plan (see Chapter 12 opening photo).

Standing space	Open floor space where a person can stand to access shelving, counters, equipment, etc.
Stations	Truncated word for workstations or cubicles.
Storage cabinet	An item of furniture, constructed in metal, generally used in back office areas or storage rooms.
Storage room	A room with open floor space or shelving for storing any assorted number of items as needed.
Storage units	An item of furniture, often constructed of wood, used in offices for additional storage.
Stud	One of a series of vertical structural members, either wood or metal, that act as the supporting elements in a wall or partition.
Supply room	A room or area to store bulk supplies, primarily office supplies, but also selected furniture items such as an extra chair or file cabinet.
Support rooms	Rooms, areas, or functions that help support the client's business, such as copy room, library, computer room, etc.
Systems furniture	Similar to or the same as furniture systems. See also *workstations, cubicle, cubicals, furniture systems, landscape furniture, modular furniture, open-office furniture, panel systems,* and *stations.*
Tax write-offs	In a company's accounting procedures, a write-off, taken on income tax returns, refers to the reduced or zero value of an asset.
Team area	An area or room with table and chairs, lounge seating, or other furniture where employees can come, either spontaneously or prearranged, to work and collaborate together on individual or joint projects.
Tear sheet	See *cut sheet.*
Telephone booths	Small cubicles or enclosed rooms with a small counter or table, task or lounge chair, P&D connections, and possibly a telephone that can be used by visitors or employees to make private or personal telephone calls. Also called *quiet rooms, focus rooms,* and *private conversation rooms.*
Telephone closet	A small room stacked vertically on each floor in part of the building core that allows direct wire connection from the local telephone supply source to each tenant on a floor of the building.
Tenant	A business, organization, company, or firm that occupies floor space and pays rent in a building.
Test fit	A quick study to determine how a client's program requirements might lay out in various selected building floor plates.
Time frame	**1.** A period of time that is required to complete a task; **2.** A period of time that will lapse before a task or action can or will start.
Training room	Dedicated or makeshift rooms used for training employees via computer, internet, projection screens, or other medium.
Transaction shelf	A ledge or shelf on the front of a reception desk unit, at either standing or seated height, that can be used by a visitor to sign in or to hold business cards, the company signage, etc.
Travel distance	The maximum distance that a person can travel inside a building to reach an exit for egress.

Typical layouts	Drawings, often enlarged in scale, that show a single room or area that is duplicated throughout a floor plan. See also *typical room layout*.
Typical private office layout	A floor plan drawn at ¼-in. scale that shows a single office with furniture to demonstrate what the layout or arrangement of the furniture might look like in a typical private office.
Typical room layouts	See *typical layout*.
Typical workstation layouts	A floor plan drawn at ¼-in. scale that shows a single workstation or cubicle to demonstrate what the layout or arrangement of components and worksurfaces might look like in a typical workstation.
UL approved	Underwriters Laboratories (UL) is an independent product safety certification organization, one of several companies approved by a US federal agency to test and analyze product safety, particularly for electrical devises and components.
Unassigned space	Any leftover floor space or a specific floor area that has not been assigned to any particular room, area, or function. See also *leftover space*.
Upcharge	A separate or extra charge that is added by the manufacturer to the normal price of an item when any deviation is requested for and made to a standard product, such a special finish, size, or style variation.
Updated budget	Applying newly received costs, quantities, or items to a budget in progress.
Usable square feet (USF)	The net square footage plus circulation and any leftover or unassigned floor space (see Box 12.1).
Use group	The classification of a building or structure based on the purpose for which the building or structure is used (see Box 2.1).
Utility closets	Either separate or combined closets containing various utility wiring, including telephone, electrical, cable, and fiber-optic wirings.
Variance (code)	Permission granted by the building permit office to allow an exception to a particular code requirement for a particular project.
Vending room or area	A room or area containing one or more vending machines; often found in public areas.
Vertical file	A 15 in. or 18 in. wide storage unit with two to five drawers used to store and file letter or legal sized papers, manila folders, or hanging folders.
Void spaces	See *dead space*.
Walking space	Floor space used for walking from one area to another area, either within a room or as a corridor, aisle, or hallway.
Wall units	Either built-in or freestanding storage units used to house audio/visual equipment and other items in a conference room.
War room	A room often used for strategic planning or other conference meetings. It is generally equipped with chart holders, white board or easel writing surfaces, and computers.
Warm lit shell	A building, generally commercial, with minimally finished interior spaces, including ceiling tiles; light fixtures; some walls and electrical outlets; and carpet. Tenants will generally move into these conditions or pay for minimal renovations. See also *cold lit shell*.

Wet areas	Areas, such as a coffee room counter, which have the potential to get wet due to the presence of localized water supply as in a sink with a faucet. Backsplashes are normally installed along the backs and sides of these counters to help control water damage. See also *non-wet areas*.
Wet column	An interior column along which a potable water pipe rises vertically throughout the building.
Work area	**1**. Any area occupied by an office worker and used as the primary work area or space; **2**. private offices, individual or shared workstations, and cubicles with low, high, or no panel dividers, counter spaces in workrooms, libraries, mailroom, etc., and telecommuting areas such as a home office.
Work area mix	The number or ratio of offices and workstations to be planned within the floor space.
Workroom	A designated area or room often containing a photocopier, counter, storage, and other provisions that support the daily operations of a business. Similar to copy room.
Workspace, Workplace	New terminology used to describe alternative work-style areas for performing work-related tasks.
Workstations	Individual work areas, assembled with panel system components, using either low or high panels. Although there is no official designation as such, workstation is probably a slightly more formal term than some other terms with which it is used interchangeably. See also *cubicle, cubical, panel systems, furniture systems, landscape furniture, modular furniture, open-office furniture, systems furniture*, and *stations*.
Worksurface	A horizontal surface hung from or on panels, typically 29 in. above the floor, in a workstation and used as the primary work area by the workstation occupant.
Wrapped corridor	See *donut corridors* or *looped corridors*.
X-ref	In computer drafting, a plan from a non-opened file that is linked into an open file as an inactive background.
Z- corridor	A corridor that connects one exit stairwell to another exit stairwell through the elevator lobby.

REFERENCES

PREFACE

1. NCIDQ definition of interior design. Available at http://www.ncidqexam.org/about-interior-design/definition-of-interior-design/, June 12, 2015.

CHAPTER 1

1. http://www.britannica.com/art/interior-design.
2. Edmund N. Bacon, *Design of Cities*, rev. ed. (New York: Penguin Books, 1980), 29.
3. John Wood, the Younger, *A Series of Plans for Cottages, Habitations of the Laborer* (1792), as cited by Edmund N. Bacon, *Design of Cities*, rev. ed. (New York: Penguin Books, 1980), 29.
4. Based on seventeenth-century engraving, as cited by Edmund N. Bacon, *Design of Cities*, rev. ed. (New York: Penguin Books, 1980), 28.
5. Furniture plan, "Arthur Andersen & Co." Griswold, Heckel & Kelly Associates, Chicago, IL, 1987, p. F-5-1, with annotations added by Mary Lou Bakker to show design thought process.
6. "Phillips Janson," *Interior Design*, April (1993): 112.
7. Holly Richmond, "Work Hard, Play Hard," *Contract Magazine*, November/December (2009): 61.
8. Linda Burnett, "Spa Healing," *Contract Magazine*, October (2007): 58, 60.
9. Karin Tetlow, "Shared Conferencing," *Interiors*, August (1992): 80.
10. Amy Argetsinger and Roxanne Roberts, "Day for a Queen," *Washington Post*, May 6, 2007, Section D, D1.
11. Definition from GreenBuilding.com. Available at http://www.greenbuilding.com/#.
12. "Green Building," *Wikipedia*. Available at http://en.wikipedia.org/wiki/Green_building.
13. U.S. Green Building Council, LEED Reference Guide for Green Interior Design and Construction, Version 4v, 2013, 5.
14. Based on the replication of drawing by design director, Heery International Inc., Washington, DC, 2003.

15. Differences Between Left and Right Hemisphere. Accessed at http://www.mtsu.edu/~studskl/hd/hemis.html, July 11, 2007.

16. Kevin Lynch, *Site Planning*, 3rd ed. (Cambridge, MA: MIT Press, 1990), 128, 129, 137.

17. Ian L. McHarg, *Design with Nature* (New York: John Wiley & Sons, Inc., 1992), 103.

18. Edmund N. Bacon, *Design of Cities*, rev. ed. (New York: Penguin Books, 1980), 35.

CHAPTER 2

1. "Thinking Outside the Box: Architects Discover They Can Do More than Make Buildings" (Washington, DC: AIA, 2002), 5.

2. Jerrold M. Sonet and Alan M. Siegel, "Compromising Positions Part II," *Interior Design* (June 1990), 86.

3. IBC, International Building Code (IBC), 2015, Section 302.1, 41.

4. IBC, 2015, Section 303, 41.

CHAPTER 3

1. A CAD drawing by Cherlye Rome, based on a conceptual plan developed by Mary Lou Bakker, in a building in Chicago, IL.

CHAPTER 4

1. Paul Cornell, *Dynamic and Task Seating* (Grand Rapids, MI: Steelcase, Inc.), 2.

2. U.S. Green Building Council, LEED Reference Guide for Green Interior Design and Construction, Version 4v, 2013, 239.

CHAPTER 5

1. International Building Code (IBC), 2015, Ordinance, xix.

2. IBC, 2015, Section 1006.3.2 and Table 1006.3.2(2), 255–256.

3. "Rules and Regulations, Part III," *Federal Register*, Vol. 56, No. 144 (Washington, DC: U.S. Department of Justice, Office of the Attorney General, July 26, 1991), 35544.

4. "Rules and Regulations, Part III," *Federal Register*, Vol. 56, No. 144 (Washington, DC: U.S. Department of Justice, Office of the Attorney General, July 26, 1991), 35544.

5. 2010 ADA Standards for Accessible Design (ADA), 2010, Overview, 1.

6. ADA, 2010, 2010 Standards, 31.

7. ADA, 2010, Telephones, 74, 194 or http://www.ada.gov/regs2010/2010ADAStandards/2010ADAStandards_prt.pdf.

8. IBC, 2015, Section 202, Definitions, 15.

9. IBC, 2015, Section 1020, Corridors, 279.

10. Tracings based on Charles W. Harris and Nicholas T. Dines, *Time-Saver Standards for Landscape Architecture* (New York: McGraw-Hill, 1988), 210–213.

11. ADA, 2010, Walking Surfaces, 117–118 or http://www.ada.gov/regs2010/2010ADAStandards/2010ADAStandards_prt.pdf.

12. IBC, 2015, Section 1003, General Means of Egress, 28, 250.

CHAPTER 6

1. IBC, 2015, Section 1208, Interior Space Dimensions, 314.

2. ADA, 2010, Doors, Doorways, and Gates, 119–123 or http://www.ada.gov/regs2010/2010ADAStandards/2010ADAStandards_prt.pdf.

CHAPTER 7

1. U.S. Green Building Council, *LEED, Reference Guide for Green Interior Design and Construction*, Version 4v, 2013, 391.

CHAPTER 8

1. Based on Conference Room, "Hutchison Corporation," Reel/Grobman & Associates, Los Angeles, CA, (1989). Hand drafted by Mary Lou Bakker.

2. Based on Conference Room and Reception Area, "Laurus Strategies," Chicago, IL, (2006). Hand drafted by Cheryle Rome.

CHAPTER 9

1. Based on Reception Area, "At Kearney, Inc.," Reel/Grobman & Associates, Los

Angeles, CA, (1989). Hand drafted by Mary Lou Bakker.

2. Based on Entry Presentation, "Pharmacia Ophthalmics," Reel/Grobman & Associates, Los Angeles, CA, (1989). Hand drafted by Mary Lou Bakker.

CHAPTER 10

1. ADA, 2010, Lavatories and Sinks, 107–111, 110–111, 170–171.
2. The National Coffee Service Association, *Coffee Breaks + Architecture*, 1992, Vienna, VA.
3. U.S. Green Building Council, LEED, Reference Guide for Green Interior Design and Construction, Version 4v, 2013, 223.
4. Based on Joseph De Chiara, Julius Panero, and Martin Zelnik, *Time-Saver Standards for Interior Design and Space Planning*, 2nd ed., (New York: McGraw-Hill, 2001), 342.
5. The National Coffee Service Association, *Coffee Breaks + Agriculture*, 1992, Vienna, VA.
6. U.S. Green Building Council, *LEED, Reference Guide for Green Interior Design and Construction*, Version 4v, 2013, 323.

CHAPTER 11

1. Xerox Corporation, *Power Requirements—Quick Reference*, (Norwalk, CT, 2007), 1.
2. United HealthCare Mail Services Guidelines, *Exhibit I*, Minneapolis, MN, 1996.
3. Lighting Systems, *A Lighting Design*, p. 1. Available at http://www.3sgconsulting.net/lighting-design-an-art-and-science/. Gotham Architectural Downlighting, *A Technical Bulletin: Reflector Manufacturing*. Accessed at www.gothamlighting.com/pdf/techbulletins/reflectormanufacturing.
4. AIA Best Practices, *Lactation Room Design*, 10-5-2010, 1–2.

CHAPTER 12

1. Interior/Architectural Design Process, (Heery International, Washington, DC, 2002), 7, 8.
2. Interior/Architectural Design Process, (Heery International, Washington, DC, 2002), 9, 10.

CHAPTER 13

1. International Building Code (IBC), 2015, Section 1108, 302–304.
2. IBC, 2015, Chapter 2, 25.
3. IBC, 2015, Section 403, 57–58.
4. IBC, 2015, Section 1009, 258.
5. IBC, 2015, Chapter 2, 30.
6. IBC, 2015, Section 1004, 251.
7. IBC, 2015, Section 1006, 253–355
8. IBC, 2015, Section 1005, 252–253.
9. IBC, 2015, Section 1017, 277.
10. Existing floor plan, "Musick, Peeler & Garrett LLP." Reel/Grobman & Associates, Los Angeles, CA, 1990. Redrawn on CAD by Mary Lou Bakker.
11. IBC, 2015, Chapter 2, 15–16.
12. IBC, 2015, Section 1029, 289.
13. IBC, 2015, Section 1004, 252.
14. IBC, 2015, Section 1016, 276.
15. IBC, 2015, Section 1020, 279.
16. IBC, 2015, Section 1007, 256.
17. IBC, 2015, Section 1010, 261.
18. Based on floor plan, "Laurus Strategies," C. Rome Design, Chicago, IL, 2006.

CHAPTER 14

1. Wall Street Journal. Available at: http://online.wsj.com/article/SB119578134568501693.html.
2. Do Green Buildings Enhance the Well Being of Workers, *Environmental Design and Construction*, (July 2000): 5–9.
3. U.S. Green Building Council, LEED, Reference Guide for Green Interior Design and Construction, Version 4v, 2013, 403-404.

4. Ibid., 419.

5. *International Code Council*, available at: http://publiccodes.cyberregs.com/icod /igcc/2012/.

6. International Building Code (IBC), 2015, Section 1016, 276.

7. IBC, 2015, Section 1003, 250.

8. IBC, 2015, Section 1208, 315.

CHAPTER 15

1. Marketing Plan, GHK, Chicago, IL, 1986. Redrawn on CAD by Cheryle Rome.

2. Space Plan, "Hutchison Corporation," Reel/Grobman & Associates, Los Angeles, CA, 1989, color pencils applied by Mary Lou Bakker.

3. Space Plan, "AT Kearney, Inc.," Reel Grobman & Associates, Los Angeles, CA, 1988, redrawn on CAD by Mary Lou Bakker.

4. Jerry Cooper, "Color and Collage," *Interior Design*, May 1988, 264.

5. Based on Entry, "Pharmacia Ophthalmics," Reel/Grobman & Associates, Los Angeles, CA, 1988, drafted and colored by Mary Lou Bakker.

6. Model, "AT Kearney, Inc.," Reel/Grobman & Associates, Los Angeles, CA, 1988, built by Mary Lou Bakker.

APPENDIX B

1. U.S. Green Building Council, LEED Reference Guide for Green Interior Design and Construction, Version 4v, 2013, 51.

2. U.S. Green Building Council, LEED Reference Guide for Green Interior Design and Construction, Version 4v, 2013, 59.

3. Marketing Package for 77 W. Wacker Drive, Chicago, Illinois, The Prime Group, 1991.

4. Marketing Package for 77 W. Wacker Drive, Chicago, Illinois, The Prime Group, 1991.

5. Marketing Package for 77 W. Wacker Drive, Chicago, Illinois, The Prime Group, 1991.

6. Computer drawing by author, based on building floor plans, for building at 77 W. Wacker Drive, Chicago, Illinois.

GLOSSARY

1. Definition from 2013 District of Columbia Construction Codes, available at: http:// publiccodes.cyberregs.com/icod/igcc /2012/icod_igcc_2012_2_sec002.htm

PHOTO CREDITS

Illustrations by Cheryle Rome and
Mary Lou Bakker

CHAPTER OPENERS

1. © Francis Dzikowski/Esto; PM by Jeffrey Jorge Cohen, AIA, LEED AP
2. Photo by Bill Crofton; Design by Cheryle Rome
3. Photo by Ron Solomon; Design by Kevin Wyllie, RA, NCIDQ, LEED AP - ID+C
4. Photo by Jeff Howard; Design by Cheryle Rome
5. Photo and design by Kevin Wyllie, RA, NCIDQ, LEED AP - ID+C
6. Photo courtesy of Hartman Design Group; Design by Todd Howard Ezrin, NCIDQ, LEED AP
7. Copyright Paul Bielenberg, photographer; Design by Wirt Design Group, Inc.
8. Photo by Matthew Nichols; Project: Department of Justice, Office of Justice Programs, Washington, DC
9. Photo by Dan Cunningham, Architectural Photographer; CA by Mary Lou Bakker, AIA, IIDA, LEED AP
10. Copyright Joshua Perrin, photographer; Design by Wirt Design Group, Inc.
11. Photo and design by Kevin Wyllie, RA, NCIDQ, LEED AP - ID+C
12. Graphics by Mary Lou Bakker, AIA, IIDA, LEED AP
13. Photo by Michael Given, LEED AP
14. Photo by Ernst Pierre-Toussaint; Project: The Field Museum, Chicago, IL
15. Copyright Paul Bielenberg, photographer; Design by Wirt Design Group, Inc.

APPENDIX B

1. Michael Hanson/Getty Images

TEXT ART

1.2 Illustration by Vanessa Han

INDEX

building code, 81-82, 82*b. See also* code(s)
building footprint efficiencies, 241
building history, in space plan, 8
building location. *See also* location(s)
    LEED and, 341*b*, 342*b*
    site location and, 248
    in space plan, 6*f*, 7, 7*f*
    tour of, 248
Building Officials and Code Administrators
    (BOCA), 82*b*
built-in wall units, 149
bum wad (sketch or trace paper), 13, 281
business. *See* client(s)
buzzer system, 174

C

cabinets, 52
    base, in food rooms, 182-83, 183*f*, 183*t*
    in circulation plan views, 364
    framed, 182, 183*f*
    frameless, 182, 183*f*
    upper, in food rooms, 183*t*, 184-85, 184*f*
cable trough, 132, 133*f*
cafeteria, 198. *See also* food room(s)
cantilever brackets, 59, 59*f*
card pass system, 174
casegoods, 42-47, 44*it*-46*it*, 47*f*
casters, 70
ceiling heights, 312, 313*b*
centerline, 102-03
chain of command, 32-33
chairs. *See* seating
circulation, 365-67. *See also* space
    assigning, 83
    calculation of, 239*b*
    in conference rooms, 146, 147*f*
    factors, 240*b*
    file cabinet, 217-19
    in file rooms, 208
    internal departmental, 238*b*
    plan views, 89, 362-74
    in Program Report, 237, 237*t*, 238*b*
    primary, 238*b*
    secondary, 238*b*
    sitting space in, 86, 87*it*, 88*t*
    in space plan, 10
    in space planning procedure, 296
    standing space in, 86, 87*it*, 88*b*, 88*t*
    types of, 83-89, 84*b*, 84*f*, 85*f*, 86*b*, 86*f*, 87*it*,
        88*b*, 88*t*
    walking space in, 84-86, 84*f*, 85*f*, 86*f*
    with workstations, 287
clear dimensions, 103-04, 103*f*
client(s)
    "baggage," 9
    basic makeup of, 19
    budget, 9, 18
    business of, 8
    chain of command with, 32-33
    classifications, 19-22
    clientele of, 20
    contact, 27-28
    desired ambience of, 8-9
    desires, 18-19
    discovery process with, 31-38, 35*f*
    kickoff meeting with, 32
    lease review with, 18
    legal classifications of, 19-21
    listening to, 18-19
    macro topics for, 17
    with multiple locations, 18
    needs, 18-19
    organization charts, 224-25, 224*f*, 225*f*

organization size, 20
philosophy, 20-21, 24-25
profiles, 335-40
programming requirements, 8, 20, 33
questionnaires, 33-35
schedule, 9
single-location, 18
in space plan, 6, 8-9
in space plan analysis, 301-03, 300*f*, 302*f*
understanding, 19
use classifications, 21-22, 21*b*, 22*b*
walk through with, 38
work area mix of, 22-26
clinics, job titles in, 27*b*
closed shelving, 74*it*, 75
closets, in reception areas, 170-71, 170*f*
closing, 331-32
clothing, 331
coat closet, in reception areas, 170-71, 170*f*
code(s). *See also* International Building Code (IBC)
    building, 81-82, 82*b*
    compliance, 312-13
    corridor widths in, 84, 84*b*, 85, 85*b*
    in project information, 249-50
    purpose of, 81
    in space plan, 10
    in space plan analysis, 306-13, 308*f*-12*f*, 311*b*, 313*b*
    variances, 21-22
    year, 249-50
coffee brewers, 186-87, 187*f*
coffee rooms, 193-96, 194*f*. *See also* food room(s)
    location of, 179-80
    organization size and, 180
collaborative areas, 139-40, 152-53, 214, 214*f*, 215*f*
collaborative seating, 71*it*, 72
collating area, 203, 203*f*
color, in presentation plans, 322-23
columns, 93-94, 94*f*, 95*f*, 97*f*
common path of travel, 254-57, 255*b*, 255*t*, 259*f*
compact refrigerators, 188-89
company. *See* client(s)
company logo/name, in reception areas, 168-70
computer-aided design and drafting (CADD), 14,
    283-84, 284*f*, 326
computer room. *See* technology rooms
concealed wall units, 149-50, 151*f*
conceptual phase, 2*b*
concrete construction, 250
conference chairs, 69*t*, 70
conference rooms
    acoustics in, 157
    blackout for, 154
    boardrooms as, 150-51, 151*f*
    circulation in, 146, 147*f*
    collaborative rooms as, 152-53
    credenzas in, 146, 147*f*
    depth of, 154
    doors in, 155
    equipment in, 144*b*, 148-49
    finishes for, 157
    general, 152, 153*f*
    glazing walls in, 154-55
    as individual, 143
    interior location of, 154
    items in, 143-44, 144*b*
    layout drafting, 157, 158*f*
    layouts of, 153-57, 153*f*, 155*f*, 156*it*
    light provisions for, 154
    main, 151-52
    number of, 143
    number of people for, 144*b*
    in questionnaire, 353
    scheduler, 148-49
    sizing of, 144-50, 145*it*, 146*b*, 147*f*, 148*t*, 151*f*

training rooms as, 152
types of, 150-53, 151*f*, 153*f*
videoconferencing in, 152
wall units in, 149-50, 150*f*, 151*f*
width of, 154
windows in, 153-54
conference tables, 63*it*, 64-65, 144-46, 145*it*, 146*t*, 148*t*
connectors, panels, 54-58
construction, in space plan, 10
construction costs, workstations and, 23
construction documents, 321, 327
construction document phase, 2*b*
construction type, 250
continuous windows, 91, 93*f*
contract administration phase, 2*b*
contract furniture, 41-42
contract workers, in questionnaire, 351
copier room, 202-06, 203*f*, 204*f*, 205*t*
core, building, 236*b*, 261, 262*f*
core and shell buildings, 1, 91
corner units, 60, 60*f*
corner worksurfaces, 118, 119*it*
corporate philosophy, 241
corridor(s)
    dead-end, 264, 266*b*, 266*f*, 308, 308*f*
    donut, 263-64, 265*f*
    doors, 264-67, 268*b*, 268*f*, 269*f*
    existing, 263, 264*f*
    looped, 263-64, 265*f*
    new, 263
    public, 263-64, 263*b*, 265*f*, 266*b*, 267*f*
    in space plan analysis, 306-08, 308*f*
    widths, 84, 84*b*, 85, 86*b*, 254*t*, 256*b*
    wrapped, 263-64, 265*f*
    Z, 263, 265*f*
counters
    in copier rooms, 203, 203*f*
    in food room, 180-82, 181*f*, 182*f*
    reception, 165
courts, job titles in, 27*b*
cover letter, in Program Report, 224
credenzas, 43-45, 45*it*, 47*f*, 105, 146, 147*f*
creep, in measurements, 93
    files and bookcases, 218-19
    panels, 126
creeping dimensions, 93*f*
cross-section
    coffee counters, 185*f*
    reception desk, 166*it*
    walls, 156*it*
cubicles. *See* workstations
curtain wall, 91, 92-93, 92*f*, 93*f*
curtain wall perimeters, 93
curved walls, 292, 292*f*
custom desks, 164-65, 165*f*, 166*t*
custom furniture, 42, 75-76
custom tables, 63*it*, 65

D

data capabilities. *See also* A/V equipment
    in copier rooms, 205-06, 205*t*
    in tables, 63*it*, 65
    in workstations, 128-30, 129*f*
daylight harvesting, 12, 304, 304*b*, 305*f*
dead-end corridors, 264, 266*b*, 266*f*, 308, 308*f*
delivery and mail room, 206-07, 207*f*
demising partitions, 272-73
department, in organization chart, 225
design development phase, 2*b*, 5, 293
design philosophy, 3
desks
    custom, 164-65, 165*f*, 166*t*
    executive, 43, 44*it*